APPLIED ETHICS:
A READER

Edited by
Earl R. Winkler and Jerrold R. Coombs

BLACKWELL
Oxford UK & Cambridge USA

First published 1993

Blackwell Publishers
238 Main Street, Suite 501
Cambridge, Massachusetts 02142
USA

108 Cowley Road
Oxford OX4 1JF
UK

Library of Congress Cataloging-in-Publication Data

Applied ethics: a reader / edited by Earl R. Winkler and Jerrold R. Coombs.
    p.   cm.
    Includes bibliographical references and index.
    ISBN 0-631-18832-0. —— ISBN 0-631-18833-9 (pbk.)
    1. Ethics. I. Winkler, Earl R. (Earl Raye), 1938– .
II. Coombs, Jerrold R.
BJ1031.A67   1993
170——dc20   92-36936
                                            CIP

British Library Cataloguing in Publication Data
A CIP catalogue record for this book is available from the British Library.

Typeset in 10½ on 12 pt Ehrhardt
by Photo·graphics, Honiton, Devon
Printed in Great Britain by TJ Press, Padstow, Cornwall

This book is printed on acid-free paper

Contents

II General Issues Related to the Fields of Applied Ethics

Business Ethics

Environmental Ethics

Biomedical Ethics

Notes on the Contributors

Annette Baier is Professor of Philosophy at the University of Pittsburgh. Her books are *Postures of the Mind: Essays on Mind and Morals* (1985) and *A Progress of Sentiments: A Re-reading of Hume's Treatise* (1991). Her recent work in ethics has taken as its focus the concept of trust.

Dale Beyerstein teaches philosophy at Vancouver Community College in Vancouver, British Columbia. His major interests are critical thinking and medical ethics. In addition to publishing essays in the *Skeptical Inquirer*, *Canadian Journal of Psychiatry*, and *Canadian Journal of Psychology*, he has written several position papers for the British Columbia Civil Liberties Association.

Jerrold R. Coombs is Professor of Philosophy of Education at the University of British Columbia and is a founding member of the Association for Values Education and Research. He edited *Philosophy of Education* (1979) and co-edited *Ends in View* (1990). He has co-authored a number of reports of research on moral and law-related education funded by Canadian government agencies and has published many articles and chapters in books dealing with moral education and ethical issues in education. He is a former President of the Philosophy of Education Society of North America.

Peter Danielson is Associate Professor of Philosophy and Senior Research Fellow of the Centre for Applied Ethics at the University of British Columbia. He is the author of *Artificial Morality* (1992) and of various articles concerning ethical theory and applied ethics, particularly in the area of ethics and technology.

Nancy (Ann) Davis is Associate Professor of Philosophy and an Associate of the Center for Values and Social Policy at the University of Colorado at Boulder. Her interests lie primarily in moral theory, applied ethics, and moral methodology. Her recent publications include essays on moral theory and motivation, deontological moral theories, reproductive technologies, and sexual harassment. She is currently working on a series of essays on the morality of abortion and a book on sexual harassment in the university.

Bent Flyvbjerg is Associate Professor with the Department of Development and Planning, University of Aalborg, Denmark. He has done extensive work in applied ethics in the fields of environmental policy and planning, transportation, and city planning. In addition to having done research and teaching at the University of California, Los Angeles and Harvard University, he has worked as an advisor to business and government in Scandinavia, Africa, Asia and South-East Asia. His latest book is *Rationality and Power* (1991).

Kenneth Goodpaster holds the Koch Chair in Business Ethics at the college of St Thomas, St Paul, Minnesota. His research has spanned a wide range of topics from conceptual studies of ethical reasoning to empirical studies of the social implications of management decision-making. He is the author of a number of books including *Perspectives on Morality* (1976), *Ethics in Management* (1984), and *Policies and Persons: A Casebook in Business Ethics* (1985). Work in progress includes a monograph on management and moral philosophy entitled *The Moral Agenda of Management*.

Lori Gruen is completing her PhD in Philosophy at the University of Colorado at Boulder, where she is associated with the Center for Values and Social Policy. She has taught environmental ethics, feminist philosophy, and applied ethics, and has published on ethics and animals, feminist critiques of science, and ecofeminist philosophy. She is currently co-editing, with Dale Jamieson, *Reflecting on Nature: Readings in Environmental Philosophy*, due to appear in 1993.

Barry Hoffmaster is Director of the Westminster Institute for Ethics and Human Values in London, Ontario, and is Professor in the Department of Philosophy and Associate Professor in the Department of Family Medicine at the University of Western Ontario. His areas of academic interest include the relation of social sciences to bioethics and philosophy of law. He is co-author with Ronald Christie of *Ethical Issues in Family Medicine* (1986) and co-editor with Benjamin Freedman and Gwen Fraser of *Clinical Ethics: Theory and Practice* (1989). He has published a number of articles in both philosophy and social science journals.

Alison M. Jaggar is Professor of Philosophy at the University of Colorado at Boulder, where she also teaches in women's studies. Her books include ▸

Feminist Frameworks, co-edited with Paula Rothenberg (1978; 2nd edn 1984), *Feminist Politics and Human Nature* (1983), and *Gender/Body/Knowledge: Feminist Reconstructions of Being and Knowing*, co-edited with Susan R. Bordo (1989). Currently she is working on *Feminism and Moral Theory*, supported by a fellowship from the Rockefeller Foundation. Jaggar was a founding member of the Society for Women in Philosophy and currently chairs the American Philosophical Association Committee on the Status of Women.

Dale Jamieson is Associate Professor of Philosophy at the University of Colorado, Boulder, Adjunct Scientist in the Environmental and Societal Impacts Group at the National Center for Atmospheric Research, and former Director of the Center for Values and Social Policy at the University of Colorado. He is the author of many articles on practical ethics; an anthology on environmental philosophy, *Reflecting on Nature: Readings in Environmental Philosophy*, co-edited with Lori Gruen, is to appear in 1993.

Matthias Kettner is Professor of Philosophy at Johann Wolfgang Goethe University, Frankfurt. He has written a number of articles in applied ethics and philosophical psychology. Other areas of specialization include Hegel's theoretical philosophy, Freudian psychoanalytic theory, and hermeneutics. Since 1985 he has worked directly with Karl Otto Apel and in close collaboration with Jürgen Habermas on the application of discourse ethics.

Edward W. Keyserlingk is Associate Professor of Humanities and Social Studies in Medicine at McGill University, Montreal, and Director of the Contemporary Family Program at McGill's Centre for Medicine, Ethics, and Law. Before taking up the position at McGill he directed the Health and Environmental Law Project of the Law Reform Commission of Canada. His publications include two books, *Sanctity of Life or Quality of Life in the Context of Ethics, Medicine and Law* (1979) and *The Unborn Child's Right to Prenatal Care* (1984), and numerous articles and reports in the areas of health, law, and ethics, and environmental law and ethics. Among the topics he has addressed are euthanasia, the right of unborn children to prenatal treatment, non-treatment of newborn children, and crimes against the environment.

Alistair M. MacLeod is Professor of Philosophy and Head of the Department of Philosophy at Queen's University, Kingston, Ontario. His areas of academic interest include moral, social, and political philosophy and business ethics. He is author of *Paul Tillich: An Essay on the Role of Ontology in his Philosophical Theology* (1973) and has written a number of articles on rights, distributive justice, equality, rationality, and business ethics.

Michael Philips is Professor of Philosophy at Portland State University.

His work in ethics and applied ethics has appeared in numerous philosophical journals and has been reprinted in several anthologies. He has recently
completed a manuscript on the problem of how to evaluate moral codes,
which develops and defends the approach he outlines in this volume. He
is currently writing a book on personal identity in collaboration with R. I.
Sikora.

James Rachels is Professor of Philosophy at the University of Alabama
at Birmingham. He is the author of numerous articles, the best known of
which is "Active and Passive Euthanasia," which appeared in the *New
England Journal of Medicine* in 1975. He has written three books, *The
Elements of Moral Philosophy* (1986), *The End of Life: Euthanasia and Morality*
(1986), and *Created from Animals: The Moral Implications of Darwinism*
(1990).

Holmes Rolston III is University Distinguished Professor of Philosophy
at Colorado State University, Fort Collins. His publications include five
books, the most recent being *Philosophy Gone Wild* (1986) and *Environmental
Ethics* (1988), and numerous articles and contributions to books. Much of
his work has been translated into other languages and republished in
many different parts of the world, both in academic publications and in
newspapers and periodicals. Recently he was named distinguished lecturer
for the 28th Nobel Conference, October 1992.

R. I. Sikora is Professor of Philosophy at the University of British Columbia. His academic interests include ethics, philosophy of mind, epistemology, and metaphysics. He is co-editor with Brian Barry of *Obligation to
Future Generations* (1978) and author of numerous articles in philosophical
journals. He is currently writing a book on rule utilitarianism and applied
ethics and collaborating with Michael Philips on a book about personal
identity.

Robert C. Solomon is Quincy Lee Centennial Professor of Philosophy
at the University of Texas at Austin. He is the author of several books
about business ethics including *Above the Bottom Line* (1983), *It's Good
Business* (1985), and *Ethics and Excellence* (1991). He is also the author of
The Passions (1976), *In the Spirit of Hegel* (1983), *About Love* (1988), and
A Passion for Justice (1990). He regularly consults and provides programs
for a variety of corporations and organizations concerned about business
ethics.

Roger Wertheimer is Associate Professor of Philosophy at California
State University at Long Beach. He is the author of *The Significance of
Sense* (1972) and of numerous articles in theoretical ethics, applied ethics
(biomedical and criminal justice), and other areas of philosophy. His

current research includes a general study of justification, explanation, and proof.

Earl R. Winkler is Associate Professor of Philosophy and Senior Research Fellow in the Centre for Applied Ethics at the University of British Columbia. He is co-editor with James E. Thornton of *Ethics and Aging* (1987), has chapters in several books, and has published numerous articles in philosophical journals, particularly in ethical theory and applied ethics. He is a member of the Advisory Council on Ethical Issues in Health Care for the British Columbia government, a member of the Permanent Consultative Council on Ethical Issues for the Law Reform Commission of Canada, and a founding member of the Canadian Bioethics Society.

Langdon Winner is Professor of Political Science in the Department of Science and Technology Studies at Rensselaer Polytechnic Institute, Troy, NY. In addition to his two books, *Autonomous Technology* (1977) and *The Whale and The Reactor* (1986), he has written many articles and reviews for academic journals and for other publications including the *New York Times Book Review, Science, Village Voice, Atlantic Monthly*, and *Rolling Stone*.

Michael Yeo is Associate Director for Administration at the Westminster Institute for Ethics and Human Values, London, Ontario. He is chief co-author of *Concepts and Cases in Nursing Ethics* (1991) and has published a number of articles in applied ethics, particularly concerning business and professional ethics. His current research includes co-directing a project on ethics in journalism.

Introduction

Earl R. Winkler and Jerrold R. Coombs

I

Interest in increasing our understanding of ethical issues concerning health care, business, the professions, and the environment has grown markedly over the last quarter century. When considering the main forces giving rise to this increased interest in applied ethics, one naturally thinks first of biomedical ethics, the most mature and well defined of the divisions of applied ethics. Although abetted by the "liberation" movements of the 1960s and 1970s, biomedical ethics emerged principally in response to various issues and choices that were created by new medical technologies. The traditional values and ethical principles of the medical profession came to be regarded as inadequate in these new situations, because they often seemed to require decisions which appeared to be clearly wrong.

There are obvious and important differences, at a general level, between the main divisions of applied ethics. Biomedical ethics is focused within a particular institutional setting and concerns the practices of a closely associated set of professions. Business ethics is broader in scope because the field of business is much more diverse than the medical field. Environmental ethics obviously has an even broader purview, including the attitudes and behavior of all of us, particularly our basic social patterns of resource use and consumption, and our fundamental moral attitudes toward other animals and the natural world.

In spite of these and other differences, however, business ethics and environmental ethics still have the same basic provenance as biomedical ethics. Within the context of traditional assumptions and values, modern industrial and technological processes, formerly seen as the very engines of progress, have led to global crisis. The *raison d'être* of environmental ethics is to criticize and improve the values and principles in terms of which we understand our responsibilities to future generations, our relationship to non-human animals and other living things, and our place in nature generally. Traditional values and principles of Western business practice have also come to seem inadequate to the complex realities of the modern world. This is particularly true regarding the social responsibilities of business, especially those concerning public health and safety and environmental risks. Scandals on Wall Street and the like may prompt endowments for ethics education in business schools, but they are not significant enough to explain the high level of interest business ethics currently enjoys. A more likely explanation will concentrate on such things as the realization that the traditional corporate obligation to maximize profits for shareholders, within the limits of applicable law, can lead much too easily to tragedies such as that at Bhopal.

Viewing the rise of applied ethics generally in this light, it is not surprising that as moral quandaries grew, first in bioethics and then in the other areas, hope for progress shifted from tinkering with traditional values to moral philosophy and foundational ethical theory.

II

As applied ethics has grown into an established field of study and practice, a number of important questions have arisen concerning the nature of the field and the problems within it. Paradoxically perhaps, one of the most fundamental of these concerns the usefulness of ethical theory. Traditional moral philosophy has virtually identified the possibility of genuine moral knowledge with the possibility of universally valid ethical theory, and has supposed that all acceptable moral standards, of every time and place, can be rationally ordered and explained by reference to some set of fundamental principles. *Perfect* theoretical unity and systematization may be impossible to obtain, because there may be a plurality of basic principles that resist ordering. But it is generally assumed that such principles will be few in number, such that substantial and pervasive order may be discovered. A corollary to this conception of moral knowledge is the view that moral reasoning is essentially a matter of deductively applying basic principles to cases. However, contrary to the expectations created by these methodological assumptions, many philosophers who ventured into clinics and boardrooms were chagrined to discover how little usefulness this deductive approach had in the confrontation with genuine moral problems.

Efforts to resolve real moral problems in medicine with some version of Kantian or utilitarian theory, for example, immediately confront the problem of the abstractness and remoteness of general ethical principles. Of course one wants best to serve the important interests of all concerned and to respect the personhood of the affected parties; but for real problems of practice the most important and difficult question often is how best to understand the current situation in just these terms. What, for example, could it mean to respect properly the personhood of a potential anencephalic organ donor? In the experience of many philosophers actually working in medical ethics, most of the real work of resolving moral problems occurred at the level of interpretation and comparison of cases. Recourse to abstract normative principles seemed never to override case-driven considered judgment. On the contrary, conflict between a putative principle and the extensive consideration of cases seemed always to result in refining the interpretation of whatever abstract principle was involved. This eventually led to a serious if not widespread erosion of confidence in the power of traditional normative theory to decisively guide the resolution of real practical problems.

In the field of biothetics, experience of this sort has given rise to a family of mid-level theories which claim to be grounded in our central traditions of normative theory but whose principles also claim to offer enough content to guide practical judgment. Similar theorizing is now being attempted in some quarters of business and professional ethics. Gradually, however, many philosophers and others who have worked extensively in applied ethics have moved in a different direction, toward a rejection of the traditional idea of developing and applying general normative theory. Their experience in the field has convinced them that the appearance of universality achieved by general normative theory is necessarily purchased at the price of too rigidly separating thought about morality from the historical and sociological realities, traditions, and practices of particular cultures. A result of this separation, as already mentioned, is a level of generalization and abstraction that makes traditional ethical theory virtually useless in guiding moral decision-making about real problems in specific social settings. Moreover, these critics see essentially the same problems of ahistoricism and abstraction reappearing with the standard mid-level normative theories in bioethics and elsewhere.

Concerns about ahistoricism and abstractness, and the problems of application that they create, have produced a powerful skepticism about the very possibility of constructing a perfectly general normative theory. By now this ancient philosophical quest appears to many to be inconsistent with the most immediate, natural, and defensible conception of morality. Viewed from the perspective of modern history, sociology, and anthropology, moralities are seen as social artifacts that arise as part of the basic elements of a culture – its religion, its social forms of marriage and family, its economy, and so forth. Morality is thus an evolving social instrument that serves a variety of very general ends, which are associated with different domains of social life and are pursued within the context of changing historical circumstance and significant epistemic limitations. As such, a morality may be criticized in terms of how well or ill it serves identifiable and worthy social ends. But, by the same token, what is good or right in some realm of life, within a given cultural setting, must be a function of a highly complex set of conditions, including psychological factors and patterns of expectations that are themselves created by social custom and convention.

In light of the very different historical origins of diverse social forms, across so many different cultures, there seems to be no good reason to assume that all defensible moral standards will be explicable in terms of a deductive relationship to some more or less unitary set of basic principles with more or less determinate normative content. Although such a theoretical reduction or reconstruction may be possible, in spite of cultural diversity and in spite of the overwhelming failure of all previous efforts to gain general acceptance of any set of fundamental moral principles, many now regard this enterprise as exceedingly doubtful, even philosophically naïve.

III

Skepticism about the possibility of normative theory on the grand scale and growing doubts about the feasibility of solving moral problems by deductively applying general principles has given rise to a plurality of approaches and ways of conceptualizing problems within the field of applied ethics. One general approach to practical moral decision-making that is currently gaining favor is *contextualism*. As variously developed in the current philosophical literature, contextualism is primarily critical of established beliefs about ethical theory rather than constructive of better and deeper models of moral reasoning and justification. From this point of view, it is unnecessary to strive for a universally valid ethical theory since there are more realistic ways of accounting for moral rationality and justification. In place of the traditional, essentially top-down model of moral reasoning and justification, contextualism adopts the general idea that moral problems must be resolved within the interpretive complexities of concrete circumstances, by appeal to relevant historical and cultural traditions, with reference to critical institutional and professional norms and virtues, and by relying primarily upon the method of comparative case analysis. According to this method we navigate our way to a practical resolution by discursive triangulation from clear and settled cases to problematic ones.

Closely associated with questions concerning the usefulness of general normative theory is the question of how we should conceive of the enterprise of living and acting morally. While Kantians and utilitarians focus on following appropriate rules and principles, an increasing number of philosophers in the field of applied ethics argue that we should focus on acquiring virtues appropriate to fulfilling our roles in particular cultural and institutional settings. This conception is consistent with a general contextualist orientation in rejecting the deductive model of moral deliberation. In so far as proponents of this position are concerned with ethical theory at all, it is a much more empirically oriented theory than moral philosophers have traditionally sought. Such theory seeks to understand the instrumental effects of various ways of conceptualizing and judging action and character within the context of the social and institutional roles persons play.

Another question which divides practitioners of applied ethics is where we should look in our quest for standards of justification for moral judgments. For some, the turn away from the deductive model of problem-solving in applied ethics has spurred renewed interest in procedural aspects of group moral deliberation and decision. They have begun to consider much more seriously the question of what features a decision procedure must have if its conclusions are to be regarded as morally justified. There seems to be considerable support for the view that a justified moral judgment must represent, in some sense, a free and informed consensus of all interested parties. The central problem is to gain a fuller understanding of the nature of the biases and distortions that affect decision procedures in particular social and cultural contexts, and thus to clarify the conditions under which we can be confident that we have at least approximated such a consensus.

Clearly, rejecting the deductive model of moral problem-solving does not entail rejection of all moral theory. Significant moral reform in social life depends upon securing some kind of theoretical purchase on established practice and institutional arrangements. Ethical theory in a form that is sufficient to this purpose is therefore necessary. It is necessary in many other ways as well. For example, theory of some sort is necessary even to approach the problem of moral status – what gives something moral standing such that it is an object of moral consideration in its own right. And only ethical theory can illuminate or resolve such questions as whether the distinction between killing and letting die is morally relevant in itself, or whether actual or hypothetical consent under certain ideal conditions is more important in justifying certain kinds of social institutions and policies. These questions, and countless others like them, simply are theoretical questions that arise naturally and unavoidably when attempting to make moral headway in a complex and changing world. Theories dealing with such questions as these, however, do not provide decision procedures for solving moral problems. Rather, they help us to extend and deepen our understanding of the complex set of moral concepts in terms of which we interpret our problems and dilemmas, and so point the way to improving our values and social practices.

The most relevant and useful theoretical constructions are likely to be those that are impelled by an informed understanding of the real conflicts and difficulties of practical life. The recent history of moral philosophy's contributions in the world of practice bears this out. Responses to particular theoretical issues arising in connection with problems like abortion and euthanasia, or concentrated efforts in areas like environmentalism and animal rights, have produced moral philosophy's most significant contributions to the important moral issues of the day. Moreover, the best work of this kind in applied ethics is currently exerting considerable influence on some of the most interesting work concerning ethical theory.

One of the consequences of the turn toward contextualism and virtue ethics has been a renewal of efforts to better understand the nature of practical moral reasoning and the norms governing it. This kind of exploration is presently fostering a kind of redirected *meta-ethics*. Rather than concentrating on the analysis of basic ethical concepts and the meaning of moral propositions, the focus is on the structure of actual moral reasoning, including comparisons with law and science, on the conditions for properly evaluating moral precepts and rules, and on the limits of rational decidability in morals. Meta-ethical theory of this kind, which might strive ultimately to systematically illuminate what abstract conditions social moralities, or their parts, must meet in order to be reasonable or defensible, may be philosophically very valuable. This kind of theory can at least serve, if not finally fulfill, a powerful intellectual desire for ordered, systematic understanding. And it could be helpful indirectly in practical terms as well.

IV

The majority of the papers in this volume are concerned with taking a fresh look at applied ethics, either in terms of its overall conception and methodology or in terms of methodological issues of narrower scope. A number of papers, both in part I and in part II, bear directly on the question of the relationship between ethical theory and moral practice, though in different ways and with different intentions. Taking another tack, some papers represent efforts to say something about procedures of rationality and consensus formation within practical ethics generally. Several papers in part I share this theme while also collectively representing both Anglo-American and European philosophical orientations to this topic. Papers having as their focus methodological issues related to individual fields of applied ethics make up the three sections of part II. Many of the positions represented in this part, however, are generalizable to other fields or have important implications for them, and they reveal numerous connections with the more general themes of part I.

The intensely practical and consensus-driven nature of applied ethics would alone serve to raise a question of its critical and reformative potential, but given the current trend toward meta-level contextualist accounts of moral reasoning and justification this issue becomes acute. From such a perspective, how can applied ethics avoid being inherently conventional and conservative? How, in other words, can applied ethics secure a sufficiently critical perspective on conventional moral and evaluative practices to be capable of genuine and, if necessary, radical reform? Environmental ethics perhaps deserves special attention in this regard because so much of its thrust is directed at deep, even revolutionary reform in moral attitudes toward other animals and the natural world. The general topic of the critical potential of applied ethics is the central concern of Rachels' paper in part I (chapter 6) but is also addressed less directly in several other papers in both parts.

Certain fields of applied ethics have developed to include professional consultation and the representation of so-called "ethicists" within institutional settings, on government commissions and committees, and in the media and the courts. This has resulted in much recent discussion of the whole issue of moral expertise. Can there be any such thing as a moral expert, or experts on the important ethical dimensions of certain domains of practice? Of course, if moral reasoning and decision-making were primarily a matter of defending some general principle and applying it to cases in a predominantly analytical way then, presumably, the skills associated with this process would constitute a sort of moral expertise which could be linked to certain sorts of training and preparation. In particular, training in the history of normative theory and analytic philosophy would appear especially relevant, even indispensable. On the other hand, a more contextualist approach to the processes of moral reasoning will recognize a central role in moral discourse for a variety of skills and intellectual and emotional resources beyond those that are typical of the moral philosopher. Psychological understanding and sensitivity will be seen as crucial, as will sociological knowledge, knowledge of religions, of political realities, and so forth. This point of view, therefore, sees applied ethics as inherently multi-disciplinary because it is impossible to locate all the skills and attributes necessary to progress in social morality in the training and skills that are typical of any single profession.

Although the issue of moral knowledge and expertise is the dominant theme only in Wertheimer's paper in part I (chapter 8), several other chapters throughout the volume address this issue either directly or tangentially. Interest in this issue, moreover, is not unrelated to a more general renewal of interest in "moral psychology" as philosophy has, in certain periods, concerned itself with this field. What, for example, are the principal sources of moral hypocrisy in our times, or how much does the credibility of one's moral views depend on their being based on certain kinds of relevant experience? The papers by Baier and Davis in part I (chapters 7 and 9) represent this dimension of recent work in applied ethics.

Thus far there is too little in contemporary moral philosophy that strives for a systematically balanced reconciliation of the claims of ethical theory in certain forms and the claims of contextualism. The individual papers in this book, with perhaps a few exceptions, do not greatly reduce this deficiency. Taken as a whole, however, in terms of recurring central themes, repeated contrasts, and interesting examples and suggestions, we hope that this volume helps to stimulate more work of this integrative kind.

For each chapter we include a brief summary of its main argument, together with suggestions concerning thematic comparisons with other papers in the volume.

ACKNOWLEDGEMENTS

In the summer of 1990 the University of British Columbia hosted an international conference on "Moral Philosophy in the Public Domain." Many of the papers in this volume originated as presentations at this conference, some especially commissioned for this purpose and most undergoing considerable revision since. This conference was part of a much larger undertaking aimed at the establishment of a permanent Centre for Applied Ethics; this was formally accomplished the following year. The editors wish to acknowledge the generous endowments of W. Maurice Young of Vancouver which served to fund this conference (in addition to providing the major impetus behind UBC's plans to found a Centre for Applied Ethics).

We also wish to thank Howard Jackson, chairman of the Philosophy Department at UBC, for his keen editorial advice; Michael McDonald, the current director of the Centre for Applied Ethics, for his help and encouragement; and Louise Stuart, the administrative secretary of the Centre, for her gracious and unfailing help in the preparation of the manuscript for this book. Lastly, we thank all of the contributors to this volume for their papers and their patience.

Part I
Methodology, Critical Potential, and Skeptical Doubts

1
Aristotle, Foucault and Progressive Phronesis: Outline of an Applied Ethics for Sustainable Development

Bent Flyvbjerg

Bent Flyvbjerg enters the debate on the nature and methodology of applied ethics through a consideration of the proper function of social science. His point of departure is the long-standing conflict over whether or not social sciences can establish general knowledge claims. They cannot be theoretical sciences, he argues and the attempt to pursue them as though they were has led to an emphasis on instrumental rationality and the neglect of rational inquiry concerning the value or desirability of our practices and institutions. He proposes that we see social science as essentially practice-guiding – as enabling us to find out what is desirable so we can choose and act wisely.

Conceived in this manner, social science is a kind of applied ethics, but it is not to be carried out by attempting to apply ethical theories or principles to particular problems. Rather, it should rely on the study and analysis of particular cases to discern what it is desirable to do. On this point Flyvbjerg is in agreement with the kinds of views presented by Winkler and Hoffmaster in this volume (chapters 19, 20) and argued at length by Albert Jonsen and Stephen Toulmin in their book, *The Abuse of Casuistry*.[1] Taking Foucault's work as exemplary, he argues further that the methodology of applied ethics should include consideration of the mechanisms of power operating in the case under consideration.

Flyvberg's argument that social science should be viewed as a kind of applied ethics should be compared with Hoffmaster's discussion of the relevance that ethnography, as a branch of anthropology, has for medical ethics.

No practical discussion is going to take place unless you understand the relevance of phronesis. *But no practical philosophy can be adequate for our time unless it confronts the analysis of power and how it operates in our everyday lives.*

Richard J. Bernstein

Asking Simple Value-rational Questions: A Lost Virtue

We live in an unprecedented historical period. Within the past few decades the actions of mankind have become, for the first time ever, a threat to life as we know it; not only through nuclear disasters that may or may not happen but through changes in the global ecology that *are* happening. Earlier the continuance of life on the planet was taken as given rather than subject to a question-mark. No wonder, then, it has been said we live in a *post*-era: post-rational, post-enlightenment, post-modern, post-foundationalist, post-structuralist. If any one phenomenon distinguishes the start of a new era and a *post*-condition, it is this: humanity's newly achieved ability to effectively destroy its own sustenance. The world has become post-immortal; not in the sense that life on the planet is necessarily mortal but rather that there is no longer any assurance of its immortality. We live in a world-at-risk, where life has become contingent upon our own actions.[2]

In this unique situation the need has never been greater to skillfully pose, answer, and act upon simple value-rational questions like the following:

- Where are we going?
- Who gains, who loses?
- Is it desirable?
- What should be done?

Ironically, the capacity for dealing with such questions has never been less developed than is currently the case – which, of course, is at the heart of the problem. Thinkers as different as Weber, Foucault, and Habermas have pointed out that for more than two centuries instrumental rationality has increasingly dominated value rationality, leading to what has been called the civilization of means without ends.

More than two thousand years ago Aristotle was keenly aware that the inability to think and act value-rationally could seriously impair the social and physical existence of individuals, communities, and societies alike. In the *Nicomachean Ethics* Aristotle discussed the social role of what he called "intellectual virtues" and focused, in particular, on three such virtues called *episteme*, *techne*, and *phronesis*. It is interesting to note that the terms *episteme* and *techne* are still found in current language, for instance in the words epistemology and epistemic, technology and technical, whereas *phronesis* has no direct modern counterpart.[3] This fact is telling of what has happened historically: the "virtues" still with us in words and in deeds are the ones central to scientific and instrumental rationality, whereas the lost virtue *phronesis* is the virtue related to value rationality and *praxis*. Aristotle found that any well-functioning society would be dependent on the effective workings of all three intellectual virtues in science, craft/art, and ethics, respectively. Yet Aristotle emphasized *phronesis* as the most important virtue, "for the possession of the single virtue of prudence [*phronesis*] will carry with it the possession of them all [all the intellectual virtues]."[4]

With the rationalistic turn of the past two or three centuries *phronesis* and value rationality have become marginal practices. Today one strategy for dealing with this problem is to go back through the rationalistic turn asking what can be learned about the present from the past and how the modern concept of rationality can be reformulated and enlarged from this experience. The aim is not to develop a historical understanding of Aristotle or other ancient Greeks, nor to present Greek philosophy or ancient Greek society as an ideal to be striven for today. The point is, simply, to ask what can be learned about our present situation from a current reading of Aristotle.

Aristotle on *Episteme, Techne* and *Phronesis*

In the English translation of the *Nichomachean Ethics* the words used for *episteme* are "science" and "scientific knowledge." Aristotle defines *episteme* as knowledge that is universal, eternal, and can be demonstrated to be true from first principles, i.e. knowledge that in Aristotle's own words is fixed and "cannot be otherwise than it is."[5] This is the definition of science as "pure" science and the ideal of absolute knowledge that has dominated epistemology and science for more than two thousand years, often to a degree where the ideal would be considered the only legitimate model for "real" science. Recently the ideal of fixed knowledge has been shown to be an *idée fixe* and has been set in motion even in the natural sciences, first by Kuhn's uncovering of a universal hermeneutics in the production of scientific knowledge and since by the chaos theorists of physics. But unlike modern science, Aristotle did not limit his concept of truth to *episteme*: he saw *techne* and *phronesis* as two additional dimensions to what truth is.

Techne today is typically translated into two meanings that in ancient Greece were one, namely art and craft. Aristotle says that *techne* is "a productive state that is truly reasoned" and that *techne* always concerns bringing something into being that was not.[6] As distinct from *episteme*, which aims at uncovering how things are that cannot be otherwise, the product of *techne* is always capable of being otherwise or "of being or of not being."[7] Therefore, according to Aristotle, *techne* concerns what is variable, not what is fixed; it concerns pragmatics, not universals.

Where *episteme* concerns universal *knowledge* and *techne* concerns the *production* of things, *phronesis* concerns "*action* with regard to things that are good or bad for man."[8] Accordingly, the point of departure for *phronesis* is an analysis of values and their implications for action. *Phronesis* is the type of knowledge and reasoning that forms the basis for *praxis*. With respect to the question of who, in particular, possesses this intellectual virtue, Aristotle says: "We consider that this quality belongs to those who understand the management of households or states."[9]

Like *techne*, *phronesis* has its main focus on that which is variable and particular, that which requires deliberation and judgment. More than anything else, *phronesis* requires experience and practical common sense. It is worth quoting Aristotle at length on this point:

> Prudence [phronesis] is not concerned with universals only; it must also take cognizance of particulars, because it is concerned with conduct, and conduct has its sphere in particular circumstances. That is why some people who do not possess theoretical knowledge are more effective in action (especially if they are experienced) than others who do possess it. For · example, suppose that someone knows that light flesh foods are digestible and wholesome, but does not know what kinds are light; he will be less likely to produce health than one who knows that chicken is wholesome.[10]

In this passage Aristotle emphasizes a number of characteristics of intellectual work that, in my judgment, are crucial to the development of situational and applied ethics:

- The importance of what is particular and context-dependent is emphasized over what is universal.
- The importance of what is concrete and practical is emphasized over what is theoretical.
- Aristotle immediately practises what he preaches by giving a concrete example in support of his argument. Aristotle, here as elsewhere, is clearly conscious of the "power of example".
- The example concerns human health and takes as its point of departure something which is at the same time specific and fundamental to the way human beings function. Both are typical for the ancient Greeks.

Below we will return to these and related points *in extenso*. At this stage what should be observed is that, important as these points may be to the development of situational and applied ethics, in many areas of social science and philosophy they are highly controversial. My guess is that in many quarters one would be the laughing-stock of colleagues if one chose to support arguments by examples similar to Aristotle's chicken example. Supposedly the very task of science and philosophy is to uncover universals; in addition it is conventional, but misguided, wisdom that one cannot generalize from the particular, for instance the singular case; finally, working with theory is typically considered more prestigious than doing empirical or practical work – in most fields the development of theory is considered the ultimate goal and pinnacle of scientific endeavor. The problem is that Aristotle is explicitly anti-Socratic and anti-Platonic on these points, while for more than two thousand years, despite pockets of dissent, the Socratic–Platonic tradition has influenced science and philosophy more than any other tradition. For this reason Aristotle's line of argument regarding the relationships among science, art/craft, and ethics does not seem to resonate with mainstream social science and philosophy today. Yet, this is the very kind of argument we need in order to develop situational and applied ethics.

Beyond Relativism and Nihilism

Before moving on to the more specific discussion of developing methodological guidelines for an applied ethics, I want to address a question as old as science itself: Can the study of man and society be scientific in the same sense as the study of natural objects, or must one speak of two fundamentally different activities in relation to the two types of object? According to Aristotle, it makes a difference whether one studies man or things. If he is wrong on this point, his argument for the importance of ethics is severely weakened.

But the passage of time suggests Aristotle is right. The study of man and society is not, never has been, and, most likely, never will be scientific in the sense of the natural sciences, i.e. comprised of predictive theory. It is highly improbable, for instance, that the "dubious" science of economics will ever be able to predict and engineer changes in the exchange rate between deutschmarks and US dollars in a fashion similar to the way physics can predict and engineer a moon landing. The reason is that the object of the social sciences, man, is self-interpretive, whereas physical objects, to the best of our knowledge, are not; the object of the social sciences is, in effect, a subject. Thus the social sciences involve what Anthony Giddens has called a "double hermeneutic": What counts as a relevant fact or feature is dependent on the interpretation of both researchers *and* the people being studied.[11] In the natural sciences only a "single hermeneutic" is at work, that of the researchers, since physical objects do not "answer back." The self-interpretations of people being studied in the social sciences are inherently unpredictable because they are always already context-dependent and cannot be reduced to a set of rules.[12] Predictive theory *must* be context-independent and rule-based, otherwise the independence of specific time and space required for prediction cannot be established. Social "theory" *cannot* be context-independent because what counts as a relevant feature to the theory is context-dependent. There goes the epistemic ideal and the possibility that someday the social "sciences" can be constructed based on cumulative refinements of theory like the natural sciences.

To many this conclusion will be unacceptable since from a conventional point of view the very identity and *raison d'être* of science is to be found in the epistemic ideal. Those seeing things this way may agree that the social sciences are not *as yet* predictive and that these sciences have not reached the level of the natural sciences but will argue that this is because the social sciences are younger than the natural sciences, their study object is more complex, their experiments more difficult to control, etc. In due time, when the social sciences reach the level of maturity of the natural sciences, the social sciences will be epistemic and perform as well as the natural sciences, or so the argument goes. The comfort of this position is obvious: the ideal to be striven for is clear, and in many academic settings prestige, money, and power depend on acceptance of this view.

The thought of giving up the epistemic ideal, with its focus on fundamental universals and predictive theory, seems to generate in many what Richard Bernstein has called Cartesian Anxiety, i.e. the fear that in so doing one opens the door to relativism and nihilism.[13] In fact, the door is already wide open because the mainstream social sciences have not come to terms with the fact that despite several hundred years of attempts at establishing themselves as epistemic sciences the epistemic ideal still seems to be an illusion; and obviously a sound bulwark against relativism and nihilism cannot rest on an illusion. The consequence is highly volatile non-cumulative social sciences susceptible to political and academic whims.

A sounder basis for the social sciences can, in my judgment, be found in a contemporary interpretation of the concept of *phronesis*. In a discussion of the differences between different kinds of sciences in relation to *episteme* and *phronesis*, Aristotle explicitly states that "the political sciences are species of prudence [*phronesis*]," and that sound sciences in this area cannot be based on *episteme*.[14] Being an accomplished scientist in the epistemic sense of the word is not enough when it comes to the political sciences, since "although [people] develop ability in geometry and mathematics and become wise in such matters, they are not thought to develop prudence [*phronesis*]."[15] The role of the political sciences, according to Aristotle, is to clarify values and interests and, on this basis, deliberate about what is good for man and society. Just as *phronesis* is considered the most important among intellectual virtues, so to Aristotle political science is indispensable to a well-functioning society because "it is imposs- ible to secure one's own good independently of . . . political science."[16]

This reading of the role of political science can, in my judgment, inspire contemporary social science and philosophy as a species of *phronesis*. In this role social science and philosophy would ask and analyze, as a basis for social action, simple value-rational questions such as those mentioned in the first section above. The questions would be asked in relation to specific areas of polity, economy, technology, ecology, and culture. To mention but one obvious example, the questions would be asked in relation to the currently pressing issue of establishing a global development pattern that is "sustainable" with respect, for instance, to the depletion of the atmosphere's ozone layer or a possible greenhouse effect.[17] Social science and philosophy practised in this manner would, in fact, be applied ethics and would in many ways resemble what has been called "social science as public philosophy" by Robert Bellah and his colleagues, "practical philosophy" by Richard Bernstein and others, "situational ethics" by Hub- ert and Stuart Dreyfus, and "applied philosophy" by the Academy for Applied Philosophy in Denmark.[18] Epistemic sciences, to the degree that post-Kuhnian and post-chaos-theory natural sciences can be called epis- temic, currently have little to offer in relation to the value-rational analysis of applied ethics because of their singular focus on instrumental rationality.

With the reintroduction of *phronesis* into the discussion of what science is and ought to be, the picture often drawn of impotent social sciences and potent natural sciences is seen to be misleading. Social science and natural science have their strengths and weaknesses along fundamentally different dimensions and should not be compared on the single dimension of *episteme*. The social sciences have much to contribute to social, economic, technological, ecological, political, and cultural development when prac- tised as *phronesis*, but little when practised as *episteme*. This, of course, renders the endless but futile attempts at making these sciences epistemic all the more unfortunate because they take up resources that could be used meaningfully elsewhere. The natural sciences, vice versa, have a proven track record of comparatively cumulative and stable epistemic results but have very little to offer as *phronesis* in relation to the most pressing issues of the day, these issues often being a result of natural science made instrumental in technologies with negative side-effects on nature and society.

Max Weber was the first social scientist to offer a comprehensive and systematic account of the one-sided development of instrumental rationality at the cost of value rationality in modern society. Weber spoke of "Occiden- tal" rationalism, that is, the "specific and peculiar rationalism" that distinguishes Western civilization from any other.[19] Today it no longer seems pertinent to describe this rationalism as a singularly Western phenomenon, unless the purpose is to describe its historical roots, for this rationalism is becoming increasingly global, especially with respect to its consequences. Weber was particularly interested in the social and cultural effects of instrumental rationality, for instance as they appeared in what he saw as alienation and an undermining of traditional values that contributed to a general "disenchantment of the world." Since Weber, these effects, by most accounts, have become more pronounced, and within the last few decades a whole new complex of problems in relation to ecology and nature has been added, posing a serious risk to the very existence of the living world, disenchanted or not.

The problem of ecology and natural resources is rarely mentioned in connection with Weber's work. He saw, however, with impressive foresight, that the burning of fossil fuels was central to the workings of instrumental rationality and the existence of what he called "the vast and mighty cosmos of the modern economic order." In fact, Weber thought it likely that what he called the "iron cage" of instrumental rationality could not be broken out of and that value rationality would not regain importance "until the last ton of fossilized fuel is burnt."[20] Weber could not foresee the greenhouse effect and global warming, the main cause of which is the burning of fossil fuels. Today, however, we can add to Weber's insights that there probably is no time to wait for the last ton of fossil fuel to be burned before bringing to an end the dominance of an instrumental rationality that has, in many ways, gone astray. More than ever there is a need for value rationality to balance instrumental rationality.

Foucault as a Paradigmatic Case

Around the time of publishing *The Order of Things* in 1966 Michel Foucault was deeply involved with the question of whether the study of man, society, and government could become scientific in the epistemic sense of the word.[21] Influenced by French structuralism, then in its heyday, Foucault seemed to think that epistemic social sciences could be achieved. However, in an interview published two years before his death in 1984, Foucault said he no longer was interested in this question, and continued: "I am not even sure if it is worth constantly asking the question of whether government can be the object of an exact science."[22] Instead, Foucault told the interviewer, "what interests me more is to focus on what the Greeks called the *techne*, that is to say, a practical rationality governed by a conscious goal."[23] Foucault did not say in the interview, or elsewhere, what the reasons were for his shift in interests from *episteme* to *techne*. His work after *The Archaeology of Knowledge* (1969) indicates, however, an eventual realization that structuralism would not live up to its promise of becoming a scientific methodology, and that there were no signs to be found anywhere in the sciences of man and society that these "sciences" were on their way to becoming, or would ever become, epistemic.[24]

After *The Archaeology of Knowledge* Foucault no longer seemed interested in epistemology and theory, but turned to developing his genealogical method in the famous studies of prisons and sexuality.[25] Foucault's method was now developed by actually applying it, not talking about how it *should* be applied.[26] And Foucault was explicit that the aim with his studies of power was "to move less toward a 'theory' of power than toward an 'analytics' of power."[27] A dense understanding of the particulars of power relations in specific domains was at the heart of his analysis and the movement from theory to analysis was paralleled by a movement from asking the structurally inclined *why* of power to the more dynamic *how*: in other words, there was a movement from explanation to narrative. Foucault's studies after 1970–1 are highly selective case studies based on in-depth empirical analysis and interpretation of vast primary source materials. Foucault now lets the studies tell their own story to the extent this is possible, but the fact that he does not attempt to generalize the studies theoretically does not mean they have no value outside their specific domains. With obvious support in the work of Nietzsche, Foucault chose his cases with great acumen as to their strategic importance: how better to get at the root of understanding a society than by showing, for example, how it defines crime and controls criminals, how it defines mental disease and isolates the mentally ill, how it defines and controls sexuality? Foucault's studies gain their general interest by uncovering metaphors and paradigmatic cases of the workings of society, not by any attempt at theorizing.

In this reading of Foucault, an important lesson of his work before 1970–1 is that the study of man and society cannot be epistemic and, accordingly, that in the social sciences *techne* cannot be thought of as applied epistemic science, even if this is the conventional conception of the relationship between *episteme* and *techne*, or pure science and applied science. The later Foucault studied *techne* directly – without the superstructure of *episteme* – as a practical rationality governed by a conscious goal. By linking *techne* to goals Foucault now approached it "from the other side," that is, from *phronesis*, and by analyzing in detail the relationships between different kinds of *techne* and different kinds of power the purpose was "to criticize the workings of institutions, which appear to be both neutral and independent" and, ultimately, to change the workings of these institutions.[28] Thus, by approaching *techne* in this manner Foucault came to practise a method which in many ways is similar to that of *phronesis* with its emphasis on goals, values, interests, and *praxis* instead of on theories and epistemic knowledge. In fact, Foucault expanded the concept of *phronesis* considerably by indirectly giving it an interpretation more fused with power issues than any earlier interpretation of the concept.[29] As James Bernauer has pointed out, whatever conclusions his future readers may draw, Foucault's work has made it more difficult to think unhistorically, non-politically, and non-ethically, that is, irresponsibly, about *praxis*.[30]

Methodological Guidelines for an Applied Ethics

Few researchers seem to reflect explicitly on the strengths and weaknesses of the social sciences practised as *episteme*, *techne*, and *phronesis*, respectively. Even fewer are carrying out actual research on the basis of such reflection, and fewer still have explicated what the methodological guidelines would be for social science practised as *phronesis*. In fact, it seems that researchers practising *phronesis*-like methods have a sound instinct for getting on with their research and not getting involved in methodology, a case in point being the sparseness of methodological considerations and guidelines in Foucault's work mentioned earlier. None the less, given the above interpretation of the actual and potential role of the social sciences, it is an essential task in the development of these sciences toward social usefulness that such guidelines are developed as a basis for an applied ethics.

One way of approaching this problem would be to carry out a reading of the method implicit in select examples of *phronesis*-like research. The methodological guidelines given below are based on such a reading of, among others, Michel Foucault, Hubert Dreyfus, Clifford Geertz, and Robert Bellah, who, however different on other matters, all practise social science as "public philosophy." The readings indicate that an applied ethics based on a contemporary interpretation of *phronesis* would focus on the following points, as methodological guidelines for practical research:

● *Values*. By definition, an applied ethics inspired by *phronesis* should focus on values, for instance by means of the simple value-rational questions mentioned earlier: Where are we going? Is it desirable? What should be done? The basic purpose is to balance instrumental rationality by enhancing the capacity of individuals, communities, and societies for value-rational action.

● *Power*. In addition to asking the three questions mentioned under "values," an applied ethics inspired by *phronesis* should also ask: Who gains and who loses? By virtue of which mechanisms of power? What are the possibilities for changing existing power relations, if desirable? Of what kind of power relations is the applied ethics itself a part? An applied ethics needs to ask these questions in order to avoid the voluntarism and idealism typical of many schools of ethical thought.

●*Closeness*. Researchers practising applied ethics inspired by *phronesis* should get intimately close to what they study and embed their research in the relevant context in order to ensure a hermeneutical "fusion of horizons." This holds true for both contemporary and historical studies. For contemporary studies researchers should get physically close to what or whom they study, both when gathering data and when publishing results; researchers should expose themselves to reactions – positive and negative – to what they are doing and to the learning this potentially involves. Researchers should, to a certain extent, become part of what they study, without the result necessarily being simple action research or "going native." For historical studies researchers should physically work where the relevant historical material is located and should immerse themselves deep in archives, annals, and individual documents.

●*Minutiae*. Researchers should, as a point of departure, ask "small questions" and focus on extensive description of minutiae, even if this often seems trivial. This methodological guideline, which runs counter to much conventional wisdom on "important issues" and "big questions," is based on the lesson from phenomenology that small questions often lead to big answers and that details often, when scrutinized closely, are pregnant with metaphor. Research should be as detailed and as general as possible, finding what is big in what is small, and vice versa.

●*Practices*. Research should focus on practical activity and practical knowledge in daily life situations. This *could* mean, but is in no way limited to meaning, a focus on traditional sociological concepts of "everyday people" or "everyday life." What it *does* mean is a focus on the actual daily practices that constitute a given area of interest, be it the dynamics of Wall Street, Greenpeace, or a small-town parent–teacher association. Practical rationality in action is considered more fundamental as an object of study than discourse and theory.

●*Concrete cases*. Research should focus on case studies, precedents, and exemplars. *Phronesis* is based on practical rationality and judgment. As argued elsewhere, practical rationality operates mainly on the bases of in-depth case experience and there is no way of understanding practical rationality except through cases.[31] Judgment can be cultivated and communicated only by exposure to exemplars. As Richard Rorty has pointed out with John Dewey, the way to re-enchant the world may be to stick to the concrete.[32]

●*Context*. Research should focus on context, since practices and cases can only be understood in their proper context. In this interpretation, applied ethics is always situational ethics. The focus is on tradition, and on *Sittlichkeit* more than on *Moralität*.[33]

●*How-questions*. Research should take its point of departure in how-questions more than in why-questions; in *verstehen* more than in *erklären*. Outcome is always understood in close relation to the dynamics of process.

●*Narrative/history*. "History" is important in both meanings of the word in an applied ethics inspired by *phronesis*: both as the narrative of an *histoire* with specific actors and events, and as the recording of historical development.

●*Actor/structure*. Research should focus on both actor and structure without becoming trapped in the dualisms actor–structure, hermeneutics–structuralism, voluntarism–determinism.[34] A movement beyond these dualisms is needed.[35]

●*Dialogue*. By definition, dialogue is important in an applied ethics inspired by *phronesis*. The whole purpose of such an ethics is to contribute to *praxis* via public dialogue, since according to Aristotelian thought, greater trust is placed in the public sphere than in the authority of science. At a minimum, four levels of dialogue can be distinguished in research with this purpose: dialogue in relation to those being studied, in relation to fellow researchers, in relation to policy-makers, and, last but not least, in relation to the general public.

Progressive Phronesis and Sustainability

I want to suggest the term "progressive phronesis" for an applied ethics working according to these methodological guidelines. The term "progressive" is added in order to stress the contemporary character of the concept, attributable not least to the inclusion of power issues. Aristotle did not enclose in his conception of *phronesis* explicit considerations on power. This may not have been a problem for practising *phronesis* among the elite in the Greek *polis*. But as Richard Bernstein rightly has pointed out in an evaluation of Hans Georg Gadamer's conception of *phronesis*, which also does not include issues of power, if today we are to think about politics and what can be done to the problems of our time, as we clearly are when we talk about the world-at-risk and sustainable development, there is no way to avoid progressing from the original conception of *phronesis* to one explicitly including issues of power: "No practical discussion is going to take place unless you understand the relevance of *phronesis*. But no practical philosophy can be adequate for our time *unless it confronts the analysis of power and how it operates in our everyday lives.*"[36] This is one reason why the work of Michel Foucault, with its explicit and consistent emphasis on issues of power, is particularly relevant to a current interpretation of what *phronesis* is and should be.

The general task of an applied ethics practised on this basis would be to give concrete examples and detailed narratives of who is getting and using power for what purposes, and to suggest how others might get it and use it for other purposes. The task is to clarify the problems we face and to outline how things can be done differently in full knowledge that we cannot find grounds for final answers to these questions. In relation to the question of sustainable development, the task would be to focus examples and narratives on the specific problems of this issue: ensuring that essential needs for jobs, food, energy, water, and health are met globally, conserving and enhancing the earth's resource base, protecting the atmosphere so that it can protect us, and reorienting the development of technology to serve these purposes.[37] Ultimately the task is to make the world-at-risk less risky to live in. My own research on these problems indicates that even though technical issues and the development of effective technical solutions to the sustainability problem are and will continue to be important, and even if they are the issues most often discussed in professional and political circles alike, they are not the main obstacle in moving toward sustainability. Developing local and global power relations that will allow for the implementation of effective technical solutions to the sustainability problem is the primary challenge before us.

This centrality of power relations was apparent at a recent United Nations conference held in Bergen, Norway, to put into action the World Commission's recommendations on sustainable development, in particular as they bear on a possible greenhouse effect and depletion of the atmosphere's ozone layer. Attended by representatives from 34 countries, the conference failed to lay down specific goals on carbon dioxide emissions, the main cause of a possible greenhouse effect, because action was blocked by the USA. The US objection to specific goals was couched in scientific terms: evidence on the greenhouse effect is insufficient, and more research needs to be done before action can be taken. However, a closer look reveals the issue of power. The US level of carbon emissions per capita in 1987 was approximately 140 percent higher than that of Japan, 70 percent higher than that of West Germany, and 2,550 percent higher than that of India.[38] The USA is the world leader in carbon dioxide emissions and may have more to lose from restrictions on emissions than other countries. Currently the "American way of life" depends on a high level of burning of fossil fuels and, accordingly, on a high level of carbon dioxide emissions, and the 60–80 percent reduction in these emissions identified as necessary to prevent global warming could be seen as threatening the American living standard. Thus the USA currently has a vested interest, however short-sighted it may be, in a no-restrictions policy on carbon dioxide emissions. Among many expressions of this interest was a US government memorandum of April 1990 on "discussions to be avoided" on global environmental issues. It encouraged officials to manage discussions by focusing on the many uncertainties in research that need clarification.[39]

In opposition to this attempt at "discourse management," the majority of countries at the Bergen conference wanted to act on the basis of a "principle of caution," giving the benefit of doubt to the environment. These countries wanted, but did not get, an agreement among participating countries on quantitative goals and deadlines for carbon dioxide emissions. Sweden, one of these countries and historically a leader in environmental and social policy, has already approved a policy to freeze carbon dioxide emissions at 1988 levels, to tax emissions by 1991, and to reduce by 50 percent over the next decade emissions of nitrogen oxides, a main cause of ecological damage to water, soil, and vegetation. Even on as mundane a level as that of the Stockholm Street Traffic Office one already finds a fully fledged action program for necessary changes to vehicles and traffic in the greater Stockholm region in pursuit of the implementation of national goals. The program is based on the obvious, but rare, insight that if every city and region does not work toward the national goals, it will be impossible for the country as a whole to meet them. The difference between Sweden and the USA is not that science is further advanced in the former than in the latter, but that, instead of the power-in-the guise-of-science strategy that the USA is currently following on the "greenhouse" question, Sweden is following its tradition for following the principle of caution, established not by scientific evidence, but by a tradition of open political and public debate of the issues involved, that is, by a tradition of *phronesis*, in which greater trust is placed in the public sphere than in the authority of science.

Another noteworthy point arising from the Bergen conference is that the scientific community at the conference, in endorsing the "principle of caution," abstained from the conventional epistemic ideal of neutral instrumental-rational sciences. The spokesperson for the scientific arm of the conference was a philosopher, and the scientific community very strongly played the phronetic role of clarifying values and interests as a basis for action, underscoring the point made earlier that philosophy and social science have an important role to play in relation to the problems of our time. This is not to say that natural scientists cannot or do not have an important role to play in this respect. They do, and they did at the Bergen conference. However, when they do, they are practising not natural science, but applied ethics. To a certain extent this was the course Einstein, Bohr, and many other socially concerned physicists took when the atomic bomb and its consequences became reality in the 1940s, and they got involved in the political and ethical issues of reducing the risk of repeated use of the bomb. Today the possibility of global warming, depletion of the atmosphere's ozone layer, and other environmental threats are having a similar effect on natural science, social science, and philosophy alike, making more and more scientists and philosophers ask the simple value-rational questions introduced at the beginning of this chapter. Aristotle would have us deliberate about "what is good for man and society"; in our times, this entails also asking: "What is good for the world-at-risk?"

NOTES

1   Albert Jonsen and Stephen Toulmin, *The Abuse of Casuistry: A History of Moral Reasoning*, Berkeley and London: University of California Press, 1988.
2   Thanks are due to Neal Richman for assistance in finding the appropriate words to describe this situation.
3   In English *phronesis* is typically translated (if translated at all) into the awkward term "prudence."
4   Aristotle, *The Nichomachean Ethics*, Harmondsworth: Penguin, 1976, 1144b33ff. To Aristotle man has a double identity. For "human man," i.e. man in politics and ethics, *phronesis* is the most important intellectual virtue, according to Aristotle. To the extent that man can transcend the human condition, contemplation is most important: 1145a6ff; 1177a12ff.
5   *Nichomachean Ethics*, 1139b18ff.
6   Ibid., 1140a1ff.
7   Ibid., 1140a1ff.
8   Ibid., 1140a24ff, emphasis added.
9   Ibid., 1140a24ff.
10 Ibid., 1141b8ff.
11 Anthony Giddens (1984): *The Constitution of Society: Outline of the Theory of Structuration*, Cambridge: Polity Press, pp. xxxv, 284.

12   The argument is fully developed in Bent Flyvbjerg (1987): "Teori og metode i studiet af menneske og samfund," Working Paper, Institute of Development and Planning, University of Aalborg. See also Hubert Dreyfus (1984): "Why Current Studies of Human Capacities Can Never be Made Scientific," *Berkeley Cognitive Science Report*, vol. 11, and Pierre Bourdieu (1977): *Outline of a Theory of Practice*, Cambridge: Cambridge University Press, esp. chs 1, 2.

13   Richard J. Bernstein (1985): *Beyond Objectivism and Relativism: Science, Hermeneutics, and Praxis*, Philadelphia: University of Pennsylvania Press.

14   *Nichomachean Ethics*, 1141b8ff.

15   Ibid., 1142a12ff.

16   Ibid., 1142a12ff.

17   See e.g. World Commission on Environment and Development (1987): *Our Common Future*. Oxford: Oxford University Press, or the many reports and papers from the Worldwatch Institute, Washington, DC, on these and related matters.

18   Robert N. Bellah et al. (1985): *Habits of the Heart*, Berkeley: University of California Press, pp. 297ff; Bernstein: *Beyond Objectivism and Relativism*, p. 40; Hubert and Stuart Dreyfus (1991): "Sustaining Non-Rationalized Practices: The Body, Power and Situational Ethics," an interview by Bent Flyvbjerg; *Praxis International* Vol. 11, No. 1. Academy of Applied Philosophy (1987): *Statement of purpose*, Klampenborg, Copenhagen.

19   Max Weber (1958): *The Protestant Ethic and the Spirit of Capitalism*, New York: Scribners, p. 26.

20   Ibid., pp. 180–2.

21   Michel Foucault (1973): *The Order of Things: An Archaeology of the Human Sciences*, New York: Vintage Books. (First published 1966.)

22   Michel Foucault (1982): "Space, Knowledge and Power," an interview by Paul Rabinow, in Paul Rabinow, ed. (1984): *The Foucault Reader*, New York: Pantheon, p. 255.

23   Ibid.

24   Michel Foucault (1972): *The Archaeology of Knowledge and the Discourse on Language*, New York: Pantheon. (First published 1969.)

25   Michael Foucault (1979): *Discipline and Punish: The Birth of the Prison*, New York: Vintage. Michel Foucault (1980–4): *The History of Sexuality*, vols 1–4, New York: Vintage; Paris: Gallimard.

26   Two of the few works with explicit methodological considerations are Michel Foucault (1971): "Nietzsche, Genealogy, History," in Rabinow, ed.: *The Foucault Reader*, and Foucault: *The History of Sexuality*, vol. 1, part 4, ch. 2 (first published 1976). The importance of these works to an understanding of the project and method of the later Foucault cannot be overestimated.

27   Foucault: *The History of Sexuality*, vol. 1, p. 82.

28   Noam Chomsky and Michel Foucault (1974): "Human Nature: Justice versus Power," in Fons Elders, ed.: *Reflexive Water: The Basic Concerns of Mankind*, London: Souvenir Press, p. 171.

29   For a more comprehensive reading of Foucault's work as *phronesis* and for

an explication of his methodology in the study of power, see Bent Flyvbjerg (1991): *Foucault's erfaring, Nationalitet oi MACT*, Vol I, Copenhagen: Academic Press.

30 James W. Bernauer (1988): "Michel Foucault's Ecstatic Thinking," in James W. Bernauer and David Rasmussen, eds (1988): *The Final Foucault*, Cambridge, Mass.: MIT Press, p. 75.

31 Bent Flyvbjerg (1989): "Socrates Didn't Like the Case Method, Why Should You?," in Hans E. Klein, ed.: *Case Method Research and Application: New Vistas*, World Association for Case Method Research and Application, Needham, Mass. See also the excellent analysis of this point in Alisdair MacIntyre (1977): "Epistemological Crises, Dramatic Narrative and the Philosophy of Science," *Monist*, vol. 60.

32 Richard Rorty (1985): "Habermas and Lyotard on Postmodernity," in Richard J. Bernstein, ed.: *Habermas and Modernity*, Cambridge, Mass.: MIT Press, p. 173.

33 See also Dreyfus and Dreyfus: "Sustaining Non-Rationalized Practices."

34 An "actor" can be either an individual person or a collective entity, e.g. an organization.

35 Regarding what a movement beyond these dualisms might mean, see the excellent analysis in Hubert Dreyfus and Paul Rabinow (1982): *Michel Foucault: Beyond Structuralism and Hermeneutics*, Brighton: Harvester Press. See also Thomas McCarthy's considerations on hermeneutics and structural analysis in his introduction to Jürgen Habermas (1984): *The Theory of Communicative Action*, vol. 1, Boston: Beacon Press, pp. xxvi–xxvii.

36 Richard Bernstein (1989): "Interpretation and Solidarity," an interview by Dunja Melcic, *Praxis International*, vol. 9, no. 3, p. 217, emphasis added.

37 World Commission on Environment and Development: *Our Common Future*, ch. 2.

38 Christopher Flavin (1989): *Slowing Global Warming*, Washington, DC: Worldwatch Institute, pp. 26ff.

39 *Information*, May 14, 1990.

2
Scientific Knowledge, Discourse Ethics, and Consensus Formation in the Public Domain

Matthias Kettner

Matthias Kettner's essay is explicitly grounded in the "discourse ethics" of Apel and Habermas. In his view the job of the moral philosopher is not that of solving moral problems – that is to be done through practical discourse aimed at consensus. However, any agreement brought about by practical discourse is morally justified only to the extent that it represents a rational consensus. The philosopher's task is to provide the procedural norms which practical discourse must fulfill if its conclusions are to be regarded as rational. Accordingly, Kettner formulates five standards for evaluating the moral adequacy of any process by which consensus about public policy is formed. In the second part of his paper, he uses these five standards to evaluate the processes by which support for the development of nuclear power was secured in Europe and the United States.

Kettner's essay presents an interesting contrast to the essay by Jagger (chapter 4). Although they have very different emphases, both focus on the importance of rational dialogue in moral problem-solving. The crucial difference between the two is one that divides many moral philosophers. Whereas Kettner attempts to show that there is a practical use for philosophers' criteria of rational practical dialogue, Jaggar thinks they are relatively pointless, since there is little hope of approximating them in any actual situation. Another important comparison is with Winner's paper (chapter 3) concerning the absence of opportunity for citizen participation in decisions about the introduction and use of technology.

Discourse ethics as developed by Karl-Otto Apel and Jürgen Habermas postulates a number of procedural conditions for rational consensus formation with regard to both normative and factual issues. In the first part of this paper I present an outline of the theoretical and the practical levels of discourse ethics. I claim that discourse ethics provides a critical yardstick

Prepared for the conference on Moral Philosophy in the Public Domain held at the University of British Columbia, June 1990. The author thanks Peter Mostow for valuable comments.

for evaluating processes of consensus formation about public policy decisions. I introduce the normative concept of the "consensual etiology" of an existing institutional arrangement. In the second part of the paper I apply the concept of a consensual etiology in order to critically evaluate the history of public consensus formation about the civil use of nuclear power, showing that public consensus formation about nuclear power falls short of certain morally relevant constraints. Furthermore, I discuss how political decision-making concerning nuclear power relies on "mandated science," i.e. science used or interpreted for the purposes of making policy, as a questionable surrogate of morally required consensus.

2.1 The Structure of Discourse Ethics

Discourse ethics is a normative moral theory developed by Karl-Otto Apel (Apel 1972, 1978, 1979, 1982, 1988, 1990) and Jürgen Habermas (1989, 1990). Discourse ethics has been characterized as deontological, pro-cedural, universalistic, and cognitive (see Habermas, 1989). More important perhaps than these features, which discourse ethics shares with a number of other post-conventional normative moral theories, is a structural feature: discourse ethics is a two-level theory. On the first ("theoretical") level, discourse ethics is a specific program of meta-ethics and normative philosophical ethics. Its objective is to specify and justify prescriptive contents that can then serve as regulative ideas, i.e. as rationally justified operative idealizations, on the second level ("level of practical discourse"). It is up to philosophy to theoretically specify the concept of practical discourse; practical application of this concept in the non-ideal actual world proceeds through the social practices of persons whose moral life is not up for philosophy to control. Discourse ethics thus distinguishes between the role of the moral philosopher as theorist and the role of someone involved in the resolution of actual moral problems. The main point of this distinc-tion is to avoid intellectual paternalism. Sections 2.1.1–2.1.4 contain a description of the two levels of discourse ethics, inevitably somewhat condensed as a result of the limited space available here.

2.1.1 The Theoretical (I) Level: Deriving Prescriptive Contents from Presuppositions of Argumentation

On the philosophical or theoretical level, discourse ethics attempts to delineate a range of prescriptive contents for which a rationally definite grounding can be expected, to spell out such contents, and to establish their presumably universal validity by ascertaining their rationally definite grounds.

Such grounds, it is claimed by Apel, can be found in the very activity of argumentation itself, i.e. they can be ascertained when people involved in argumentation (e.g. about the truth of a proposition p, or the rightness of some normative arrangement n) reflect on operative presuppositions that have to be shared in their exchange of argumentative speech acts in order for this exchange to be meaningful as argumentation. Such presuppositions are thus non-contingently related to argumentation.

Apel calls such non-contingent presuppositions of argumentation "transcendental–pragmatic" presuppositions: "pragmatic" inasmuch as they pertain to and are operative in a communicative *praxis*, namely argumentation; "transcendental" inasmuch as commitment to those presuppositions is unavoidable for any speaker whose utterances are made according to those action-concepts that belong to our concept of communicative rationality, i.e. to a concept that is itself indispensable for and irreplaceable in every possible discursive world.[1]

In argumentation, we are dialogically and cooperatively trying to arrive at the *best reasons* (e.g. to hold true that p, or to hold right that S ought to do A). Hence we are trying to furnish reasons that we assume, under ideal conditions, would convince everybody competent with regard to the disputed issue of why such and such ought rationally be held to be valid, or invalid. Argumentation, then, is a dialogical procedure whose outcome tends to reflect not unequal powers, differences in social status, or divergent intellectual abilities of the participants but rather the force of the better argument only. Argumentation that operates under this regulative ideal Apel and Habermas call "discourse."

Apel claims that there are transcendental–pragmatic presuppositions of argumentation that are morally relevant and have universal normative validity. Consider, for example, the fact that participants in discourse necessarily presuppose, with regard to all beings capable of speech and argumentation, their reciprocal recognition as free and equal persons, namely as persons who are equally entitled to, and equally free to, express consent or dissent to validity claims entirely on the basis of their rational evaluations of reasons and arguments. Furthermore, in argumentation over validity claims we presuppose that the intrinsic aim of our activity is the settling of disputed validity claims by rational agreement reached entirely through uncoerced dialogue. Although dialogue in the actual world is always bound to be dialogue within a limited community of particular persons, the audience that is being addressed in terms of counterfactual intentions is a "virtually infinite community of communication" (see Apel

1981). Apel has made this point in terms that draw on Charles S. Peirce's seminal idea of an infinite community of investigators.

Both these morally relevant presuppositions are strongly counterfactual: Though any real episode of argumentation will conform to these presuppositions by virtue of its being an episode of argumentation, it will not always be evident to the participants that they make these presuppositions, nor can they be sure that these presuppositions are in fact sufficiently fulfilled within the confines of their actual community of communication. However, if someone substantially doubts their fulfillment with regard to a particular episode of argumentation (say, a participant in a discourse concerning the truth of some proposition p learns that potentially valuable contributors have been shunned or that relevant evidence has been suppressed) then she has *prima facie* good reason to withhold consent and to criticize the impaired communicative rationality embodied in that particular episode.

The nature of transcendental–pragmatic presuppositions can be clarified by comparison to Kant's "regulative ideas." The aim of this paper, however, is to apply rather than to theoretically defend discourse ethics. Therefore I will not pursue this point here. Instead, I conclude my exposition of the first ("theoretical") level of discourse ethics by briefly introducing some points that Apel hopes can be defended by appeal to transcendental–pragmatic presuppositions of argumentation (see Apel 1987).

2.1.2 Discourse as Product and as Process

Ideally, the outcome of discourse will be a rational consensus. However, any particular consensus as the product of a concrete, historically situated and hence limited community of communication is fallible. Hence in principle it must be open for revision. Consensus can be spurious in a number of ways. If the communicative rationality that was presumed to have been exercised in some specific consensus-oriented process can be shown to have been flawed, or if new arguments relevant to the contents of some particular consensus should emerge, discourse has to be taken up again. Discourse is thus an open-ended project.

The authority of any discursively reached consensus is the authority of rational agreement, i.e. any discursively reached consensus, despite its fallible nature, will be taken to manifest whatever has in its favor *our best reasons*. We take "our" good reasons to be good reasons judged from everyone's perspective, not just from our own perspective. With regard to truth, any discursively reached consensus about the truth of some proposition p will manifest the best reasons anyone can have to agree to p's being true (*p* is, then, what everyone *ought rationally* to believe). With regard to moral rightness, any discursively reached consensus about the moral rightness of some prescriptive content *n* (e.g. a particular norm of action) will manifest the best reasons anyone can have to consider *n*'s being morally binding on everyone (*n* is, then, what everyone *ought morally* to abide by).

Discourse ethics accounts for the social binding force of moral commitments only to the extent to which such commitments can be justified by appeal to universalizably good reasons. Moral commitments, of course, may and do rest on many other force-giving sources. And not every moral commitment is by the nature of its particular content addressed to everyone. The accounts of moral psychologists and sociologists abound with explanations of societal or intrapersonal sources and mechanisms which generate forces that the individual perceives as morally binding. Anthropologists especially have a lot to say about group-specific moral commitments. The contention of discourse ethics is, rather, to spell out the cognitive kernel of morality: if morality has a rational core at all, then that core will have to manifest itself in the ideas that govern our procedures for discursively reaching consensus about the validity of prescriptive claims.

In the next section I introduce two principles that serve to pinpoint the Kantian heritage in discourse ethics.

2.1.3 Dialogical Universalizability and the Practical Discourse Demand

Discourse ethics modifies the Kantian principle of universalizability into a principle of dialogical universalizability. Instead of asking what an individual moral agent could, or would, will without self-contradiction to be a universal maxim for all, real people have to determine by engaging in uncoerced discourse which norms or normative institutional arrangements can be freely willed by everyone concerned.

This dialogical reading of Kant's categorical imperative yields the following criterion of moral rightness ("normative validity"): Every valid norm must satisfy the condition that all persons or parties affected can accept the consequences and side-effects that its general observance can be anticipated to have for the satisfaction of everyone's interests (cf. Habermas 1990). This idea captures and transforms the Kantian notion of a *test* for moral worthiness of maxims of action.

Discourse ethics modifies the Kantian position in yet another important respect. In discourse ethics, Kant's notion of the "good will" and the *imperative* side of Kant's categorical imperative are taken up in the notion of a morally rooted demand for a specific way of conflict resolution. Discourse ethics holds the following action-guiding principle as binding on every (real or possible) member of the (virtually infinite) community of communication: Whenever interests conflict, attempt to resort to practical discourse for resolving the issue!

On the first, or theoretical, level discourse ethics postulates that the morally obligatory course of action is to try to transform conflicting interests into *competing claims* over such *norms* that would, if valid, regulate conflicts in a way that all people affected would be able to acknowledge as morally right. For brevity, I shall refer to this demand as the "practical discourse demand." With this general action-guiding principle supplemented by the dialogical principle of universalizability, moral theory limits its domain of special authority. It is obvious that the practical discourse demand as it stands cannot be "applied" like a recipe to be followed or be "implemented" in domains of moral life by moral experts.

2.1.4 Prescriptive Contents for the Practical (II) level

The normative notion of a consensual etiology On the practical level, then, discourse ethics does not generate concrete moral principles, norms of action, or value-orientations. Instead, discourse ethics imposes a number of morally relevant constraints on the rational acceptability of any proposed or already entrenched substantive moral principles, concrete norms of action, value-orientations, etc. On the strength of the practical discourse demand, their rational acceptability is constrained by how they conform to practical discourse as a regulative idea: Any prescriptive content commanding universal allegiance that (we have good reason to suspect) *could not* have come into such a position via the route of dialogical universalizability will (to that extent) be disqualified for failing the practical discourse demand set up for moral rightness by discourse ethics.

I suggest we can best think of this demand in terms of a "consensual etiology": discourse ethics constrains the rational acceptability of any normative order, or institutional arrangement tied to a certain normative order, by requiring it either to have a consensual etiology, or to be conceivable as, or be an equivalent of, something that could have a consensual etiology. The idea of a consensual etiology should not be misunderstood for a utopian idea. Rather, the idea of a consensual etiology of x (some established normative order or existing arrangement) is a critical yardstick for evaluating the moral acceptability of x. The moral credit x deserves depends crucially on an evaluative comparison between the potential of opportunities for practical discourse that were bound up with the emergence of x on the one hand, and how x really made its way into the actual world on the other. To see how the practical discourse demand is relevant with regard to x in a certain episode of x's emergence is to see how the practical discourse demand could be attended to in that episode. How it is actually dealt with, or whether it is dealt with at all, has to be evaluated against this background. For instance, x's moral acceptability will be found to be impaired to the extent that absence of or distortions in the procedural conditions for practical discourse in relevant episodes can be explained as effected by agents with vested interests in the emergence of x.

To see the critical force of the practical discourse demand we can take a closer look at the notion of practical discourse. Below I point out five constraints that provide content to the notion of practical discourse. The five constraints I wish to underline make clear some important respects in which practical discourse differs from less demanding moral conversations and from practical deliberation in general. Those constraints also have momentous political implications with regard to public policy-making. In section 2.2 I will explore some of those implications specifically with regard to the issue of nuclear power.

Five morally relevant constraints of practical discourse

1 *Generality constraint* Practical discourse over an issue ought to be open to *all* competent speakers whose interests are or will be affected by regulations adopted to resolve the issue. I will call this feature of practical discourse the generality constraint. The generality constraint does not imply that any and every person affected will have to be heard; rather, what it implies is that the arguments put forward by the *actual* participants will have to be fairly representative of the arguments that *all others concerned* would or could present. The best way to ensure this is, of course, to make participation as widely inclusive as possible. Where the interests of future generations are at issue and direct participation is impossible, proxy or surrogate participants will have to step into their argumentative place in the discourse. It is debatable whether the representational capacities that are institutionalized in the parliamentary systems of modern democracies are adequate for these tasks.

2 *Autonomous evaluation constraint* Practical discourse provides its participants with symmetrical chances to introduce and challenge assertions and to express their needs, wishes, and interests. This implies a principle of non-paternalism. Practical discourse starts with the very terms in which the participants themselves construe the issue in question, their respective interests, and their moral commitments. Unlike objectifying moral theories such as (for example) preference utilitarianism, practical discourse does not replace the concepts under which people really intend their actions to be moral actions by some dogmatic format. This does not imply that each individual's needs, wishes, and interests as expressed go unchallenged.

To have the last word on one's interests in no way precludes improving on what one's first word would have been. Concepts can be questioned, for example when they are descriptively inadequate. Individual as well as collectively shared values and ideals can be challenged, for example when they dogmatically rule out alternatives. Interests can be considered illegitimate, for example when the needs, wishes, or beliefs on which they are based can be shown to be irrational. This feature of free accessibility of critical evaluations under non-paternalistic conditions I will call the *autonomous evaluation constraint* of practical discourse.

Related to the autonomous evaluation constraint are two further points, namely that practical discourse requires that the participants are subject neither to internal nor to external coercion. I shall address the absence of internal coercion first.

3 *Role-taking constraint* Participants must be able to adopt a hypothetical stance toward their own interests, values, needs, etc., as well as to those expressed by others. Internal coercion (e.g. strong neurotic fixations) will prevent people from adopting such a stance. To be capable of taking an interest in each other's interests, and to be prepared to let one's own interests be radically questioned, calls for what Kohlberg (1990) and others have termed "ideal role taking."

4 *Power-neutrality constraint* Absence of external coercion, on the other hand, means that existing power differentials between participants have to be bracketed or neutralized in some way so that they have no bearing on an issue within the cooperative pursuit of rational agreement through argumentation. To illustrate: if, for example, a South African farmer were seriously to debate the alleged moral rightness of slavery with his black servant he could not without pragmatic self-contradiction refer to his (still) superior power-position in order to prove his point, unless the discursive position were given up and turned into a position of collective bargaining or, in the worst case, to strategic threatening.

5 *Transparency constraint* The final feature of practical discourse that I wish to underline here is the incompatibility of practical discourse with purely strategic action. Strategic action is success-oriented action by an agent who treats others as limiting her conditions of operation or merely as means to the agent's ends. Practical discourse requires participants to share a full understanding of their goals and intentions relevant to the issue. As strategic action, overt or covert, is incompatible with unreservedly cooperative pursuit of rational agreement, strategic action has no place in practical discourse. Goals and intentions whose effectiveness requires their not being shared (e.g. lying, betraying, deceiving, pretending,

persuading, making believe) belong to latent strategic action, not to the consensual action that is required for practical discourse. I shall call this incompatibility the *transparency constraint* of practical discourse.

Section 2.2 applies discourse ethics as outlined so far to the issue of nuclear power.

2.2 Scientific Knowledge and Consensus Formation about Nuclear Power

National energy politics is an area of political decision-making that obviously affects the interests of the entire population. That such decisions, e.g. the decision to embark on ambitious nuclear power programs, are in fact momentous should be apparent to virtually everyone. In the USA at least since the Harrisburg reactor incident of 1979, in Britain since the disclosure of massive hazards caused by leaking radioactive wastes at Sellafield, and in Europe generally since the Chernobyl catastrophe of 1986 that exposed many European countries to intense radioactive emissions. The *political* fall-out of Chernobyl has forced public policy-makers in the energy sector to address resurgent anti-nuclear opposition and to confront a public that is increasingly aware of the potential costs and risks of an energy path that for a long time had seemed for the majority to be unquestionably worth pursuing.

Looking at how political thematization of momentous scientific and technological issues such as nuclear power unfolds historically, one detects a certain pattern. In an early phase, physical, scientific and economic considerations form the dominant aspect of rationality under which such issues are thematized. In time, such considerations are "replaced in importance by sociopolitical questions, which, in turn eventually give way to moral and ethical issues that become crucial" (Del Sesto 1979, p. 69). With nuclear power, we are presumably in this third stage now. This puts on the agenda a critical review of the surprising fact that only now do moral issues surrounding nuclear power technology gain importance. In the beginnings of the "natural history" of nuclear power technology, were there no moral issues to be addressed? Or have such issues been with us all along, their importance being realized only recently, and literally by accident? And if so, is this a morally irrelevant fact about the vicissitudes of technological experience, public awareness, and policy-making? Or does this fact rather reveal some morally relevant deficiencies that are part and parcel of the kind of rationality that is embodied in technological experience, in public awareness, and in policy-making?

One way to raise these questions is to judge the "natural history" of nuclear power and its political thematization against the normative model of practical discourse. In the light of the practical discourse demand, the "natural history" of nuclear power and its political thematization should be reconstrued as either embodying, or failing to sufficiently embody, a consensual etiology.

2.2.1   Economic Interests and Ideological Factors

The first thing to note in our attempt to discover a consensual etiology of nuclear power is that need and safety have been, and still are, the pivotal concepts in establishing either support for or opposition to nuclear power (Thompson 1984, p. 58). In the early days of nuclear power, political consensus rested mainly on energy need interpretations that were couched in terms of economic necessity with strong utilitarian overtones. It was argued, both in the USA and in Germany, that opting for nuclear power was an unrivalled means of ensuring the vital national objective of energy self-sufficiency and promoting economic growth. Later this argument gained some additional backing with the perceived threat of being black-mailed by the oil-producing countries of the Middle East. Furthermore, it was argued that the use of nuclear power was a means of avoiding the increased costs of fossil fuels, which would be rapidly ascending toward the end of the century due to the depletion of natural resources; and that nuclear power was the only option available for maintaining a high standard of living and for making such a standard available to all segments of society.

What a minority called a "Faustian bargain" was generally fairly well received as a great bounty for mankind: as a promise of "the greatest future ever spread before mankind with dazzling possibilities of life, liberty, and the pursuit of happiness" (Merriam 1947), providing virtually limitless energy that would be "too cheap to meter," as the enthusiastic phrase went (Del Sesto 1979, ch. 2). Yet what in these phrases is presented as embodying a morally worthy general interest was in fact never put to the test of dialogical universalizability. The utilitarian prophets helped to sell nuclear power to the masses by providing an ethical rationale for favorable attitudes; they did not, however, care to ask the public or to help people to critically consider their long-term interests, nor did they encourage people to make their own decisions for or against risks, costs, and benefits that were determined *for* them by experts in economics and physics. Hence, important decisions were made on behalf of the people affected, and neither the generality constraint nor the autonomous evaluation constraint was fulfilled.

In capitalist societies there is, of course, general agreement that people as contractors of goods and services are morally permitted to do as they please without critically considering their long-term interests. The "free market" will gauge needs, values, wants, risks taken, and products offered. Yet the very question, which ranges of goods and services the people agree to be subsumed under market conditions and which not, remains morally relevant. Even on a very narrow economic construal of nuclear power as, say, a promising technologically innovative product it is obvious that anybody's chance to express consent or dissent by means of buying or refusing to buy was unduly diminished as government goals ("national self-sufficiency") coincided with the power industry's vested interests to produce protection of those interests on a massive scale.[2]

In retrospect, the early political consensus in favor of nuclear power, and public policy-making based on that consensus, appear to have been driven by some powerful ideological motives. Such motives internally coerce practical discourse and give rise also to shortcomings with respect to the role-taking constraint. Most prominent in the case of nuclear energy are violations of the role-taking constraint *vis-à-vis* future generations. Among the motives that may contribute to an explanation of these violations are:

- the motive of embarking upon a thrilling technical challenge, based on a strong and ambitious faith in science and technology;[3]
- the motive of turning the curse of nuclear power into a blessing: the desire to shift the definition of nuclear energy from an evil military application to something that could benefit mankind;[4]
- the belief in the unlimited capacity of human intelligence to manage self-imposed problems and, generally, a "deeply embedded belief in the utility of science for achieving practical goals" (Del Sesto 1980, p. 50).

This third motive serves to throw into relief the prominent role of scientific expertise in public policy-making.

2.2.2 Mandated Science

In a world in which science coupled to technology has become the dominant productive force, policy-making and scientific expertise have become inextricably entwined. We depend on scientists to tell us whether we should be worried about radiation, whether nuclear power plants are safe, whether the greenhouse effect can be overcome, etc. It has widely been argued not only that scientific knowledge is intrinsically valuable, but also that because it is the only truly valid type of knowledge it necessarily leads to practical benefit (Weingart 1970). Science, so the story goes, is unique in its cumulative acquisition of unquestionable facts obtainable only so long as scientists are allowed to approach the study of nature with values that curb human tendencies toward bias, prejudice, and irrationality. This selective characterization of science in the political context amounts to the creation of a professional ideology. Values inherent in science are described by scientists in terms such as independence, emotional discipline, impartiality, and objectivity. For a long time, sociology of science has uncritically taken these self-interpretations at face value without questioning them as rhetoric that scientists use in order to preserve their prominent position in society's distribution matrix of power and prestige (Mulkay 1979).

The entry of scientists into the political arena affects them today in at least three ways:

- it influences their definition of technical problems, definitions which cannot themselves be decided by observation and systematic inference alone;
- it influences the choice of assumptions introduced in the course of informal reasoning and the informal acts of interpretation that are essential to give meaning to "purely scientific" findings (an example of this is the "linear" vs the "threshold" model in the debate over permissible radiation standards);
- it subjects scientists to the requirement that their conclusions be politically useful (cf Mulkay 1979, p. 114).

The last of these points indicates a redefinition, or social role change, with which scientists have to cope once they come to operate as experts or expert advisers in the political context. In that context they are being perceived as purveyors of certified knowledge; they have nothing to offer other than the supposed certainties of science. If they were to present their conclusions as no more than plausible guesses based on uncertain foundations they would carry little political weight.

Liora Salter, a Canadian sociologist who has extensively studied the role of science in the making of standards, has coined the term "mandated science" for science used or interpreted for the purposes of making policy (Salter 1988). Mandated science transforms scientific knowledge into policy recommendations. On the one hand, scientific backing for policy recommendations is simply necessary for factually informed decision-making. On the other hand, because of the symbolic moral capital vested in the scientific image, scientific backing for policy recommendations often serves to enhance trust in a preferred option and to morally discredit proponents who advocate alternative options but are unable to marshall scientific evidence in their favor.

I will now point out three structural features of mandated science, and their moral relevance for a consensual etiology account of public policy based on mandated science.

2.2.3 Why Mandated Science Fails as a Substitute for Morally Relevant Consensus

1 *Uncertainty* The first important feature of mandated science is uncertainty due to the fallible nature of proper empirical scientific knowledge. Uncertainty, which in non-mandated science is a tenet of adequate science, an assumption of its working practitioners, causes problems for regulators and those who want to use science to support their decisions. Mandated science is thus directed toward closure, toward the production of conclusions that would support decisions taken in a non-scientific sphere of activity. If scientific research is essentially an open-ended exploration of the characteristics of natural phenomena, the result presumably will be an ever more complex and indeterminate account of that reality.

The Rasmussen Report on reactor safety nicely illustrates this point.[5] For proponents as well as opponents of nuclear power, this report (and its magical number of 1.7×10^{-4}) has become a fixed point of reference in the debate over need and safety. This has tended to obscure critical issues of evaluation that are implicit in the seemingly technical terms "need" and "safety" in which the debate is framed. Why should it not turn out that nuclear power may be safe, but unnecessary? Or necessary, but unsafe? And if necessary, "necessary" in what sense? Necessary, perhaps, in order to "continue the expression of Western values of wealth, economic freedom, and opportunity through the development of industrial technology" (Thompson 1984, p. 68; see also Henderson 1981)? By narrowly focusing on the quest for certainty, mandated science contributes to failure to fulfill the autonomous evaluation constraint.

2 *Communicative irresponsibility* A second vulnerable point of mandated science can be seen in its notorious problems with communicative responsibility, i.e. problems inherent in the presentation of scientific findings to non-scientific audiences. "In order to maintain their credibility as scientists, participants in mandated science must . . . speak as if they were speaking with other scientists. To be effective in the policy arena, however, these same scientists . . . must speak with an awareness that others – whose preoccupations and interests are quite different – will use what they say to further goals that are unrelated to science" (Salter 1988, p. 8), and

that will probably create immense moral costs for the public. Failure to live up to communicative responsibility can amount to violations of both the role-taking and the transparency constraints.

Again the Rasmussen Report serves well to illustrate the point. Many laypersons with attitudes favorable to nuclear power took the message of the report to be simply that reactor safety had been *proven*, thus confusing empirically based extrapolation with proof. An even worse misunderstanding can be traced to a confusion of the estimated *probability* of an event (such as a melt-down) with the predicted *frequency* of such events: the report was used by some politicians to assuage anti-nuclear fears with the argument that a melt-down would be expected to occur not earlier than 10,000 years from now.

We should note in passing that it seems in practice impossible for a scientist in mandated science to act both in the role of scientists and in the role of a moral adviser: inasmuch as he or she is perceived to express moral value commitments his or her scientific trustworthiness will wane (Salter 1988, p. 193 provides an example). Therefore, the locus of moral reflection within mandated science will have to be occupied by persons who are specifically acknowledged in that role, not by the scientists themselves.

3 *Multiplication of dissent*   Another morally significant feature of mandated science is its tendency to multiply dissent such that it cannot be dealt with in ways prescribed by the epistemic nature of proper science. According to many studies of the use of science in external political settings (such as political debates), scientific knowledge eventually does not reduce the scope of political action. Rather, scientific knowledge becomes a resource which can be interpreted in accordance with political objectives (Mulkay 1979, p. 114; Nelkin 1971, 1975). Opposing parties in political disputes involving technical issues can usually all obtain the services of reputable scientists who will provide data to buttress their policy and to undermine that of their opponents. Within the political arena, the problem of unwanted scientific dissent-multiplication can be solved only by flat ("enough is enough") or by strategic action (e.g. by outbuying expertise, suppressing counter-expertise, etc.), thus violating the transparency constraint, or the power-neutrality constraint, or both.

2.2.4   After Chernobyl

I conclude with some brief remarks about the public debate in Germany after Chernobyl.

In order to meet the generality constraint of practical discourse, three obstacles to informed public discussion would have to be overcome, namely:

(1) lack of full public information; (2) lack of adversarial scientific expertise within proper science; and (3) unwillingness of the government to foster discussion of a topic which the government considers either too complex and technical for laypeople or more appropriate for a public relations program to allay public anxiety. The repercussions of the Chernobyl disaster have gone a long way towards overcoming the first and second obstacles. An extensive survey of public opinion changes from 1986 to 1988 (Peters et al. 1990) revealed that the majority of the German population did not shut their eyes to contradictions in the published information about the disaster. The public was (and still is) oriented both toward statements from established institutions (government sources, the nuclear power industry, nuclear research centers, etc.) *and* toward statements from alternative institutions (ecological institutes, the Green Party, Citizens' Action Committees Against Nuclear Power, etc).[6] This result may be interpreted as a widespread readiness to be critical of information and a preference for using different information sources with different perspectives (cf Peters et al. 1990, p. 128–9). However, the third obstacle (the government's unwillingness to foster critical discussion with the widest participation possible among those affected) remains crucial. Unless such discussions can take place, neither the generality constraint nor the autonomous evaluation constraint of practical discourse will be fulfilled.[7]

I cannot within the scope of this paper discuss any substantial proposal (such as, e.g., "science courts") for making informed public discussion about nuclear power more congruent with the exigencies of practical discourse. But certainly such proposals will have to reflect the spirit of John Stuart Mill, who once remarked: "The only way in which a human being can make some approach to knowing the whole of a subject is by hearing what can be said about it by persons of every variety of opinion, and studying all modes in which it can be looked at by every character of mind."[8]

NOTES

1   A "discursive world" is a world in which (1) there is an exchange of speech acts between at least two persons P_1 and P_2 that we can conceptualize as an episode of argumentation (about an utterance for which universal validity claims are raised) (2) such that P_1 and P_2 mutually share an understanding of their exchange as an episode of argumentation, and (3) P_1 and P_2 could share their mutual understanding with us.

2   "The technology came into being as a result of governmental investment and is growing as a consequence of governmental support. Its hazards to the health and safety of the public are not reflected in its costs because of the exculpatory effect of the Price-Anderson Act. [A parallel holds for Germany.]

Since the absence of market restraints deprives the public of the opportunity to vote with its dollars on the question of risks versus benefits, the public can participate in the risk/benefit determination only through its vote at the polls. The public is entitled to this vote and to the maximum feasible articulation of the risk/benefit problem in the political arena . . . why, in a democracy, should the public not have the full opportunity to decide for itself, rationally or irrationally, what benefits it wants and what price it is willing to pay?" (Green 1970, pp. 137–8).

3 Pro-nuclear "testimony was dominated by this faith in science and technology; one need only look at the masses of technical detail marshalled by pro-nuclear witnesses to get some idea of its importance. For example, AEC and industry witnesses framed their testimony almost entirely in terms of high complex scientific and technical data. In fact, over 80% of all testimony given by pro-nuclear witnesses was couched in terms of technical, facts-and-figures, or administrative expertise, as compared to some 17% for anti-nuclear groups" (Del Sesto 1980, p. 48).

4 For a discussion of various psychoanalytic explanations of pro-nuclear consensus, see Kettner 1989.

5 The Rasmussen *Reactor Safety Study* (1975) was and still is the primary evidence for proponents of nuclear power to redeem their safety claim. The Rasmussen study derives a mathematical frequency for accidents by extrapolating upon data for failures of specific components in safety systems – it is by no means a *proof* of reactor safety. Although Rasmussen did "a poor job of translating the method and results of the study into common sense terms" (Thompson 1984, p. 66), and despite a very critical review by the US Nuclear Regulatory Commission (*Risk Assessment Review Group Report to the US Nuclear Regulatory Commission*, Washington, DC: USNRC, 1978), the Rasmussen study cannot be said, as some would have it, to be thoroughly discredited: "A complete formal and epistemological critique of risk assessment methodology would be required to document opposition to safety claims based upon its results" (Thompson 1984, p. 66). However, the Chernobyl incident has provided such massive *prima facie* evidence against the safety conclusion that many people now consider Chernobyl as an informal or inductive *reductio ad absurdum* of any safety study, no matter how it is conducted methodologically.

6 Ambivalent awareness of competing opinions and options must be regarded as rationally preferable to single-minded ignorance of alternative opinions and options. The latter condition characterized media discourse and public opinion on nuclear power in the USA at least up to 1966 (Gamson and Modigliani 1989, p. 15).

7 One of the lessons that the German parliament drew from the cognitive dissonances that riddled the mass media after Chernobyl was to implement new regulations to the effect that information policy concerning nuclear hazards would henceforth be centralized at the federal government. This constitutes, in my opinion, a clear violation of the autonomous evaluation constraint (it is a paternalistic decision that sparing people some anxiety is

to be preferred over giving them unimpeded access to "all the news fit for print"). In fact, asked "whether they would prefer a more centralized or a more decentralized information policy in cases similar to the Chernobyl disaster, about 62% of the respondents . . . expressed their preference for a decentralized policy" (Peters et al. 1989, p. 10).

8 See esp. Shrader-Frechette 1985, ch. 9, and p. 313 for the quote by J. S. Mill. For an example of a workable framework for public deliberation about a complex bioethical issue, see Crawshaw et al. (1990).

REFERENCES

Apel, K.-O. (1972): The apriori of communication and the foundations of the humanities. *Man and World*, vol. 5, no. 1, pp. 3–37.

Apel, K.-O. (1978): The conflicts of our time and the problem of political ethics. In F. R. Dallmair (ed.), *From Contract to Community: Political Theory at the Crossroads*. New York: Marcel Decker.

Apel, K.-O. (1979): Types of rationality today. In T. Geraets (ed.), *Rationality Today*. Ottawa: Ottawa University Press, pp. 307–40.

Apel, K.-O. (1981): *Charles S. Peirce: From Pragmatism to Pragmaticism*. Amherst: University of Massachusetts Press.

Apel, K.-O. (1987): The problems of philosophical foundations in light of a transcendental pragmatics of language. In K. Baynes, J. Bohman, and T. McCarthy (eds), *After Philosophy: End or Transformation?*, pp. 250–90. Cambridge, Mass.: MIT Press.

Apel, K.-O. (1988): *Diskurs und Verantwortung*. Frankfurt: Suhrkamp.

Apel, K.-O. (1989): Normative ethics and strategical rationality. The philosophical problem of political ethics. In R. Schürmann (ed.), *The Public Realm. Essays on Discursive Types in Political Philosophy*. N.Y.: State Univ. of N.Y. Press pp. 107–131.

Apel, K.-O. (1990): Is the ethics of the ideal communication community a utopia? In S. Benhabib & F. Dallmayr (eds), *The Communicative Ethics Controversy*. Cambridge, Mass.: MIT Press.

Crawshaw, R., Garland, M., Hines, B., and Anderson, B. (1990): Developing principles for prudent health care allocation: the continuing Oregon experiment. *Western Journal of Medicine*, vol. 152, pp. 441–6.

Del Sesto, S. L. (1979): *Science, Politics and Controversy*. Boulder: Westview.

Del Sesto, S. L. (1980): Conflicting Ideologies of Nuclear Power: Congressional Testimony on Nuclear-reactor Safety, *Public Policy*, vol. 28, no. 1, pp. 39–70.

Gamson, W. A., and Modigliani, A. (1989): Media discourse and public opinion on nuclear power: a constructionist approach. *American Journal of Sociology*, vol. 95, no. 1, pp. 1–37.

Green, H. P. (1970): Nuclear power and the public. In M. Foreman (ed.), *Nuclear Power and the Public*. Minneapolis: University of Minnesota Press.

Habermas, J. (1989): *Moral Consciousness and Communicative Action*. Cambridge, Mass.: MIT Press.

Habermas, J. (1990): Discourse ethics: notes on a program of justification. In S.

Benhabib and F. Dallmayr (eds), *The Communicative Ethics Controversy*, pp. 60–110. Cambridge, Mass.: MIT Press.

Henderson, H. (1981): The challenge of decision making in the solar age. In D. Brunner et al. (eds), *Corporations and the Environment: How Should Decisions be Made?* Los Altos: William Kaufman.

Kettner, M. (1989): Ausstrahlungen. Psychologische Argumente in der Tschernobyl-Diskussion. In H. J. Wirth (ed.), *Nach Tschernobyl*, pp. 99–122. Frankfurt: Fischer.

Kohlberg, L. (1990): The return of stage 6: its principle and moral point of view. In T. Wren (ed.), *The Moral Domain: Essays in the Ongoing Discussion between Philosophy and the Social Sciences*, pp. 151–81. Cambridge, Mass.: MIT Press.

Merriam, C. E. (1947): On the Agenda of Physics and Politics. *American Journal of Sociology*, vol. 53, pp. 167–73.

Mulkay, M. (1979): *Science and the Sociology of Knowledge*. London: Allen & Unwin.

Nelkin, D. (1971): Scientists in an environmental controversey. *Social Studies of Science*, vol. 5, pp. 245–61.

Nelkin, D. (1975): The political impact of technical expertise. *Social Studies of Science*, vol. 1, pp. 245–261.

Peters, H. P. Albrecht, G., Hennen, L. and Stegelmann, H. U. (1989): "Chernobyl" and the nuclear power issue in West German public opinion. Preprint, Kernforschungsanlage Jülich GmbH.

Peters, H. P., Albrecht, G., Hennen, L. and Stegelmann, H. U. (1990): "Chernobyl" and the nuclear power issue in West German public opinion. *Journal of Environmental Psychology*, vol. 10, pp. 121–134.

Rasmussen, N. C. et al. (1975): *Reactor Safety Study: An Assessment of Accident Risks in U.S. Commercial Power Plants*. U.S. Nuclear Regulatory Commission, WASH-1400 (NUREG-75/014). Washington, D.C.: Government Printing Office.

Salter, L. (1988): *Mandated Science: Science and Scientists in the Making of Standards*. Dordrecht/Boston/London: Kluwer.

Shrader-Frechette, K. S. (1986): *Science Policy, Ethics, and Economic Methodology*. Dordrecht: Reidel.

Thompson, P. B. (1984): Need and safety: the nuclear power debate. *Environmental Ethics*, vol. 1, pp. 57–70.

Weingart, P. (1970): *Die Amerikanische Wissenschaftslobby*. Düsseldorf: Bertelsmann Universitätsverlag.

3
Citizen Virtues in a Technological Order

Langdon Winner

Winner's central concern is with understanding how a democratic citizenry can and should participate in decision-making about technology. This is the fundamental first step for an ethics of technology. Unfortunately, he claims, the Western tradition of moral and political philosophy has little to offer on this score. Most thinkers in our tradition have placed technology and politics in separate domains, isolating citizens' roles from the realities of technical practice and technical change. Winner insists that any attempt to discuss technology as a topic in moral and political philosophy must begin by considering how this crucial separation occurred historically and how it impairs our sense of possibilities. Winner sketches two distinct paths leading to the separation of politics and technology: the ancient view, focused particularly in Plato and Aristotle, and the modern view, beginning with the renewal of political philosophy in the sixteenth century and eventuating in the ideas of classical political liberalism as represented in the work of John Locke and Adam Smith. Paradoxically, the first separation is an expression of distrust or devaluation of techne, and the latter an expression of liberal trust and elevation of it. But the result, today, is that there is no moral community or public space in which technological issues are topics for deliberation and common action. After elaborating on the diminished quality of citizenship resulting from the gulf between the political and technical spheres, Winner closes by speculating on how democratic citizenship might be expanded to include greater participation in defining the common good regarding technological policy.

This paper should be compared with those of Kettner (chapter 2), Flyvbjerg (chapter 1), and, less directly, Jamieson (chapter 17).

As it ponders important social choices that involve the application of new technology, contemporary moral philosophy works within a vacuum. The vacuum is created, in large part, by an absence of widely shared understandings, reasons, and perspectives that might guide societies as they confront the powers offered by new machines, techniques, and large-scale technological systems. Which computer applications are desirable and

This article was originally published in *Inquiry*, vol. 35, nos 3–4, Autumn 1992.

which ought to be avoided? How can one weigh the risks of introducing a new chemical into the environment as compared to the benefits of its use? Should there be limits placed upon the ability of biotechnology to alter the genetic structure of plant and animal life? As we ponder issues of this kind, it is not always clear which principles, policies, or forms of moral reasoning are suited to the choices at hand.

The vacuum is a social as well as an intellectual one. Often there are no persons or organizations with clear authority to make the decisions that matter. In fact, there may be no clearly defined social channels in which important moral issues can be addressed at all. Typically, what happens in such cases is that, as time passes, a mixture of corporate plans, market choices, interest-group activities, lawsuits, and government legislation takes shape to produce jerrybuilt policies. But given the number of points at which technologies generate significant social stress and conflict, this familiar pattern is increasingly unsatisfactory.

Philosophers sometimes rush in to fill the void, offering advice that reflects their training and competence. They examine cases in which some feature of a present or emerging technology raises questions about right and wrong in individual choices and social policies. They take note of properties of the new technology that have important consequences for social life, properties that raise interesting philosophical issues; for example, issues about the rights and responsibilities of those who develop or use the technology in question. From there they can develop a variety of theories, principles, and arguments that may help people decide what to do.

Proceeding in this way, philosophers may find themselves involved in an exercise that is essentially technocratic. The complicated business of research, development, and application in modern life includes a moment where the "value issues" need to be studied and where the contributions of knowledgeable, degree-carrying experts can be enlisted. In the United States, for example, The National Science Foundation has for many years included a program on "ethical and value studies" that supports university scholars who do research of this kind. The underlying assumption seems to be that this is an important area that the nation needs to cultivate. The sponsors may hope that officially designated "values experts" will eventually be able to provide "solutions" to the kinds of "problems" whose features are ethical rather than solely technical. This can serve as a final tune-up for working technological models about to be rolled out the showroom door. "Everything else looks good. What are the results from the ethics lab?"

Philosophers sometimes find it tempting to play along with these expectations, gratifying to discover that anyone cares about what they think, exhilarating to notice that their ideas might actually have some effect. But is it wise to don the mantle of values expert? Although philosophers may be well equipped to help fill the intellectual emptiness arising from the lack of moral understandings, ethical reasoning, and community guidelines, there remains the social and political vacuum that so often surrounds discussions about the moral dimensions of technological choice. After one has addressed the range of social theories, empirical analyses, philosophical arguments, and ethical principles about the possibilities of Technology X, there remains the embarrassing question: Who in the world are we talking to? Where is the community in which our wisdom will be welcome?

Consider the following passages from two prominent writers addressing urgent ethical questions for our time. The first is from a well-known biologist reflecting about the ethical dimensions of developments in his own field:

> Given the nature of our society, which embraces and applies any new technology, it appears that there is no means, short of unwanted catastrophe, to prevent the development of [human] genetic engineering. It will proceed. But this time, perhaps we can seek to anticipate and guide its consequences.[1]

The second passage was written by a professional philosopher, exploring avenues for the new field of computer ethics:

> We are open to invisible abuse or invisible programming of inappropriate values or invisible miscalculation. The challenge for computer ethics is to formulate policies which will help us deal with this dilemma. We must decide when to trust computers and when not to trust them.[2]

Both these passages are notable for the way they employ the pronoun "we" in contexts where moral issues about technology are open for discussion. But who are the "we" to whom the writers refer? Both writers seem to mean something like "people in general" or "society as a whole." Or perhaps they mean something like "those who work in a particular field of technical development and have privileged access to the decisions that matter."

I raise this point not to call attention to the way writers, including this one, loosely deploy first person plural pronouns. What matters here is that this convenient "we" suggests the presence of a moral community that may not, in fact, exist at all, at least not in any coherent, self-conscious form. If "we" scholars find ourselves talking about a collectivity of others who are not in fact engaged in decisions, then it is time for "us" to look around and find out where "they" have gone. That is the important first task for the contemporary ethics of technology. It is time to ask: What is the identity and character of the moral communities that will make the crucial, world-altering judgments and take appropriate action as a result?

This question is, in my view, one about politics and political philosophy rather than about ethics considered solely as a matter of right and wrong in individual conduct. For the central issues here concern how the members of society manage their common affairs and seek the common good. Because technological matters so often become central features in widely shared arrangements and conditions of life in contemporary society, there is an urgent need to think about them in a political light. Rather than continue the technocratic pattern in which philosophers advise a narrowly defined set of decision-makers about ethical subtleties, today's thinkers would do better to re-examine the role of the public in matters of this kind. How can and should a democratic citizenry participate in decision-making about technology?

Unfortunately, the Western tradition of moral and political philosophy has little to recommend on this score, almost nothing to say about the ways in which persons in their roles as citizens might be involved in making choices about the development, deployment, and use of new technology. Most thinkers in our tradition have placed technology and politics in separate categories, defining citizen roles as completely isolated from the realities of technical practice and technical change. There have been two distinctive paths to this conclusion, one characteristic of thinkers in antiquity, another strongly advanced in modern times. But whether we are pondering ancient *techne* or today's megatechnics, any attempt to discuss technology as a topic in political and moral philosophy needs to pause long enough to appreciate how this crucial separation occurred and how it impairs our sense of possibilities.

Technology and Citizen: The Ancient View

At the beginning of Western moral and political philosophy speculation about *techne*, the realm of the practical arts, played a prominent but largely negative role. As Socrates, Plato, and Aristotle sought to define the nature of knowledge, the good, political society, justice, rulers and citizens, and the form of the best state, they frequently drew on comparisons to *techne*, the realm of the arts and crafts, viewing it with a mixture of awe and suspicion. Foremost among their concerns was the belief that technical affairs constituted an inferior realm of objects, knowledge, and practice, one that threatened to infect all who aspired to higher things.[3]

Thus, Socrates argues that philosophical inquiry needs to focus upon moral and political matters rather than consider questions of natural philosophy or the practical arts. One must seek higher wisdom, knowledge of the pious, the just, the good, rather than mastery of material things.

In the *Symposium*, Socrates recalls that this was a central lesson revealed to him by the priestess Diotima. Eros, or Love, she taught, is directed toward the higher, transcendent realm. Those who follow Eros may eventually attain knowledge of transcendent good. "For god mingles not with man; but through Love all the intercourse and converse of God with man, whether awake or asleep, is carried on. The wisdom which understands this is spiritual; all other wisdom, such as that of the arts and crafts, is mean and vulgar."[4]

Plato goes even further specifying why the realm of *techne* is both inferior and potentially dangerous. True knowledge, he argues, is not that of worldly, mutable, material things, but knowledge of the realm of unchanging ideas, *eidos*. Thus, he explains in *The Republic*, the real table is not that made by a craftsman, but the table that exists as an ideal form in the transcendent realm. Attempts to define the good society must understand this, seeking true rather than debased foundations for political practice. For that reason, Plato places the arts and crafts in the lowest of three social classes, and removes from them any chance of holding power. While he recognizes that agriculture, medicine, architecture, and the other practical arts are necessary to the life of the state, he denies that they offer anything of value in ruling a good society. In both *The Republic* and *The Laws*, Plato advises those who would rule to stay as far away from mundane technical activities as possible.[5]

Arguing for a position that was to become commonplace in antiquity and throughout much of the Middle Ages, Plato also criticizes the practical arts for their tendency to produce innovations, for being a source of harmful, potentially boundless change in human affairs. Political philosophy seeks to establish good order and to maintain it against the world's tendency toward chaos and decay. "Change, we shall find, is much the most dangerous thing in everything except what is bad – in all the seasons, in bodily habits, and in the characters of souls."[6] In the first century BC Lucretius echoes these sentiments, lamenting the destructive role of new techniques in warfare. "Tragic discord gave birth to one invention after another for the intimidation of the nations' fighting men and added daily increments to the horrors of war."[7]

Of all the classical arguments calling for the separation of technology from political affairs, the most significant is Aristotle's. For, unlike Plato, Aristotle explores the possibilities of a broadly based citizenship in political societies of many different kinds, perhaps even ones that resemble our own. As he defines the roles and virtues of a citizen, however, the crucial differences between technical and political life stand out.

Aristotle's view that "man is by nature a political animal" means that humans are creatures naturally suited to live in a polis or city-state.[8] Drawing upon studies of some one hundred and fifty city-states of his time, he argues in the *Politics* that the polis is the highest form of human organization, one that completes the development of other forms of association, the household and the village. Political life is a gathering of freemen and equals. Each man is free in the sense that there is no master to dictate his activities. Each one is equal as well, equal in legal standing, access to public office, and right to speak in political matters. Political life concerns matters that all citizens have in common. In the public sphere one's attention moves beyond personal or family interests to seek the good of the whole community. "One citizen differs from another, but the salvation of the community is the common business of them all."[9] Citizenship, active participation in public life, fulfills man's highest potential. The *bios politicos* realizes a greater good than more primitive forms of human existence ever attain.

Having defined politics in this manner, Aristotle goes on to explore the specific roles and virtues of the citizen. He notes the traditional distinction between the rulers and the ruled and concludes that the citizen must be different from both. Citizenship in his view must include both roles within each person.

> The excellence of the two is not the same, but the good citizen ought to be capable of both; he should know how to govern like a freeman, and how to obey like a freeman – these are the excellences of a citizen. And although the temperance and justice of a ruler are distinct from those of a subject, the excellence of a good man will include both.[10]

Looking at a range of existing constitutions, Aristotle concludes that a good constitution will allow the rotation of citizens in office so the "excellences" or "virtues" he recommends will become common in actual practice.

In the same passages that offer his definition of citizenship Aristotle takes care to specify which persons are not capable of holding this role. He points to the menial duties and craft work that were handled by slaves and foreign workers in Greek city-states of the time. Physical toil and use of the practical arts bind one to the realm of material necessity, a condition incompatible with the unencumbered freedom needed for citizenship. While slaves and craftsmen are necessary for the existence of the state and while some city-states recognize them as citizens, a good society will not extend citizenship in this way, "for no man can practice excellence who is living the life of a mechanic or labourer."[11]

Aristotle goes even further, arguing that citizens should avoid learning the practical arts because that would be degrading. "Certainly the good man and the statesman and the good citizen ought not to learn the crafts of inferiors except for their own occasional use; if they habitually practice

them, there will cease to be a distinction between master and slave."[12]
Thus, the making of useful things and the activities of public life must
forever remain separate.

While the ideas of Socrates, Plato, and Aristotle did not by themselves
define the understanding of the Greeks and Romans on such matters,
entirely similar notions about technology and economics were common in
antiquity. The sphere of technical affairs was closely associated with slavery
and menial labor and was, therefore, something that persons of the ruling
classes sought to avoid. In fact wealthy Romans normally left the day-to-
day handling of private economic affairs to their slaves, the origins of what
we today call "management."[13] While Romans sought material wealth, it
was usually gained through landed property and commercial trade, economic sources that did not require recurring technical change. Indeed,
technological innovation was widely regarded with suspicion. Suetonius
tells of a time when a creative soul came to the emperor Vespasian with
a device for carrying heavy columns into Rome at a low cost. Although
Vespasian rewarded the man for his invention, he refused to use it,
exclaiming, "How will it be possible for me to feed the populace?"[14] As the
historian M. I. Finley concludes, "Economic growth, technical progress,
increasing efficiency are not 'natural' virtues; they have not always been
possibilities or even desiderata, at least not for those who controlled the
means by which to try to achieve them."[15]

Technology and Citizen: The Modern View

With the renewal of political theory in the sixteenth century and since,
the prospects for social and political life were gradually redefined. Concepts
of power, authority, order, liberty, equality, and the state came to be
deployed in ways that we now consider distinctly modern. The attempts
of Machiavelli, More, Hobbes, Locke, Montesquieu, Bentham, and Marx
to create a new understanding of politics corresponded to path-breaking
work in the natural sciences that produced new ways of thinking about
the physical world. Strongly associated with these intellectual movements
was a thoroughgoing re-evaluation of the sphere of technical practice and
its economic settings, a re-evaluation in which the pessimism of ancient
and medieval views eventually yielded to an unbridled optimism. In this
ferment of ideas, the traditional view of the relationship between politics
and technology was overthrown and a new one imagined.

A leader in promoting respect for technical activity was Francis Bacon.
In *The New Organon* Bacon surveys the state of knowledge in his time,
criticizing the hold of the ancient philosophers over the minds of moderns.

He argues that the supposed wisdom of the Greeks is suspect precisely because it lacks any practical, material value: "It can talk, but it cannot generate, for it is fruitful of controversies but barren of works."[16] As an alternative Bacon sets forth a new program of knowledge and practice, one based upon careful study of particular phenomena, adherence to method, inductive logic, controlled experiment, naturalistic explanation, and a specialized division of labor among scientists. The ultimate purpose of such activity, he makes clear, ought to be the conquest of nature and expansion of human powers. Natural philosophy must go beyond the quest for knowledge as an end in itself and seek fulfillment in the practical arts.

As a former politician who had fallen from power in disgrace, Bacon enthusiastically praises the superiority of the new scientific and technical pursuits in contrast to affairs of state. Comparing the contributions of history's political heroes to those who have made wonderful discoveries and inventions, Bacon concludes that the highest honors go to scientific and technical innovators, "For the benefits of discoveries may extend to the whole race of man, civil benefits only to particular places; the latter last not beyond a few ages, the former through all time."[17]

Although Bacon's expectations about the directions the arts and sciences ought to pursue were not always prescient, his promotional views won numerous followers in later generations. Explicitly taking his advice, many French *philosophes* of the eighteenth century took great care to stress not only the practical value of technical pursuits but their intellectual strengths as well. In his *Preliminary Discourse to the Encyclopedia of Diderot*, Jean Le Rond D'Alembert notes the widespread contempt that surrounds the mechanical arts, an outlook that even the artisans themselves seem to share. He argues that, in fact, "it is perhaps in the artisan that one must seek the most admirable evidences of the sagacity, the patience, and the resources of the mind."[18]

Closely linked to a more favorable view of the practical arts and technical innovation is a change in attitude toward commerce and material self-interest. During the Middle Ages, avarice was often identified as both a sin and a source of civil unrest. While medieval societies were often quite open in their quest for wealth, the dominant view among clerical, political, and intellectual elites was that such motives should be carefully contained. A significant development in modern social and political thought was to annul this distrust and to recast ideas about wealth and commerce in an entirely favorable light. The pursuit of economic gain, some philosophers began to argue, is actually a force for moderation, helping to nurture more rational, peace-loving attitudes among both rulers and subjects. Persons with an economic stake in such trade and manufacturing were now thought to be healthy contributors to stability and justice in political society.[19] As Baron de Montesquieu argues in *The Spirit of the Laws*, "the spirit of commerce is naturally attended with that of frugality, economy, moderation, labor, prudence, tranquillity, order, and rule. So as long as this spirit subsists, the riches it produces have no bad effect."[20] Commerce, he argues, has another beneficial effect, binding nations together in a pattern of mutual need that discourages conflict.

Ideas of this sort, increasingly common in seventeenth- and eighteenth-century political theories, helped justify the modern optimism about economic self-interest and faith in the beneficence of economic growth which lie at the foundation of modern liberal thought. In the new understanding, wealth is good not only for its material benefits, but also because its pursuit produces better rulers and better citizens.

The idea that self-interested economic activity is fundamental to politics is strongly expressed in the writings of John Locke. In *The Second Treatise of Government*, Locke's conception of man is that of an acquisitive creature who subdues nature and makes it his property. Men leave the "state of nature" when they come to realize that their possessions are insecure. They form a society and, as a second step, submit to the rule of a government which recognizes their rights, particularly the right of property. From this point of view, the function of political society and government is that of defending the holdings of what are in essence private individuals. If it turns out that government is not useful in achieving these purposes, it can be rightfully overturned in revolution.

At the center of Locke's theory of political society and of modern liberal theory in general is a conception of human life that C. B. MacPherson has called "possessive individualism."[21] In this vision, acquisitiveness emerges as a positive, civilizing force. For as people pursue material gain, they become more rational, industrious, peaceful, and law-abiding. Hence the purely private virtues appropriate to a market society and capitalism are the virtues that build a stable political order. Of the activities that help produce a good society, none are superior to technical pursuits. As David Hume explains in his essay, "Of Refinement in the Arts," "In times when industry and the arts flourish, men are kept in perpetual occupation, and enjoy, as their reward, the occupation itself, as well as those pleasures which are the fruit of their labour. The mind acquires new vigour; enlarges its powers and faculties ... "[22] For that reason Hume advises rulers to encourage the development of manufacturing, even in preference to agriculture. Dynamic new enterprises are more civilizing than the bucolic traditions of farming.

An important feature of this persuasion in contrast to classical notions is that politics is assigned a relatively low position in the broader scheme of human affairs. For Locke, government is an instrument with no intrinsic value. Its role is to protect the rights of "life, liberty and property" by serving as an umpire when disputes arise. Attending to governmental matters is certainly not a sphere in which individuals can realize their highest potential. Locke finds no higher meaning in the realm of citizen action. One enters the public realm merely to express one's private interests. In contrast to Aristotle's view, Lockean liberalism recognizes neither goods nor virtues that stem from one's being as a public person.

In *The Wealth of Nations* Adam Smith develops the belief in the primacy of private affairs to its logical conclusion, viewing all public interference with scorn. Government measures, he argues, have "retarded the natural progress of England towards wealth and improvement."[23] Government is the source of extravagance, misconduct, and countless ill-conceived projects, while the "uniform, constant and uninterrupted effort of every man to better his condition"[24] is identified as the wellspring of most private and public good.

> It is the highest impertinence and presumption, therefore, in kings and ministers to pretend to watch over the economy of private people, and to restrain their expense, either by sumptuary laws, or by prohibiting the import of foreign luxuries. They are themselves always, and without any exception, the greatest spendthrifts in the society. Let them look well after their own expense, and they may safely trust private people with theirs.[25]

Ideas of this kind underlie basic institutions of politics and economics in modern liberal democracies, posing strong barriers to attempts to think about the public dimensions of technological choice. Technological change, defined as "progress," is seen as an ineluctable process in modern history, one that develops as the result of the activities of men and women seeking private good, activities which include the development of inventions and innovations that benefit all of society. To encourage progress is to encourage private inventors, entrepreneurs, to work unimpeded by state interference. As later theorists in the liberal tradition modify this understanding, they notice "market externalities" that cause stress in the social system or environment. This does not alter the fundamental attitude toward economic and technical choices. The burden of proof rests on those who would interfere with beneficent workings of the market and processes of technological development.

If one compares liberal ideology about politics and technology with its classical precursors, an interesting irony emerges. In modern thought the ancient pessimism about *techne* is eventually replaced by all-out enthusiasm for technological advance. At the same time, basic conception of politics and political membership are reformulated in ways that help create new contexts for the exercise of power and authority. Despite the radical thrust of these intellectual developments, however, the classical separation between the political and the technical spheres is strongly preserved, but for entirely new reasons. Technology is still isolated from public life in both principle and practice. Citizens are strongly encouraged to become involved in improving modern material culture, but only in the market or other highly privatized settings. There is no moral community or public space in which technological issues are topics for deliberation, debate, and shared action.

Technology and the Quality of Contemporary Citizenship

The hollowness of modern citizenship, the paucity of citizen roles, and the lack of opportunities for direct participation in politics is now a general condition, not limited to technology policy-making alone. Many writers have lamented structures of representative democracy that effectively exclude ordinary people from significant involvement in public affairs. Thus, Hannah Arendt notes with approval Thomas Jefferson's proposals that American government include "elementary republics" that might have brought small-scale political assemblies into the realm of everyday life. "What he perceived to be the mortal danger to the republic was that the Constitution had given all power to the citizens, without giving them the opportunity of *being* republicans and of *acting* as citizens."[26]

In contemporary political science, low voter turnout, citizen apathy, the triviality of political campaigns are often cited as consequences of the failure of modern democracies to include citizens in meaningful activities. Much of the recent discussion among social scientists about "participatory democracy" and "strong democracy" speculates about ways to remedy these shortcomings.[27] But apart from noticing the pungent effects of television upon election campaigns and the pervasive effects of modern consumerism, social scientists seldom take note of the connection between the hollowness of modern citizenship and the social relations of technology.

In fact, the political vacuum evident in the lack of citizen roles, citizen awareness, and citizen speech within liberal democratic society is greatly magnified within today's technology-centered workplace. Devices and systems commonly used in factories, fields, shops, and offices seek productivity and profit by controlling human behavior. In such settings the spontaneity and variability of workers' activities are regarded as a cause of uncertainty and a risk for business. For that reason the physical movements and decision-making abilities of employees are subject to rational planning and centralized guidance. Rather than encouraging personal autonomy, creativity, and moral responsibility, many jobs and machines are designed to eliminate these qualities altogether.[28]

One might suppose that the technical professions offer greater latitude in dealing with the moral and political dimensions of technological choice. Indeed, the codes of engineering societies mention higher purposes of serving humanity and the public good, while universities often offer special ethics courses for students majoring in science and engineering.[29] As a practical matter, however, the moral autonomy of engineering and other technical professionals is highly circumscribed. The historical evolution of modern engineering has placed most practitioners within business firms and government agencies where loyalty to the ends of the organization is paramount. During the 1920s and 1930s there were serious attempts to change this pattern, to organize the various fields of engineering as truly independent professions similar to medicine and law, attempts sometimes justified as ways to achieve more responsible control of emerging technologies. These efforts, however, were undermined by the opposition of business interests that worked to establish company loyalty as the engineer's central moral concern.[30] Calls for a higher degree of "ethical responsibility" among engineers are still heard in courses in technical universities and in after-dinner speeches at engineering societies. But pleas of this sort remain largely disingenuous, for there are few legitimate roles or organized settings in which such responsibility can be strongly expressed.

One could expand the inventory of social vocations in which moral issues in technological choice might be deliberated and decided, to include business managers, public officials, and the citizenry at large. Alas, there is little evidence that anything about these roles adds qualities of ethical reflection or action which are missing for ordinary workers or technical professionals. The responsibility of business managers is to maintain the profitability of the firm, a posture that usually excludes attention to the ethics of technological choice. Where questions of responsibility arise, businesspeople usually listen to hired lawyers who explain their legal liabilities. Elected officials, similarly, find little occasion to consider the moral dimensions of technological choices. Their standard approach is to consult the opinions of scientific and technical experts, judging this information in ways that reflect a variety of economic and political interests. The general public may have a vague awareness of policy choices in energy, transportation, biomedical technology and the like. But its response is increasingly apathetic, reactive, and video-centered.

Under such circumstances it is not surprising to find that people who call for moral deliberation about specific technological choices find themselves isolated and beleaguered, working outside or even in defiance of established channels of power and authority. At the level of individual action one finds the hero of much contemporary writing about technology and ethics – the "whistleblower," an employee who notices something troubling in the day-to-day workings of a sociotechnical system and tries to call it to the attention of a reluctant employer or the news media. By all accounts, such behavior is often severely punished by the organizations whose actions and policies the whistleblowers criticize. When they cannot be simply ignored, whistleblowers are isolated, fired from their jobs, and then black-balled within their professions. Their lives become embroiled in exhausting efforts to show the truth of their claims and re-establish their value as employees.[31] For career-minded students who study the stories of whistleblowers in university ethics courses, the underlying message is (regardless of what their teachers may intend): this is what happens if you speak out.

At the level of collective social action the method commonly used for expressing moral concerns about technological matters is that of "public interest" or "citizens'" groups. Organized around key issues of the day, such groups take it upon themselves to express the interests and concerns of an otherwise silent populace about such matters as the arms race, nuclear power, environmental degradation, abortion, and many other issues. Ralph Nader, Helen Caldicott, and Jeremy Rifkin are among the contemporary figures who have become skillful in using this persuasive approach. It is characteristic of interest groups of this kind to be external to established, authoritative channels of decision-making power. The explicit purpose of groups identifying themselves with the "public interest" and "social responsibility" is to apply pressure, external pressure, upon political processes that otherwise move in what group members see as undesirable directions.

While the activities of public interest groups are clearly an exercise of the right of free speech and while they are obviously important to the effective operation of modern democracy, the very existence of these groups points to the lack of any clear, substantive meaning for the term "public." In this conception, the "public" takes form in an *ad hoc* manner around certain points of social stress. One can claim to speak for "the public" simply by staging a demonstration or appearing on morning television news programs. The ease with which activists appropriate the word "public" leads to charges that particular groups are, in fact, unrepresent-ative, that "they don't represent *my* idea of the public interest." Neverthe-less, public interest organizations offer the most direct means liberal democracies now have for focusing and mobilizing the concerns of ordinary people about controversial technologies.

The lack of any coherent identity for the "public" and of well-organized, legitimate channels for public participation contribute to two distinctive features of contemporary policy debates about technology: (1) futile rituals of expert advice; and (2) interminable disagreements about which choices are morally justified.

Disputes about technology policy often arise in topic areas that seem to require years of training in fields of highly esoteric, science-based knowledge. A widely accepted notion about science is that it offers a precise, objective understanding of the world. Because technology is regarded as "applied science" and because the consequences of these applications involve such matters as complicated scientific measurements and the interpretation of arcane data, a common response is to turn to experts and expert research findings in the hope of settling key policy questions.

This faith in scientific and technical advice involves much frustration in actual practice. Often it turns out that deep-seated uncertainties cannot be dispelled by consulting the experts; for the search for an objective answer brings a plurality of responses rather than a simple consensus. Studying the probable effects of background radiation, for example, different fields of scientific research give very different estimates of possible hazards. Problems of this kind are compounded by the fact that expertise is often indelibly linked to and biased by particular social interests. For example, looking at the problem of toxic waste disposal at Love Canal near Niagara Falls, New York, in the late 1970s, different social interests proposed different scientific models of the boundaries of the question and produced drastically different estimates of the hazards to citizens living in the area.[32] If, as contemporary sociologists claim, scientific knowledge is socially constructed, then scientific findings used in policy deliberations are doubly so. To an increasing extent, law-makers and bureaucrats see scientific studies merely as resources to be deployed in ongoing power struggles.

What this suggests is that political disputes about technology are seldom if ever settled by calling upon the advice of experts. At public hearings held before legislative bodies, different social interests parade carefully chosen scientists and technical professionals. All of them speak with a confident air of "objectivity," but the experts often do not agree. Even where there is agreement about the "facts," there are still bound to be disagreements about how the "facts" are to be interpreted or what action is appropriate as a consequence.

Another characteristic of contemporary discussions about technology policy is that, as Alasdair MacIntyre might have predicted, they involve what seem to be interminable moral controversies. In a typical dispute, one side offers policy proposals based upon what seem to be ethically sound moral arguments. Then the opposing side urges entirely different policies using arguments that appear equally well grounded. The likelihood that the two (or more) sides can locate common ground is virtually nil. Consider the following arguments, ones fairly typical of today's technology policy debates.

1 (a) Conditions of international competitiveness require measures to

reduce production costs. Automation realized through the computerization of office and factory work is clearly the best way to do this at
present. Even though it involves eliminating jobs, rapid automation is
the way to achieve the greatest good for the greatest number in
advanced industrial society.

(b)   The strength of any economy depends upon the skills of people
who actually do the work. Skills of this kind arise from traditions of
practice handed down from one generation to the next. Automation
that de-skills the work process ought to be rejected because it undermines the well-being of workers and harms their ability to contribute
to society.

2   (a)   A great many technologies involve risks of one kind or another.
Judging the risks of chemical pesticides, one must balance the social
benefits they bring against the risks they pose to human health and
the environment. Considering the whole spectrum of benefits and risks
involved, the good in using pesticides far outweighs their possible
dangers.

(b)   Persons have a right to be protected from harm, including possible
harm that may stem from useful technological applications. The use
of pesticides subjects consumers to health hazards over which they
have little or no control. Regardless of the larger good that the use
of pesticides might bring, their use should be curtailed to prevent the
risk of harm to individual consumers.

Positions of this kind involve a mixture of what may be highly uncertain
empirical claims combined with philosophical arguments about which there
is little consensus. Parties who square off in disputes of this kind usually
believe that their side draws upon the very best data available and strong
moral principles as well. But as the combatants circle each other in the
ring, there is often a gnawing feeling that the various lines of moral
reasoning have been concocted on the spot, used to justify positions that
could be better described as emotional judgments or matters of sheer self-
interest. In this way debates about technology policy confirm MacIntyre's
argument that modern societies lack the kinds of coherent social practice
that might provide firm foundations for moral judgments and public
policies.[33]

What usually happens in such cases is a process of "muddling through."
Interest groups apply pressure on politicians, gaining influence in proportion to the amount of money each group has to spend on the effort.
Lawsuits are filed on one side or the other or both. Lawyers and judges
sort through the flagrantly one-sided legal briefs, seeking precedents that
might be patched together to provide a framework for deciding the case
at hand. Television ads bombard viewers with flashy image and ten-second

"sound bytes." Public opinion polls monitor the level of support for various proposals. Candidates for election sometimes take stands on issues that can then be included among the influences that sway voters in one direction or another. Eventually a policy outcome of some kind evolves, but it is seldom one that contains any experience of social learning that might be applied to similar episodes in the future.

Redefining Citizenship

In summary, I have argued that as moral philosophy confronts contemporary technology-related issues, it does so in an intellectual and social vacuum, one located in a deep gap between the technical and political spheres established by both ancient and modern philosophers. I have pointed to some of the consequences of this situation for thinking about technological choices and technology policies in our time. From this point of view, the technocratic approach I mentioned earlier – rushing forward with philosophical expertise to clarify moral categories, theories, and arguments in the hope that policy-makers or the public will find them decisive – is a forlorn strategy. For the trouble is not that we lack good arguments and theories, but rather that modern politics simply does not provide appropriate roles and institutions in which the activity of seeking the common good in technology policy is a legitimate project.

Under these circumstances a more fruitful path for philosophy is to begin exploring ways in which publics suited to renewed discussion about technological choices and policies might be constituted. Rather than echoing the judgments of Aristotle and Adam Smith that political and technical affairs are essentially different, contemporary philosophers need to examine that question anew.

Some interesting possibilities arise in the fact that at long last the conceptual and practical boundaries between technology and politics upheld in both ancient and modern theory have begun to collapse. In the world of the late twentieth century, the spheres of technical and political life have merged in a variety of ways, woven together in situations in which common forms of human living have become dependent upon and shaped by technological devices and systems in telecommunications, computing, medicine, mass production, transportation, agriculture, and the like. To an increasing extent the qualities of technical artifacts reflect the possibilities of human living, what human beings are and aspire to be. At the same time, people mirror the technologies which surround them. Each day we see a widening of the kinds of human activities and consciousness that are technically embedded and technically mediated.

Although this rapidly growing, planetary technopolis strongly influences what our lives contain, few have tried to imagine forms of citizenship appropriate to this way of being. Some observers are content to point out the obvious, namely that technology is already highly politicized, that the development, introduction, and use of technologies of various kinds are always shaped by conflicts, negotiations, and machinations among powerful social interests. But to notice this fact is by no means to acknowledge the technopolitical sphere as a public space where citizen deliberation and action ought to be encouraged. To take that step, one must move beyond supposedly neutral sociological descriptions and explanations of how technologies arise and begin raising questions about the proper relationship between democratic citizenship and the shaping of technological order.[34]

Attempts of this kind have been launched recently in several modest experiments within the Scandinavian social democracies. These experiments are interesting in their own right, but also show the promise of creating citizen roles in places where private calculations of efficiency and effectiveness, costs, risks, benefits, and profits usually rule the day. A prototype of this variety of technological citizenship took shape at a research institute in Stockholm, Sweden, the Center for Working Life. The basic goal of the Center's work was to expand the scope of Scandinavian ideals of worker democracy in which technological innovation was likely to occur. They were encouraged by Swedish laws passed in the mid-1970s that recognized the right of all parties in the workplace, managers and workers alike, to negotiate about matters that affect the quality of working life. The "co-determination laws" cover such areas as job allocation, training, and work environment. Beginning in the 1970s, legal rights of this kind were carried in a novel direction by a group of labor unions working with university-educated computer scientists and systems designers. Realizing that computerization was likely to transform Swedish factories, shops, and offices, fearing the loss of jobs and workers' skills, the teams set out to investigate the new technologies and to explore possible ways of using them.[35]

In one such case, the UTOPIA project of the early 1980s, workers in the Swedish newspaper industry – typesetters, lithographers, graphic artists, and others – joined with representatives from management and with university computer scientists to design a new system of computerized graphics used in newspaper layout and typesetting. The first phase of the project surveyed existing work practices, techniques, and training in the graphics industries. The group then formed a design workshop to consider possibilities for a new system, using a paper and plywood mock-up as the model of a newspaper workstation. From there they produced a 48-page technical document giving precise design specifications to the computer suppliers.

The pilot system, installed at Stockholm daily newspaper *Aftonbladet*, offered a pattern of hardware, software, and human relationship very different from that which would have been produced by managers and engineers alone. It allowed graphics workers considerable latitude in arranging texts and images, retaining many of their traditional skills, but realizing them in a computerized form. In their deliberations, project members considered but rejected the pre-packed graphics programs promoted by vendors from the United States because they reflected an "anti-democratic and de-skilling approach."[36] As project member and computer scientist Pelle Ehn observes, "What was new was that these technical requirements were derived from the principle that the equipment should serve as *tools for skilled work* and for production of *good use quality products*." [37]

The "Scandinavian approach" to participation in design is interesting not only for its tangible results, but also for what it suggests about a positive politics of technology seen in broader perspective. In a small and tentative manner, the UTOPIA project created a public space for political deliberation about the qualities of an emerging technical artifact. A diverse set of needs, viewpoints, and priorities came together to determine which material and social patterns would be designed, built, and put into operation. As Pelle Ehn points out, the important step in this process was to find a "project language game" in which all the participants, from very different vocations, professions, and social backgrounds, could speak to each other.[38] True, it was a fairly limited public that was constituted here. But it was far more inclusive than is normally the case in the printing industry or elsewhere.[39]

The creation of public spaces of this kind is, of course, predicated on modifying the right of owners of private property to have exclusive or even primary control of the shape of new technologies that affect how others live. That condition is, to a great extent, an accomplishment peculiar to Scandinavian social democracy, a product of political conflicts and agreements over the past several decades. It is now a condition sustained by the fact that more than 80 percent of Swedish workers are union members.[40]

Another achievement of the "Scandinavian approach" has been to eliminate what I noted earlier as one of the most troubling features of contemporary technology policy: the ritual of expertise. In the UTOPIA project and others similar to it, a person's initial lack of knowledge of a complex technical domain does not create a barrier to participation. The information and ideas needed to participate are mastered as part of a process in which the equality of team members is the established norm. Conversely, those who came to the process with university degrees and professional qualifications explicitly rejected the idea that they were the designated, authoritative problem-solvers. Instead they offered themselves as persons whose knowledge of computers and systems design could contribute to discussions conducted in democratic ways.

This approach may also help dispel the second disturbing feature of contemporary technology policy debates, the interminable moral controversies they tend to generate. Here the guiding assumption is that if people with diverse viewpoints and conflicting social interests come together as equals in a situation that presents a common problem to be solved, an agreement will eventually evolve. As Ehn describes a typical predicament, "Management introduces new technology to save manpower. Journalists, graphics workers, and administrative staff confront each other in the struggle over a decreasing number of jobs. Is there a basis for solving these demarcation disputes across professional and union-based frontiers? Can a new way of organizing work create peaceful coexistence in the borderland?"[41] The answer seems to be yes. However, the answer is never as simple as one set of philosophically well-grounded prescriptions winning out over another. Instead what happens is a negotiated political agreement among those whose interests will be affected by the change.

What the Scandinavian projects have done in an experimental way is to institute technopolitical practices from which new citizen virtues can emerge. Within small communities constituted for the purpose, choices about technologies that will influence the quality of social life are carefully studied and debated. This involves no expectations of political heroism, only the sense that ordinary people, regardless of background or prior expertise, are capable of taking a turn in making decisions of this kind.[42] The vision of knowledge and social policy that underlies these efforts strongly resembles Paul Feyerabend's anarchistic proposals for "committees of laymen" involved in science.[43] In this instance, however, there was an opportunity to test the ideas in actual practice.

As revealed by Ehn's engaging treatise, the role of philosophy in this process is a limited but useful one. It attempts to clarify the basic conditions that undergird practices of work and discourse within the design projects. By seeking to understand these practices at a deeper, more general level, philosophical inquiry may shed light on ongoing negotiations as they occur. Thus, Ehn draws upon the writings of Heidegger, Wittgenstein, Habermas, and other philosophers to illuminate his central concerns.[44] In the ideal case, philosophical reflection becomes one element in the process, although not one given privileged status. For it is understood that the key insights, lessons, and prescriptions must arise from a process in which project members, regarded as equals, join to explore the properties of both technical artifacts and social arrangements in a variety of configurations.

A criticism that might be raised about approaches like that pursued by Ehn and his Scandinavian colleagues is that they work at a superficial level within the technologies they confront. As history of technology Ulrich Wegenroth has noted, there is today a widening gap between "professionalization" and "trivialization" in many fields of technological development. Deeper, more complex levels of technical design and operation – the making of computer chips, for example – are accessible to and acted upon by only a handful of technical professionals. The same technologies are, however, restructured at the level of the user interface and present themselves there in a deceptively friendly form. As Wegenroth observes, "If a new technology is met by suspicion and resistance in society, its acceptance is not won by reducing its complexity to make it intelligible and thus controllable by the general public, but by reengineering its interface to trivialize it."[45]

Do the Scandinavian projects merely re-tailor interfaces to make them more agreeable to workers while leaving the deeper structures of the technology as something given? The question cannot be answered in this brief overview. It is worth noting, however, that within the domain of computer programming the innovations of the Scandinavian researchers appear to have been fairly fundamental. Thus, members of the UTOPIA project rejected an American firm's software package because it contained entrenched forms of hierarchical work organization, features that the group found "anti-democratic and de-skilling." Rather than try to weed out the deep-seated authoritarianism of American computer programs, the UTOPIA participants elected to start from scratch.[46]

It is perhaps too early to characterize the virtues of citizen participation that might emerge from practices of this kind, too soon to specify whether this experience might be successfully applied to realms of technological choice usually governed by the merciless logic of economic and technical rationalization.[47] Members of the UTOPIA project appear to have developed a sense of cooperation, caution, and concern for the justice of their decisions. They were especially conscientious in trying to find effective designs that could take advantage of computer power while preserving the qualities of traditional workmanship. The members realized that conditions expressed in the design of a new system were conditions they would eventually have to live with. In that way their work echoes Aristotle's definition of the virtue of the good citizen, namely an understanding of both how to rule and how to be ruled. At a time in which politics and technology are thoroughly interwoven, perhaps a similar definition of virtue of citizens is that they know both how to participate in the shaping of technologies of various kinds and how to accept the shaping force that these technologies will eventually impose.

From this viewpoint the creation of arenas for the politics of technological choice is much more than a way of solving unsettling problems that arise in the course of technological change, although steps of this kind certainly might do that. It is also more than finding alternatives to the increasingly absurd logic of efficiency, productivity, and control that now drives technological choices in the global economy, although there is certainly a need for such alternatives. Even more important, the creation of new spaces and roles for technological choice might lead us to affirm a missing feature in modern citizenship: the freedom experienced in communities where making things and taking action are one and the same.

NOTES

1   Robert Sinsheimer, "Genetic Engineering: Life as a Plaything," in *Contemporary Moral Controversies in Technology*, ed. A. Pablo Iannone (New York: Oxford University Press, 1987), p. 131.

2   James H. Moor, "What is Computer Ethics?" *Metaphilosophy*, vol. 16, no. 4 (Oct. 1985), p. 275.

3   My treatment of classic and modern attitudes toward technology draws upon Carl Mitcham's excellent survey, "Three Ways of Being-with Technology," in *From Artifact to Habitat: Studies in the Critical Engagement of Technology*, ed. Gayle Ormiston (Bethlehem, Pa.: Lehigh University Press, 1990).

4   Plato, *Symposium*, trans. Benjamin Jowett (New York: Library of the Liberal Arts, 1948), 203a.

5   See my discussion of Plato's views in *The Whale and the Reactor: A Search for Limits in an Age of High Technology* (Chicago: University of Chicago Press, Chicago 1986), ch. 3.

6   Plato, *The Laws of Plato*, trans. Thomas L. Pangle (Chicago: University of Chicago Press, 1980), 797d.

7   Lucretius, *The Nature of Things*, trans. Ronald Latham (Baltimore: Penguin, 1951), p. 211.

8   Aristotle, *Politics*, trans. Benjamin Jowett, in *The Complete Works of Aristotle*, vol. II, ed. Jonathan Barnes (Princeton: Princeton University Press, 1984), p. 1987.

9   Ibid., p. 2026.

10   Ibid., p. 2027.

11   Ibid., p. 2028.

12   Ibid., p. 2027.

13   M. I. Finley, *The Ancient Economy* (Berkeley: University of California Press, 1973), pp. 75–6.

14   Ibid., p. 75.

15   Ibid., p. 84.

16   Francis Bacon, *The great Instauration*, in *The New Organon and Related Writings*, ed. Fulton Anderson, (Indianapolis: Bobbs-Merrill Co., 1960), p. 8.

17   Ibid., p. 117.

18   Jean Le Rond D'Alembert, *Preliminary Discourse to the Encyclopedia of Diderot*, trans. Richard N. Schwab (Indianapolis: Bobbs-Merrill, 1963), p. 42.

19   See Albert O. Hirschman, *The Passions and the Interests: Political Arguments for Capitalism before Its Triumph* (Princeton: Princeton University Press, 1977).

20 Baron de Montesquieu, *The Spirit of Laws*, trans. Thomas Nugent, rev. edn, vol. I (New York: P.F. Collier & Son, 1900), p. 46.

21 C. B. MacPherson, *The Theory of Possessive Individualism: Hobbes to Locke* (Oxford: Clarendon Press, 1962).

22 David Hume, "Of Refinements in the Arts," in *The Philosophical Works*, vol. 3, ed. T. H. Green and T. H. Grouse, reprint of the new edition of 1882, (Aalen: Scientific Verlag, 1964), p. 301.

23 Adam Smith, *Wealth of Nations*, books I–III, intr. Andrew Skinner (Harmondsworth: Penguin, 1970), p. 446.

24 Ibid., p. 443.

25 Ibid., p. 446.

26 Hannah Arendt, *On Revolution* (Harmondsworth: Penguin, 1977), p. 253.

27 See, for example, Benjamin Barber, *Strong Democracy: Participatory Politics for a New Age* (Berkeley: University of California Press, 1984).

28 For poignant descriptions of circumstances that often face workers, see Barbara Garson, *Electronic Sweatshop: How Computers are Transforming the Office of the Future into the Factory of the Past* (New York: Simon and Schuster, 1988).

29 See, for example, *Ethical Issues in the Professions*, ed. Peter Windt et al. (Englewood Cliffs, NJ: Prentice-Hall, 1989) and *Ethical Issues in Engineering*, ed. Deborah G. Johnson (Englewood Cliffs, NJ: Prentice-Hall, 1991). My essay, "Engineering Ethics and Political Imagination," in *Broad and Narrow Interpretations of Philosophy of Technology*, ed. Paul T. Durbin (Dordrecht: Kluwer Academic Publishers, 1990), pp. 53–64, criticizes the approaches often used to teach ethics for technical professionals.

30 Edwin Layton, *Revolt of the Engineers: Social Responsibility and the American Engineering Profession* (Cleveland: Case Western Reserve University, 1971), chs 1, 2.

31 Myron Glazer and Penina Glazer, *The Whistleblowers: Exposing Corruption in Government and Industry* (New York: Basic Books, 1989).

32 Beth Savan, *Science Under Siege: The Myth of Objectivity in Scientific Research* (Montreal: CBC Enterprises, 1988).

33 Alasdair MacIntyre, *After Virtue: A Study in Moral Theory*, 2nd edn (Notre Dame: University of Notre Dame Press, 1984), chs 14, 15.

34 For a critique of the new sociology of technology, see my "Social Constructivism: Opening the Black Box and Finding It Empty," *Science as Culture*, no. 16 (Autumn 1992).

35 For a description of Scandinavian experiments in democratic participation in design, see Pelle Ehn, *Work-oriented Design of Computer Artifacts* (Stockholm: Arbetslivcentrum, 1988).

36 Ibid., p. 345.

37 Ibid., p. 339 (emphasis in original).

38 Ibid., p. 17.

39 In fact, problems arose within the UTOPIA because it was not inclusive enough, excluding the participation of journalists. As Ehn notes, the future of the project "depends upon whether the graphic workers and journalists

succeed in overcoming their professional clash of interests, and together develop a common strategy." Ehn, *Work-oriented Design*, p. 357.

40   Peter Lawrence and Tony Spybey, *Management and Society in Sweden* (London: Routledge & Kegan Paul, 1986), p. 85. For an overview of the relationship between technology and work in Sweden, see Åke Sandberg, *Technological Change and Co-determination in Sweden: Background and Analysis of Trade Union and Managerial Strategies* (Philadelphia: Temple University Press, 1992). An excellent discussion of the moral issues confronting Scandinavian social democracy can be found in Alan Wolfe, *Whose Keeper?: Social Science and Moral Obligation* (Berkeley: University of California Press, 1989).

41   Ehn, *Work-oriented Design*, p. 342.

42   For a general exploration of tensions between technical expertise and direct democracy, see *Democracy in a Technological Society*, ed. Langdon Winner (Dordrecht: Kluwer Academic Publishers, 1992) and Frank Fischer, *Technocracy and the Politics of Expertise* (Newbury Park, Ca.: Sage, 1990).

43   See Paul K. Feyerabend, *Science in a Free Society* (London: New Left Books, 1978) and his suggestions in "Democracy, Elitism, and Scientific Method," *Inquiry*, vol. 23, no. 1 (1980), pp. 3–18.

44   Arguments and conclusions similar to Pelle Ehn's can be found in Terry Winograd and Fernando Flores, *Understanding Computers and Cognition* (Reading, Mass.: Addison-Wesley, 1987).

45   Ulrich Wengenroth, "The Cultural Bearings of Modern Technological Development," in *Humanistic Perspectives on Technology, Development and Environment*, ed. Francis Sejersted and Ingunn Moser (Oslo: Centre for Technology and Culture, Report Series no. 3, 1992).

46   Ehn, *Work-oriented Design*, pp. 344–5.

47   Methods of organizing people and machinery in the mode of "just-in-time" and "lean production" now gaining momentum in the global market economy point in directions very different from those pursued by Scandinavian workplace reformers. The workplace regimes created within this mode of production could well achieve levels of rationalization and centralization that would make Frederick W. Taylor and Jacques Ellul blush. See J. P. Womack, D. T. Jones, and D. Roos, *The Machine that Changed the World* (New York: Rawson Associates, 1990).

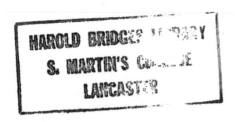

4
Taking Consent Seriously: Feminist Practical Ethics and Actual Moral Dialogue

Alison Jaggar

Alison Jaggar writes from within the feminist tradition in ethics, a tradition she characterizes as "opposing perceived male bias in ethics." She notes that within that tradition there is considerable debate over the usefulness of contractualist approaches to moral philosophy of the sort practiced by Rawls, Gauthier, Gewirth, and others. These approaches attempt to justify some set of fundamental moral principles by showing that under certain ideal conditions rational persons would freely agree to them. Jaggar does not enter this debate directly, but instead focuses on a central intuition of contractualism, namely, the intuition that "free and informed consent is a necessary, if not sufficient, condition of moral acceptability." This intuition she regards as in accord with Western feminism's interest in emancipation. After canvassing the advantages and disadvantages of feminists' interpreting the consent requirement as requiring hypothetical rather than actual consent, she provides a number of reasons for rejecting hypothetical in favor of actual consent. Acknowledging the impossibility of achieving real-life moral consensus that is fully informed and uncoerced, she nonetheless regards it as a useful ideal, and recommends that feminists actively pursue dialogue aimed at consensus. Such dialogue must, however, be practiced with due awareness of the ways in which it may fail to be fair, i.e., may fail to ensure that all points of view are actually given equal consideration.

Jaggar's paper should be compared with Kettner's (chapter 2). Although very different in aim and emphasis, both focus on the importance of rational dialogue and consensus in social morality.

This paper began from my interest in discovering whether contractualist moral theory could be useful to contemporary feminists addressing practical issues of so-called applied ethics.[1] Contractualist moral theory is distinguished, of course, by its concern for free and informed consent but, because of the conceptual and practical problems endemic to establishing that empirical instances of consent really are free and informed, most contemporary versions of moral contractualism have utilized philosophical constructions of hypothetical consent given in idealized circumstances. In this paper, I indicate why the theoretical device of hypothetical consent initially may be attractive to feminists working in practical ethics but then go on to show why, despite its initial attractions, hypothetical consent is an inappropriate conceptual tool for this sort of feminist ethical work. In spite of my rejection of hypothetical consent in practical ethics, I find the intuition that constitutes the distinctive moral core of contractualism extremely valuable to feminism. Hypothetical consent is only one theoretical elaboration of this intuition and I conclude by suggesting that the intuition might be developed more usefully, at least in the area of practical ethics, by renewed attention to the notion of actual consent based on actual moral dialogue.

I

Contractualism

Contractualism in moral philosophy is a development of the social contract tradition in political philosophy. It seems safe to say that contractualism is currently the most popular approach to ethics in contemporary Anglo-American philosophy.[2] Precisely because of its popularity, it is not easy to specify exactly what is and what is not involved in contractualism: different theorists interpret and develop the tradition in a wide variety of ways. However, I shall take as my starting point a characterization offered by Thomas Scanlon in a thoughtful defence of contractualism. According to contractualism, Scanlon writes, "an act is wrong if its performance under the circumstances would be disallowed by any system of rules for the general regulation of behaviour which no one could reasonably reject as a basis for informed, unforced general agreement" (Scanlon 1982: 110). Scanlon's characterization brings out the central feature of contractualism on which I shall focus here, namely its emphasis on the importance of general consent or moral consensus in distinguishing right from wrong. It also makes explicit the requirement, elaborated by almost all post-Hobbesian contract theorists, that expressed consent or actual consensus alone has no particular moral weight. Scanlon, like most contractualists, stipulates that in order to gain the legitimacy required to generate moral obligation, consent be given or consensus achieved only under certain conditions, conditions that typically are spelled out in terms of information, rationality (expressed here in the stipulation that agreements must be reasonable), and the absence of coercion. Of course, the questions of what should count as being appropriately informed, rational, and uncoerced themselves are further topics for philosophical investigation and provide much of the ground for dispute between, for instance contractualists who are politically liberal and those who are politically radical or conservative.[3]

Feminism

The feminist tradition in ethics, like the contractualist tradition, has developed over a period of several centuries, although its history, unlike that of contractualism, is not well known and is only now being recovered. The philosophical literature on feminist ethics, like that on contractualist ethics, is currently expanding rapidly and is marked by wide variety and lively debate (Jaggar 1989, 1990b). Common to all feminist approaches, however, is an explicit commitment to opposing perceived male bias in ethics. Thus, on the normative level the feminist ethical literature rejects any rationalizations of women's subordination; on the theoretical level, it engages in serious and respectful, though not uncritical, reflection on the moral experience of women as well as of men (Jaggar 1990b).

It is sometimes believed that feminist interests in practical or applied ethics are restricted to a sub-set of moral or public policy issues, often labelled "women's" or, sometimes, "feminist" issues. Such a belief is mistaken for several reasons, however; one of these is its presumption that moral or public policy issues can be divided cleanly into those that are and those that are not of special concern to women or feminists. This presumption is false on two grounds. On the one hand, since men's and women's lives are inextricably intertwined, there are no "women's issues" that are not also men's issues; the availability or otherwise of childcare and abortion, for instance, has significant consequences for the lives of men as well as of women. On the other hand, since men and women typically are not what lawyers call "similarly situated" relative to each other, it is difficult to think of any moral or public policy ("human") issue in which women do not have a gender-specific or feminist interest. For instance, such issues as war, peace, and world starvation, though they are certainly general human issues in the sense of affecting entire populations (actually, not only populations of humans), nevertheless have special significance for women because the world's hungry are disproportionately women and children, because women are primarily those in need of the social services neglected to fund military spending, and because women benefit relatively little from militarism and the weapons industries.

Feminist interests in practical ethics, therefore, are not restricted to a limited ethical domain. On the contrary, contemporary feminism has *enlarged* the traditional concerns of practical ethics by introducing both new issues and new perspectives on "old" ones. What does distinguish feminist approaches to practical ethics is that they consistently raise concerns, in a wide range of contexts, about whether certain social arrangements or moral or public policy recommendations might subordinate or disproportionately disavantage either women in general or some group of women in particular.

The Promise of Contractualism for Feminism

While some contemporary feminists draw deeply on the contract tradition, a considerable number dissent from it sharply.[4] Some, including myself, have been critical of its use in political philosophy (Jaggar 1983; Pateman 1988); others have criticized contractualist approaches in moral philosophy, complaining that they typically involve assumptions antithetical to kinds of moral experience often said to be distinctively feminine (e.g. Baier 1984; Held 1987). For instance, feminists have argued that existing contractualist theory presupposes unrealistic or morally undesirable, as well as characteristically masculine, conceptions of moral subjectivity and moral motivation, and a narrow (and also allegedly masculine) focus on moral principles combined with a neglect of the moral significance of interpretation and character. How far these feminist criticisms of contractualism are justified and whether contractualists can develop answers to them are questions that I shall not address here. Instead, I shall focus on one element central to contractualist moral theory, namely the intuition that free and informed consent is a necessary, if not a sufficient, condition of moral acceptability.

This fundamentally egalitarian and anti-authoritarian intuition springs from the same interest in emancipation that has always inspired at least Western forms of feminism. Contemporary contractualism has developed the intuition in ways designed to guarantee that morality be impartial and objective, that it be public and consensual, and that moral obligation be assumed autonomously. Some recent work in feminist ethics has been critical of impartiality and autonomy, at least as these ideals have been interpreted in nonfeminist moral theory, but many other feminists are working to rethink prevailing understandings of these concepts rather than reject them entirely (Jaggar 1989). Commitment to at least some version of impartiality and objectivity seems presupposed by the persuasive feminist critiques of male bias in existing moral theory, while a commitment to something like autonomy seems implicated in feminism's hostility to coercion and domination and its concerns about ideological manipulation. For these all reasons, as well as feminism's suspicion of the public/private distinction, contractualism might be expected to qualify as an approach to ethics that deserves serious feminist attention.

In addition, contractualism promises a way of avoiding *both* the most blatant forms of ethnocentrism *and* the moral skepticism associated with unconstrained cultural relativism. On the one hand, since it is likely that many different sets of principles could pass the test of being accepted by informed and uncoerced individuals, contractualism is compatible with a degree of cultural relativism (Scanlon 1982: 112). On the other hand, its insistence that actual agreement, unconstrained by morally motivated limits, is inadequate to ground moral obligation is supposed to enable it to transcend conventionalism. These features fit comfortably with the feminist commitment to respecting cultural diversity at the same time as condemning women's subordination.

From Actual to Hypothetical Consent

In real life, of course, morality is rarely if ever a matter of consensual agreement between fully informed and uncoerced individuals. Apart from the obvious logistical problems of even consulting everybody, most of the real-life societies with which we are acquainted are characterized by deep inequalities between individuals in information, rationality, and power. For these familiar reasons, theorists in the contractualist moral tradition have felt themselves compelled to resort to the notion of hypothetical consent: that is, to rely on constructions of what people *would* agree to *if* they were, contrary to fact, appropriately informed, rational, and uncoerced.

How does anyone know what people would agree to in a counterfactual situation? Some moral philosophers offer a kind of reversibility test, which involves putting oneself imaginatively in the place of others. For instance, R. M. Hare recommends that we project ourselves imaginatively into the perspectives of others in order to comprehend the situation from their points of view (Hare 1981: 91–5). The usefulness of such (deceptively) simple thought experiments is limited, however, both by their imprecision, a consequence of the limits of our moral imagination, and by the fact that the real-life people with whom we are instructed to identify may not themselves be fully informed, rational, and uncoerced.

In order to overcome these problems, a number of contemporary moral theorists have recommended much more elaborate thought experiments, demanding the imaginative construction of worlds entirely different from our own. Robert Nozick, for instance, asks his readers to imagine them-selves into a fictional state of nature (Nozick 1974), Bruce Ackerman describes a fictional spaceship (Ackerman 1980), and John Rawls is well known for his account of a hypothetical "original position," in which individuals with no knowledge about their own situation discuss the prin-ciples that will regulate the basic institutions of the society they are to inhabit (Rawls 1971). All these elaborate thought experiments are designed as philosophical idealizations, abstracting those features of real-life situ-ations that distort actual moral thinking, so that hypothetical agreements can be projected that are both more precise or determinate and more morally adequate or reliable than actual or even imagined agreements between real people in real-life situations.[5]

The move from actual to hypothetical consent is attractive because it promises to avoid the problems associated with both actual agreement and actual disagreement. On the one hand, hypothetical consent offers the basis for a critique of existing or conventional morality, even when this seems to be the object of general popular assent, and thus promises to indicate a route out of conventionalist ethics. On the other hand, hypothetical consent points to a way of moving past the deadlocks often resulting from actual disagreement. Thus it seems plausible to suppose that appeal to hypothetical consent may permit the derivation of substantive and morally justifiable public policy recommendations.

Feminism and Consent, Assumed or Expressed

The recent history of Western feminism provides some vivid illustrations of the conceptual and moral or political difficulties that surround attempts to establish the moral legitimacy of empirical instances of actual consent. Reminding ourselves of this history explains why the move from actual to hypothetical consent might well make contractualist approaches appear even more attractive to feminist practical ethics.

The first decade of contemporary feminism (roughly from the late 1960s to the late 1970s) began to make visible a system of gender domination that shaped both daily life and its theoretical articulations. Feminists revealed the ways in which both gendered and apparently gender-blind norms of social organization (e.g. both sexual double standards and the length and structure of the working day) operated to render women dependent on, and thus subordinate to, men. They also demonstrated the ways in which much existing scholarship either failed to mention women explicitly or else portrayed them as marginal, deviant, or even pathological, thus obscuring or rationalizing women's subordination.

Central to feminism's moral critique of this situation was the claim that the acquiescence that women historically seemed to have displayed in these arrangements – and that many women, determinedly and even ostentatiously, continued to display – could not be taken to represent free and informed consent. Feminists began to analyze the complex system of both blatant and subtle threats and inducements that constrained and manipulated not only women's actions but also their thinking, influencing them not only to stay with abusive partners, for instance, but also to interpret control as caring and abuse as love. Drawing on a variety of traditions, including gender socialization theory, Marxist notions of economic coercion, cultural hegemony and false consciousness, psychoanalytic notions of unconscious motivation, and Foucauldian analyses of the relations between power and the discourses of knowledge, feminists showed how the familiar notion of consent was problematic, theory-laden, and contestable.

The invention of the conceptual tool of gender encouraged feminists to focus their social and textual analyses on the differences between the social situations of women and men, and the consequent apparent differences in men's and women's "natures." In the exhilarating days of feminism's first upsurge, many claims were made about "women": women's needs, women's interests, women's capacities, women's psychology, women's ways of knowing. Feminist theorists enjoyed a heady sense that discoveries of sexual difference were shattering paradigms as it were right and left. But this early excitement was moderated when successive groups of women, including some feminists, questioned the initially unqualified generalizations. Such generalizations best described, so they said, the experience of a limited group of women: those who were white, middle-class, and able-bodied. Working-class women claimed that home-making was often more fulfilling than paid labour; black women interpreted reproductive rights less in terms of abortion than in terms of freedom from forced sterilization; disabled women pointed out that there could be a positive side to being viewed as what the prevailing feminist jargon called a "sex object." The so-called "problem of difference" came to be conceived of less as a problem between women and men than as a (cluster of) problem(s) between women and women. Ironically, the very feminists who had challenged men's presumption in speaking for women now were told that they themselves were presuming too much when *they* claimed to speak for women.

The second decade of feminism was marked by sharp disputes between feminists – disputes in which the notion of consent continued to be central, although in new ways. For instance, in the sometimes acrimonious feminist debate over pornography feminists were divided less over assumptions of tacit consent than over interpretations of expressed consent. Feminist critics of pornography described adult female pornographic models as victims trapped in such hopeless circumstances that genuine consent was impossible. The models' participation in the production of pornography was thus interpreted as a form of rape – as, often, was prostitution and, sometimes, even marriage or any form of heterosexual intercourse. Feminists who defended pornography argued that this description of adult pornographic models infantilized them by discounting their assertions of choice, and thus perhaps dehumanized them even more effectively than the pornography. In addition, the defenders of pornography asserted that at least some women enjoyed "consuming" pornography – to which the critics replied that such women were brainwashed by male culture.

This short excursus into recent feminist history highlights some of the conceptual and moral or political problems associated with empirical consent. It shows not only that unexpressed consent cannot be assumed, because of the difficulty of projecting ourselves into other people's shoes, especially people distinguished from us by barriers of gender or class or ethnicity, but that even expressed consent is not beyond challenge. Can the theoretical device of hypothetical consent in idealized circumstances fulfill its promise of avoiding these problems and so provide a workable moral decision procedure for feminist practical ethics? I turn next to considering some difficulties confronting feminists who might seek to use the notion of hypothetical consent in this way. Some of these difficulties are not serious but some of them I view as insurmountable.

II

Problem 1: Hypothetical Consent as Philosophically Contested

The notion of hypothetical consent in idealized circumstances is designed precisely to avoid the problems we have noted with empirical consent. In so doing, however, it is forced to depend on very general claims about human needs, human capacities, and human motivations, claims that in turn involve highly controversial philosophical theories about human nature and human rationality. A quick glance not just at the history of philosophy but even at its present situation will remind us of just how controversial and contested such theories are. In terms of human motivation, for instance, think of the deep disagreements manifest between Marxists, Freudians, Christians, sociobiologists, and feminists. It is true that idealized hypothetical consent is postulated not on the basis of theories of empirical motivation but rather on the basis of philosophical constructions of rational motivation, but these are equally, if not more, uncertain and contested. Indeed, the whole history of Western philosophy could well be construed as a debate over the nature of rationality. Is reason essentially normative or is it restricted to instrumental calculation? Can or should it be defined in terms of self-interest? Should the so-called laws of logic be revised in the light of how real people actually draw inferences? Is reason universal or is it culturally constituted, consisting primarily in sets of traditional practices that reflect social agreements about what kinds of inferential moves are acceptable?

In the context of contractualist moral theory, claims about rational motivation are inseparable from claims about people's needs and interests – and ultimately from a vision of human flourishing. But notions of needs and interest, too, are endlessly contested. Regarding interests, for instance, it is clear both that individuals do not always know their own interests well and that they are often betrayed by those who claim to know them better. Moreover, some interests, arguably like some needs, are morally legitimate while others should not be met. If an attempt is made to identify legitimate interests in terms of human needs, we find not only that such claims, too, are the object of much theoretical debate in academic disciplines such as sociology, psychology, anthropology, and philosophy; they are also the object of practical political contest. I have in mind here not only the familiar Marxist point that abstract statements of human needs, such as the need for food and shelter, carry very different practical implications in different cultural contexts. Even within the same cultural context, questions of need are disputed on a daily basis by advocates of labor, the unemployed, schoolchildren, the military, welfare mothers, the disabled, and so on.[6]

It is implausible to suppose that philosophical argumentation will ever establish conceptions of rationality or of human needs and capacities that are at once sufficiently abstract to be universal and sufficiently specific that they will not invite endless disputes over their interpretation. Issues of rationality and human nature are central to the continuous reconstitution of moral and political life and will remain perennial subjects of debate not only in academic philosophy but also in practical politics. Thus, philosophical theories of idealized consent will always be both historically limited in applicability and essentially contested.

Accepting these limitations, however, does not make theories of idealized consent any less reputable than other philosophical theories, which are also historically limited and essentially contested. And acknowledging the impossibility of final resolutions does not commit us to abandoning either philosophical theory or political and ideological struggle. On the contrary, part of what it means to be a feminist is precisely to dispute these political and philosophical issues; and contemporary feminists are doing just this, in political as well as philosophical arenas. Let us suppose for the sake of argument, then, that appropriately feminist interpretations of the contested concepts could be agreed for a time, within a particular historical context. Let us then ask again whether it is possible in this case for the notion of idealized consent to be useful to feminist practical ethics.

Problem 2: Hypothetical Consent and Basic Social Institutions

Feminists who seek to utilize the notion of hypothetical consent in practical ethical contexts immediately face the problem that most contemporary contract theorists, including John Rawls, regard the device of idealized consent as useful less for resolving day-to-day moral issues than for designing the "basic structure" and "major institutions of society" (Rawls 1971: 7). One might naturally think that designing the basic structure and major institutions of society is an enterprise in which relatively few individuals ever engage and then only in periods of social revolution. Thus, one might conclude that appealing to the notion of hypothetical consent for resolving the practical issues of daily life is simply misusing, even abusing, a theoretical tool designed for quite different purposes.

My own view is that this objection to using the notion of hypothetical consent in practical ethics is not conclusive, since I believe, though I cannot argue it here, that the line between basic institutions and specific practical issues is so permeable that, in an unspectacular way, the basic institutions of any relatively open society are being redesigned all the time. Moreover, feminists, in my view, are among those who engage most consistently and self-consciously in such redesign. Many, pehaps most, of the issues with which feminists are concerned raise questions about basic social institutions, questions that go far beyond relatively straightforward issues of overt discrimination on the basis of sex. For instance, the issue of abortion raises questions about the nature and extent of privacy rights and civil liberties; the issue of comparable worth raises deep questions about appropriate criteria of just distribution; the issues of childcare or domestic partnership raise questions about the institution of the family; the issue of pornography raises further questions about civil liberties; and so on.

Because I view general principles and specific applications as ultimately inseparable, it seems to me that the fact that the theoretical device of hypothetical consent was developed initially to justify very general principles of social organization does not necessarily mean that it might not also illuminate more specific issues in practical ethics.

Problem 3: Hypothetical Consent in Circumstances of Male Domination

The most serious questions about how the notion of idealized hypothetical consent might be useful to feminist work in practical ethics come, in my view, not from the fact that this notion typically is used in reasoning about the basic structure and major institutions of society. They come rather from the fact that this reasoning is about ideal rather than actual societies. The project of theorists reasoning in this way is to elaborate what John Rawls calls "perfect justice": i.e. the principles that characterize well-ordered societies in favorable circumstances (Rawls 1971: 245). Such theorists typically assume "strict compliance" with these principles from the inhabitants and refrain from addressing situations of injustice or "partial compliance" (Rawls 1971: 8). They hope to guide social reform not by developing specific strategies for social change but rather by offering "a vision to aim at" (Rawls 1971: 246). As Rawls puts it, they are working on the level of "ideal" rather than "nonideal" theory.

The very notion of developing a distinctively feminist perspective in practical ethics, however, presupposes our habitation of a pre-feminist world that by definition is far from ideal. This world is characterized by male domination and its inevitable concomitants of brutality, exploitation, and ideological distortion. Feminists daily confront the realities of rape, prostitution, pornography, and incest, as well as environmental destruction, war, and grotesquely unequal access to world resources. Reflection on the notion of hypothetical consent may be able to demonstrate (if demonstration be needed) that these atrocities would not characterize the perfectly just society, that they are morally wrong, unjust, and/or irrational; but it seems capable of giving little moral guidance in dealing with them when they occur.

Moreover, contemporary feminists in the real world must negotiate with people quite unlike the free, informed, and reasonable individuals postulated by hypothetical (idealized) contact theory. Instead, feminists must deal with people constituted through institutions of domination such as gender, race, and class. Such people, and they include ourselves, are not only unequal in knowledge and power but often also prejudiced and confused – even brutal or sadistic. Nor are they are about to comply with the recommendations of feminist ethics. No matter how impeccable the political insight and philosophical argumentation by which feminist ethical recommendations are established, feminists can predict that they will frequently be derided as utopian, dismissed as special pleading or so-called reverse discrimination, and flouted by powerful individuals whose privileges are exposed as unjustified.

It is true that feminist ethics always has to reconcile two elements: the utopian and the pragmatic. The utopian element provides visions of a longed-for feminist future, while the pragmatic element offers guidance in the painfully pre-feminist present (Jaggar 1990a). The utopian element in feminist ethics so far has come largely from two sources: from socialist feminist dreams of a society without gender, race, or class, on the one hand, and from radical feminist science fiction, on the other. Neither of these traditions pretends to justify its visions with philosophically rigorous argument; instead, both assume that the moral desirability of the worlds they envision is amply demonstrated simply in describing them. I do not here dispute that the device of idealized hypothetical consent, given suitably feminist interpretations of the crucial assumptions, may enable feminist philosophers to offer a distinctively philosophical contribution to the vision-ary or utopian element in feminist moral thinking.

For feminists working in practical ethics, however, and thus seeking to bridge the gap between utopia and reality, appeals to hypothetical consent seem distinctly unpromising. As we have seen already, we can never be sure what real-life individuals think without actually asking them, let alone what they would think if their situations were different: indeed, we do not even know what we ourselves would think if our own situations were different. Moreover, if people's situations, and so their thinking, were *very* different, we might wonder if they retained their identity and were still the same people. And when we attempt to avoid these problems with empirical consent by postulating abstract, perfectly rational, fully informed, and uncoerced individuals in a simplified and ideal world, it is hard to see what those individuals have to do with us, very concrete people who are only partially free, rational, and informed – often, indeed, quite ignorant, damaged, and corrupted – and who inhabit an extremely complex world that is conspicuously far from ideal.

Problem 4: The Implicit Elitism of Hypothetical Consent

In addition to the difficulty of establishing relevance to the practical moral and public policy issues that confront contemporary feminists on a daily basis, reliance on the notion of idealized hypothetical consent raises problems of moral inequality and authoritarianism – this despite the fact that contractualism's emphasis on mutual consent is designed precisely to avoid such problems. There are at least two ways in which these problems may arise in the context of contractualist theory.

First of all, we have seen already that it is no simple matter to operationalize the method of hypothetical consent. The recommendation that we should refrain from acting in ways incompatible with norms that could be accepted by informed and unforced individuals offers no guidance in the absence of means for discovering what such individuals might accept. But the reasoning of real individuals is unpredictable, as we have seen, while the conclusions of individuals in idealized circumstances can be established only on the basis of sophisticated philosophical argument. Even supposing it possible, contrary to my last argument, for philosophical projections of idealized consent to generate normative conclusions that were both generally accepted and relevant to the issues at hand, the arguments establishing and validating such conclusions would have to be developed by feminists with advanced philosophical training. In other words, the method of idealized consent is not a moral decision procedure equally available to all, thus enabling every person equally to be a full moral agent. The method is not accessible, for instance, to most graduates of US high schools, let alone to those whose literacy skills are only minimal.

To put the point most dramatically, for feminists to utilize the method of idealized consent seems to require the services of feminist ethical experts – or "philosopher queens!"

Faith in our constructions of hypothetical consent may also lead us to discount the actual consent or dissent of real individuals, such as pornographic models or prostitutes. Hypothetical consent is designed, after all, to avoid the moral defects that damage the legitimacy of many instances of actual consent. From here, it is only a short step to rationalizing compelling people to conform to agreements to which, it may be asserted, they certainly *would* consent if only they were more rational or their circumstances were more favorable than in fact they are – forcing people, so to speak, to be free. Contractualist moral theory is grounded on the intuition that legitimate moral obligation can only be self-imposed, and I have claimed that this is an anti-authoritarian and egalitarian intuition entirely in accord with the emancipatory spirit of Western feminism. When reliance on actual consent is replaced by appeal to hypothetical consent, however, contractualism reveals an elitist subtext that lends itself easily to authoritarianism.

III

Taking Consent Seriously: Actual vs Hypothetical Dialogue

Up to this point, I have been arguing that the theoretical device of hypothetical consent is unlikely to be useful to feminists seeking to discover or justify what is to be done in the applied ethical contexts of daily life. My argument does not entail, of course, that the notion of hypothetical consent may not occasionally be helpful on a commonsense, nontheoretical level, as a rough and ready guide to what is morally permissible. We appeal to something like this notion whenever we try to arouse intuitions of sympathy or fairness by asking ourselves or each other or our children, "How would you like it if someone did that to you?" or "What if everyone did that?" Reflecting on how we would feel if we were in another person's shoes, or even speculating about what free and rational persons could hypothetically consent to, may sometimes be useful for pointing us in the right moral direction, even if they cannot confirm that we have arrived at our moral destination.

While there may be some heuristic value in conducting a hypothetical dialogue in one's head or on one's computer, however, we must never forget that consent given hypothetically is never the moral equivalent of actual consent. Constructions of hypothetical consent have no independent moral force, any more than hypothetical experiments have independent evidential force. If we have no one else to talk with, then there may be no harm in trying to imagine what other people might say. But just as a thought experiment can never be a substitute for empirical investigation, so a hypothetical dialogue is likely to be far less fruitful than an actual dialogue – and for many of the same reasons.

Bearing this in mind, I suggest that feminists (and others) who work in practical ethics and who are inspired by the egalitarian and anti-authoritarian ideals that motivate the contract tradition should refrain from speculations about hypothetical consent and devote their energy instead to reflecting on and indeed actively pursuing real-life moral consensus. Of course, I mean consensus reached legitimately, in the sense recognized by the contract tradition.

Few modern philosophers so far have turned their attention to this task; perhaps because it seems so hopeless. People in the real world obviously have sharply divergent values; the starting point of contemporary liberal theory, indeed, is the undisputed fact that modern societies are characterized by a plurality of conceptions of the good. People in the real world also have interests that conflict in very real ways – which is not to say that they do not also share some significant interests. For example, people are divided, as we have seen, by enormous inequalities of resources and power, and they are unlikely to agree on how these should be redistributed. For these reasons, moral consensus ordinarily is regarded as a utopian ideal, achievable, perhaps, by small groups of people, self-selected by their shared values, when they engage in some well-defined and limited project, such as running a food co-op or opposing a nuclear power station, but hopelessly impractical even for many families, let alone for administering modern nation-states or resolving international conflicts.

One prerequisite for legitimate moral consensus is moral dialogue under fair conditions, a requirement necessary to ensure that all points of view are given equal consideration. Contractualism generally acknowledges this insight, just as it has also seen that real-life moral dialogue rarely takes place in anything approximating fair conditions. Few of our actual moral discussions resemble even the relatively fair circumstances of a philosophy seminar – and all who have participated in such discussions can testify that socially constructed inequalities set powerful constraints on our dialogue even there. It is undoubtedly because of their awareness of the dialogical distortions that occur in real life that most contract theorists have avoided discussing actual dialogue and have preferred speculating, instead, about hypothetical dialogue. At least one influential contemporary theorist, Bruce Ackerman, even denies explicitly that morality (unlike politics) requires dialogue since, he says, "a little talk may go a long way; a lot may lead nowhere" (Ackerman 1989: 6). Talking to others is not, in Ackerman's view, "of supreme importance in moral self-definition" because "the key decisions are made in silence: Whom to trust? What do I really think?" Ackerman concludes that "a morally reflective person *can* permissibly cut herself off from real-world dialogue" (Ackerman 1989: 6).

In sharp contrast with Ackerman, Jürgen Habermas emphasizes that intersubjective dialogue is indispensable and recommends what he calls a communicative ethics of need interpretation (Habermas 1983). Like contemporary Anglo–American theorists who work in the contract tradition, Habermas specifies the "ideal speech situation" that would give moral authority to the conclusions emerging from such dialogue, but he departs from the Anglo-American tradition of idealized hypothetical consent by asserting that the dialogue should be actual rather than hypothetical. The conditions under which Habermas would regard the conclusions of such dialogue as morally legitimate are so stringent, however, that they can rarely, if ever, be met in the world we inhabit and Habermas provides no practical guidance for individuals in speech situations that are less than ideal. In the absence of such guidance, his supposedly communicative ethics is little more helpful than the device of idealized consent for addressing immediately pressing issues in practical ethics.

Feminist Marilyn Friedman is one of the few contemporary philosophers who have sought to move beyond a negative critique of what Habermas calls the "monologism" characterizing much Anglo-American moral epistemology. She has argued recently that actual dialogue is indispensable for fulfilling the requirement of impartiality (Friedman 1989). Philosophers have often recommended that we seek an impartial perspective by putting ourselves imaginatively in the places of others, as we have seen, but Friedman notes the difficulties, discussed already, of discovering strangers' views in substantive detail. She speaks, too, of the difficulty of presenting the full force of motives we have never felt or even find repugnant – the motives, for instance, of child molesters, Satanic cultists, or advocates of the "final solution." One could add to these difficulties the problem of reasoning according to standards that one does not share. Friedman concludes that these practical problems are so intractable that they render many of the most influential contemporary theories that recommend impartiality so indeterminate as to be vacuous.[7]

I regard Friedman's argument as well taken. Given the inevitably limited nature of human experience and knowledge, including our limited knowledge even of our own capacities, needs, and motivations, it seems indisputable that actual dialogue, despite its significant shortcomings, is not just necessary but perhaps the most important vehicle, not only for the moral education of children but also for our own moral development. Only through actual dialogue or even confrontation can we, for instance, come to see the inevitable biases and prejudices of our own moral thinking and not only learn what others views as rational and necessary but move closer to discovering what we ourselves really think and need.

Faced with the seemingly insuperable difficulties in the way of achieving within any foreseeable future even moral dialogue under anything approximating fair conditions, let alone achieving actual moral consensus, I still would oppose feminists retreating to what I see as the epistemologically barren and morally dangerous project of projecting hypothetical or idealized moral consensus. The dream of actual moral consensus has its own dangers, of course, most notably the danger of discouraging tolerance of differences of opinion. But nothing is proof against abuse, and so long as we are clear that actual consensus is only a dream, like the dreams of perfect freedom or equality or democracy, it may serve, like these other dreams, as a valuable heuristic ideal.

One advantage of concentrating on the notion of actual rather than hypothetical moral consensus is that it encourages us to focus on the practical obstacles that stand in the way of actual agreement. We have seen already that many of these obstacles are easy to identify. Most prominent among them are the socially constructed inequalities that make impossible not only moral consensus but even the fair moral dialogue that is the prerequisite of consensus. We already have good reasons for working politically to reduce such inequalities but, if actual dialogue is taken as crucial to feminist practical ethics, considerations of moral epistemology may now be added to these reasons. It becomes even clearer that moral progress is inseparable from political progress and feminist ethics from feminist politics.

In conclusion, then, I think that reflection on the strengths and weaknesses of contractualist approaches to moral philosophy offers several lessons for feminist ethics. First, such reflection shows us that there is no rationalistic short cut or tidy and unproblematic procedure, even in principle, for figuring out the right thing to do. However, by attending to the moral intuition that is the core of contractualism we are encouraged to enlarge our moral insight by listening respectfully to other people – and then, in the absence of anything close to an ideal speech situation, to evaluate their words critically in the context of who they are and what are their situations. Developing contractualism in the direction of actual rather than hypothetical consensus helps us realize that moral knowledge is inseparable from practical – especially political – wisdom: wisdom that enables us to weigh the claims of people who are never fully rational or uncoerced, but never completely puppets either, people who are, in addition, always in some power relation respective to us. Only such wisdom can tell us when, and especially with whom, it is morally incumbent to engage in dialogue, as well as when it is necessary to end the dialogue and to commit ourselves to practical action. Developing such wisdom may also assist our philosophical theorizing in moving past the originally suggestive but now ossified and conflict-perpetuating dichotomies of freedom and coercion, consent and dissent.

NOTES

1 In developing the ideas for this essay, I have benefited enormously from discussions over several years with Marcia Lind. Marcia's tenacious commitment to the feminist promise of contractualism has forced me to clarify my own agreements and disagreements with her position. I acknowledge with gratitude the comments I received on earlier drafts of this paper from Marilyn Friedman, Virginia Held, Marcia Lind, and Linda Nicholson. Virginia was kind enough to discuss the drafts with me at length and made a number of extremely helpful suggestions.

2 Contemporary theorists who rely on some form of contractualism include: Ackerman 1980; Beitz 1989; Dworkin 1977; Gauthier 1986; Gewirth 1978; Nozick 1974; Rawls 1971; Reiman 1990; Scanlon 1982.

3 O'Neill (1985) provides a useful discussion of some of these issues.

4 Theorists seeking to appropriate the contract tradition include Hampton 1991; Lind forthcoming; Okin 1989a, 1989b.

5 Though not all of these theorists would acknowledge themselves Kant's heirs, these aspects of their work may perhaps be seen as attempts to operationalize the Kantian principle of universalizability, which requires the moral agent to develop a perspective acceptable to all.

6 And one might note that even the abstract statements usually are not as transhistorically "pure" as they are often thought to be. For instance, is clothing really a human need, in all historical circumstances? And why is companionship or even children so often omitted from such lists constructed by male philosophers?

7 Friedman accepts Hare's assertion that the difficulties identified pose practical rather than principled problems to moral theories (such as contractualism) that recommend the adoption of an impartial standpoint, but it seems reasonable to me to regard them as problems in principle with any moral method that requires beings who are less than omniscient to reason from other people's points of view.

REFERENCES

Ackerman, Bruce, 1980. *Social Justice in the Liberal State*, New Haven and London: Yale University Press.

Ackerman, Bruce, 1989. "Why Dialogue?", *Journal of Philosophy*, vol. 86, no. 1.

Baier, Annette, 1984. "What Do Women Want in a Moral Theory?", *Nous*, Vol. 18, no. 1.

Beitz, Charles R., 1989. *Political Equality: an Essay in Democratic Theory*, Princeton, NJ: Princeton University Press.

Dworkin, Ronald, 1977. *Taking Rights Seriously*, Cambridge, Mass.: Harvard University Press.

Friedman, Marilyn, 1989. "The Impracticality of Impartiality," paper read at the Eastern Divisional meeting of the American Philosophical Association, Atlanta.

Friedman, Marilyn, 1989. "The Impracticality of Impartiality," *Journal of Philosophy*, vol. 86, no. 11.

Gauthier, David, 1986. *Morals by Agreement*, New York: Oxford University Press.

Gewirth, Alan, 1978. *Reason and Morality*, Chicago: University of Chicago Press.

Habermas, Jürgen, 1983. *Moralbewusstsein und kommunikatives Handeln*, Frankfurt: Suhrkamp.

Hampton, Jean, "Feminist Contractarianism," in Louise M. Antony and Charlotte Witt eds. *Feminist Essays on Reason and Objectivity*, Boulder, CO: Westview Press, 1993.

Hare, Richard M., 1981. *Moral Thinking*, New York and Oxford: Oxford University Press.

Held, Virginia, 1987. "Non-Contractual Society," in Marsha Hanen and Kai Nielsen, eds, *Science, Morality and Feminist Theory*, Calgary: University of Calgary Press.

Jaggar, Alison M., 1983. *Feminist Politics and Human Nature*, Totowa, NJ: Rowman and Allanheld.

Jaggar, Alison M., 1989. "Feminist Ethics: Some Issues for the Nineties," *Journal of Social Philosophy*, vol. 20, nos 1/2.

Jaggar, Alison, M., 1990a. "Sexual Difference and Sexual Equality," in Deborah L. Rhode, ed. *Theoretical Perspectives on Sexual Difference*, New Haven and London: Yale University Press.

Jaggar, Alison M., 1990b. "Feminist Ethics: Projects, Problems, Prospects," in Herta Nagl-docekal and Herlinde Pauer-Studer, eds, *Denken der Geschlechterdifferenz: Neue Fragen und Perspektiven der Feministischen Philosophie*, Vienna: Wiener Frauenverlag. Reprinted in Claudia Card, ed., *Feminist Ethics*, Lawrence, Kansas: University of Kansas Press, 1991.

Lind, Marcia, forthcoming.

Nozick, Robert, 1974. *Anarchy, State and Utopia*, New York: Basic Books.

Okin, Susan Moller, 1989a. *Justice, Gender, and the Family*. New York: Basic Books.

Okin, Susan Muller, 1989b. *Gender, the Public and the Private*. Toronto, Ont.: Faculty of Law, University of Toronto.

O'Neill, Onora, 1985. "Between Consenting Adults," *Philosophy and Public Affairs*, vol. 14, no. 3.

Pateman, Carole, 1988. *The Sexual Contract*, Stanford, Ca.: Stanford University Press.

Rawls, John, 1971. *A Theory of Justice*, Cambridge, Mass.: Harvard University Press.

Reiman, Jeffrey, 1990. *Justice and Modern Moral Philosophy*, New Haven and London: Yale University Press.

Scanlon, T. M., 1981. "Contractualism and Utilitarianism," in Amartya Sen and Bernard Williams, eds, *Utilitarianism and Beyond*, Cambridge and New York: Cambridge University Press.

5
Rule Utilitarianism and Applied Ethics

R. I. Sikora

Sikora argues that there is a dire need in applied ethics for a general theoretical framework capable of adjudicating between conflicting particular judgments and intuitions. He outlines a version of rule utilitarianism, comparing its strengths to other principal forms of ethical theory and, at the same time, commenting on its methodological relations to commonsense morality. Turning then to his central task, he attempts to demonstrate the practical power of rule utilitarianism by showing how it can be effectively deployed in the abortion debate, the debate over animal rights, the controversy over the moral relevance of killing vs letting die, and, via a general attack on Kantian autonomy, in the debate over the place of autonomy in medical ethics. Sikora closes with a defense of rule utilitarianism against its most common criticism, the "rule worship" objection. Strictly speaking, rule utilitarianism is itself an abstract formula for the determination of substantive moral rules to be applied within a given society. Thus, Sikora's paper reflects a powerful commitment to the traditional, essentially deductive model of the relationship between ethical theory and rational moral practice.

The deductive model of moral reasoning defended in this paper contrasts sharply with the views of moral reasoning presented by Rachels (chapter 6), Winkler (chapter 19) and Hoffmaster (chapter 20), and with the views of expertise in applied ethics advanced by Baier (chapter 7) and Wertheimer (chapter 8). Concerning the relation between ethical theory and received morality, this paper should be compared with Philips's section on "ethics as social policy" (chapter 10).

There is a deep and pervasive problem in applied ethics. While there is no lack of stylish literature, there is a dire need for a rationale to adjudicate between a scatter of conflicting intuitions. I believe that Brandt's form of rule utilitarianism can provide such a rationale.[1] For Brandt an action is right in a given society if and only if it is in accord with the most beneficial morality for members of the society to subscribe to, in the sense of following it as well as one could expect those people to do. This is in contrast with act utilitarianism (AU), which holds that an action is right if and only if it is in accord with the morality that would be most beneficial if it were followed perfectly. Brandt rejects AU, holding that if we subscribed to AU rather than a pluralistic code our actions would not be sufficiently predictable and we would have too much room for rationalization.

I shall defend a version of rule utilitarianism that resembles Brandt's but that is concerned with the welfare of all sentient beings, not just with the welfare of the society that would subscribe to it. My version also differs from Brandt's in explicitly allowing for rights as well as obligations; and in recognizing that actual social circumstances may make it wrong to follow the morality to which it would be most beneficial for a society to subscribe.[2] For convenience I shall call my view rule utilitarianism (RU) although it is only one version of the doctrine.

RU justifies moral rules derivatively on the grounds that subscribing to them would tend to maximize happiness rather than offering them as basic deontological principles that would hold in all possible worlds. The rules would be firm rather than inviolable but opposed to mere rules of thumb that could be broken whenever it seemed best to do so. And the set of rules would be short enough and simple enough for an average person to learn.

Since different moralities would be beneficial in different cultures, it may seem that RU is a form of cultural relativism. But it is not, since its goal – the maximization of happiness – would remain constant, and actual moralities could always be criticized in terms of that goal. Even so, RU is naturalistic in that Brandt defends his hedonistic goal on the grounds that it is what we would desire if we were fully rational. Unlike deontologists, he does not need to appeal to non-natural, distinctively ethical qualities either explicitly, like W. D. Ross,[3] or implicitly, like many current writers on applied ethics.[4] And since even opponents of RU usually grant that consequences have considerable weight in determining whether an action is right, it would seem that they should also grant that the consequentialist reasons that RU offers for having certain rules rather than others must also have considerable weight. In which case it follows, by all accounts, that the questions that rule utilitarianism asks are well worth investigating.

Despite its advantages, RU is commonly neglected because of the rule worship objection, and the objection that it cannot justify the distribution of goods and evils in terms of desert. I will return to these problems in sections V and VI. Another reason for neglect is the common assumption that RU cannot yield interesting results in applied ethics. My main objective here is to show that this assumption is false. Using RU as a basis, I will defend abortion, argue that animals used for experimentation or raised for food have a right to lives worth living (which means that factory farming cannot be justified), and defend the common view that killing is worse than letting die. I will also show that Kantian autonomy is logically impossible and that, because of this, no form of retributivism is justifiable and that the role of autonomy in medical ethics should be reconsidered.

I believe too that RU has clear implications in regard to many other issues, including nuclear deterrence, terror bombing (and terrorism generally), distributive justice, infanticide, euthanasia, and the resuscitation of terminal patients, as well as the problems of means vs side-effects and helping vs harming. Furthermore, it can provide a basis for the formation of principles to deal with problematic choices forced on us by various technological advances, particularly in medicine.

Before turning to the main body of this article, I should note that I am at work on a book in which, besides developing RU more fully and considering these additional applications, I take account of numerous objections that I lack the space to consider here.[5]

I Rule Utilitarianism and Commonsense Morality

It is desirable that a theory in applied ethics, besides being broadly applicable, should be capable of winning widespread acceptance. One approach has been to argue that the main ethical theories of our philosophical tradition are largely extensionally equivalent; another has been to try to show that most disputes in applied ethics can be resolved by careful analysis; a third has been to hold that ethical theory can safely be ignored. Unfortunately, the initial optimism in regard to these approaches has largely dissipated.

As for RU, although it is obviously considerably closer than AU to most actual moralities, critics have objected that, even so, deontological theories, theories that ascribe great intrinsic value to autonomy, or contractarian theories are better suited than RU to the defence of commonsense morality. It is usually assumed that if commonsense morality, i.e. those principles that are accepted by most people in most cultures, is used to evaluate a moral theory, all of commonsense morality should be treated with either equal respect or equal disrespect. This is a mistake. The main effect of most moral principles is on the people who subscribe to them. If such a principle is accepted by most people in most cultures, though it should not be treated as sacrosanct, it should be taken very seriously. It would be unlikely to acquire such widespread acceptance if most people did not find it reasonably satisfactory. Thus the parts of commonsense morality that concern relations between people cannot be rejected lightly. But this favorable presumption clearly does not carry over to moral rules that downgrade the interests of animals; nor does it apply to commonly accepted rationales which may typically be used to explain moral principles. Given this general view of the strengths and limitations of commonsense morality, RU can justify what there is about it that should be taken seriously, including important principles that cannot be justified by any other major moral theory.

For example, despite recent philosophical arguments to the contrary, it is commonly believed that killing is worse than letting die. I will show that this can be justified as a derivative RU principle but not as a basic deontological principle. The same applies to various commonsense principles that rely on the active/passive distinction, and also to the principle that actions that employ objectionable means are worse than actions with bad side-effects. All these principles are, of course, open to exceptions in special sorts of cases. But RU provides a basis for determining which sorts of exceptions are acceptable, namely, those that should be built into the most beneficial moral code, taking account of the need to avoid undue complexity. RU can also justify a firm derivative rule to the effect that rewards and punishments should only go to those who deserve them, even though, as I will argue, it is logically impossible for us to have the kind of freedom that would justify *basic* rules founded on desert. Furthermore, RU comes closer to commonsense morality than Rawls's widely influential theory of economic justice.[6] Rawls's maximin principle is solely concerned with maximizing the lot of those at the economic bottom of society, while RU can attribute value to goods going to people above the bottom – though this value would, of course, decrease as one ascends the scale economically.

Many of the most important moral controversies, like that in medical ethics about the value of autonomy vs happiness, or the controversy over abortion, obviously involve far too much disagreement for there to be commonsense moral views for an ethical theory to either defend or oppose. There is, however, one major respect in which I advocate a marked change from commonsense morality, namely from the widespread view that our pleasure and pain should count more than those of animals. However, this will not count against RU, if it is shown that the part of commonsense morality that deals with our treatment of animals does not deserve our respect. The general problem with this part of commonsense morality has already been mentioned. In contrast with principles that apply to people, whose survival shows them to be reasonably satisfactory to most people in most cultures, principles applying to animals can survive regardless of whether they satisfy the legitimate interests of animals.

I will often support principles that follow from RU by showing that they are in accord with more or less common moral intuitions. Such support is strongest if the principle in question, for example, the view that killing is worse than letting die, has centrally to do with people and is in accord with the widely shared beliefs of commonsense morality. There is less support, of course, if the principle accords with less widely shared moral beliefs, ones accepted only in some cultures and not others, for example. Furthermore, if a principle followed from RU but deviated from the actual morality of a society for which it would be beneficial, one would still have to take account of the costs of transition in terms of conflict, psychological stress, and the like, before advocating change. To justify an attempt to bring about moral change, the value of the change will have to exceed these costs. In addition, this net benefit multiplied by the likelihood of success in bringing about the change will have to exceed the costs of an unsuccessful attempt multiplied by the likelihood of failure. Obviously such calculations have to rely heavily on subjective probability judgments, but the same is true of most practical decisions. If RU were found to be in direct conflict with some part of commonsense morality that deserves to be taken seriously this would pose a serious problem for this part of my theory. But even here one should not exclude the possibility of adequately explaining the need for improvement.

The role that I give to commonsense morality differs from the role ascribed to moral intuitions in wide reflective equilibrium theory. In contrast to this popular methodology, I provide a naturalistic justification for systematically ascribing much more weight to some moral intuitions than to others, and for ascribing virtually no weight to the common intuition that the suffering of animals counts less than the suffering of persons.

II The Bearing of Rule Utilitarianism on Killing vs Letting Die

Most deontologists hold that, at the level of basic morality, killing innocent persons (henceforth referred to simply as persons) is worse than letting them die. I shall argue instead that killing is worse derivatively in any world that is not radically different from our own, but that killing is not worse at the level of basic morality.

Jonathan Bennett has also defended the view that these actions are on a par at the level of basic morality. He argued that the difference between killing and letting die has to be morally neutral because it consists solely in the fact that in killing only a small proportion of the movements one could make in the circumstances would eventuate in death, while in letting die most of one's movements would do so.[7] In claiming this, Bennett had in mind the following sort of case for letting die: A sees B drowning in a swimming pool. No one else is there. Instead of moving in one of the relatively few ways that would enable A to save B's life, A moves in one of the many ways that would eventuate in B's death. For killing, Bennett had in mind something like this: A has a loaded gun pointed at B, and in pulling the trigger A moves in one of the relatively few ways that would eventuate in B's death.

However, Bennett's account of the ground of the distinction is wrong. Consider the following case: A and B have been sailing. Their boat sinks; they are alone in the water, miles from land, and there is only one life-preserver. If A doesn't get it he will drown; the same holds for B. A takes the life-preserver (moving in one of the relatively few ways that would enable him to get it) – and thereby *kills* B? Surely not; he lets B die.

There is much more to be said about the analytic aspect of the distinction between killing and letting die, but I want to turn now to the ethical aspect of the distinction. Although Bennett was wrong in holding that killing invariably falls in the "few-of-many" category and that the opposite is true of letting die, his theory is roughly correct. This has implications at the derivative level of morality which justify the view that killing is normally worse. Since killing usually falls in the few-of-many category, you can normally go about your affairs without killing people. But this is seldom true of saving lives, since in this case it is the thing that does not eventuate in a death that usually falls in the few-of-many category. In addition, there are so many lives to be saved that a corresponding obligation to save lives would leave one little time for anything else.

Putting it simply, avoiding killing is usually easy, while saving even a small fraction of the lives one theoretically *could* save would be extremely hard, and it is reasonable to expect more compliance with an easy rule than with a hard rule. Furthermore, in any world that is not radically different from ours, it is more important to have other people kept from killing us than to have them disposed to save our lives. Accordingly, it is socially beneficial for us to treat killing as worse than letting die.

It might seem that the active form of letting die that I used to refute Bennett's number-of-ways theory would be an exception to this principle since, unlike the more usual passive form, it falls in the few-of-many category. But in the active form of letting die the movements that you must avoid in order not to let the person die include the very movements that you want to make to go about your affairs.

There is another important difference between the two forms of letting die. In the passive form, which amounts to refraining from preventing a death, it will still count as letting the person die even if you refrain from preventing his death because you want him to die. In contrast, if you prevent someone from preventing a death because you want the person to die, although your action will not count as killing, you will have *brought about* his death rather than merely letting him die. To illustrate this point, let me alter my life-preserver case: This time A could survive without the life-preserver, but he wants B to die. He takes the life-preserver for himself to prevent B from using it. It would still be wrong to say that A killed B, but it would also be wrong to say that A let B die. Rather, A brings about B's death, and we would normally regard this as on a moral par with killing B.

Let us go back to the question of whether deontologists are right in thinking that killing is worse than letting die at the level of basic morality. If killing were worse at the level of basic morality it should be worse in all possible worlds, but this is not so. There could be a world in which killing would not be worse, namely, a world in which it was as easy to save lives as to avoid killing people, and in which promoting the saving of lives was as important as preventing killing.

The Number-of-ways Theory of the Active/Passive Distinction and Harming vs Helping

Although Bennett accepts my counterexamples to the number-of-ways theory of killing vs letting die, instead of giving up the number-of-ways distinction he has applied it to the active/passive distinction.[8] It is still vulnerable, however, to counterexamples such as the following. A asks B to sit still to have his picture taken, but B moves at the crucial moment in order to spoil the picture. Clearly the spoiling would be active rather than passive; but almost any movement would spoil it, so Bennett's theory would force him to say that the spoiling was passive. I suspect, though, that there are fewer exceptions to the number-of-ways account of the active/passive distinction than to such an account of killing vs letting die. However, here, as in the case of killing vs letting die, even though the number-of-ways account is only roughly accurate, it is significant morally because it means that it is usually easier to avoid contributing to something actively than to avoid contributing to it passively. And since both harming and helping are active, this supports the view that harming is worse than not helping, for it means that avoiding harming is usually easier than helping.[9]

Killing as a Side-effect vs Killing as a Means

Besides justifying the view that killing is worse than letting die, RU can show why some sorts of killing are worse than others, and why some sorts of exceptions should be built into a code and others not. Killing as a side-effect is usually less bad morally than killing as a means, because side-effects are usually less certain and because side-effects tend to be linked by longer causal chains from the initiating action than are means, making it harder to avoid them than to avoid objectionable means. Thus we tend to make an exception when the side-effect occurs as certainly as if it were a means and as soon as the means would occur. For example, we regard it as sophisticated to treat killing a fetus by a craniotomy in order to save the life of the mother as worse than causing a fetus to die as a side-effect of saving the life of the mother. However, we should be hesitant about using reasoning like this in support of an equivalence between killing civilians as a means in terror bombing and killing them as a side-effect in tactical bombing, because allowing terror bombing (and terrorism in general) increases the number of potential victims in wars and revolutions.

As we become more sophisticated we tend to allow an increasing number of utility-oriented exceptions to our rules. Decisions in regard to possible exceptions are often called for in response to novel medical cases, for example. Concerning the general defense of RU, however, we should recognize that it would never be beneficial to allow anything approaching the vast number of exceptions that would be required to render a pluralistic code, defensible in RU terms, extensionally equivalent to AU.

III A Rule-utilitarian Defense of Abortion on Demand

The main problem in defending abortion is to show that killing fetuses is permissible even though it is wrong to kill innocent individuals who are rational or have been rational in the past (to whom I will refer in this section simply as persons[10]). To do this, I need to show (a) that there is a sufficient reason for forbidding the killing of persons that does not apply to fetuses, and (b) that there is not some other reason that is sufficient for banning abortion.

The first part of the task is surprisingly easy. It is enough to call attention to the obvious but commonly ignored fact that *allowing the killing of persons (except for euthanasia) would have disastrous consequences that would be fatal to civilization, while this is not true of allowing abortion on demand.*[11] Thus I can concentrate on (b), on trying to show that there is not some other reason that would justify banning abortion.

However, I will show first that, although there is no adequate utilitarian reason to bar abortion as things currently stand, there might be sufficient reason for banning it in an underpopulated world. It is obvious that abortion is bound to be a distressing operation to perform and that the psychological effects on the mother may be even worse than the physical. Furthermore, unlike most defenders of abortion, I believe that, other things being equal, it is wrong to prevent the existence of a person who would have good prospects for a happy life.

I have a simple argument for this. It is generally agreed that you should prevent the existence of a person if you knew that his or her life would be utterly miserable. But it is also generally agreed that if you could prevent the existence of a very large number of persons – as the Pope could, for example, by advocating birth control – even if you knew that a few of them would be utterly miserable, it would be at least permissible, other things being equal, not to prevent their existence if you also knew that the rest would be very happy. But if preventing the existence of miserable persons is good, preventing the existence of happy people must be bad in order for it to be morally permissible not to prevent the existence of the group taken as a whole.

Nevertheless, the world is now so dangerously overcrowded that allowing abortion tends to increase rather than decrease the total amount of happiness. This would be true even if the aborted fetuses would have had average prospects for happiness; but it seems likely that the prospects for most of them would be far below average once we take account of the generally poor prospects for unwanted children, children of impoverished parents, children without a father, or children suffering brain damage in the womb from alcohol, cocaine, or other drugs. Furthermore, we should also take account of the possibility, for most pregnant teenagers, of their having children with better prospects for happiness later. Finally, a law against abortion is hard to enforce, easily evaded by those who can afford to travel (and therefore unfair to those who cannot), likely to lead to dangerous back-alley abortions, and likely to undermine respect for the law among those who regard abortion as justifiable.

However, such utilitarian considerations would not daunt most "pro-lifers," for they would hold that fetuses have a right to life that would make it wrong to allow abortion even if allowing it would be, on the whole, highly beneficial. They would note that we do ascribe a right to life to children and adults, and argue that it is inconsistent for us not to ascribe the same right to a fetus. But it is perfectly consistent for RU to justify this right for children and adults on the basis of indirect considerations that apply even to individuals whose lives are not worth living, yet hold that in an overcrowded world it cannot justify the ascription of such a right to fetuses.

Advocates of the view that fetuses (and perhaps embryos, and even zygotes) do have a right to life can appeal to either actual or potential characteristics, but both approaches lead sooner or later to severe problems for all but the most extreme pro-life theories. If they rely on potential features, they must hold that it is wrong to destroy even a single-cell zygote, a view rejected by all but the most extreme conservatives. If instead they rely on actual features, they can rely either on features that would be morally relevant in other species as well as our own, or on the fact that a fetus, embryo, or zygote belongs to the same species as ourselves. The latter leads to speciesism which, as I will show in section IV below, is a self-oriented prejudice like racism or sexism. And those who reject speciesism appear forced to admit that any morally relevant characteristics of fetuses, let alone embryos and zygotes, are also shared by various animals that it is permissible to kill for far less significant reasons than those used in defence of abortion.

However, Eike-Henner Kluge insists that late fetuses have structural capacities for reasoning, etc., that distinguish them from animals even though they do not yet exercise those capacities.[12] On this basis he argues that, since an adult in a deep coma or under anaesthesia counts as a person and retains the right to life because she retains the distinctively human neurological system, once fetuses have attained the same neurological system, the same right should apply to them.

But suppose that because of a brain injury, multiple sclerosis, or Alzheimer's disease you no longer had that sort of neurological system. If your life, however primitive, were still worth living, it would be agreed generally that you would still have a right to it, while Kluge would have to hold that you had lost that right. In contrast, RU can hold that you would retain the right because of the danger to society of allowing individuals who had functioned as persons to be killed even if they could no longer so function. (Euthanasia is an exception to this, but only for persons whose lives are not worth living.)

As for the extreme position that even a single-cell zygote has a right to life, it has a consequence that most of us would reject. Suppose that you knew that a given zygote was flawed and would eventuate in a person with reduced prospects for happiness but that it could be replaced by a flawless zygote. The extreme conservative would have to hold that it would be wrong to replace it.

IV   Rule Utilitarianism and Animals

The Pain of Animals Shouldn't Count Less than Our Pain

In a backlash against the animal liberation movement, some philosophers have claimed that speciesism, unlike sexism or racism, is morally justifiable. But this violates common moral intuitions as well as utilitarianism. Suppose that we found an island inhabited by creatures that resembled us in their level of rationality and in the various other characteristics that we value in human beings but that they belonged to a different species. Surely we would not hold that their suffering counted less than ours?

It has also been argued that the pain of animals should count less than our pain because animals are not rational. But this too is unjustifiable for, as Peter Singer has shown, this is inconsistent with our attitude toward the suffering of people, since we do not count the suffering of even the least rational of human beings as less important than the suffering of the rest of us.[13]

Derivative Rules for Animals Should Be Different from Those for Persons

Though we inflict appalling amounts of unnecessary suffering on people, we inflict a far greater amount of unnecessary suffering on animals. If I had to choose between preventing the unnecessary suffering of human beings and the unnecessary suffering of animals, I would be forced with great anguish to make my choice in favor of animals. Fortunately such a choice is unnecessary, even if it were possible. By far the two worst things that we do to animals are defiling their environment and factory farming. In the first, we harm ourselves as well as animals; and factory farming could be eliminated with comparatively little loss to human beings. It is true that the price of meat would rise if we raised food animals in a way that gave them lives worth living, but most meat-eaters would be healthier if they ate more complex carbohydrates and less meat. Better still, we could become vegetarians and become healthier, eat more interesting food, and produce much more food at far less cost to the environment.

But while the prevention of animal suffering should take high priority for us – perhaps even top priority in the case of factory farms – our moral rules for the treatment of animals should be different from those applying to persons, and closer in some respects to AU. It is not that the interests of animals should count less than our own interests at the level of basic morality. Rather, derivative rules in regard to animals would not be beneficial if they ignored the numerous differences between animals and persons.

Killing Persons vs Killing Animals

As I've argued, people are on the whole better off with killing treated as worse than letting die. In some areas this would also apply to animals since, as in the case of people, it is easier to avoid killing animals than to save their lives. However, while it would be wrong, for example, to kill one person to save several other persons, this kind of action may be justifiable in the case of animals, because animals, unlike people, would be better off with such a rule. It is reasonable, for instance, to be much less reluctant to kill animals to prevent the spread of a fatal disease to other animals than to kill persons to prevent the spread of a fatal disease to other persons. These differences are best understood in the light of various utilitarian reasons why killing people should be treated as far worse than killing animals.

Besides the fact that it is important to give people a sense of security, killing innocent people is likely, as in terrorism, to evoke a response in kind that can have a snowballing effect. This does not apply to killing animals. There is also a more obvious reason for holding that killing people is worse than killing animals, namely that the lives of persons tend to be more valuable than the lives of animals. But this reason is weaker than is commonly supposed. While most persons have a greater remaining life expectancy than most animals, this does not apply to very old people; and many persons have lives that are not worth living or are barely worth living, while many animals appear to have lives that are very much worth living.

It is commonly believed that it is a person's desire to go on living rather than the quality of his future life that determines its value. But one need not hold that a miserable person's life is valuable *per se* to defend the view that it would be wrong to kill him. Even miserable persons become anxious and insecure if they are not protected by rules against murder, and this is enough to justify a firm rule against killing them. This is not true of animals, which is why it may be far worse to kill a miserable person than a happy animal.

Laboratory Animals Have a Right to a Life Worth Living

Some opponents of animal experimentation that involves suffering and/or death would oppose it, even if it would prevent more suffering than it would cause, on the grounds that we would not tolerate similar experiments on people. There is a good reason to give people a right not to be subjected to such experiments. Forcing people to submit to them against their will would have catastrophic indirect effects. But this is not true of animals, so the issue is more complicated than in the case of people. This does not mean that the interests of animals count less than those of people. The point is rather that some practices would promote overall utility in the case of people but not animals, while others would promote it in the case of animals but not people.

In trying to determine what sorts of animal experimentation, if any, are morally acceptable, the following categorizing of experiments on animals bred for the purpose of experimentation into four groups may prove helpful:

1 Animal experimentation that ends in death but does not involve pain for an animal that is given a life worth living.
2 Animal experimentation that does involve some pain for an animal but in which the animal is given a sufficiently good life in other respects for it to be relatively clear that on the whole it has a life worth living. It should be noted here that human beings can suffer a great deal in the course of long lives and still have lives that are on the whole worth living; but since the animals used for experiments typically have short lives, much smaller amounts of pain may prevent their lives from being worth living. Also, while it is at least arguable that human beings can have lives worth living even if they have much more pain than pleasure, this is hardly plausible in the case of animals. Animals seek to survive even if their lives are miserable, but this only reflects the evolutionary advantage of instinctual response to perceived threats.
3 Animal experimentation in which the animal has a good life outside the experimentation but where there is enough pain to make it unclear whether its life is on the whole worth living.
4 Experimentation where, even if the animal is treated as well as is compatible with the nature of the experiment, it is fairly clear that it does not have a life worth living because the experiment is terribly painful or because it causes most of the animal's life to be miserable.

It is generally accepted that we should be concerned with the health of animals used for experiments and that they should not be caused to undergo unnecessary suffering, but very little is said about giving them the positive experiences that their lives must have to be worth living. The quality of life of rodents used for medical experimentation tends to be much better than that of battery hens, for example, because rodents are kept in much larger cages in proportion to their own size than battery hens. However, it is not regarded as necessary to provide "toys" for them to amuse themselves. It may seem sentimental in a world with billions of deprived human beings to suggest that we need toys for rodents. But such toys would be cheap and could be used for many generations of animals. Furthermore, if we give them lives that are clearly worth living such experiments can be justified fairly easily, while the justification of experiments that do not satisfy this requirement is bound to be impossible in some cases and problematic in others. Also, the toys should be designed to give as much pleasure as possible. This could require a good deal of thought and research, but given the number of animals involved, the hedonic payoff could be far greater than in many far costlier ways of benefiting animals.

Even a person thinking solely in terms of the lives of the animals in question could justify experiments in the first two categories, but we need to look very carefully at the possible gains from experiments where we cannot be at all sure that the animals in question would have lives worth living. Obviously it is experiments in the fourth category that are the most problematic. As a utilitarian, I cannot hold that such experiments should never be performed, but I think that we should extend to animals used for experiments a right to a life worth living that can be violated only in extreme cases. This means that experiments in the fourth category should be permitted only when an exceptionally strong case can be made that the experiments are a necessary means to the prevention of far more suffering than they cause.

I realize that I am using the notion of rights in a broader way than many philosophers will countenance. Among other things, I do not require the possessors of rights to be able to make contracts or to have the capacity to forgo their rights. But the notion of a right has been extended so broadly in ordinary usage that lesser claims are likely to be ineffectual. Furthermore, I have retained the most important element in a right, an element that AU could not accept, namely powerful protection against violations except in extreme cases. Of course, the right in question is not as yet backed by convention. It is, as it were, a candidate right, a right that has not been given to animals but that should be given to them. Our obligations in regard to candidate rights are often different from our obligations in relation to established rights. To a large extent they will be obligations to do things to get the candidate rights accepted.

Animals Raised for Food also Have a Right to a Life Worth Living

Setting aside altogether the interests of animals, it would be better for people if we became vegetarians. Far fewer people would starve; most of us would be healthier; and we would do much less damage to the environment. However, the transition to vegetarianism is bound to be gradual, so we need to determine how animals raised for food should be treated in the meantime. The case for the right of an animal to a life worth living is even stronger when animals are raised for food than when they are used for medical experimentation. Medical experimentation, unlike raising animals for food, may enable us to save lives or prevent greater suffering.

A Very Short Life with a Very Harsh Death Must be Very Happy Indeed to be a Life Worth Living

In determining whether an animal has a life worth living a lot depends on what sort of death is in store for it. Death in a slaughterhouse is a very harsh death indeed. The actual killing may be quick, but the broken bones coupled with rough handling that typically precede such a death are likely to entail acute suffering extended over many hours. If an animal with a very short life faces such a death then, for its life as a whole to be worth living, the rest of it must be far better than if it faced instead the painless death of most rats and mice used for medical experimentation.

If one is concerned with the overall quality of a life, the nature of the death of an animal having a very short life is far more important than in the case of most persons. Since we live much longer than most animals, a day of suffering in the course of dying is a much smaller fraction of the life of an average human being than it is, for example, in the life of a "broiler" that is killed within weeks of its birth or of a spent battery hen that is killed well before it is two years old. It follows that for the life of an animal who will face a harsh death to be worth living overall, most of its life must involve much more pleasure than pain. But it is grossly implausible to hold that this is true of life on a factory farm. This is enough by itself to show that factory farming is morally unacceptable.

When these considerations are combined with the fact that roughly a hundred times as many animals are raised on factory farms as are involved in animal experimentation, it becomes obvious that the animal movement should focus chiefly on factory farming. Furthermore, the stiffest resistance to the animal movement is aroused by opposition to medical experiments. Paradoxically, then, attacking medical experimentation for its use of animals may often be counterproductive in the current climate, causing animals more harm than it prevents.

V Rule Utilitarianism and the Impossibility of Kantian Autonomy

Advocates of the Kantian view that autonomy is intrinsically valuable fault utilitarianism for ascribing value to autonomy only in so far as it is conducive to happiness. Similarly, it has been argued that utilitarianism must be wrong because it cannot ascribe intrinsic value to the distribution of goods and evils in terms of desert. I shall argue that these objections are unjustified if we lack the kinds of freedom and desert that Kant had in mind, and that we do lack these kinds of freedom and desert, for Kantian freedom and desert are incompatible with both determinism and indeterminism and, therefore, logically impossible.[14]

My main task is to show that libertarians are right in holding that freedom and desert are incompatible with determinism since they have in mind the Kantian kinds of freedom and desert rather than the kinds described by compatibilists. I shall rely mainly on a kind of meta-level argument to the effect that the traditional arguments for the incompatibility of freedom and desert with determinism pertain to Kantian freedom and desert and are sound on that interpretation. But first I will present a series of imaginary cases designed to show the difference between the Kantian notions of freedom and desert and compatibilist notions of them.

According to the Greek myth, Zeus created Minerva full grown and wise, with all the attributes of a mature person. Suppose instead that he created a mature Iago and a mature Desdemona who then *fully rationally, on the basis of desires with which they identify themselves and in accord with their basic values* perform the actions depicted in *Othello*. Would Iago be free and would he deserve to be treated worse than Desdemona? If "freedom" and "desert" are used in their Kantian senses he would not, because he would not be ultimately responsible for his actions. If anyone was, it would be Zeus. However some of us (sometimes) use "desert" in a compatibilist sense in which Iago would deserve to be treated worse, although this kind of desert only provides a utilitarian justification for punishment and cannot justify any form of retributivism.

Suppose now that, instead of being created full grown by a god, people were normally born full grown. Surely there too, Iago would not deserve (in the Kantian sense) to be treated worse than Desdemona, though he would certainly deserve it in any compatibilist sense.

Next suppose that instead of creating Iago and Desdemona full grown, Zeus arranges to have them born in the usual way in a deterministic world with everything needed to guarantee their characteristic behavior. I suggest that Iago would still deserve to be treated worse than Desdemona in terms of compatibilist forms of desert but not in terms of Kantian desert. But would this not also be true even if a god were not responsible for the situation? The only point of introducing a god was to make it perfectly clear that the ultimate responsibility would not be Iago's. But the same must be true without a god, since Iago would be in the same situation. The only difference is that without a god no one would be ultimately responsible.

Turning now to the traditional arguments, I have in mind, among others, the familiar argument that if determinism is true we can never act differently from the way we do act; that if we can never act differently from the way we do act we are not free; so that if determinism is true we are not free. Note first that if the argument is sound in terms of Kantian freedom, it is reasonable to construe it in this way. Otherwise one has to hold, as compatibilists implausibly do, that numerous sophisticated philosophers and others over generations have made the simple-minded mistake of failing to notice a switch in the premises of the argument from the categorical to the hypothetical sense of "can."[15] Furthermore, *if the argument is about Kantian freedom, compatibilists need not reject it, for they have no need to defend that kind of freedom.*

Even so, compatibilists might object that whereas they are able to give internally consistent, sufficient conditions for their various sorts of freedom, this has not been done for the Kantian kind of freedom. Hence there is no real *content* for such a notion, so "freedom" is never used in a Kantian sense. The Kantian notion does have content, however. An action is free in the Kantian sense if (a) the agent could (in the categorical sense) have acted differently and (b) the agent is ultimately responsible for the action. I believe that these conditions are inconsistent with one another, but it does not follow that there is no concept of Kantian freedom. Rather, it is an incoherent concept like the concept of squaring a circle.

It is also possible to explain why we have this concept. Most ordinary people believe that various forms of discrimination based on desert, rather than utility or fairness, are justified if the individual in question has acted freely, believing also that they are not justified *unless* conditions (a) and (b) are satisfied. So these conditions are built into their notion of freedom.

It follows from this account of the Kantian concept of freedom that the traditional argument given above is sound in terms of that kind of freedom; for determinism entails that there is no chance of our acting differently in the categorical sense as (a) requires. Furthermore, while indeterminism may satisfy (a), by leaving room for uncaused or partially uncaused actions, such actions would not satisfy (b), because, in so far as an action was uncaused, one would not be responsible for it. Since the same would seem to apply to uncaused or partially uncaused character traits, and other characteristics that might influence one's behavior, the Kantian kind of freedom would seem to be logically impossible.

It may be objected that the plain man's notion of freedom cannot be incoherent since he regards many actions as free. But when he uses the term in his daily life, he only employs upper-level criteria like those offered by compatibilities. At a deeper level he believes that no actions would be free if determinism were true, but he operates on the assumption that it is not and fails to see the futility of an appeal to indeterminism.

I have defended what might be called "partial compatibilism," the view that determinism is compatible with some kinds of freedom and desert but not with the Kantian kinds, and that the plain man has the latter in mind when he finds the traditional arguments for the incompatibility of freedom and determinism persuasive. "Total compatibilists" assume instead that no kind of freedom or desert is incompatible with determinism and therefore that the traditional arguments for their incompatibility cannot possibly be sound. They infer that to bring an end to the dispute they need only point out the fallacies that *must* underlie the traditional arguments and show that we should be satisfied with the kinds of freedom and desert that are compatible with determinism.

It was useful to show that there *are* kinds of freedom and desert that are compatible with determinism, and recent total compatibilists have described deeper kinds of freedom than were recognized in the past, hoping at last to satisfy libertarians and hard determinists. However, total compatibilism has been as unsuccessful in this respect for philosophers like Harry Frankfurt or Gary Watson as it was for their numerous predecessors from Hume and Mill through Schlick and Stevenson.[16] Libertarians and hard determinists will not be satisfied until it is admitted that the traditional arguments are sound – as they are when they are aimed at Kantian freedom and desert.

Returning to the objections to utilitarianism, if I am right about the impossibility of Kantian autonomy, advocates of a Kantian evaluation of autonomy who base this evaluation on a Kantian view of the nature of autonomy are obviously in trouble. And those who accept the Kantian evaluation of autonomy but reject Kantian autonomy are not entitled to assume that the Kantian evaluation should carry over to a compatibilist kind of autonomy. Instead they should ask themselves whether, or to what extent, their Kantian evaluation of autonomy is defensible regarding the radically different kind of autonomy offered by compatibilists. As for RU, it can ascribe a good deal of extrinsic value to the kind of autonomy that is possible, and while a purely hedonistic version of rule utilitarianism like Brandt's cannot ascribe any intrinsic value to it, that does not necessarily apply to other versions, including my own.

I hold that something is intrinsically valuable for an individual if she would value it intrinsically if she were fully rational in the sense of not being influenced by logical errors, ignorance of concepts, factual errors or ignorance, or failure to have a vivid idea of the sort of thing in question. On this basis, I believe that pleasure and freedom from pain are intrinsically valuable for everyone, and the most important intrinsic values for most of us, but that people would differ in regard to other putative intrinsic values, such as knowledge, mystical experiences, aesthetic experiences, as well as the kinds of autonomy that are possible.

As for the ascription of intrinsic value to distributions of good and evil in terms of desert, although proving that we cannot have Kantian freedom (which would make us ultimately responsible for our actions) shows that such a distribution is only extrinsically valuable, RU, unlike AU, can still justify giving innocent persons a right not to be punished that can be violated only in very extreme circumstances. Also, it is surely a gain rather than a loss if proving that Kantian freedom is impossible shows, at the same time, that positive retributivism is unjustifiable.

VI   The Rule-worship Objection and the Error Theory

Although RU avoids most of the counterintuitive consequences of AU, it does so by requiring us to treat its rules as firm rather than mere rules of thumb. Act utilitarians respond with the charge of rule worship. Brandt replies that subscribing to RU (in the sense of following it as well as one could expect actual people to do) would come much closer to maximizing utility than subscribing to AU, a formidable objection to a view which regards maximizing utility as the goal of morality.[17] However, he also holds that though this is the goal of morality, it is usually wrong to break the rules even if you believe that breaking them would have the best results. This would seem to be irrational. Is Brandt guilty of rule worship after all? I will argue that he is not.

When a rule utilitarian believes that it is wrong to break a rule, he sometimes believes that adhering to it would be optimific and sometimes not. When he believes that it is, he behaves exactly as if he were an act utilitarian. He only behaves differently when he follows a rule even though he believes that breaking the rule would have better results. But RU maintains that his overall pattern of behavior in following the rules will have better results than if he followed AU. This superiority cannot be explained in terms of the part of his behavior that matches that of an act utilitarian. The only possible explanation is that when he behaves differently by following a rule although he thinks that breaking it would have better results, this belief is wrong sufficiently often and/or his errors are sufficiently serious to make his policy of adhering to the rules yield better results.

I call this explanation the "error theory." Subscribing to RU is more beneficial than subscribing to AU if and only if the error theory is true. And Brandt has argued persuasively that your behavior is likely to be more beneficial if you subscribe to RU than if you subscribe to AU, since AU leaves too much room for rationalization and our behavior would therefore not be sufficiently predictable. In a world of subscribers to AU, it would be hard for anyone to be at all sure what others would do in various circumstances where we need reliable predictions.

It does not follow, however, that RU never commits us to irrational behavior. Because of our fallibility it would always be rational to follow a set of rules tailored to counteract our own particular weaknesses, but the need for predictability makes it necessary (except for certain professions) to have the same rules for an entire society. Such a code must be suitable for average persons so that while any member of a society would probably come closer to maximizing utility by subscribing to such a code rather than to AU, it could not possibly be tailored perfectly for everyone. Thus it may sometimes be rational for individuals who are less prone to error than average persons to violate the morality to which it is most beneficial for their society to subscribe.

An example may be useful here. Any RU code allows us to deviate from its rules in extreme circumstances. In such cases you are not violating the rule because the rule allows for such deviations. Since the notion of extreme circumstances is vague and since circumstances that would count as extreme for some rules would not count as extreme for others, there will be cases where it is not clear whether you should deviate from the rule or not. But suppose that it is a case of punishing a police officer who, despite appearances to the contrary, is innocent, in order to prevent a riot in which dozens of innocent people would be killed. Suppose, too, that you believed that the best morality for your society would allow you to punish the police officer only if you believed that the alternative was thousands of deaths. In such a case, if you had good grounds for believing that you were far less prone to error in this sort of situation than an average person in your society would probably be, it might be rational to punish the police officer. Nevertheless, given the need for predictability, and the fact that one would be all too likely to rationalize in assessing one's degree of proneness to error, such situations are sufficiently unusual not to present a serious practical problem.

Still one would prefer to have a code that never prescribed irrational behavior. This may seem to reveal a fault in RU; but the fault lies instead in the common assumption that despite the sort of world we live in, the best morality can give us everything that we would like. That is, we normally assume that the best morality for a society as a whole will also be perfectly suited to the capacities and circumstances of every individual in it, and that the morality that it would be best for a society to conform to perfectly will also be the most beneficial morality for a society of fallible individuals to subscribe to. Instead, we should recognize that the best sort of morality for our imperfect world has minor disadvantages as well as far more important advantages.

Summary

I have argued that in so far as we test moral principles in terms of our intuitions, we should be concerned primarily with principles that apply to our treatment of people (as opposed to animals) and that are accepted by most people in most cultures. I believe, though this is not my main reason for accepting RU, that RU is better equipped than deontological theories to justify firm principles that pass this test. I argued that this is the case for the view that killing is worse than letting die, that harming is worse than not helping, and in defence of the common principle that innocent persons have a right not to be punished. In addition, I rejected the common view that animal suffering should count less than the suffering of people and argued that animals raised for food or for experimentation should have a right to lives worth living. I have also defended abortion by showing that there is a conclusive utilitarian reason for forbidding the killing of persons that does not apply to fetuses; by arguing that RU can consistently justify a right to life for persons without ascribing a similar right to fetuses; and by giving a rule-utilitarian defence of the view that their past as persons gives temporarily comatose and anaesthetized persons, and even persons who are no longer rational, a right to life not possessed by fetuses. Since AU cannot accept either firm rules or rights, none of these views is consistent with AU. In addition, I have argued that Kantian autonomy is logically impossible and that it follows that no form of retributivism is justifiable. Furthermore, if Kantian autonomy is impossible, advocates of a Kantian view of the value of autonomy should ask themselves whether it is justified if we can only have the kinds of autonomy that are compatible with determinism, that is, whether it is reasonable to retain the Kantian evaluation of autonomy while rejecting the kind of autonomy that Kant had in mind.[18]

NOTES

1   R. B. Brandt, *A Theory of the Good and the Right* (Oxford: Oxford University Press, 1979).
2. There are reasons why it may sometimes be wrong to follow the morality to which it would be most beneficial for one's society to subscribe. That ideal morality will usually differ from the actual morality of a society, and there may be rules that it would be beneficial for a society to change but that one should follow until the change is brought about. Also the ideal morality may include some rules that it would be desirable to have in place but such that the costs of the transition would be too great. And even if the costs of a transition to a new rule would not be too great, so that it is desirable to make the change, such a proposed rule – call it a candidate rule – is likely to impose very different obligations from rules that are actually in place. For example, one's obligation might be largely a matter of campaigning for the new rule by writing, giving speeches, arguing with people, going on marches, engaging in acts of civil disobedience, etc. In this paper nothing much turns on this added difference between myself and Brandt except in the section on animals where I argue that animals bred for our purposes have a right to a life worth living, meaning by this that they have a candidate right to this rather than an established right.

3   W. D. Ross, *Foundations of Ethics*. (Oxford: Clarendon Press, 1939).

4   For a devastating critique of the sort of meta-ethical theory that deontologists must rely on, see P.F. Strawson, "Ethical Intuitionism," *Philosophy*, vol. 24, no. 88 (Jan. 1949) pp. 23–33.

5   In the book I concentrate particularly on issues involving a choice between life and death. Besides abortion, I consider the question of infanticide in the case of neonates with spinal bifida or Downe's syndrome, assisted suicide and the use of extreme measures to prolong the lives of terminally ill patients. I also look at the measurement of utility – particularly in determining how to allocate limited medical resources – and argue that, even at a practical level, it is more feasible to make a rough measurement of pleasure and pain than to do so in regard to the fulfillment of interests. Although I show that a good deal can be done with RU in applied ethics, there is great deal more to be done. My hope is to convince other philosophers in applied ethics that there is gold, a lot more gold, in the rule utilitarian mine.

6   J. Rawls, *A Theory of Justice* (Cambridge, Mass.: Harvard University Press, 1971).

7   Jonathan Bennett, "Whatever the Consequences", *Analysis*, vol. 26 (1966).

8   Jonathan Bennett, "Accountability," in Zak Van Stratten, ed., *Philosophical Subjects: Essays Presented to R. F. Strawson* (Oxford: Clarendon Press, 1980).

9   The exceptions are cases where the failure to act is egregiously wrong, as in the case of a mother who deliberately fails to feed a newborn child.

10   I do not claim that this is what "persons" means. I am using the word as a technical term. Nothing in my argument hinges on the question of what it means in ordinary usage.

11   It may be objected that allowing abortion should be compared with allowing members of certain specific groups of innocent persons to be killed rather than with allowing the killing of innocent persons in general. But while allowing the killing of members of specific groups would have less catastrophic effects than allowing the killing of innocent persons in general, even if this practice were limited to unhappy persons, the indirect effects of allowing it would be enough to make it wrong, while there are not corresponding indirect effects from allowing abortion.

12   Eike-Henner Kluge, "Infanticide as The Murder of Persons," in Marvil Kohl, ed., *Infanticide and the Value of Life* (New York: Prometheus Books, 1978).

13   Peter Singer, *Animal Liberation: A New Ethics For Our Treatment of Animals* (New York: Avon Books, 1977).

14   Kant may be interpreted instead as holding that there are free actions but that it is a category mistake to hold that they are either determined or not determined. I find this view highly implausible. At any rate it is clearly not the plain man's notion of freedom, and it is not the notion of freedom with which I am concerned.

15   The usual compatibilist approach to this argument is to claim that it derives its plausibility from an equivocation on "can," with the term used in the categorical sense the first time and the hypothetical sense the second time,

so that the premisses are true but the argument is invalid. An alternative approach is to claim the argument is valid because "can" is used in the categorical sense both times, but that it is not sound because the claim that you cannot act differently in the categorical sense does not imply that you are not free. This claim would be backed up by showing that inability to act differently in the categorical sense is compatible with the various sorts of freedom offered by compatibilists. An obvious problem for this response is that it does not account for the plausibility of the argument. A libertarian can hold that while inability in the categorical sense to act differently is compatible with the various "freedoms" offered by compatibilists, this inability is not compatible with the Kantian kind of freedom. This is shown by the fact that compatibilist kinds of freedom cannot justify any form of retributivism.

16 See H. Frankfurt, "Alternative Possibilities and Moral Responsibility," *Journal of Philosophy*, vol. 66 (1969), pp. 828–39.

17 Brandt, *A Theory of the Good and the Right*.

18 This paper has benefited from discussions with Richard Brandt, D. G. Brown, Mark Dickson, Andrew Irvine, Jeff McMahan, Roland Otterstein, Leo Paquin, Michael Philips, Paul Russell, Peter Singer, Nick Sleigh, and Earl Winkler.

6
Moral Philosophy as a Subversive Activity

James Rachels

After reviewing the pitfalls of attempting to found moral theory on either received morality or self-evident moral axioms, Rachels proposes a model of moral reasoning without foundations. Using the metaphor of "the web of belief" Rachels argues that no element of the web of moral belief is immune from potential criticism or revision, but some beliefs, both general and particular, are nearer the center of the web, and therefore more secure, while others lie nearer the fringes. In reasoning morally we strive for a systematic harmonization within the full network of belief, including beliefs about history, science, human psychology, and sociology as well as general and particular moral beliefs. Rachels borrows the metaphor of "the web of belief" from Quine but his overall view has close affinities with Rawls's initial idea of "reflective equilibrium" and, especially, with Norman Daniel's extension of the Rawlsian idea in terms of "wide reflective equilibrium theory."

Rachels' paper bears comparison with several others in this collection that illustrate, in different ways, the kind of working back and forth within the web of moral belief that Rachels has in mind. Concerning the general issue of the relation between theory and practice, compare the papers of Sikora (chapter 5), Hoffmaster (chapter 20), and Winkler (chapter 19); concerning the critical potential of moral philosophy, compare with Philips's outline of how social moralities can be properly evaluated in his section on "ethics as social policy" in chapter 10.

Pyrrho the Skeptic taught that, for every argument that can be given in favor of any proposition, an equally good argument can be given for its opposite. Therefore, he concluded, the wise man will suspend judgment about everything, and believe nothing. Such a view has its charms, but it also seems to have alarming practical implications: for example, if I have no greater reason to believe there is a truck coming at me than to believe there is no truck coming, and moreover no reason to believe it is more to my advantage to go on living than to die, why should I get out of the truck's way? Why shouldn't I just stand in the highway and see what happens? Surely, one might think, Pyrrho could not have meant to be saying *that*. But according to Diogenes, that is exactly what he meant:

Pyrrho led a life consistent with his Skepticism, going out of his way for nothing taking no precaution, but facing all risks as they came, whether carts, precipices, dogs or what not, and generally, leaving nothing to the judgment of the senses. But he was kept out of harm's way by his friends who used to follow close after him.[1]

One story is that Pyrrho once came upon his elderly teacher, from whom he had learned his skepticism, stuck in a ditch. Unable to think of any good reason to rescue him, Pyrrho did not do so. Another passer-by did pull the old man from the ditch and castigated Pyrrho for his heartlessness. The teacher, however, commended Pyrrho for having learned his lesson well.

We do not know whether these stories are true (in keeping with Pyrrho's own teaching, we might be skeptical about them); but we do know that Pyrrho was a philosopher who did not believe that one's philosophical theorizing should be insulated from one's everyday beliefs and practice. If there are good philosophical reasons for doubting the reality of space and time, he thought that this means we should not be so sure that we are here now, since "here" and "now" refer to space and time. Pyrrho's skepticism was epistemological; it was a view about what we can know, or not know; however, the primary recommendation of his philosophy was ethical: the suspension of judgment about matters of truth and falsity, about good and evil, is said to lead to a state of tranquility which is the only secure path to happiness. Pyrrho seems to have been absolutely serious about this – no matter how much one might doubt that not avoiding carts and precipices leads to happiness.

Pyrrho's assumption, that what we think and what we do go hand in hand, was shared by most thinkers throughout Western history. In the twentieth century, however, we have become accustomed to a different way of understanding philosophical ideas. Today, if a philosopher doubts the reality of space and time, or the legitimacy of our usual ways of talking about space and time, this is taken to be no reason at all for him or her not to apply for a sabbatical next year. Somewhere along the way we learned to insulate our philosophical thinking from our first-order beliefs, and we even developed theories about the nature of our enquiry to justify this. (It is sometimes said, for example, that philosophical questions are different *kinds of questions* from those asked by practical people.) When did this happen? Who invented insulation? Myles Burnyeat has written a splendid paper about this question, in which he argues that the answer is: Kant did it.[2] But that is not what I want to discuss in this essay. Instead I want to discuss insulation as a continuing practice in philosophical thinking about ethics. Most moral philosophers today, especially those who do applied ethics, would probably say that they do not believe in insulation.

After all, if you are trying to formulate and justify a position about a specific practical issue, you will not want to say that your ethical theory is irrelevant to your conclusions. But as we shall see, this is a complicated business.

Moorean Insulation

There is an argument of G. E. Moore's with which all students of philosophy are familiar. Faced with skeptical doubts about the reality of time, Moore responded: today I had breakfast before I had lunch; therefore, time is real.[3] In its day, this was regarded as a powerful *riposte*. Following Moore, it became fashionable for philosophers to say that simple facts such as this one are far more certain than any sophisticated arguments that might be marshalled against them. Today this is no longer so fashionable; instead, it is commonly said that Moore was naïve to think that the skeptical arguments could be refuted so easily. The philosopher's claims about time, it is now said, are different sorts of claims from the ones that ordinary people make about breakfast coming before lunch. Therefore, nothing follows from the ordinary judgments about the philosophical issues.

Burnyeat comments that any philosopher who thinks he is not an insulator should consider his reaction to Moore. Moore was not an insulator; he thought that philosophical claims do have straightforward implications for first-order judgments, and vice versa. Those who consider Moore's argument to be naïve apparently disagree. But Moore *was* an insulator of a more limited kind. Let me explain what I mean by making a distinction between doing philosophy *safely* and doing philosophy *with risk*.[4] Those who do philosophy safely proceed in such a way that their first-order beliefs are never called into doubt. They begin with the assumption that they know a great many (first-order) things to be true, and for them, philosophical thinking involves (only?) a search for principles and theories that would justify and explain what they already know. Those who do philosophy with risk, on the other hand, expose their first-order beliefs to the perils of thought. Everything is up for grabs. Any belief may have to be rejected, if reasons are found against it; and one cannot say, in advance, what reasons might turn up for doubting what beliefs.

Those who do philosophy safely are insulators, but for them insulation works in only one direction. Their philosophical views will be tailored to accommodate their first-order beliefs, but the first-order beliefs are themselves held sacrosanct. They are not placed at risk. Moore was an insulator of this qualified sort. An ordinary belief might discredit a theory, but not the other way around. In his honor, if it is an honor, we might call this *Moorean insulation*.

Moorean insulation, when applied to the traditional issues of metaphysics – to questions about space and time, about physical objects, and so forth – is an appealing doctrine. It does seem right to say that we know breakfast comes before lunch, and so on; and it is tempting to conclude straightaway that any philosophical doctrine that says otherwise might be false. But when we turn to moral philosophy, Moorean insulation loses much of its appeal. The moral beliefs that are common in our society, and which we philosophers perforce share (or at least which we begin by sharing), may be in part the result of sensible thinking. But they are also in large part the products of historical and psychological processes that have involved superstition, selfishness, false religion, bad science, and bad metaphysics. Moorean insulation would protect these beliefs from revision. It is, therefore, a profoundly conservative approach, bent on justifying whatever moral views we already happen to have, whatever they might be.

Moorean insulation has been associated, throughout twentieth-century moral philosophy, with a certain style of argument, again familiar to all students of the subject. I refer, of course, to the familiar method of argument by counter-example. A thesis about morality will be advanced, together with arguments in its favor, and this will be met by the claim that the thesis cannot be true because it is contrary to a commonly-held moral belief. Act utilitarianism has been "refuted" a thousand times by this method: "Act utilitarianism says that we should do whatever will produce the best results; but it might sometimes produce the best results to secure the judicial execution of an innocent person; this is never right; therefore, act-utilitarianism must be rejected." One still hears this sort of argument, although the examples given have changed over the years. Recently, examples involving what Bernard Williams calls "personal integrity" have been popular weapons against utilitarianism.[5] However, many philosophers, including Williams, now regard this style of reasoning as overly crude, and recognize that it must at least be supplemented by a persuasive explanation of *why* it is always wrong to secure the judicial execution of the innocent, or why personal integrity is so important, or why whatever other example is being used has the significance it allegedly has. Happily, counter-examples alone are no longer considered so decisive as they once were.

Yet the eclipse of this style of argument does not necessarily mean the disappearance of Moorean insulation. Moorean insulation is also revealed by the extent to which, in constructing one's moral theory, one takes conformity to pre-reflective belief as a guiding consideration. It is one of the great virtues of John Rawls's work that this methodological issue is out in the open.[6] Rawls explicitly endorses the idea of using one's moral intuitions as check-points for testing the acceptability of theory. Moral theory, he has said, is like linguistics. Just as a linguistic theory should reflect the competent speaker's sense of grammaticalness, a moral theory should reflect the competent moral judge's sense of rightness. In other places Rawls backs off a bit from this strong statement, and substitutes the idea that one's considered moral judgments should be brought into a "reflective equilibrium" with one's theoretical pronouncements. But the individual judgments still play an important regulative role, and the extent to which cherished moral beliefs are really placed at risk is somewhat murky.

I said that it is a virtue of Rawls's work that in his writing this methodological issue is out in the open. Elsewhere, however, the issue may not be in the open, and Moorean insulation may do its work unnoticed. One might, for example, reject utilitarianism and prefer instead a theory that emphasizes the virtues because the latter sort of theory "does a better job of explaining" what is presumed to be our actual moral situation. The underlying conception of our actual moral situation may not be placed at risk. Instead it may simply be presented in an attractive way, that appeals to our pre-reflective sense of what moral life is like. Then the theorizing proceeds apace, and the developed theory is finally displayed as "explaining" why we should live in just the way that we thought we should all along.

Or, to take a different sort of example: recently there has been a lot of philosophical writing about the nature of personal relationships, taking it as a datum that we have special responsibilities and obligations to our parents, children, and friends. These are responsibilities and obligations that we do not have to just everybody, but to specific people in virtue of our specific type of relationships with them. A common move is to take this "fact" as a reason for rejecting any moral theory that seems to imply otherwise, and to look instead for a theory that will give these relationships, and the responsibilities they involve, a central place. Frequently it is said that, even if we do not yet have such a theory, this is a necessary condition that any acceptable theory must meet.[7]

I find this troubling, and not merely because it involves Moorean insulation. Like everyone else, I have a deep feeling, that I cannot shake, that my responsibilities to my own children are special. If I have to choose between feeding my own children, and giving the food to starving orphans, I am going to feed my own. (More than that: faced with a choice between sending my own children to college, and using the money to help feed starving orphans, I send my own to college.) It would be reassuring simply to assume that I am right to feel this way; and as a philosopher I could cast my vote in favor of a moral theory that makes things come out right on this issue. But there are disturbing arguments on the other side. After all, my children were merely lucky to have been born into a relatively affluent family, while the orphans, who have the same needs and are equally deserving, were unlucky to have gotten stuck with their situation. Why should the just distribution of life's goods, right down to food itself, be determined in this way? Why should it be counted as a virtue for a moral theory to allow so much to depend on mere luck? But taking such an argument seriously means placing the pre-reflective belief in the special importance of family relations at risk. A Moorean institutionalist could, of course, take this argument seriously in a certain sense: it could be taken as something to be seriously refuted. But if one approaches the argument with anything like an open mind, allowing the possibility that there may be something to it, then the pre-reflective belief – even so fundamental a belief as the belief about the specialness of one's duties to one's own children – is suddenly in jeopardy.

Can Moral Philosophy be Subversive?

The alternative to Moorean insulation is an approach to ethics which sees moral philosophy as, at least potentially, a subversive activity, which could undermine even the most deep-seated assumptions of ordinary morality. The advantage of such an approach is evident: it makes no sense to conduct a search for the truth by assuming from the outset that we already know what the truth is. Only by rejecting insulation can we avoid incorporating into our theory the prejudices and other irrational elements that infect our pre-reflective judgments. However, matters are not so simple. Although it sounds fine to say that we should abjure Moorean insulation, I can think of at least two reasons why it might be thought that the alternative is an impossible fantasy.

1 First Principles and Particular Judgments

The first reason is connected with the idea that in any enquiry we must have some starting point from which our reasoning proceeds. As Hume pointed out, every argument leads back to some first principle that is itself unjustified. If we ask for a justification of that principle, perhaps one can be given, but only by appealing to still another unjustified assumption. In moral philosophy this means that we must ultimately begin with some conception of what is morally important, which is itself taken for granted. A utilitarian might assume that what is important is maximizing welfare.

Someone with a different cast of mind might make a different assumption. But no one can escape reliance on some starting point, which is insulated from challenge by its very place in the scheme of reasoning.

Thus it might seem that we have only two options: either we accept one or more moral principles (our "axioms") as self-evident, and derive particular moral judgments from them; or we begin with the set of particular judgments that we find most plausible, and work backwards to the general principles that explain and justify them. Peter Singer, among others, has argued for the first alternative. Speaking of those who, like Rawls, assume that our considered moral judgments are largely correct, he says:

> Why should we not rather make the opposite assumption, that all the particular moral judgments we intuitively make are likely to derive from discarded religious systems, from warped views of sex and bodily functions, or from customs necessary for the survival of the group in social and economic circumstances that now lie in the distant past? In which case, it would be best to forget all about our particular moral judgments, and start again from as near as we can get to self-evident moral axioms.[8]

The approach suggested in this passage is about as radical as one could imagine: we are to start with self-evident axioms and then accept the particular judgments that follow from them, *no matter how far from ordinary morality those judgments turn out to be.* There are, of course, a number of objections that might be raised against this.

First, it is no obvious improvement to switch one's allegiance from self-evident judgments to self-evident axioms. Either way, our starting point is taken on faith. Furthermore, what is to prevent our choice of axioms from being influenced by the same irrational forces that infect our particular judgments?

Second, it may be observed that philosophers who have tried to do this have almost always failed. The utilitarians have come closest. Taking the principle of utility as their self-evident starting point, utilitarians have been notably critical of ordinary morality. However, we might ask exactly what is supposed to be self-evident about the principle of utility. The classic formulation of the principle – that we should act so as to maximize happiness and minimize suffering for all sentient beings – might fairly be described as self-evident. But it has never been self-evident that this is our *only* duty. Moreover, few utilitarians have stuck to the classic principle when confronted with objections. They have instead reformulated their principle in terms of such technical notions as "expected utility" or "overall preference satisfaction," and they have worried about whether it is average or total happiness that should be pursued. The result is a revised principle that is more philosophically defensible but a lot less self-evident. And furthermore, they have done this precisely to avoid unwanted implications at the level of particular judgments.

Third, and finally, Singer's suggestion seems unreasonable on its face. Moral principles tend to be vague and abstract; we hardly know what they mean until we see exactly what particular judgments follow from them. Suppose, for example, we start with an "axiom" that seems self-evident, but then, upon investigating its consequences, we discover that it leads to the conclusion that murder is permissible. If this seems far-fetched, consider the following familiar point. It seems self-evident that we should do whatever will decrease the amount of unhappiness in the world. But we might help to accomplish this by quietly murdering a few chronically unhappy people. Should we then conclude that these murders are justified? Remember that the recommendation is that we accept the consequences of our self-evident starting point, *no matter how contrary to accepted morality those consequences might be* – after all, as Singer points out, our pre-reflective judgments are tainted by all sorts of irrational influences. Plainly, though, when confronted with such implications reasonable people will conclude that their axioms need to be revised, no matter how attractive those axioms might have seemed before their implications were exposed.

Faced with all this, it is tempting to conclude that, if we *must* begin with principles that are not themselves justified, why not choose those principles that will yield the first-order judgments that one finds most plausible? This seems eminently sensible. So Moorean insulation seems not only unavoidable, but reasonable.

If this were correct, it would be a depressing thing to learn, because it would mean that moral philosophy is, in the end, just an elaborate rationalization of what we already want to believe. However, I do not believe that Hume's logical point really has this sort of significance. We do not have to choose between these two alternatives, because we do not have to think of our moral principles and beliefs as forming an axiomatic system, at least not in this simple way.

What, exactly, is the relation between our particular moral judgments and the theoretical ideas to which philosophers appeal in discussing them? The higher-order considerations typically invoked by philosophers form a large and varied group. Consider the following small sample:

that pain, frustration, and ignorance are bad;
that friendship, knowledge, and self-esteem are good;
that human life has a special value and importance;
that human interests have a fundamental importance that the interests of other animals do not have;
that people should always be treated as ends-in-themselves, and never as mere means;

that personal autonomy – the freedom of each individual to control and direct his or her own life – is especially important;

that each of us has special obligations and responsibilities to our own family and friends;

that there is an important moral difference between causing harm, and merely allowing it to happen;

that there is a difference in stringency between our strict duties and other duties which are matters of "mere" charity or generosity; and

that a person's intention, in performing a given action, is relevant to determining whether the action is right.

We need not think of these as axioms from which conclusions about particular actions are derived. Instead we may think of them, together with the multitude of particular moral judgments we make, as forming part of a network of beliefs that are connected with one another in various ways. In other words, rather than thinking of morality as a deductive system with axioms at the top and particular judgments at the bottom, we may think of it as forming part of what W. V. Quine calls the "web of belief."

Quine originally conceived of this metaphor as a way of expressing his view of the relation between empirical observations, scientific theories, and the laws of logic. He held that none of these, including the laws of logic, are immune from criticism; as new evidence is discovered, and new considerations come to light, no element of the web is protected from the possibility that it might have to be revised or even rejected. He realized, of course, that we may be more reluctant to abandon some of our beliefs than others. Let us say that these are near the center of the web, while the beliefs that we hold with less confidence are on its outer fringes.[9]

If we think of our moral system as forming part of the web of belief, it is clear, I think, that there is no firm correlation between what is near the center and what is on the fringes, on the one hand, and the difference between particular moral beliefs and general moral principles on the other hand. Some of our moral judgments about particular cases are near the center of the web. We would be extremely reluctant ever to abandon the belief that what Charles Manson's gang did was wrong. And some of our general principles are also near the center: for example, that causing pain is wrong. But there are also both general principles and particular judgments that are nearer the fringes – for exmaple, the particular judgment that Reagan's people should not have swapped arms for hostages is not nearly so certain as the judgment that Manson's people acted wrongly; and the theoretical idea that there is a difference between causing harm and allowing it to happen is not so certain as the principle that causing pain is wrong. It is an important feature of this model, however, that no belief, theoretical or practical, is absolutely insulated from revision, whatever its position in the web may be at any given time.

A moral belief or principle can be moved from the center of the web to its fringes, or even abandoned altogether. Let me mention one moral idea that used to be near the center of our common web, but which I think has now been shown to be untenable. For centuries it was part of the orthodoxy of Western thought that mere animals have no moral claim on us. A few isolated thinkers did not share this view, but they were so few that they could be ignored. So animals have been used as food, as experimental subjects, as sources of leather and wool, and in general have been treated as resources for human use and enjoyment without regard for their own interests. Indeed, to justify these practices it was sometimes even argued that mere animals *have no* interests that could be figured into our moral calculations. Within the past two decades, however, this belief has been challenged so effectively, by philosophers such as Peter Singer and Tom Regan, that it has (in my view at least) been rendered virtually untenable.[10] At the very least, one can no longer simply assume, as philosophers did for centuries, that the interests of non-humans can be ignored.

It is not merely philosophical argument that has brought about this change. Our moral views are connected, in our overall web of belief, with all sorts of non-moral considerations. Charles Darwin did as much to call this particular part of moral orthodoxy into doubt as anyone, by showing that human beings share a common origin, and common characteristics, with the members of other species. A short time ago the presumed "difference" between human life and interests, and those of other animals, might have been cited as one of those central moral "facts" that could be used to test the acceptability of moral theory, but no longer. Even if it still occupies a place in one's web of belief, it certainly has been moved much farther toward the periphery.

Before leaving this topic, I want to add two further comments. First, it might be thought that, in urging a shift away from conceiving of morality as a deductive system toward thinking of it as a part of the overall web of belief, I am recommending abandonment of the traditional conception of the philosopher's task as that of developing moral *theories*. Some contemporary thinkers such as Thomas Nagel and Bernard Williams have argued against the traditional conception of moral theory, urging instead that morality has multiple and incommensurable sources that cannot be neatly systematized in the way that philosophers have supposed.[11] They might find what I have been saying congenial. But I do not mean to be aligning myself with them on this point. What I have been saying is, I think, neutral with respect to the possibility of developing a theory in the traditional sense. It might still be possible, when surveying the web at any given time, to systematize what one finds there in the traditional way. It could turn out, for example, that all the actions one regards as right conform to the principle of utility, in which case utilitarianism would be vindicated. But if one adopts the strategy I have suggested, one would not have reached this conclusion by taking the principle of utility as a self-evident starting point. Instead, that principle would have been subjected to the same scrutiny as every other element of the web. It would simply have survived the critical process.

A second and related point is that if even if one accepts some general theory such as utilitarianism, the way of thinking I have sketched still has its advantages, since it is well suited to provide an explanation of the connection between the main principles of the theory and other beliefs associated with it. Consider the familiar problem that arises when we ask for a justification of the principle of utility. This seems impossible, because if the principle is justified in terms of some other principle, then that other principle, and not the principle of utility, becomes the ultimate standard. Thus one might conclude that nothing much of interest can be said. Yet individual utilitarians have had quite a lot to say here. They have argued, variously, that utilitarianism should be accepted by people of a benevolent temperament; that it is consonant with a properly "scientific" way of viewing the world; that it is the only moral view that fits the logic of moral language; that it is a natural ethic for a species formed by Darwinian evolution; and that alleged "duties" which are not compatible with utilitarianism may be explained away as the products of superstition and false religion. Notoriously, even if all this were true, none of it would be a proof in the sense of deducing the principle of utility from higher-order moral principles. So what is to be made of such arguments? What is going on here, I suggest, is that connections are being found between the principle of utility and other beliefs in those philosophers' total webs. The connections are weaker than logical entailment, but they are nonetheless important. If sound, these considerations provide reasons in favor of accepting the ultimate principle, without strictly entailing it. Such considerations have more to do with showing that one's total set of beliefs form a consistent and satisfying whole than with proving that one's ultimate principles are true.

2   Rationality and Tradition

There is another reason why one might doubt the viability of abandoning Moorean insulation in favor of an approach which sees moral philosophy as radically subversive. The latter approach, it might be argued, expects too much of reason alone. It involves the idea that moral truth may be sought by the exercise of reason without dependence upon some previously agreed-upon (and therefore unchallengeable) set of values. But this idea may itself appear to be nothing but a philosophical fantasy.

Alasdair MacIntyre, in his recent book *Whose Justice? Which Rationality?* argues just this point. The idea of impartial reason, justifying norms of conduct binding on all rational people, is, according to MacIntyre, an illusion fostered by the Enlightenment. In reality there is no such thing as a reason – for belief or action – that must be acknowledged by every rational being as such; rationality is possible only within a historical tradition, which sets standards of enquiry for those working within that tradition.

> What the enlightenment made us for the most part blind to and what we now need to recover is, so I shall argue, a conception of rational enquiry as embodied in a tradition; a conception according to which the standards of rational justification themselves emerge from and are part of a history in which they are vindicated by the way in which they transcend the limitations of and provide remedies for the defects of their predecessors within the history of that same tradition.[12]

Thus, in MacIntyre's view, the reasons that would be adduced by a modern liberal in arguing, say, that slavery is unjust, would not necessarily be acceptable to an Aristotelian, whose standards of rationality are different; and the search for standards that transcend the two traditions is a fool's quest. No such tradition-neutral standards exist, except, perhaps, for purely formal principles such as non-contradiction, which are far too weak to yield substantive ethical results.

At first hearing, this sounds like a familiar view: relativism. But it turns out that MacIntyre is no relativist. Relativism is one of the modern ideas that MacIntyre, who now describes himself as an Augustinian Christian, rejects. One of the major challenges confronting the reader of *Whose Justice? Which Rationality?* is to figure out how, after embracing this view of rationality, MacIntyre can escape being a relativist. His idea seems to be this: traditions confront one another historically, and one tradition succeeds in establishing its superiority over its rival by demonstrating that it can solve the problems internal to the other tradition, while at the same time incorporating within itself everything in the other tradition that survives the dialectical examination.

This, however, only invites an awkward question: MacIntyre represents the confrontation as involving rational debate, and not mere institutional power – Augustinian Christianity displaces Aristotelianism, on his view, not merely because of the combined political power of church and state, but because it could be demonstrated to be superior, even to the partisans of the other tradition. But if there are no standards of practical rationality that are neutral between the two traditions, how is this possible?

MacIntyre believes that an abstract answer to this question is not to be found; for an answer one must look to history for examples of how the process has actually taken place. So the bulk of his book is occupied by an examination of four traditions (the Aristotelian, the Augustinian Christian, the Scottish, and the modern liberal) and the various clashes between them. To assess MacIntyre's argument, then, we would have to examine the details of the historical debates and see whether their outcomes did or did not depend on the application of standards of rationality which were not merely tradition-bound. Obviously, that is too much to attempt here. Nevertheless there are several relevant points that might be made.

First, the type of confrontation that MacIntyre pictures as taking place between traditions is possible only because the partisans of the different traditions have a lot in common. If they were not trying to solve the same problems, then it would make no sense to say that one tradition does a better job of solving a problem than does another; and if the traditions had no common content, it would make no sense to talk about one tradition's incorporating within itself the worthy aspects of its rivals. What people in different traditions have in common might, therefore, form the basis of a shared rationality that makes possible the development of common norms.

Aristotle, who epitomized a tradition MacIntyre rejects, believed that this is so. Aristotle observed that all humans face danger and fear death, and so have need of courage; that all have bodily appetites that are sometimes difficult to control, and so have need of ways to manage themselves; that none is self-sufficient, and so all have need of friends. Surveying the various ancient societies, he declared: "One can see in one's travels to distant countries the experiences of recognition and affiliation that link every human being to every other human being."[13] Aristotle thought that such universal elements of human experience provided the basis for an ethic that was not simply local to one culture. He did not, however, expect universal agreement about that ethic. (He did not make the mistake of confusing the question of whether a moral argument of universal validity can be constructed with the very different question of whether people can be persuaded to accept that argument.) The fact that people do disagree about norms – the endless disputation which MacIntyre says is typical of modern, rootless humans – was as familiar to Aristotle as it is to us. But as Aristotle knew, there is more than one possible explanation of that disagreement. Indeed, the best explanation is probably that such disagreement stems from a combination of causes, significantly including the ignorance, poverty, disease, and political and religious oppression that have plagued a large proportion of human beings throughout history.

But this argument cannot continue forever at such an abstract level. Sooner or later the challenge will be heard: if you think that there are norms which are binding on all humans – if you think that reasons can be given to show that a certain practice is right, or wrong, such that those reasons must be accepted by every rational person, regardless of the tradition in which he or she participates – then give us an example of such a norm. The challenge is daunting, but it cannot be avoided. So I will offer as an example the matter that I mentioned before: the condemnation of slavery. It is easy, of course, to construct an argument against slavery from a modern liberal point of view. But is that argument tied only to modern liberal values? Or does it appeal rather to considerations which any reasonable person should accept?

As I conceive it, the argument against slavery is, in bare outline, as follows. All forms of slavery (and it must be remembered that "slavery" is a general name for a fairly wide range of historical practices, which have differed significantly from one another) involve setting apart a class of humans for treatment that is systematically different from that accorded other members of the community. Deprivation of liberty is the feature which these various practices have most in common, although slaves have also been subject to a variety of other unwelcome treatments. Now the argument is that it is unjust to set some people apart for different treatment unless there is a relevant difference between them that justifies the difference in treatment. But there is no general difference between humans that would justify setting some of them apart as slaves. Therefore slavery is unjust.

Is this argument only a product of modern liberal thought? Or should it be compelling even to those who live in different sorts of societies, with different sorts of traditions? To test this, we might consider a slave society such as Aristotle's. According to one estimate, there were as many slaves in Aristotle's Athens, in proportion to the population, as there were in the slave states of America before the civil war. Aristotle himself defended slavery. Yet the rational resources available within his tradition seem to have been sufficient for an appreciation of its injustice. Aristotle himself reports that "Some regard the control of a slave by a master as contrary to nature. In their view the distinction of master and slave is due to law or convention; there is no natural difference between them: the relation of master and slave is based on force, and being so based has no warrant in justice."[14]

But, as is well known, Aristotle did not share this enlightened view. A slave-owner himself, he held that slavery is justified by the inferior rationality of the slave. Because they are not so rational as other humans, slaves are fitted by nature to be ruled rather than to rule. Aristotle also knew that many slaves are inclined to revolt, but he attributed this not to any sense they might have of the injustice of their position, but to an excess of "spiritedness." In his sketch of the ideal state, near the end of the *Politics*, he suggests that farm labor should be provided by slaves, "but slaves not drawn from a single stock, or from stocks of a spirited temper. This will at once secure the advantage of a good supply of labour and eliminate any danger of revolutionary designs."[15] But Aristotle was not of a single mind about this, for he also supported provisions for manumission. After recommending that farm labor be performed by slaves, he adds that "It is wise to offer all slaves the eventual reward of emancipation." In his will Aristotle provided for the emancipation of his own slaves. This is an unexpected concession from someone who held that slaves are fitted for their station by nature itself.

Plainly, Aristotle accepted the principle that differences in treatment are unjustified unless they are correlated with differences between individuals that justify those differences in treatment. In fact, this is just a modern version of an idea that he advanced in the *Nicomachean Ethics*, namely that like cases should be treated alike and different cases differently. That is why he felt it necessary to defend slavery by contending that slaves possess an inferior degree of rationality. But this is a claim that can be shown to be false by evidence that should be counted as evidence as much by Aristotle as by us. Therefore, even on Aristotle's own terms, slavery should be recognizable as unjust. In arguing this we are not simply transporting our standards of rationality back into a culture that was "different," although we might well cite information about the nature of human beings that we have now, but which was unavailable to him.

Of course, showing that this argument should be accepted by Aristotle is not the same as showing that it should be accepted by all reasonable people. The possibility still remains that MacIntyre is right, and that there are partisans of some traditions for whom this type of argument could have no effect. But I see no good reason to believe this; the argument I have outlined appeals to such a basic principle of reasoning that I think it should always have some force. At any rate, as we have seen, Aristotle held the sensible view that people in different traditions have enough in common, in virtue of their shared humanity, to make the achievement of common norms a reasonable goal. On its face, this seems at least as plausible as the idea that the incompatible standards of different traditions cannot be overcome.

Philosophers as Commentators on Public Events

Moral philosophers who specialize in "applied ethics" often discuss the behavior of politicians, physicians, and businesspeople. I want to conclude by saying something about actual human behavior, but not the behavior of these who are so frequently criticized. Instead I want to say something about the behavior of the moral philosophers themselves.

As moral philosophy has become more concerned with practical matters during the past twenty years, philosophers have sometimes found themselves in the heady position of being called upon by newspaper reporters to comment on the latest public controversies. When this happens, the reporters usually are not much interested in detailed analysis or lengthy qualifications – a short, pithy quote is what is wanted. Nor are they eager to hear reassurances that some apparently alarming development really is not alarming. That does not make good copy. What makes good copy is the idea that a new development is morally troubling, or worse. And frequently philosophers are available to provide just such comments. It seems to me that, more often than not, this combination of reporters' interests and philosophers' snap judgments has a profoundly conservative effect. New developments are viewed as troublesome against the background, not of careful analysis, but of accepted wisdom.

In March 1990 a story appeared in the US newspapers about a Los Angeles couple who had decided to have another child in the hope that the baby's bone marrow cells could be used to save the life of their teenage daughter. Abe and Mary Ayala, who are in their forties, had not intended to have an additional child; in fact, Abe Ayala had had a vasectomy. But their 17-year-old daughter, Anissa, was dying of leukemia, and a bone marrow transplant was her only hope. After two years of searching in vain for a suitable donor, they decided to have another child because there was a one-in-four chance that the new family member would be a suitable donor. So Abe Ayala had his vasectomy reversed and Mary Ayala became pregnant. The baby, a girl named Marissa, was born on April 6 and she was indeed a compatible donor. The transplant procedure, which was to be accomplished a few months later, would involve little risk for the baby, and Anissa's chances of surviving would rise from zero to between 70 and 80 percent.

The Ayalas were understandably elated to learn that Anissa's life might be saved. However, the newspaper stories prominently featured quotations from medical ethicists who labeled their decision "troublesome" and even "outrageous": "The ideal reason for having a child," said a well-known figure in the field, "is associated with that child's own welfare – to bring a child into being and to nurture it. One of the fundamental precepts of ethics is that each person is an end in himself or herself, and is never to be used solely as a means to another person's ends without the agreement of the person being used." The Ayalas' baby "is not seen as an end in itself, but as a means to another end. The fact that the other end is laudable doesn't change that." Another expert was quoted as saying that the Ayalas' decision means "we're willing to treat people like objects" – and, he added, "I don't think we ought to do that."[16]

Now the Ayalas are real people, not characters in a made-up classroom example, although their plight does sound like one of those fictional cases philosophers sometimes invent: "You say you don't want any more children? Well, would you have another baby if it were necessary to save the life of your teenage daughter?" The Ayalas *were* desperately trying to save the life of their teenage daughter, and they didn't much care for the ethicists' comments. Mrs Ayala said that the ethicists ought to be worrying more about the shortage of marrow donors, and less about their decision. Anissa herself was asked what she thought about all this, and she said that she was "sort of troubled" by the criticism, but added that "We're going to love our baby."

If Anissa were trained in philosophy, she might have found the criticisms less troubling. She might have observed that people have always had babies for all sorts of reasons other than the "ideal" one. Real life rarely lives up to philosophers' expectations. People have children so that the children can share in the family's work, to please the grandparents, or just because it's expected of them. They sometimes have second children because they don't want the first to be an "only child." None of this is strange or unusual; it is just the way life is. What is important is, as Anissa insists, that once born the children are loved and nurtured within good families. Anissa might also have pointed out that her mother, in fact, had wanted another baby anyway – it was only her father's wish to have no more children. And finally, she might have expressed some appropriate skepticism about the idea that an individual "is never to be used solely as a means to another person's end without the agreement of the person being used." Does this mean that, if Anissa already had a baby sister, the baby could not be used as a donor because the baby was not old enough to give permission? Should Anissa herself be left to die, for the sake of respecting this principle? Perhaps the ethicist quoted in the *New York Times* thinks so; he was quoted as saying "It's outrageous that people would go to this length."

Curiously, there is an argument, proceeding from principles frequently endorsed by the most conservative pro-life advocates, that supports the Ayalas' decision. This argument invokes the idea that we are conferring a benefit on someone by bringing them into existence. The new baby, not

Anissa, seems the really big winner here: after all, if her parents had not decided to have her, so that Anissa could get the stem cells, the baby would have not got to exist. Those who oppose abortion sometimes ask: Aren't you glad your mother didn't have an abortion? The answer, of course, is that most of us *are* happy that our mothers did not do that; otherwise we would not be here now. The people who ask this question think that something follows about the morality of abortion, although it is not clear what; but they usually fail to notice that we could just as well ask: Aren't you glad that your parents didn't practice birth control? (Orthodox Catholics, at least, are consistent on this point.) We should be equally happy that contraceptives were not used by our parents, and for the same reason: otherwise, we would not be here now. Similarly, Anissa's little sister might some day be asked: Aren't you glad that your parents decided to have you? Aren't you fortunate that Anissa needed those stem cells? Perhaps this means that conservatives who take a pro-life view ought to have been happy with the Ayala's decision, rather than being critical of it.

It might be doubted, however, that this is a sound argument. The idea that we are conferring a benefit on someone by bringing them into existence is easily disputed. I would rather rest my defense of the Ayalas' decision on a different sort of reasoning. First we may consider two separate questions:

1 Suppose a couple, before having any children at all, is trying to decide whether to have one child or two. They slightly prefer having only one. But then they are told that if they have only one child it will die when it is a teenager. However, if they have two, both will probably live full lives. Would it be wrong for the couple to decide, for this reason, to have two children?
2 Suppose a couple already has two children, one a teenager dying of leukemia, and the other an infant who is the only available bone marrow donor. The infant cannot give its permission, of course, but then again it would not be harmed at all by the procedure. Would it be wrong, under these circumstances, to use some of the infant's stem cells to save the teenager's life?

It seems to me that it would be easy enough to argue that the answer to both these questions is no. Then the inference to the permissibility of the Ayalas' decision would be obvious.

But this is a peripheral point. My main interest here is in the performance of philosophers – "ethicists" – as commentators on public events. Sometimes they do what we might think philosophers ought to do: challenge the prevailing orthodoxy, calling into question the assumptions that people unthinkingly make. But just as often they function as orthodoxy's most sophisticated defenders, assuming that the existing social consensus must be right, and articulating its theoretical "justification." And when all else fails, there is a familiar argument that can be relied upon: the slippery slope. Any departure from business-as-usual can be pronounced "troubling" because of what it might lead to. The Ayalas' decision was also criticized on this ground. It was said that it might lead to "fetus farming," or to abortions so that the aborted fetus could be used for life-saving purposes.

Of course, we do not know exactly what will happen to the Ayala family, or to social values, in consequence of decisions such as theirs. But two comments seem pertinent. First, there is nothing new about their sort of decision. In the publicity surrounding the Ayala case, it was revealed that other families had been making similar decisions for quite some time. Dr Robertson Parkman, head of the division of research immunology and marrow transplantation at Los Angeles Children's Hospital, told a reporter that he personally knows of cases going back to 1974 in which families have had additional children to obtain marrow transplants. But until now there has been little publicity about it. The new publicity also revealed that, in earlier cases, medical ethicists have been able to do much more than merely complain about such decisions after the fact. In 1986 a California woman, Phyliss Baker, who had had a tubal ligation, asked a physician to reconnect her Fallopian tubes so that she could have another child. The physician, knowing that Mrs Baker was trying to save the life of her three-year-old son, who needed a marrow transplant, consulted a bioethicist and then refused to do the operation. The physician's and the bioethicist's moral scruples were preserved, and Travis, the three-year-old, died.[17]

Second, the recent history of medical ethics is dotted with episodes in which ethicists have reacted with alarm to new developments, predicting dire consequences that never occurred. Greg Pence's recent book, *Classic Cases in Medical Ethics*, recounts several such episodes.[18] A review of these cases suggests caution, lest our quick-and-easy comments today look silly tomorrow. In 1978, for example, Louise Brown was the first baby to be born as a result of *in vitro* fertilization. This important event prompted alarmed and highly critical responses from physicians, theologicans, and philosophers that are embarrassing to look back upon today. Pence reminds us of a whole series of exaggerated statements and predictions: terrible consequences were sure to follow for the parents, the child, and the society. But today Louise is a normal, happy, active child, and so are many others like her.

What will happen to the Ayalas? One plausible scenario is that Anissa will be saved, the new baby will grow up happy – or at least with the same mixture of happiness and unhappiness that characterizes most of our lives – and the Ayalas, like the Browns, will forever after think that ethicists are jerks. If further terrible consequences transpire, then of course it might turn out that they were wrong. But in their particular circumstances, I do not see how they could have been wrong to weigh their daughter's life more heavily than the philosophers' vague fears.

NOTES

1 Diogenes Laertius, *Lives of Eminent Philosophers*, vol. II, Loeb Classical Library (Cambridge: Harvard University Press, 1955), p. 475. Diogenes immediately adds, however, that "Aenesidemus says that it was only his philosophy that was based upon suspension of judgment, and that he did not lack foresight in his everyday acts." Then Diogenes recounts a number of stories about Pyrrho's "everyday acts," the gist of which seems to be that although Pyrrho tried hard to maintain an attitude of indifference, he did not always succeed.

2 M. F. Burnyeat, "The Sceptic in his Place and Time," in Richard Rorty, J. B. Schneewind, and Quintin Skinner, eds, *Philosophy in History* (Cambridge: Cambridge University Press, 1984), pp. 225–54.

3 G. E. Moore, "A Defence of Common Sense," in *Philosophical Papers* (New York: Collier, 1962), ch. 2.

4 I owe this terminology to Gareth Matthews.

5 Bernard Williams, "A Critique of Utilitarianism," in J. J. C. Smart and Bernard Williams, *Utilitarianism: For and Against* (Cambridge: Cambridge University Press. 1973), sect. 5.

6 John Rawls, *A Theory of Justice* (Cambridge, Mass.: Harvard University Press, 1972).

7 See, for example, various essays in George Graham and Hugh LaFollette, eds, *Person to Person* (Philadelphia: Temple University Press, 1989). My contribution to this volume, "Morality, Parents, and Children," defends the alternative view which is sketched in the next paragraph.

8 Peter Singer, "Sidgwick and Reflective Equilibrium," *The Monist*, vol. 58 (1974), p. 516.

9 This is, of course, a departure from Quine's original way of characterizing what is near the center of the web and what is on its fringes. Quine originally said that beliefs along the edge "impinge on experience," while those in the interior are less directly connected with particular experiences. W. V. Quine, *From a Logical Point of View*, 2nd edn (Cambridge, Mass.: Harvard University Press, 1961), p. 42.

10 See Peter Singer, *Animal Liberation*, 2nd edn (New York: New York Review Books, 1990); and Tom Regan, *The Case for Animal Rights* (Berkeley: University of California Press, 1983).

11 See, for example, Thomas Nagel, "The Fragmentation of Value,' in H. Tristram Engelhardt, Jr, and Daniel Callahan, eds, *Knowledge, Value and Belief* (Hastings-on-Hudson, NY: The Hastings Center, 1977), pp. 279–94.

12 Alasdair MacIntyre, *Whose Justice? Which Rationality?* (Notre Dame: University of Notre Dame Press, 1988), p. 7.

13 Quoted in Martha Nussbaum's "Recoiling from Reason" (a review of MacIntyre), *The New York Review of Books*, Dec. 7, 1989, p. 41. In this paragraph I am heavily indebted to Nussbaum's excellent discussion.

14 *The Politics of Aristotle*, trans. Ernest Barker (London: Oxford University Press, 1946), p. 9.

15 Ibid., p. 306.

16 *New York Times*, Feb. 17, 1990, p. 1.

17 *Birmingham News*, Apr. 16, 1990, p. 4D.

18 Gregory E. Pence, *Classic Cases in Medical Ethics* (New York: McGraw-Hill, 1990), This book is a valuable corrective in another way as well: Pence demonstrates how the facts about these cases are often very different from what philosophers assume them to be.

7
Trust and Distrust of Moral Theorists

Annette Baier

Annette Baier's essay is one of several in this volume that question the practical usefulness of much recent theorizing in ethics. The target of her criticism, unlike that of Winkler (chapter 19) and Hoffmaster (chapter 20), is not abstract theory *per se*. Rather it is the tendency of moral theorists to adopt an ahistorical, impersonal viewpoint in their writing. The credibility of a moral theory and its usefulness in guiding conduct, she argues, are dependent upon the theorist's having relevant experience concerning the moral issue being addressed. Moreover, although a theorist may strive for the stance of an impartial observer, success in this endeavor cannot be guaranteed. Consequently, readers must be given enough information about the theorist's relevant experience to enable them to identify and discount bias in the theorist's view.

In insisting on the importance of the author's revealing his or her relevant experiences and point of view, Baier is defending a position widely shared among feminist philosophers. Moreover, this position has the effect of blunting the sharpness of the common philosophical distinction between *explaining* why one holds a moral view and *justifying* the holding of it. In this way Baier's paper touches on issues concerning the importance of narrative (in this case personal narrative) in moral dialogue, discourse, and reasoning.

Adam Smith advocated that professors, including professors of ethics, should, after acquiring a license to teach, be supported not by salaries, but by the fees of those students who chose to study with them, because such study helped them to acquire whatever licenses they were seeking, and so presumably equipped them to think clearly in the professions that they planned to enter – law, business, medicine, or whatever. Our moral theorists are largely salaried moral theorists, whose theories' relevance to the lives and professions of those whom they teach is even more tenuous than it would be under Smith's scheme. For even under Smith's scheme, if the same professors who, to support themselves, must win students, are the judges who decide on the licensing of the students they are trying to win and keep, then what is achieved by the hidden hand of the academic market will be the usefulness of their classes to their students' success in getting a degree or license, not their usefulness to them in the profession in which they hope to become licensed practitioners. Does our system provide for any sort of feedback between moral theory and its discovered relevance or helpfulness in real life? Are our "best sellers" among the books of moral theory the ones that are most helpful to moral agents? Are our most highly recompensed moral theorists the ones who offer the best guidance in the "moral mazes" of professional and everyday life?

The very question will be rejected. Admirers of Adam Smith though many of our moral theorists themselves profess to be, they do not usually want academia to be treated as a marketplace, or rather not one in which those whom we teach are the "buyers" who determine the "sellers' " profit. Universities may trade in professors, and professor may haggle with university administrations, but do we trade with our students? Do we wish to depend upon the *sale* of our philosophical wares to students who have a choice of whom to buy from, a choice of *whose* courses, with *which* set books, they will take in order to graduate? That, as far as I am aware, has not been advocated by even our most market-oriented moral theorists.

The voluntary purchasers that a typical writer of a book on moral theory, one that will be reviewed on philosophy journals such as *Ethics*, hopes to get are fellow theorists and their graduate students, who have the same acquired taste for theory that the author has, often also the same acceptance of the informal understanding that none of this clever stuff is supposed to have much to do with real life, or with actual moral issues facing anyone. I say "he" quite deliberately, for this entrenched practice of turning the study of ethics into an intellectual, sometimes largely formal, game, a variant of chess, is one that, like most entrenched philosophical practices, men have invented and invested in. It has a long history. The sort of course in ethics that David Hume got at Edinburgh University in the 1720s from William Law or John Pringle was a course in "Pneumatical and Ethical Philosophy," in which the pneumatics included (for Pringle), "(1) metaphysical inquiry into such subtle and material substances as are imperceptible to the senses and known only through their operations; (2) proof of the immortality of the soul; (3) nature of created beings not connected with matter; (4) natural theology, or the demonstration of the existence of God."[1] The "ethics" built on this pneumatic foundation was a study of the texts of Roman moralists such as Cicero and Marcus Aurelius, and natural law as expounded by such modern thinkers as Pufendorf. At least Cicero's *Offices* had a fairly direct link with his *own* society and the social roles his readers might fill, if a much less direct link to any offices in eighteenth-century Scotland, and Pufendorf would be a good basis for the study of civil law and Scottish law for the would-be lawyers in Pringle's classes. (Hume and Smith – who took a similar sort of course from Hutcheson in Glasgow – both pretty clearly benefited from that part of the course, if not so much from the pneumatics proper. Smith chose to model his lectures on jurisprudence, at Glasgow, on the sort of thing he had been taught by Hutcheson before him in Glasgow.) Our modern pneumatics is game theory, and the theory of rational choice. Since Kant, reason and rational will has been the subtle imperceptible substance that is known only by its operations, and our current versions of natural theology and the immortality of the soul are the theory of super strategies and their winning ploys. Contractarians and utilitarians alike both need to rely on this sovereign immaterial reason, on this modern soul substance. So typically books of moral theory such as my colleague David Gauthier's *Morals by Agreement*, or John Rawls's *A Theory of Justice*, or Derek Parfit's *Reasons and Persons*, or Russell Hardin's *Morality within the Limits of Reason*, devote an early chapter to expounding prisoner's dilemma, maximin, or minimax relative concession, or some other such bit of pneumatics of the rational soul.[2]

A refreshing exception is Allan Gibbard's *Wise Choices Apt Feelings*, in which such pneumatics is confined to footnotes.[3] But just how close Gibbard's meta-ruminations on our moral ruminations are to ordinary persons' moral problems is not so clear. Although eschewing formalisms, he does not thereby avoid abstractness, and it may be too much to hope that anyone trained as we philosophers are trained will lose the taste for pneumatics. And after all, in fairness to our contemporary moral theorists, it should be said that they do not even *purport* to be offering guidance to the morally perplexed, but only reflective thoughts *about* morality to the philosophically inclined. Should one expect moral wisdom from those who undertake to explicate what wise moral choices are really like? Perhaps not. Intellectual not moral subtlety may be all that it is fair to look for, so that any who trust moral theorists to provide moral wisdom may get only the let-down that the foolishly trusting deserve.

Still, for *anyone* to reflect even intellectually about moral choices, they must have some experience of them. They must themselves have *some* sort of record of wise or less wise choices, apt or non-apt feelings, and have learned something from their own experience and reflection on it. In our tradition it is not thought good form for a moral theorist to refer very directly to such experience. The assumption seems to be that we all have much the same sort of experience, so theory can take it for granted, without descending to the details of what experiences were (or were not) influential on a given theorist's own reflections. But do we? For one thing, do men share the sorts of moral learning that women do? Do the powerless learn the same way that the powerful do? Can the moral experience of the poor be the same as that of the rich? Or that of the colonizers or colonizers' descendants the same as that of the colonized, the enslaved, and their descendants? *Is* there a common fund of moral experience on which our relatively successful white male moral theorists are reflecting, on behalf of the rest of us?

If not, then we might still be interested in their reflections, as we are interested in reading the memoirs of other people. We can find it interesting to do a bit of moral tourism, to try to get inside the head and heart of someone quite unlike ourselves, and with an experience of a different order. But we should give no special *authority* to their methods of moral rumination. We should simply observe them, for what they reveal about the variegated array of mind-sets that our culture throws up.

At this point it may be objected that our moral theorists are *not* all white males, descendants of the colonizers. Some, like Virginia Held, are women, and some, like Laurence Thomas, are black. Fair enough. And we do then find fairly striking differences in the *modes* of moral rumination, as well as in the willingness to reveal a bit more of the personal background that provides the experience that is reflected upon. Held's recent essay on "Birth and Death" is not an impersonal essay, but one which claims a right to speak about birth that no man could have. ("Only when the conscious experiences of mothers, potential mothers, and mothering persons are taken fully into account can we possibly develop understanding that may some day merit the description 'human'."[4]) Thomas's paper on trust and moral integrity (at least in its spoken versions) refers to the experience of being *distrusted* by strangers simply because he is a black male.[5] My own work on trust also shows, directly or by implication, quite a lot about the range of foolish and less foolish trustings and distrustings I have known. This contrasts with the standard impersonality of the works of those we think of as the current paradigms of moral theorists – Rawls, Nozick, Gauthier, Nagel. Nozick did tell us about his child's instructive reaction to the Thanksgiving turkey, Nagel tells us about his repetition of Robert the Bruce's encounter with a stubborn spider, and Gauthier reveals in his preface that he was introduced to the Prisoner's Dilemma by Howard Sobel on a November afternoon in Los Angeles in 1965 (Sobel has much to answer for!), and that Clark Glymour taught him to flip a coin and so persuaded him to drop "s/he" for a supposedly random alternation of "he" and "she" (but not of "Jonathan's" and "Joanna's" when interaction constrained by the Lockean proviso is exemplified: pp. 206ff.). Otherwise the speaker in Gauthier's book is an impersonal anonymous "we." ("We shall develop a theory of morals . . .": p. 2.) As Nancy Fraser and other feminists have recently been emphasizing, the *assumption* that there is one moral community, and that any of us can speak for it, should be suspect. It cloaks the actual conflict and the actual differences of power among different groups, each of whom might appoint a spokesperson with the right to use "we." For most moral theorists, "I" is safer. For how can one know, until one's book is discussed and reviewed, for whom, besides oneself, one speaks? Even within the group of contemporary white male contractarians there is no "we," no consensus.

When we look at Rawls's influential book, we look in vain for an identifiable author, with a specific social place and a given formative history. Like Nagel's, Rawls's view purported at first to be a view from nowhere, and only latterly came to be characterized at least as a view from within a given cultural tradition. But the view from Emerson Hall is *not* the view most of us can take. Rawls's vision, from there, is a deeply humane and in some ways inspiring one, but it is not sensitive to the concerns and hypersensibilities of some of those who have been the least advantaged, that is to say women, and in particular women who are not white middle-class women. Rawls is of course a disarmingly modest and generous moral theorist, so it seems plain mean to pick on the failures rather than the achievements of his fine book. But although he does not, like Gauthier, use the royal "we," his book is as devoid as is Gauthier's of any personal revelation, any indication of what moral experiences prompted the moral reflections. We can infer that the plight of the poor, of conscientious objectors, of civil disobedients, played a role, but it will be inference only. Where Rawls *says* he comes from is not a particular niche in a particular society that has gone through specific social troubles, but "the traditional social contract theory of Locke, Rousseau and Kant" which he attempts to "generalize and carry to a higher order of abstraction." It is a particular group of dead white males that Rawls aims to speak for. That is, of course, unfair, since he assumes, and rightly assumes, that the dialectic that those thinkers advanced is one in which many of us, especially of us philosophers, see ourselves as participants. It is a live tradition. But it is more enthusiastically viewed by some than by others. Those of us who have read *Emile* as well as the *Social Contract*, Kant's *Anthropology* as well as his *Groundwork* and *Metaphysics of Morals*, may harbor some distrust of any thinkers whose attitude to *us*, to women, was as blatantly sexist as were the stances of those two great spokesmen for the sovereign voice of reason (Locke is another and cheerier story).

Thomas Nagel's *The View from Nowhere*, like *The Possibility of Altruism*, is of course a view from somewhere, presumably from somewhere near New York University, or perhaps from Brasenose College, Oxford, where Nagel's acknowledgements tell us that some of its chapters were given as Tanner Lectures, but the highest standards of impersonality and non-location are, perhaps appropriately, observed in the text.[6] "The natural place to begin is with our own position in the world," we are told on page 13, but Nagel's own position, the natural place for him to start, is not then given. The only clues we are officially given are the story about the spider in the Princeton urinal (p. 208), a list of friends, colleagues, and students who influenced Nagel's thoughts and words, and a photograph on the dust jacket. (I observe, parenthetically, that there seems to be no particular correlation between the impersonality of a philosophical book and its author's willingness to have his/her face show from the cover. The verbal self-revealers are often faceless, while the verbal self-effacers often supply the reader with images of their faces. For the record, T. Nagel, B. Williams, and L. Thomas look out from the dustjackets of their recent books, while V. Held, C. Taylor, A. Gibbard, D. Gauthier, and S. Hampshire do not. Taylor is an interesting case, since his recent collection of philosophical papers *did* come with photograph, while his more personal and self-revealing *Sources of the Self* comes faceless.)

Recent writers who reveal something of where they come from, at least in their prefaces, are Laurence Thomas and Virginia Held.[7] Held, in the second chapter of *Rights and Goods*, "The Revival of Ethics," situates her approach to the themes of the book in the social concerns of the 1970s. In chapter 4 she discusses "moral experience," and it is no more difficult, from the book as a whole, to infer the *sort* of moral experience that informs and verifies the theory presented in the book, than it is in the case of Laurence Thomas. If we did not know from the photo on the dustjacket that Thomas is black, we would know from the preface. And once we know, we can appreciate the force of many of the book's most insightful discussions – for example, those of social trust and of threats to self-esteem that come from forms of discrimination such as sexism. That the book's index has no entry under "race" or "racism," but four entries under "gender" only underscores what Thomas had earlier demonstrated: that experiencing one form of oppression can make one sympathetic to its other forms.[8] The silence in this book about racism is an eloquent silence, unlike the silence on that topic in Nagel's or Gauthier's books.

This tradition of authorial self-effacement is a variant of a very old one. When Hume published his *Treatise*, his name did not appear on the work, let alone any portrayal of the author. Still, it was a very explicitly self-revealing work, and its first reviewers accused its author (whose identity was soon guessed) of "egotism." There are egotisms and egotisms. I for one find the royal "we," the assumption that the author speaks for all right-minded persons, much more egotistical than frequent references to one's own doubts, and mental ups and downs. Works like Descartes' *Meditations* and Hume's *Treatise* present a thinker's progress (or regress), from a starting point (which may or may not be an actual historical one, once occupied by the author himself) to some at least temporary resting place. In the nature of the case the first person singular pronoun has to be used. Such "confessional" works in philosophy and moral philosophy seem to have gone out of style, and I think we are the worse for it. Non-anonymous authorship, even with a photo on the dustjacket, is a poor substitute for what Descartes called the analytic method, that shows methodically "the true way by which the thing in question was discovered," the record of how an actual historically located thinker progressed from where he or she once was to the viewpoint found worth communicating. For the worth of the communication, and our means of assessing it, depend on the journey as much as on its destination. And at least then we have *some* answer to the question "Who speaks?" Even without a name to give to the speaker, we have a definite description – in the case of Descartes, one who had come to doubt the Aristotelian and Catholic tenets he had been taught, and the superiority of the culture in which he had been raised over its neighbors; in the case of Hume, the one who hoped to "march up directly . . . to human nature itself" and build all human knowledge "on a foundation almost entirely new," seeing himself, as Descartes before him did (and as most of us also do), as a pioneer launching out into "immense depths of philosophy," but, unlike Descartes, seeing his vessel as "leaky and weatherbeaten," and eventually seeing that he needed cooperation from others if any confidence in the enterprise was to be sustained.

Such apparent self-revelations, in the text, went out of fashion, perhaps with Bentham. But at least with such writers of non-confessional moral philosophy as Rousseau and J. S. Mill, confessions and autobiography supplemented the more impersonal works, so that, in the end, the reader *is* able to situate the moral pronouncements in the life of an actual person with actual experiences that shaped, and are acknowledged to have shaped, the moral views. J. S. Mill famously tells us how in 1826 his reformist zeal, and his dedication to the utilitarian ideal imbibed from his father and from Bentham, gave way to deep depression. He describes this realization of the hollowness of the philosophy in which he had been reared in terms of awakening "as if from a dream" but it was an awakening from an energetic dream into listlessness and "dry heavy dejection." To some extent repeating the young Hume's experience of "the disease of the learned," and also repeating Hume's self-diagnosis of this ill as due to what Mill calls "analytic habits," which work as "a perpetual worm at the root of both the passions and the virtues," Mill eventually cures himself by reading memoirs and poetry, not Benthamite philosophy, and was again able to "find enjoyment . . . in sunshine and sky, in books, in conversation, in public affairs . . . ." This experience changed Mill's philosophy as well as his life. "The cultivation of the feelings became one of the cardinal points in my ethical and philosophical creed."[9]

With J. S. Mill we have the information we need in order to understand the emphasis given, for example in chapter 3 of *Utilitarianism*, to what we might call sentimental education. Like most of us, Mill as a philosopher has a bit of a hang-up on that aspect of the good life that he himself

most signally lacked, and realized he lacked. We can understand and
evaluate his moral philosophy better because of what he has told us about
his life.

I am not advocating that all moral philosophy be done in the style of
memoirs and confessions. Heaven forbid that latter-day Rousseaus flood
us with all the grubby details of their wounded psyches! But there can be
a due mean between the extreme of impersonality, the total covering of
one's tracks, and uncensored self-revelation. We should get from a moral
theorist what background biographical information *we need* to understand
the special emphases and distinctive features of the theory advanced. We
should, I think, distrust those who purport to speak from nowhere, as
much as we should distrust those whom we suspect of faking the position
from which they speak. If moral experience is to inform moral theory
sufficiently to enable the theory to have a chance of guiding *future* moral
experience, so as to improve it, then we are owed a little information from
a theorist about the *sort* of experience that has informed her theoretical
conclusions.

A nice example of this mean between undue reticence and irrelevant
self-revelation is to be found in Stuart Hampshire's recent book, *Innocence
and Experience.*[10] The introduction tells us not just about Hampshire's
middle-class family background and his childhood encounters with the
victims of the depression – "children without shoes in winter streets," the
unemployed shipbuilders who were "likely to remain unemployed for many
years, perhaps permanently unless there was another world war, which
obviously would create a demand for ships to be built in Britain . . ."
(p. 4) – but of his own war work as an intelligence officer, his interrogation
of Kaltenbrunner in Europe and later in London. "This experience altogether changed my attitude both to politics and to philosophy" (p. 8). The
book's later discussions, especially of Nazism and evil, and of pluralism
and relativism, take on special interest for the reader, given this information
about the author's own close encounters with an enemy's "evil morality"
and their "abolition of justice in public life" (p. 75). As Hampshire says
in his introduction, any moral philosopher's personal experience unavoidably plays a part in determining what and how he or she writes.

> First, he will feel at ease in writing about those aspects of common experience
> which he knows at first hand. Second, his experience will normally have
> left him with particular doubts and uncertainties, and these, when pressed
> and probed far enough, will turn into philosophical doubts and philosophical
> uncertainties. His experience will usually have left him with some particular
> bias. He will pick out the themes that recall points of stress and conflict in
> his own past and in his own thought. It is reasonable that this bias be made
> explicit. Having some fragments of biographical information, the reader will

be better able to understand why one particular set of themes has been pursued and others neglected. (p. 3)

Yes indeed. Of course the author only gives us "fragments," and his selection of what is most relevant for understanding the emphases and the silences of the work that follow may be faulty. Self-protection may lead to self-deception, and so to less than candid selection of what fragments of biographical information to reveal, so that bias remains unrevealed. Hampshire, for example, could have revealed a bit more about the techniques of interrogation used on the likes of Kaltenbrunner, just what "deceit and guile, unjust violence and sudden aggression, ingratitude in relation to allies and friends" (p. 163) were the "everyday weapons" of the branch of the military that he served in. That would help us see further than we easily can into the subtext of his discussions of Machiavelli and "the central dilemmas of power." Hampshire's "illustration" of innocence and experience in these dilemmas is not autobiographical. Yet, as he writes about these hard matters, on the basis of what experience he has, what interrogations he has conducted, what history and memoirs he has read, he includes this assertion: "A philosopher in his study is in no position to lay down rules for justified murders and reasonable treachery" (p. 177). No indeed. But none of us spends all our time in our study, and what exactly Hampshire is saying about what an intelligence officer turned philosopher is in a position say about killing and treachery is less than clear. The "doubts and uncertainties" at this point could have been illuminated by a few more relevant fragments of the author's experience, to help the more innocent of us to grasp and assess his point.

But it is inappropriate of me to complain about Hampshire's judgment of which fragments to reveal, since all who try to incorporate some "confessional" material in their moral philosophy can expect to be faulted either for undue reticence or for "egotisms," and Hampshire has stated extremely well the case for a return to this style of moral philosophy. Let me try to make his general case more specific: those who write as moral philosophers about killing, letting die, and abortion in reason owe their readers a brief account of what killings, lettings die, and abortions they have themselves been involved in, so that we can be in a position to discern bias, self-serving rationalization, or disqualifying "innocence." Those who write about deceit and guile owe us a (guileless?) account of their own record on this matter. Those who write about exploitation and domination should tell us who they are, whom they have exploited, who has exploited them. And so on. This may seem to be asking too much, to be demanding that philosophers incriminate themselves, and surely the Fifth Amendment protects moral philosophers as much as ordinary scoundrels. So a clarification should be made to my proposal, to make explicit that it is not reasonable to expect moral philosophers to set themselves up for criminal prosecution in order to establish their credentials as informed thinkers on the topics they write on. Hobbes's eighteenth "law of nature" states that "no man in any Cause ought to be received for Arbitrator, to whom greater profit, honour, or pleasure apparently ariseth out of the victory of one party, rather than of the other: for hee hath taken (though an unavoydable bribe, yet) a bribe: and no man can be obliged to trust him." If we are to know when to trust moral theorists who purport to be impartial, they must *let it appear* just what unavoidable bribes may be operating on their thinking, for surely all of us are subject to such psychic bribes.

My proposal would, I think, at least temporarily disqualify a lot of the moral philosophy currently in the public domain, and of course universities are in the public domain, so that the philosophy we teach gets included. But equally, this request for some information about how much an author knows from personal experience about the moral issue upon which he or she pronounces would also, if acceded to, give more authority to a lot of our current philosophical literature. An obviously relevant question to want answered by any social philosopher is: "What range of societies have you known at close hand?" If rootedness in some society and its folkways is the first requirement of any social philosopher, experience of uprootedness is surely also a *desideratum*, and close acquaintance with a variety of different cultures an equally obviously relevant grounding. As Descartes tells us in his *Discourse on the Method*, "the great book of the world," and acquaintance with its cultural diversity, is the proper textbook for would-be evaluators of any given culture. Very many of our social philosophers do, I surmise, satisfy this requirement, but they are often reticent about their credentials, in ways that impoverish both the content and the authority of their theories. Were they to "come out of the closet," reveal themselves as the experienced moral and social agents and patients that they actually are, in something like the way Hampshire does, and Mill did, and many feminist writers do, then I think that philosophy in the public domain would be more readily assessed for its public value, and so *have* more public value.

I began with Adam Smith and I will also end with him. Have I, in advocating a style of moral theory that explicitly ties the theory's emphases, inclusions, and exclusions to the particularities of the theorist's own experience, advocated a renunciation of the view advanced by Hume and by Smith that, when we exercise our abilities to think and judge on moral matters, we function as judicious spectators, impartial observers? No. Impartiality is of course the aim. But, short of a moral omnicompetence that none of us can pretend to have, we are very fallible about whether on a given matter we have indeed succeeded in taking up an impartial stance. To judge that, we need each other's help. The best way to approximate lack of bias is to identify and discount bias. Our own moral experience both qualifies us to have *any* moral views, and tends to bias the views we have away from full impartiality. To have any credibility, we must show that we do have the relevant moral experience. To enable others (and ourselves) to judge our credentials, and to allow for unavoidable bias in our theories, to progress toward informed and experienced impartiality, we must be, and be known to have been, reasonably judicious *participants*. Mere spectators cannot be fully judicious about the activities they watch, and participants who cover the tracks of their participation, either out of reticence or out of bad philosophical habit, inspire less trust than those who tell us who they are before telling the rest of us what to become.

A moral theory of which we are initially suspicious, because we do not trust the theorist, given his lack or non-display of relevant credentials, can still be one that, if studied, proves helpful. A theorist we fully trust can come out with a trite or unhelpful theory. The test of a theory is what it does to our thinking, feeling, and acting, and how we reflectively judge that impact. My suggestions that it would be helpful if moral theorists identified the position from which they spoke, and the range of relevant experience informing their conclusions, my criticisms of the "views from nowhere," themselves come from one who has found a lot of current moral theory unhelpful for real-life concerns and has consequently developed a general distrust of abstract moral theory and a wish to make (to use my opponents' vocabulary) some *ex ante* assessment of whether a new book of theory coming into my hands can or cannot be expected to be adequately experience-based, and adequately self-conscious about its own sources. But *ex ante* can diverge from *ex post*, and some theories have salutory effects simply from exemplifying extreme and instructive forms of their very abstractness and their pretended ahistorical and impersonal point of view. As a mere parasite on the theories I criticize, I am grateful to those who give me food for critical reflection, as well as to those who exemplify my preferred more forthrightly personal approach. For our moral thinking needs all the goads, challenges, and inputs that it can get, and it can be instructive to find out that those one reasonably distrusted in fact advanced one's insight, perhaps through the very experience of distrust, and its partial overcoming. So let a thousand theoretical flowers bloom, in styles of moral theorizing, and a thousand thousand styles of criticizing theories and their critics.

NOTES

1 Ernest Mossner, *Life of David Hume* (Oxford: Clarendon Press, 1981), pp. 3–4.

2   David Gauthier, *Morals by Agreement* (Oxford: Clarendon Press, 1986); John Rawls, *A Theory of Justice* (Cambridge, Mass.: Harvard University Press, 1971); Derek Parfit, *Reasons and Persons* (Oxford: Clarendon Press, 1984); Russell Hardin, *Morality within the Limits of Reason* (Chicago: University of Chicago Press, 1980).

3   Allan Gibbard, *Wise Choices Apt Feelings* (Cambridge, Mass.: Harvard University Press, 1990).

4   Virginia Held, "Birth and Death," in Cass R. Sunstein, ed., *Feminism and Political Theory* (Chicago: Chicago University Press, 1990), p. 112.

5   Laurence Thomas, "Trust, Affirmation and Moral Character: A Critique of Kantian Morality," in Owen Flanagan and A. Rorty, eds., *Identity, Character and Morality: Essays in Moral Psychology* (Cambridge, Mass.: MIT Press, 1990) pp. 235–257.

6   Thomas Nagel, *The View from Nowhere* (New York: Oxford University Press, 1986); *The Possibility of Altruism* (Oxford: Clarendon Press, 1970).

7   Laurence Thomas, *Living Morally: A Psychology of Moral Character* (Philadelphia: Temple University Press, 1989); Virginia Held, *Rights and Goods* (Chicago: Chicago University Press, 1984).

8   Laurence Thomas, "Sexism and Racism: Some Conceptual Differences," *Ethics*, vol. 90 (1980), pp. 239–50.

9   J. S. Mill, *Autobiography*, (London: Longman's, Green, Reader and Dyer, 1873). pp. 138, 143–4.

10   Stuart Hampshire, *Innocence and Experience* (Cambridge, Mass.: Harvard University Press, 1989).

8
Socratic Skepticism

Roger Wertheimer

Reflecting on the swiftness with which accepted theories in philosophy become contested or refuted, Wertheimer attempts to demonstrate that we have good reason to agree with Socrates' assessment that we lack philosophical understanding, that is, understanding of the basic concepts and principles we use in making decisions and judgments. History tells us that sooner or later every philosophical theory is shown to be internally incoherent. Thus our collective experience commends a fallibilist stance not only about what is true, but about what does and does not make sense and what follows from what. Wertheimer argues that skepticism about our philosophical understanding has implications concerning the expertise applied ethicists may claim, and what they must do to ply their trade with integrity.

Skepticism about our philosophical understanding leads to doubts about the justification and truth of our moral judgments and theories, for claims of moral knowledge are akin to and continuous with our other philosophical beliefs and knowledge claims. And, since no amount of expertise in logic provides expertise in practical reasoning, argues Wertheimer, no one can plausibly claim knowledge on matters of practical reasoning. Because applied ethicists know or ought to know of reasons for respecting uncertainties, they must not pretend to an authority in practical reasoning they cannot possess. If they are to maintain their integrity they must make it clear that some wisdom beyond formal logic is needed – in appraising the plausibility of moral premises, in choosing the terms in which an issue is deliberated, in casting inchoate intuitions into an inferential structure, and in considering whether some reasoning not currently recognized by our tradition might be sensible.

Wertheimer notes that the profession of applied ethics has not been concerned with developing a code of ethics for itself. Because professional applied ethicists rightly contest both first principles and concrete cases, there appears to be little common ground on which to construct such a code. He suggests that shared Socratic skepticism is likely to be a crucial premiss in deciding issues of professional integrity, and may provide a good starting point in developing a professional code of ethics.

This paper can usefully be compared, in different ways, with those of Sikora (chapter 5), Winkler (chapter 19), Hoffmaster (chapter 20), and Yeo (chapter 14). Philips's account of "ethics as social policy" with its built-in formula for the proper evaluation of moralities (chapter 10) also provides a worthwhile contrast.

1   Socrates has long served as a symbol for our discipline, practically our patron saint, revered for the profundity of his intellect and the nobility of his character. We may honor him more in our praise than our practice, and take no word of his as gospel, and yet still remain haunted by his voice, respectful of a specter that speaks to our reason and through our conscience.

The Socrates I know, the historically purest, least Platonized Socrates is the protagonist of the *Apology*. There, standing in judgment before his community, he insisted that his life's work was motivated by a singular dual insight: that no one was wise and that he was wiser than others only in that he alone recognized this fact. What did he mean by this? What is the evidence for its truth? And what follows from its truth? We may try to answer those questions in that order, but we cannot stick strictly to that sequence, since what a statement means is not isolable from what it is implied by and what is implied by it.

For us to catch the distinctive voice of Socrates through the tumult of voices he helped inspire, we need to keep noting the contrasts with others closer to our culture. The Socratic denial of popular pretensions of understanding is radical, philosophical, yet very unlike other skepticisms of ancient and modern debate. It is, in many respects, a most modest doubt, unassuming, moderate, temperate, a doubt of a man of some wisdom.

2   First, Socratic doubt is directed solely at our philosophical convictions; it denies our claims to philosophical understanding, the understanding essential for wisdom. Philosophy, for Socrates, is a quest for wisdom, for the knowledge of the self and its true good essential for human excellence. It aspires to an understanding of the basic and thus general and abstract truths about our real nature and ideal nature and their relation. This understanding is presumed testable by reason, if not acquired or transmissible thereby.

No challenge is aimed against our nonphilosophical convictions and knowledge claims. Socrates had no doubts that we all know many familiar facts and that professionals (physicians, navigators, etc.) possess valuable knowledge pertinent to their trades. Some of this expertise about techniques might constitute kinds of wisdom, but not the generic sort Socrates sought, not the understanding needed by Everyman, whatever his trade.

Socrates sought wisdom, urged others to do the same, and throughout presumed that there are truths of the sort he sought and that they are not all beyond human ken. His quest is not supposed to be a snark hunt; but, lamentably, we have not caught our quarry – not because our philosophical opinions are false, or might, for all we know, be false: some are false, and some are more or less doubtful, but Socrates accepts that poets, prophets, and seers have many fine things to say. Their/our deficiency is not *per se* a lack of true opinions.

3   Nor is it a lack of proofs for these beliefs. Socratic skepticism is more semantic than epistemic, less a doubt about truth, proof, evidence, certainty, and knowledge than about meaning, explanation, coherence, and understanding. The typical Socratic test of wisdom does not ask "How do you know? What justifies your believing that?" but instead asks for clarification of the belief, a definition of terms, an explanation of concepts and principles. Socrates demonstrated that people cannot explain their own beliefs. We fall – quickly – into confusion, incoherence, and then silence, and thereby betray little or no understanding of our own basic conceptions and principles for judgment and decision-making.

Calling Socratic skepticism "semantic" may mislead. Socrates was innocent of modern analytical categories, and his tests for wisdom were not usually explicitly semantical, not in the "formal" but rather in the "material" mode: for example, he would ask: "What is self-control (justice, piety, etc.)?" rather than "What is the definition of the/your word *self-control?*" or "What do you mean in/by calling something *self-control?*" Whether he focused on properties or predicates matters little. Either way, his dialectical inquiry does not challenge his interlocutors' answers by presenting them with new conflicting evidence that they did not already implicitly accept.

Instead it continuously elicits the interlocutors' own existing beliefs in a manner that displays the internally conflicting character of those beliefs. In its process, this examination has various ostensible objects of discussion; in its purpose it is about each respondent's own conceptions. The respondent comes to understand that he does not understand what he, himself, has been saying, thinking, meaning. His own confident conceptions have become not so much refuted as fractured, broken into incompatible fragments, so he no longer knows – or thinks that he knows – what to say, what makes sense, what in fact he had been believing or does now believe or ought to believe. Only thus does he come to think his ideas less certain or probable.

A person can know some fact while having minimal understanding of the fact. We all know that commonly happens. Socrates taught that it happens more radically and universally than we had dreamed. And sometimes, perhaps often, people's understanding may be so radically deficient that no one who makes or denies some claim knows whether it is true, because they do not know what they are talking about. They do not understand what their own judgments mean; they are unable to make good sense of their own most earnest thoughts: they and their ideas are riddled with confusion and inner conflict, dilemmas, paradoxes and contradictions.

4   We can say here – as Socrates did – either that we have no wisdom or that the little we have is a wretched specimen of little worth. Like most things, being wise is a matter of degree and kind; and we may deny that something has a property when it is a bad enough specimen of that property. Obviously some people are wiser than others, so some people are wise to some degree. Perhaps only a perfect simpleton has absolutely no wisdom. At the other extreme, while some conception of absolute wisdom may be coherent, no human can have perfect wisdom, the wisdom of an infallible, omniscient divinity.[1] But none of this is news and never was. Socrates discovered that what passes for wisdom are at best bits of knowledge too fragmented, unstable, and uncertain to merit the predicate *wisdom* and the esteem it properly inspires. But he was not intent on showing that our ideas are absolutely nonsensical, barren of all real meaning, that no good sense can be made of our thoughts.

Saying that no one is wise has more impact, but the absolutism of Socratic doubt cannot be crucial. The passion of his mission would not slacken if he faced three or 37 instances of someone catching a genuine knowledge of a philosophical truth or two (such as, for example, that no one is wise). His passion would be disproportionate if, despite no one's having a bit of bona fide wisdom, normally people had close approximations of philosophical understanding about a fair-sized chunk of important matters.

Without a hint of the hyperbolic, Socratic doubt is nonetheless radical; he deemed it a discovery of the utmost import. It says we are astoundingly benighted. It is not enough to say that even our most sophisticated leaders (statesmen, teachers, doctors, poets, prophets, etc.) know a lot less than they think they know. That does not capture the fact that we cannot fathom even the first few feet of the pit we are in. We can have no conception of our condition, not until a Socrates comes to lead us into the confusion of thought we would otherwise never have noticed. And these are confusions at the heart of our own basic concepts and principles for making decisions and judgments.

5   Other skeptics challenge us to justify our believing even what we cannot stop believing (e.g. that we have two hands, and stand on earth, in a world existing apart from us, with other persons, and a past, and causal relations, etc.) – and when we find ourselves with nothing to say, no way to justify our beliefs, we may doubt whether anything needs to be said. But Socrates challenged us to explain our conceptions, and here we do not usually start with a sense of having nothing to say, nor do we fall silent from seeing that every response we can think of only begs the question.[2]

We cannot explain our basic concepts and principles, but not as we cannot justify our elemental beliefs, despite our inability to live without them. And not as we may lack words to describe the smell of some flower, despite being able to identify it. Nor as we may struggle to put in words how to tie our shoes, despite fully knowing how to do it. Instead, we cannot explain our ideas in the sense that, when we do (try to) explain them, the dialectic demonstrates that our ideas really do not make much sense. The dialectic leaves us speechless, but does not start from there. We say what we think and mean, what seems to us obvious and certain; then we discover that what we think and mean does not mean what we thought and meant, and we do not know how to think and mean what we want to think and mean.

Our lack of wisdom is not like the normal lack of self-knowledge in the speaking of a language. We demonstrate mastery of a language by routinely identifying sentences as grammatical, meaningful, synonymous, and the like. That mastery is not impugned by our universal incompetence at self-reporting the implicit syntactic and semantic rules underlying our speech practice. A normal native speaker speaks with the confident voice of authority when she rejects plausible-sounding linguistic rules because of counter-examples certified by her linguistic sense. But when our philosophical beliefs and self-reports collide, we are commonly left speechless, unwilling to disown any of them or uncertain which to repudiate or how to do it.[3]

6   Other skeptics may resort to unconventional or unreasonable standards for justification or knowledge, but Socrates did not rely on suspect standards for wisdom. Wisdom is not cleverness, which can be an unselfconscious talent for arriving at right results. People can and commonly do grossly over- or underestimate how clever (or foolish) they really are. But while someone may be uncertain or mistaken about just exactly how wise she is, it is hard to make sense of her having much wisdom if she badly misestimates her own or believes she has none. There would be no real riddle if the Delphic oracle had said that Socrates was the cleverest of men while Socrates was sure he was not at all clever. He could solve the riddle of his wisdom only by recognizing his insight into his (and our) lack of wisdom as itself a substantial bit of wisdom.[4]

Regularly producing good choices and advice may suffice to show cleverness. It may also display wisdom, but only if the display is due to an understanding of why the choices and advice are good. Deficiencies of such understanding are demonstrated by deficient, inadequate explanations of the goodness or wisdom of the choices and advice.

The Socratic standards of adequacy are minimal. Demanding that an explanation be consistent and internally coherent is hardly unreasonable. And while discovering and displaying some inadequacies may take dialectical genius, the elegant Socratic exposés seem obvious once made. Many Socratic (or Platonic) arguments, though ingenious, are not notably subtle, sophisticated, or elaborate. And even if they were, that is no measure of the import of their implications. Whatever the conventional wisdom may assume, it is sheer foolishness to suppose that internal stresses and defects detectable only by high-powered devices must be tiny, trivial, inconsequential flaws. To accuse Socratic doubt of making unreasonable demands is to betray the common blindness he revealed, for the lack of wisdom that worried Socrates was not merely an incapacity to articulate adequate accounts of our conceptions but also an incapacity to appreciate the significance of that deficiency. Socrates' own wisdom was an appreciation of our condition, not a capacity to remedy it, to remove the riddles of our minds.

7   We are in this condition, however blind to it we be. We can continually fail to see it, despite watching it patiently pointed out. It is a classroom commonplace for a student to insist sincerely that she really had good, clear ideas, but just did not put them into words well in her essay. Sometimes she vindicates herself by her subsequent explanations. But commonly the instructor is pedagogically challenged to bring the student to recognize that, despite all her self-certainty, the real trouble is not any niceties of grammar and diction but that what she has said does not make good sense because what she is trying to say does not make good sense. Commonly, with dull or careless students, the confusion is shallow, isolated, and alien to the thinking of the better students. With the best students the challenge remains to awaken realization that their/our commonsensical concepts and principles are also confusions, less blatant but more intractable.

Socrates was adept at putting people in touch with confusions at the heart of their everyday thinking, as well as confusions in the currently reputable reflective thinking. He made people feel confused, but he did not make the confusion.

That sense of confusion is not easily conveyed by description; it has a phenomenology that needs to be experienced for the confusion to be appreciated. (Socrates felt compelled to interrogate people individually rather than lecture or publish his results.) As Wittgenstein emphasized, philosophical conceptions are like pictures that are prone – with proper prompting – to flip flop in and out of focus, vacillating wildly from seeming self-evidence to sheer incredibility or incomprehensibility.[5] Lay folk are familiar with duck–rabbit pictures and other visual analogues of such aspect switches, but those perceptual events do not automatically equip the mind to imagine the analogous experience with altering aspects of conceptual objects. Still, my favorite metaphor for this is an experience of Rogers Albritton: upon abandoning his acceptance of all sense data theory, he could not wear his eyeglassese for a week.

Few of Socrates' (or our) listeners linger long enough to appreciate the character of philosophical bewilderment. A single brief encounter with a philosophical conundrum may leave a lasting impression of only a curious puzzle. An appropriate, deep intellectual humility comes from habitual humiliations, time after time of coming to feel that you really do not know what you yourself mean by this or that previously unproblematic, seemingly innocent thought. Consider: How could it be that Socrates alone really knew that no one is wise? What about his followers, who frequently heard him say and saw him demonstrate that no one is wise, and then themselves believed and said it? Why did they not just learn it and know it, and thereby have the same claim to wisdom as Socrates? Perhaps a few did get the message; but could it be that not every philosophy PhD knows what I'm talking about?

8   If Socratic skepticism is a teachable thesis, how should we understand Socrates' disavowal of having a doctrine to teach? It is said of him that what he discovered was instead a new method. But that remark is problematic. Unlike Wittgenstein, he did not say it of himself. And his procedure was hardly a robotic routine, reducible to a set of rules or forms of argument. His initial request for an explanation of some concept is a routine, but then he had no five or ten tropes to trot out for all occasions. And his apology to his peers made no claims about the source or general structure of the broad sample of confusions he uncovered, nor any panacea. His dialectic regularly made a few reasonable demands on explanations: e.g. that our explanations be consistent with our reasonable beliefs; that identifying a few denotations does not state a definition. However, overall his critiques of people's explanations are creative *ad hoc* arguments responsive to the particulars of each person's beliefs.

Socratic skepticism is the motive and result, not the method, of Socratic practice. It is a coherent cognitive attitude expressed by a justifiable judgment. Yet, to say "No one is wise" is to say "No one (well enough) understands what I'm saying (and I understand it only well enough to say it, mean it, and know that it's true.)" That may be an assertible truth free of formal paradox, yet as a teaching it teeters on self-negation.

9   Moreover, while the Socratic method of testing someone's wisdom can be called *a priori* since it calls upon no information external to her existing beliefs, Socratic skepticism is not itself in any sense *a priori*. The claim that no one is wise is not an analytic or conceptual truth, revealed by an analysis of the concept of wisdom. It is meant to be a synthetic, empirical thesis, a merely contingent truth, and not even an empirical law (for it

doesn't say no one can become wise). And Socrates did not derive the generalization from some laws of human nature. His proof of the fact does not depend on some theory about the fact. Unlike all other famous forms of philosophical doubting, Socratic skepticism is strictly inductive.

Socrates confirmed his generalized doubt by patiently inspecting, dissecting, experimenting on the best sampling of candidates he could examine. He began by interrogating everyone commonly reputed to be wise, and each time found the reputation to be unfounded. He went on to test everyone willing to be tested, confronting each new case afresh, uncovering confusion every time, and thereby providing additional data that every case would meet a similar fate. It is a classic of enumerative induction, and thus, in some idolects, not a "philosophical" argument at all. In that sense Socratic skepticism is not a "philosophical" doctrine.

While Wittgenstein (or Kripke[6]) may have invented a new, a priori semantic skepticism, Socrates might still be the first to demonstrate that people can and do systematically fail to know what they themselves mean, and that this is not a rare or isolated phenomenon but instead universal. Yet he did not say that we could never know what we mean, because there is no fact of the matter to know or because what we mean is absolutely devoid of sense. Some a priori analyses may provide insight into the phenomena Socrates uncovered, but Socrates taught no hypothesis on this score (though Plato may have).

Other skeptics say: withhold assent from common assumptions, because they could be mistaken, since in *some* apparently similar situations, such assumptions have been shown to be shaky.[7] But Socrates says: Examine your beliefs, because, in all the most reputable cases and each of the many others examined, *every* philosophical theory we have seen has been shown to be shaky by the standards proper to the subject.

Other skeptics say we might be dreaming (or have been created a moment ago, etc.), and be unable to know it; all our criteria and tests for verifying or falsifying our hypotheses could be satisfied in either case. But Socrates is saying that we *are* dreaming, semi-conscious sleepwalkers stumbling around with occasional disaster. And we can be awakened to our condition, and perhaps to some degree awakened from it. For, while genius may be needed to devise tests to expose it, no suprahuman power is then needed to perceive it. The tests are not tricky, and the results are (relatively) clear, decisive, and readily replicated.

10   Socrates is wise, but Socrates is mortal. The logic texts do not lie. His data base was but one life's labor, perhaps enough to justify Socrates' own zeal, but by modern standards his sampling of conceptual alternatives is narrow, and his explorations cursory and lacking detail. Socrates could only scratch the surface. A score of centuries of head-scratching among

the brainiest heads has not been for naught. Socrates could not have known as well as we just how little we know.

What do we learn after all our days of dialoguing with Plato and Parfit, and our nights with gnostics and Nozick? What is it we can qualmlessly claim to know, after we have been in the business a while, not spectators, not botanizing theories and theorists, but recent responsible participants in a 2,500-year dialectical conversation?

From Socrates to Sidgwick, the half-life of promising solutions steadily declined, and, acceleratedly ever since, the data accumulate that we are soon in the dark in whatever direction we look. Our evidence-bank bulges exponentially: esteemed ideas explode unexpectedly, hallowed distinctions disappear, and now the rate of explosion is exploding. By comparison, the microphysical world seems stable, predictable, near-frozen.

There may be exceptions, some results that a professional consensus deems well settled, probably permanent contributions to human thought. Maybe a few are positive results: for example, perhaps after some 2,500 years we have now nailed down a truly adequate analysis of a mathematical continuum and a definitive resolution of Zeno's paradoxes.

But mostly, as they say, the exceptions prove the rule. Mostly, the best, central, and solid findings are discoveries of some paradox, puzzling knot, or limitation of reason. We have struck pure gold with the Prisoner's Dilemma, Newcomb's Paradox, Arrow's Impossibility Theorem, Russell's Paradox, Godel's Incompleteness Proofs, Heisenberg's Uncertainty Principle, and so on. Now all we need is some understanding of what we have uncovered; but what remains uncertain is the meaning of these results: precisely what is proven by Godel's proofs? What do his conclusions mean and imply?

11   Our attitudes about logic, reasoning, and inference remain among our most conflicted and delusional. While habitually referring to famous arguments as "proofs" of this or that, we take as a matter of course that the mass of philosophical argument is notably free of unimpeachable proofs. The dialectic mocks our well-considered intuitions and carefully crafted arguments. It is now a platitude that the results of philosophical debate are preponderantly negative, that there is more consensus on which famous "proofs" go wrong and how they do, than on which, if any, are sound. We feel, with good reason, that we may fail to spot every or any defect in some reasoning, but when we do sense one it is with a sense of certainty. Our perceptions that some argument is invalid (fallacious, illogical, wrong, or fishy) are commonly among our strongest convictions: without thinking about it, we feel that we just know that some inference does not follow, does not make sense.

Meanwhile, it has always been true, yet only lately – and still but rarely

– noted that it is a plain fact of logic that logic provides no proof procedure for invalidity.[8] In essence, the epistemology of deduction is the flipside of induction: inductive hypotheses are *a posteriori* falsifiable but not verifiable; the deductive validity of arguments is *a priori* verifiable but not falsifiable. We may know that arguments fitting certain recognized forms of inference are valid. Yet we can have no criterion for telling that a suspect argument belongs to none of the valid inference forms still unrecognized; unless we independently know the premises to be true and the conclusion false, we have no way of showing that the conclusion cannot follow, or does not necessarily follow. It might be that we are just blind to the inner coherence of some conceptual complex.

That permanent abstract possibility could hardly be more alive. Yet we keep being caught by surprise each time some intellectual relic seems stone dead, decisively refuted, and then becomes unrefuted, resurrected, and all the rage. Davidson demonstrated, in his discussion of reasons as causes, both that some intuitively sound arguments are fallacious, and also that some intuitively fallacious arguments are not fallacious, and some intuitively nonsensical ideas are not nonsensical (in any of the ways allaged).[9] Grice did the same with the causal theory of perception.[10] The literature is lit with examples.

Positivism sharpened our understanding that generally a false philosophical claim affirms something that could not possibly be true, so its sense is problematical. But positivism was plagued by its supposition that nonsense has some single, all-or-nothing nature, detectable and measurable by some criterion, when actually the very idea of there being a criterion of what makes no sense itself makes no sense. We have no *a priori* tests for the unintelligible and abundant *a posteriori* evidence that our intuitions are not reliable.

Still, there is no sure-fire method for shedding the great Cartesian delusion that our conceptual space is transparent, that the mind commands a clear and direct view of its own contents, that we are perfectly positioned to survey all its objects, aspects, and possibilities. It helps to keep in mind the discomfiting record: Kant was absolutely certain that he/we absolutely could not conceive of non-Euclidian space; Frege was blindsided by Russell's Paradox; Hilbert had not feared, for he had not imagined any theorem like Godel's; before Stevenson, Moore had not considered – what seems so simple in hindsight – construing moral disagreements as other than propositional oppositions; Rawls had not been worrying whether the concept of a person might unravel in ways that Parfit made plausible. Yet reciting this record has scant effect unless we recognize (what laymen can little appreciate) that doubts about the truth of a philosophical thesis readily devolve into debates about the conceptualization of the topic, where the very sense and relevance of all the famous questions, claims, and counterclaims come to be uncertain. Does anyone now really know what is "the" issue of realism or objectivism (or whether they are the same) in ethics? Or in science?

Experience commends a wary cognitive strategy, a thoroughly fallibilist stance about not only what is true but also what does and does not make sense, and what does and does not follow from what: beware of the next idea or argument that seems conclusive or fallacious, utterly convincing or incredible! When you cannot figure out how it goes wrong or right, not even with the help of your ten cleverest friends, it is still a virtual certainty that we will soon find some plausible refutation or reconstrual in print. No proof is needed that some powerful criticism or reconstrual must be lurking for it to be reasonably expected, for we have seen it happen so regularly that ideas that seemed settled suddenly seem shaky. We might still hold fast to some ideas and arguments and continue to assume their cogency, for no proof can be given that some unknown cogent criticism must or does exist. But, while holding fast, *we* may rightly feel shaken when some clever dialectician concocts a surprising criticism and we are utterly unprepared.

I say *we*, yet some respected professionals seem impervious to these epistemic encounters. Despite their certified familiarity with a tradition that keeps teaching the threat of conceptual surprise, they stay blissfully true believers. Many are bone-deep positivists who may authentically disavow allegiance to a verifiability criterion of meaning, yet with preterarrogant assurance they forecast for all time that some philosophical issue must be debated in such and such terms. Non-cognitivists and other positivists in applied ethics are especially susceptible to such dogmatism, since they do not recognize the possibility of an independent moral truth that may elude every algorithm we have devised. Confidence comes easily if you do not feel you are amidst endlessly aspected moral facts, where unpredictable lights may fall on shadowed facets; then you can be convinced that you can cover all the epistemic bases and know who is going to win each dialectical war, because you know exactly what battles must be fought and on what grounds, and how to assess the strengths of each position.

12   The Socratic claims seem well confirmed. We suffer delusions of understanding, and have seen it demonstrated. We do not feel alarmed because our sense of understanding is a communal delusion, socially sanctioned, and we are naturally resistant to recognizing a profoundly humbling revelation of our pretensions. We lead our lives mindlessly presuming that, if we pass all the tests that dolts and teeny-boppers trip on, our ideas are in good order, with enough sense for us to carry on with our lives as we do.

Cartesian and Humean skeptics do not chide their friends for betting on there being solid ground beneath their feet and a sun that will rise on the morrow. But Socratic skepticism is a moral skepticism, and unlike most modern doubts about moral knowledge, it is meant to enter and alter our lives. So our understanding of Socratic skepticism must look woefully vague and incomplete (or worse) until we can specify its implications, what follows about how we should live our lives in the face of its revelations.

Socrates' recorded words do not supply much specification, but neither do they silence the question. He thought the confusions uncovered to be significant enough to merit our concern, but no so severe as to be immobilizing. He would have us worry about our beliefs, but he did not recommend any systematic doubt or general suspension of belief, certainly not about what any fool knows or what an expert consensus settles on. He awakened us to see our ideas in disarray and feel torn by conflicting convictions. Then he left us with an open question what to go on thinking and doing, and what to change.

Where Socratic skepticism should take you depends on where you are when you find it (or it finds you). Its practice does not presume some epistemically privileged or purified position from which to start a search for knowledge or shoulder our responsibilities. It does not presume that we need certainties to make progress, legitimately, rationally, with a reasonable belief in our power to improve our condition. It presents an open question of whether and how a dialectically exposed debility is a liability in our intellectual or practical affairs.

Presumably that varies from case to case. This skepticism does not apply to all concepts equally, canceling through and leaving everything as is, except for some empty confession of fallibility tacked on to every conclusion. To the contrary, this skepticism derives, not from some one or few conundra recurring across our conceptual scape, but instead from an unpredictable array of puzzles, resisting reduction to any perceived pattern. A modern Socrates might well say that despite our persisting failure to make good sense of the nature of numbers, we understand enough to know endless mathematical truths, and are capable of knowing many more (if not all). Our bewilderment over the nature of numbers need not infect our confidence in the calculations with which we built our bridges. But whether we should build a bridge or burn one may take a bit of wisdom. Our consternation over the nature of value and justice is more disturbing, existentially and epistemically.

Moreover, no matter what conceptions are involved, what you should do and believe, once convinced by some demonstration, depends on what you had been doing and believing up till then, and what your peculiar circumstances, capacities, and opportunities are. Our self-contradictions present us with problems, but not an ounce of counsel on their resolutions.

However profound the naked fact of our nescience may be, it has not the power of the puniest imperative to tell us what to do. Even when allied with all principles of logic, few options are foreclosed by sheer Socratic skepticism, for it is not opposed to all progress, nor to all present belief: recognizing grounds for a reasonable doubt does not itself preclude diverse justified convictions. As with other decisions, it may take some wisdom to tell when to doubt, when to believe, when to feel certain enough to proceed with some task (and, if they are not the same thing, it may take some courage, justice, and self-control too). Philosophical theses about the kinds of evidence, clarity, and certainty needed for rational thought and action presume a wisdom Socrates denies we have and does not supply.

13 However precious Socratic wisdom deems itself compared with the pretenders it displaces, it claims to be a paltry thing by any other measure. Still, our sense that Socratic skepticism has immense human import keeps pressing us to wring grand conclusions out of our utter confusion. We are persistently tempted to find its human meaning manifested in its paradigm practitioner and to treat its import for his life as a pole star for us all.

After Socrates spent some years proving to his own satisfaction that he was uniquely wise, he then dedicated his life single-mindedly to a specific, peculiar task: proving to whomever would listen that they lacked wisdom. It is worth puzzling over why that of all things became Socrates' mission, and how he allowed himself his evident certainty on many of the most controversial matters of great importance. Yet that puzzle can promise no answer to our own problem.

Socrates wisely did not say we should become little Socrates, spreading his message as he did. He did not pretend to be perfect, infallible, or faultless. But he did think himself special, the gods' gift to his people, inspired and informed by two transrational sources: a single, public testimony from the Delphic divinity and a recurrent, private, inner signal whenever he was about to err. A Humean sceptic would question the epistemic credentials of these divine revelations, but Socrates accepted these voices as authoritative channels of truth, as many of us would in his shoes. And he did not expect others to be convinced and controlled by his personal guide as he was. Socrates' deeds do not give us much authoritative direction; their propriety is conditioned by their peculiar circumstances. Even were he a perfect Socratic skeptic, he can be only one paradigm – and properly applying that model takes considerable wisdom.

14 So too for his famous dicta, which were directed at an historically

distinctive audience. The Socrates who said that the greatest good for a man is to discuss virtue every day was not so utopian or egalitarian as to assume that this greatest good is attainable or sensibly attemptable by every human being. Nor did he declare that all such discussion can or should serve only to deflate pretensions of wisdom. He did think that dropping one's delusions of understanding is a good thing, but not that it is the only one or the best: for example, it is better to have substantial philosophical understanding than to lack it and know that you do. De-lousing ourselves of delusions is not our ultimate or highest good.

Nor need it be an essential first step. It is quite unSocratic to suppose that the slate must first be wiped clean before a true creed can be inscribed in its place, that we cannot install any new true beliefs until we are released from those they replace.[11] Perhaps some important lessons cannot be learned except by making mistakes and being corrected. Still, it is best not to have to suffer that; it is better if we are taught the truth from the outset.[12]

Most of our knowledge is a social product, produced and distributed by a division of labor. Arguably the best, perhaps the only way that mankind can get some wisdom is by enabling a select few to dedicate themselves to that end, and having the rest learn from them. Tasks and temperaments need not be uniform, even among professionals; perhaps we all profit if some intellects enjoy (and suffer) the confidence, enthusiasm, or vanity of the entrepreneurial, while others are more corporate, conservative, cau-tious, or cynical. It may be for the best for some to be not Socratically skeptical, or not to the same degree, or for the skeptical to share little else. Socrates might applaud the productivity of this pluralism – and then deny all value to every life left unexamined. However, his skepticism does not sanction the antidemocratic arrogance of that valuation of wisdom and of life not in quest of it.

15 If any valuation or directive is implicit in Socratic skepticism it is only an insistence on the virtues of integrity. Skepticism challenges unjustified claims, and takes a moral tone when it takes after fraud and pretension. But the principles of integrity are largely second-order regulations whose concrete implications depend upon more contentful valuations.[13] The specific Socratic appraisals most tightly implicated by his skepticism are, expectably, not a code for everyman, but criticisms of Socratic competitors, his fellow sophists, the professional applied ethicists of his time.

Socrates was as much a professional applied ethicist as any in terms of expertise, but he insisted on working *pro bono*, living in poverty, and ridiculing his peers for successfully selling their wares in the market of public affairs. However, no poverty is a proper point of pride, save as a symbol for another value. It is never better than a necessary evil, an unavoidable means or by-product of achieving something worthwhile. Wealth and comfort may be mixed goods, with attendant risks and costs, as most goods are. Like health or intelligence, such goods can be put to bad uses and magnify calamities. In themselves, at their worst, such goods are only excessive, temptations and distractions, seducing the self away from its best path. Likewise, Socrates' absence from public affairs and inability to look after his own are sacrifices of natural human goods, endured with dignity for something noble, and any nobility they possess is derivative of that. He suffered his sacrifices wisely, not immoderately. He dwelled in a plush poverty, in the glorious Greek clime, surrounded by wealthy admirers eager to get the tab for the best food and drink around. His monasticism has no masochism, need for redemption, lusting for the lash, glorified agony. Some people sleep better on hard beds. His temperate hardships were enjoyed with a natural tolerance and taste for a Spartan lifestyle, plus, perhaps, some pride in his hardiness.

A wisdom beyond Socratic skepticism is needed to justly say when and how much sacrifice is required or advisable for the applied ethicist – or anyone. Socrates' own rationales may dignify his own rough penchants, but they will not warrant standards of self-denial his scions need adhere to, leastwise not in a thoroughly bureaucratizing free-market democracy with its relentless professionalization of occupations. Detached from his sense of the holy, his anxious shielding of his purity of purpose is a personal extravagance and no more appropriate for his profession than for many another.

In the end his most plausible pleading was his final one, that due to the great benefits his service bestowed he deserved to be publicly subsidized. If the payments made to other sophists were improper, that is due to some fraud or failure to deliver the goods promised, and not because delivering such goods cannot merit a comfortable recompense.

16 Most modern professional applied ethicists are far too clever to be caught practicing any crude, impolitic con. They know they risk professional ridicule by billing themselves fonts of wisdom. Marketing oneself as a spout of sagacity is left to that multitude of moralists undisciplined by our academic heritage: their integrity need not be compromised by their unSocratic antics. But fraudulence has a thousand forms and faces. The question remains whether disavowals of wisdom, however sincere, immunize applied ethicists against all charges of professional malfeasance according to strictures of Socratic skepticism.

That skepticism most decidedly permits, if not encourages, professionals to speak out and take sides, with sincere and passionate conviction, on matters of great public moment. No sensible professional canon would condemn someone just for authentically acting out her well-considered moral and political judgments with all the conviction and certainty she had come to after due deliberation. Of course, crusading is constrainable in ways any conduct may be: for example, matters of time, place, and manner properly limit the free speech of everyone.

However, professional privileges and responsibilities entail extra standards of accountability. Advising or proselytizing with a fervor contrary to or in excess of one's honest convictions is generally condemnable for anyone. Professional ethicists can plead fewer exceptions to that rule and can be held to higher standards of due deliberation. Partly for these very reasons some such principle might well be included in a professional code of ethics for applied ethicists – and the mere inclusion of a prohibition in an established professional code creates an added constraint upon the behavior.

17   Instituting such a code has not been much on the ethics industry agenda. That is an incongruous omission in a guild whose bread and butter is the evaluation of codes of professional ethics. This new professional species has emerged from the turbulent seas of philosophical theory, survived and flourished over the last two decades as an adaptation to an altered occupational climate, a sudden, widespread self-consciousness about professional ethics, and a consequent development, refinement, and reliance on public codes of professional ethics. Codes were thought to have a place and in fact are now in place, not just for physicians and attorneys, but for engineers, policemen, businessmen, all kinds of counselors and therapists, and practitioners of some scholarly trades like cultural anthropology. Such codes can serve diverse social, legal, and economic purposes and are assessable by various measures. It is anything but obvious why a code for applied ethicists would be less appropriate or functional than any of those others.

One thing is certain: the absence of such a code and of all consideration of it has not been due to some well-known, albeit unstated, consensus on essentials. As things are, it would be more controversial to require sound moral character for accrediting an ethicist than for licensing a locksmith. Licensing brings in extra factors, as do testts of character, but the point is plain enough as regards no more than a code of conduct. Among professional Socratic skeptics moral controversy is bound to be the norm rather than the exception.

With so much else actually and properly in dispute, from first principles to concrete cases, common ground on which to construct a code is hard to come by. So it seems a sensible strategy to start from something (perhaps the one thing) all may already share (to one or another degree): namely, Socratic skepticism. Disputes over interpretations and applications of that basis are to be expected, and (within some limits) welcomed as properly part of the process and the content of this profession. That foundation may be too slim to take us far or wide enough to construct an entire professional code,[14] but it is apt to be a crucial premiss in issues of professional integrity.

18   This essay might serve as a first draft of the beginnings of an outline of our epistemic condition and the constraints it does or does not impose on operatives in the ethics industry. One motive for my efforts is a natural transcendental worry that nags the conscience of many a professional ethicist: the worry whether and how an applied ethics profession is at all possible. The very concept of the thing seems paradoxical. On the one hand, the concept of a professional carries with it both a claim of publicly accreditable expertise and an ethos emphasizing integrity.[15] On the other hand, the concept of applied ethics refers to an enterprise whose epistemic plight appears to put in jeopardy any claim of pertinent, public measurable expertise.[16] My aim has been to allay some anxieties with an utterly untranscendental argument that will not bury the old bugbear but may put it in a healthy perspective.

While modern ethicists explain their anxieties with doubts presumed peculiar to ethics as distinct from science, Socratic moral skepticism is a skepticism about philosophical understanding. Doubts about the justification and truth of our moral judgments and theories contrast with doubts about perceptual judgments and empirical theories, for moral beliefs and claims of moral knowledge are akin to and continuous with our other philosophical beliefs and knowledge claims. Applied ethics, normative ethical theory, meta-ethics, epistemology in general, and the rest of philosophy are all epistemical brothers, fathers, and sons in the family of philosophy.[17] Within that family, a respect for intuitions, commonsense, and current beliefs is as topic-neutral as the rules of deductive inference; and qualms about the rational resolvability of disputes have comparable sources and propriety. In her practice, the Socratic applied ethicist may confront questions from any philosophical quarter, and in much the same manner and spirit.

She may wonder whether and how someone can, with integrity, advise and proselytize when he knows or ought to know of reasons for respecting uncertainties. That general question is the seed for a tree of questions. The branch that bears our inspection is whether the applied ethicist should have some extra worry for her own soul and those of her colleagues. Is the threat to their integrity any more perilous than that for a film reviewer, fashion consultant, interior decorator, architect, or academic critic in the literary or fine arts? Elsewhere candidates may be accredited as experts by their familiarity with an esteemed tradition or by proving their own worth with performances as convincing as other traditions. The ethics business works the same way.

Applied ethicists wish to practice a craft, a skill it does not take wisdom to teach or apply. They wish to be accredited and considered eligible for employ by demonstrating expertise within a reputable tradition; few are so vain as to try doing it autodidactically. They want their work recognized by their peers as contributions to a community tradition, perhaps as departures from it, but not outside it. They aspire to be professionals, not prophets.

If the ethics industry operates on the same principles as other trades in the value business, why should its employees suffer greater misgivings? Their self-labeling signifies a slanted self-conception. The very name "applied ethics" cannot but be modeled on "applied science," "applied mathematics," and the like; the term cannot be heard without echoing connotations that enforce a particular public and self-image of cognitive prowess. Their tradition has long admired and aspired to the epistemological status of math and science, but that tradition denies them the right to call themselves moral scientists. Still, they hanker after an expertise with a rigor nearer that of an engineer or economist than an editor or architect or their colleagues practicing criticism in the humanities and arts.

Their tradition prides itself on its rationality, the purer the better. Their protracted arguments about moral arguments have not yielded publicly certified conclusions, but the evident sophistication of argumentation seems evidence of some greater understanding of moral argument, an expertise in the epistemology of ethics and the evaluation of moral argument. This training in second-order studies seems to be a higher ground, a firmer footing for claims of rational rigor.

Lay folk are likely to have some difficulty comprehending (and keeping straight) how someone can be a master evaluater of moral arguments without being a master of moral truth. They are liable to be misled by instruction in the distinction between soundness and validity, unless they are given fair notice that knowledge of anything rightly called a science of validity is quite beside the point. No amount of expertise in formal logic provides mastery of an art of practical reasoning, and only its rudiments are at all useful.

Then what honest claims of expertise in an art of practical reasoning can a professional applied ethicist make? Can she tell her students or other unsuspecting clients anything more than that, whatever her or their own considered judgment may be on some matter of moral argument, what she really knows far better than they is that no one can claim any knowledge on the matter? Perhaps sometimes she can say something more than that, but it seems to me that commonly she is duty bound to say no less. Other professions do not have that responsibility if such wisdom is not essential to their professional competence.

My own Socratic skepticism says that this self-denial needs saying (or somehow being made plain) more commonly than many ethicists are wont to do. More notice must be taken and given that some wisdom beyond formal logic is needed, not just in appraising the plausibility of moral premises, but in the prior steps of choosing the terms of debate, casting inchoate intuitions into some reputable inferential structure, and considering whether some reasoning not recognized by our tradition might yet be sensible. I fear that far too commonly professionals instruct the uninitiated in tones of authoritative finality about what the "real" moral issues are in this or that situation and how the practical problems of raw reality must be conceptualized. Too commonly their curt dismissals of common ways of reasoning and conceiving bespeak only prejudice masquerading as meta-evaluations licensed by some arcane science rather than an art whose training and standards of excellence are subject to fashions.

Colleagues embarrassed by unprofessional antics have a vested interest in policing these scams. No doubt, some of this humbuggery is mere harmless puffery, and collegial speech has separate rules, etc. The one excuse that cannot be allowed is that the fraud is not ill-intentioned but due to honest delusions, for here it matters not what the professional does know but what she ought to know, and the one thing she ought to know is that she does not.

Doubtless, here as elsewhere, deceptive practices cannot always be controlled by a written, institutionally enforceable code. Our last resort remains our first: Socratic exposure of professional impostures to public ridicule.[18]

NOTES

1 Virtues are not generally the kinds of properties for which we have conceptions of perfection. We have standards for being perfectly or absolutely flat, square, or cold. But while some people are generous or kind, and some are more so than others, talk of perfect or absolute generosity or kindness lacks any requisite standard. It seems easier to talk of being perfectly just, honest, or wise – but that may be an illusion.

2 Some philosophical questions, like "What is time (existence, etc.)?" may make for immediate speechlessness. Sometimes the thing seems so primitive, simple, like yellow, that there is nothing to say. But even then, when you do (somehow) find something to say, what seems at all plausible is likely to seem obvious and indubitable, and then the dialectic exposes dilemmas, paradoxes, and incompatibilities with much else that had seemed undeniable. Of course,

in one sense how quickly you are left speechless depends on how adept you have become at leaping over and finessing all the common false starts.

3   *Contra* Robert Nozick, who dismisses Socratic skepticism by likening philosophical confusion to metasyntactic ignorance: *The Examined Life* (Simon and Schuster, New York, 1989), p. 273. On the other hand, of course those two modes of nescience may merge in places.

4   The more famous and more general statement, "Everything I say is false," is paradoxical only because it encompasses and entails the more specific denial of possessing self-referential truths.

5   Ludwig Wittgenstein, *Philosophical Investigations* (Basil Blackwell, Oxford, 1953).

6   Saul A. Kripke, *Wittgenstein on Rules and Private Language* (Harvard University Press, Cambridge, Mass.: 1982).

7   No skeptic need claim, in arguments from illusion and the like, that we know that some of our past confident first-order beliefs have been false; suffice for the skeptic that some of our past confident first-order beliefs later became shaky, reasonably doubted. The former is no better reason than the latter for thinking that all our confident beliefs are reasonably doubted.

8   Cf. Gerald Massey's articles: "Are there any Good Arguments that Bad Arguments are Bad?," *Philosophy in Context* (Cleveland State University), vol. 4 (1975), pp. 61–77; "In Defense of the Asymmetry," *Supplement to Philosophy in Context*, vol. 4 (1975), pp. 44–56; "Logic and Linguistics," in E. Agazzi, ed., *Modern Logic: A Survey* (Reidel Publishing Co., Dordrecht, 1980), pp. 311–29; "The Pedagogy of Logic: Humanistic Dimensions," *Teaching Philosophy*, vol. 4, pp. 303–36; "The Fallacy behind Fallacies," *Midwest Studies in Philosophy*, 1981, pp. 489–500.

9   Donald Davidson, "Actions, Reasons and Causes," in *Journal of Philosophy*, vol. 60 (1963), pp. 685–700. Consider the contrasts with his discovery of a logical form by which intuitively valid adverbial arguments are shown to satisfy standards of formal validity in "The Logical Form of Action Sentences," in N.Rescher, ed., *The Logic of Decision and Action* (Pittsburgh: University of Pittsburgh Press, 1967), pp. 81–95.

10   H. P. Grice, "The Causal Theory of Perception," in *Proceedings of the Aristotelian Society*, suppl. vol. 35 (1961), pp. 121–52.

11   Again, Socratic inquiry does not call for purifying oneself of all dubious convictions in preparation for acquiring some justified certainty. The dialectic operates without a Lockean picture of knowledge acquisition, since it works from and with our existing beliefs to build a new understanding. We are often liberated from an old belief, not directly by a refutation, but rather by the attractive force of some alternative, whose implications only gradually emerge and gradually motivate rejections of incompatible ideas. As every good salesman knows, criticizing the competition is commonly a foolish strategy: beliefs are most readily revised without our recognizing it, for we are normally resistant to recognizing the loss of an old allegiance.

12   We hold to our beliefs partly and properly just because we have held them. We reasonably wish not to have been wrong. Having been wrong is a cause

for regret, except in so far as it might be a step toward something else we reasonably desire. We naturally wish not to be wrong; not caring takes a radical detachment from (or non-attachment to) one's agency. We naturally wish not to have been wrong; here not caring takes a radical detachment from (or non-attachment to) one's self as a temporal being.

13   Cf. John Rawls, *A Theory of Justice* (Harvard University Press, Cambridge, Mass.: 1971), pp. 519–20.

14   But who knows just how much can be done with it? Philosophical artisans can be surprisingly adept at weaving whole world views out of no less slender threads. In short, it is worth a try.

15   A caveat. The social reality and thus the concept of the professions are evolving matters of controversy. That instability may be inherent when the title of professional is constantly honorific. Here conceptual analyses cannot be absolutely value-free.

16   Here too, the social reality and thus the concept of applied ethics are evolving matters of controversy. That becomes apparent upon reflecting on the problems of dating its origination. Commonly a splendid strategy for exploring and explicating a concept is considering controversies over what marks the inception of the thing.

17   When normal people have basic, seemingly unsettlable moral disputes, their dispute might be due to an acceptance of incompatible ultimate moral principles or values, or it might instead be due to a difference in their general philosophies, their ways of seeing and understanding the world; and we can never prove that the former, not the latter, is the real explanation of the dispute.

18   My thanks to Bredo Johnsen for his helpful critical comments.

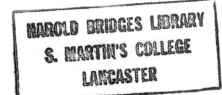

9
Moral Theorizing and Moral Practice: Reflections on Some of the Sources of Hypocrisy

Nancy (Ann) Davis

Calling our attention to the widespread moral hypocrisy in our world, Nancy Davis considers how three different conceptions of morality may give rise to such hypocrisy. One conception views moral principles or theories as telling us what we should do in an ideal, but not the actual, world. This conception gives rise to hypocrisy because it allows us too easily to justify our failure to do what we admit we (ideally) ought to do. A second conception, which views morality as demanding that individuals take effective action in solving problems like hunger and homelessness, may also give rise to hypocrisy. Because the demands of such moral principles are myriad and the likelihood that the action of one person will have any significant effect is remote, persons who have this conception of morality may cease trying to fulfill their myriad moral obligations other than by publicly endorsing the appropriate moral principles. A third conception regards the following of moral principles as praiseworthy but as requiring a significant sacrifice of one's own interests. This view gives rise to hypocrisy when its holders come to believe that the sacrifice entailed in following their espoused moral principles is greater than any person should be required to make. They therefore come to believe that honoring those who do follow their moral principles as saintly or heroic is sufficient to discharge their moral duty.

The remedy, Davis argues, is to foster conceptions of morality and moral motivation that recognize the efficacy of individual participation in concerted collective action and emphasize that fulfilling the demands of morality need not be antithetical to fulfilling one's needs and desires but can be a way of expressing them.

It is worthwhile to compare Davis's paper with that by Solomon (chapter 11), since both argue for adopting a conception of morality that sees moral goodness not as conformity to external constraints but as achieving a kind of personal excellence and fulfillment.

As I write these words, celebrations for Earth Day 1990 are reaching a fever pitch. Newspapers are full of pages of ads telling people how they personally can do things to save the planet, including imprecations to recycle those pages of ads. A television commercial for plastic bags suggests that people recycle their paper, glass, and aluminum by sorting them and placing them on the curb in the advertiser's (non-recyclable) plastic bags. A well-known chain of fast-food restaurants that contributes to global warming by razing rain forests so that they can raise cattle cheaply, and that seems to package everything, including the condiments, in plastic, urges its patrons to recycle their styrofoam packaging. On our family Earth Day walk, we passed long lines of cars waiting to find parking spaces to attend the city's Earth Day festivities. The day after Earth Day, it was widely reported that there were huge quantities of litter left behind by Earth Day revelers everywhere.

Seeking respite from the Earth Day hype, one might turn the page to read about the latest skirmish in the ongoing public war about abortion. A number of papers, including the *New York Times*,[1] reported on a 1985 poll conducted by the American College of Gynecologists and Obstetricians. Eighty-four percent of the 4,000 members polled said that they thought that abortion should be legal and widely available. But less than one-third of them (28 percent) were willing to perform abortions themselves. We might compare that result to an imagined survey of water safety instructors: suppose that 84 percent of them said they thought that apparently drowning persons should be rescued by competent swimmers, but only half of them were willing to save drowning persons themselves.

As I muse about the self-declared pro-choice doctors' reasons for not performing abortions themselves, and listen to reports about recent battles between pro-choice and pro-life demonstrators in the US, I wonder why so few of the people who identify themselves as pro-life are willing to take active steps to improve the lives of children once they are born, or the lives of the young girls for whom abortion may seem the only option. Why is there so much opposition to subsidizing childcare, when that is the only way teenage parents can afford to complete the education that they need to find employment to support the children they were implored not to abort? Why is so little effort directed toward alleviating the condition of the homeless, a sizable proportion of whom are children, who are leading truly miserable lives?[2]

Applied philosophers do all sorts of different things, but the undertaking that I wish to engage in is somewhat unorthodox and atypical. I think that reflection on the lack of fit between our everyday moral pronouncements and beliefs (on the one hand) and our practices (on the other) may produce some interesting and valuable results. Such an enterprise blends the empirical and the critical, and it yields potentially useful diagnoses and critiques. As my overview may suggest, observation of public discussion of normative and policy issues reveals that, though the use of moral language is widespread, and the importance of taking a stand and doing the right thing frequently trumpeted, things come up a bit short on the action side of the ledger. Moral language is much used, but much abused, and hypocrisy is rampant.

I shall here be concerned with some of the sources of this hypocrisy. I shall not, of course, attempt to produce a complete catalog of the sources of hypocrisy: that depressing task is well beyond the scope of this paper, as well as the scope of my competence. I shall focus on some views that I think have roots in a certain conception of morality. I hope that this will sharpen our understanding of the relations between moral theorizing and moral practice. I hope, too, that it will enhance our appreciation of the richness of the territory variously described as normative ethics, applied ethics, or practical ethics.

What picture of morality underlies people's moral pronouncements? Let us consider three different (though related) views.

(1) *Moral views (or theories or principles) provide blueprints for action in an ideal world*

According to (what I shall call) the *ideal blueprint* picture, a moral view (or theory or principle) tells us what we should do in an ideal world. Thus the claim "Lying is wrong" or the dictum "One ought not to lie" is to be understood as saying "In an ideal world, there is no lying." But if – as seems plausible – the world we live in is not ideal, but marred by ignorance, intolerance, selfishness, and suffering, then our actions need not conform with the moral principles that figure in our ideal blueprint. There is no inconsistency here. If moral principles tell us what we should do in an ideal world, we do not necessarily act wrongly or violate those principles if, in this everyday imperfect world, we choose not to do what they prescribe. Nor need the recognition that it is often better if people in the real world do not follow the ideal rules be thought to provide any grounds for thinking that the rules (principles, moral views) themselves are unten-able.

The ideal blueprint picture is attractive in several ways. First, it allows us to capture what might be called the aspirational character of morality. A moral view is supposed to give us a picture (or a vision) of how people should live, something to aspire toward. And so the recognition that we morally ought to do *x* is consistent with our not doing *x*, and indeed, with our inability to steel ourselves to do it. A moral view gives agents guidance about where they ought to aim, and what they ought to hope they can achieve next time.

The ideal blueprint conception of morality also seems to afford us a plausible way of accounting for our not doing things that we readily agree we ought to do. The world, after all, is not a perfect place, and our action plans must take that into account. And so, though one ought not to add to the pollution of this badly polluted planet, since public transportation is poor, and it is hard getting around by foot, especially in bad weather, it is permissible to drive a car, even for short distances. Similarly, since there are currently people who threaten violent reprisals, or economic boycotts of physicians who are known to be willing to perform abortions, it is permissible for physicians to refuse to perform abortions, even when they say that they support the widespread availability of abortion services, and identify themselves as being pro-choice.

There are a number of problems with the ideal blueprint conception of morality. Here I will mention just a few.

There are, first of all, conceptual or logical problems. The description of something as an ideal world does not, in and of itself, convey much information about what that world would be like, or give us an adequate basis for determining the content of the (ideal) moral principles or laws. It is not clear what it is for something to be an ideal world, and it is far from obvious that there is only one imaginable possibility. Nor is it clear that any of the imagined possibilities emerges, in the long run, as coherent or self-consistent.

Consider, first of all, the question of wrongdoing. Are the laws or principles in the ideal moral blueprint ones that allow for any wrongdoing? *Is* there any wrongdoing in an ideal world? It seems plausible to suppose not: what, after all, is an ideal world if not a world free of wrongdoing? But a little more reflection should make us hesitate. For we do not know just what it is that we are supposing when we try to imagine an ideal world, or what it would be like to have a world free of wrongdoing.

In particular, it matters how and why the world would be free of wrongdoing. Are we to suppose that, in an ideal world, all the occasions for wrongdoing are removed – that, for example, all misfortune, temptation, selfishness, and ignorance disappear – and so that people never face the pressures that induce beings like us to make bad choices and do the wrong thing? Or are we supposing that, though the opportunities and motivations for wrongful action remain plentiful in an ideal world, people always have the judgment to make the right choice and the courage to follow through on it?

Neither seems a plausible supposition. As long as we are mortal beings living in a physical world, there will continue to be danger, death, and misfortune, and all the suffering that goes along with them, and people will continue to face the pressures that make them choose and act badly at least some of the time. Nor does it make much sense to suppose that people will be, or could be, born with the sort of good judgment that would enable them always to make the right choice when faced with conflict or temptation. Moral deliberation is something one learns, and gets better at, and moral education is necessary to enable us to appreciate the complexities of the human condition and the necessity for sensitivity, farsightedness, and restraint. One can learn to choose and deliberate well only by making mistakes, and acting wrongly from time to time. We can perhaps imagine a race of beings born with the knowledge of right and wrong, and the mettle needed to always do the right thing. But such beings could not be human beings, or other biological creatures who go through childhood and the process of physical, emotional, and moral maturation. As long as we are talking about a physical world that contains human beings, we are talking about a world that contains beings who act wrongly at least some of the time,[3] and who make choices that cause suffering and harm to other creatures.

We could, however, take our lead from Leibnitzian solutions to the problem of evil and understand the ideal blueprint conception of morality as being a blueprint for the *most* perfect world *possible*: if it is not possible for human beings to learn right from wrong without making mistakes from time to time, then the most perfect world is indeed one that contains wrongdoing. On this understanding, the world is ideal when any other world would have more wrongdoing, or worse wrongdoing, in it.

It may seem to make more sense to understand the ideal blueprint view this way if we are imagining an ideal world as a physical world that contains moral agents who are human animals. But such an interpretation makes it harder to specify the content of the moral principles that should govern conduct in such a world, and indeed, it runs the risk of rendering the ideal blueprint view vacuous. It is not obvious just what is possible for us, or what represents a better (or worse) possibility. Perhaps – appearances to the contrary – this world, with its famine, disease, and suffering, cheats, crooks, and politicians – is the most perfect one possible for us. Hard as this suggestion might seem to credit, we should recall Candide's dreadful adventures in his best of all possible worlds.

And so we seem to face a dilemma. If we understand the ideal blueprint view as specifying what people ought to do in an ideal world, and an ideal world as one in which there is no wrongdoing, it is hard to see how morality could have much practical import to guide the conduct of human beings in a physical world. Moreover, unless we suppose that the ideal world does contain some wrongdoing, it is hard to see how this picture of the workings of moral principles could be sensibly (or intelligibly) applied to many of the issues that most concern applied philosophers. I have here in mind such things as the morality of (and public policy with respect to) reproductive and conservation issues, as well as other issues that involve attempts to set the parameters of the permissible. In an ideal world, abortion would presumably not be much of an issue: few, if any, pregnancies would occur that were unwanted or dangerous, no child would face the prospect of less than adequate circumstances, and, because the reorganization of society would presumably be egalitarian and humane, there would be no woman whose life plans were compromised by the bearing and raising of children. Nor would conservation issues be particularly pressing. For in an ideal world, people presumably would not hurt or abuse animals for food, or live miles away from ecosystem-damaging employment, or live profligate and short-sighted lifestyles that rely heavily on the use of fossil fuels.

If, on the other hand, we understand the ideal blueprint as allowing for the existence of wrongdoing, then it runs the risk of degenerating into vacuity: for this may be the most perfect world, and the principles that should guide our conduct in the ideal world may simply be whatever principles should govern our conduct in this world; hence the appeal to the ideal blueprint view does nothing to advance our understanding of what those are. It does not make much better sense to interpret the ideal blueprint view as directing each of us to determine what the ideal rules are, and then follow them ourselves, whether or not anyone else identifies the same rules as obligatory, or follows those rules themselves. Imagine how much self-righteous chaos such a proposal would engender.

Finally, because it is not clear that the notion of an ideal world represents a plausible or coherent picture for human beings, and because, even if it does, it represents a picture of human life that is surely very far removed from our actual human lives, the ideal blueprint view suffers from another defect, one that is particularly relevant to this discussion. It allows too much justifiable failure to do what we admit we (ideally) ought to do, and thus breeds hypocrisy. The fact that people profess to think that lying is wrong (for example) may have very little bearing on their actions. For that just means that in an ideal world, people do not lie. However, since this world is abundantly supplied with cheats, cads, and politicians, lying is often a permissible recourse. By idealizing, and thus excessively elevating, the moral standard, and understanding morality as a code of conduct for an ideal world, the ideal blueprint picture effectively lowers the standard for practice, and widens the gap between people's professed moral principles and their actual behavior. It allows us to suppose that we can assess people's moral views without looking very hard at how they actually act. As such, it is a clear source of hypocrisy in our everyday lives.

(2) *Words as constituting deeds (or: the greeting card problem): morality as performative utterance*

The ideal blueprint picture unreasonably elevates moral standards, and thus provides a ready-made excuse for lax practice. Since this is not an ideal world, we may not really be doing wrong when we fail to conform our actions to our avowed moral principles. There may thus be a large gap between our espoused moral principles and our actions.

In contrast to this, the performative utterance conception appears to posit a tighter connection between our espoused moral views and our deeds: having moral principles involves acting in accord with them, even in this non-ideal world. Though this may sound like a basis for rejecting hypocrisy, the performative utterance view has an extremely modest conception of what it is to act in accord with one's principles: we can demonstrate our commitment to a moral principle, or our espousal of a moral view, simply by stating that we have such a commitment. Thus George Bush considered that he had demonstrated concern for the poor and homeless merely by saying that he wanted a kinder and gentler America and doing nothing (else) to make America kinder or gentler. And in some circumstances, one's stated endorsement of a particular principle itself constitutes action in accord with that principle. Thus again, Bush took himself to be the environmental president because he said he was: no other planet-preserving action was necessary.

The view of moral commitment as performative utterance may be one manifestation of a more pervasive phenomenon, which might be called the "greeting card mentality." If we are to believe the greeting card companies, it is possible to express sincere affection for people (or any of a myriad of other sentiments) merely by sending them mass-produced cards that say that we have sincere affection for them. Even when we have done nothing else to show such concern, and perhaps, even when we have done many things that seem to indicate that we lack that concern, sending along a greeting card that contains a pre-printed jingle is supposed to do the trick. All one needs do to demonstrate one's love and respect for an aged parent in a nursing home is send her a card on Mother's Day. In some cities, one is invited to make a $1 contribution to the poor and homeless; that contribution entitles one to a button that says "I care." Caring can be shown by a $1 donation.

That the view of moral commitment as performative utterance may foster hypocrisy is obvious: even in these inflationary times, saying something does not make it so. George Bush was no environmentalist, and people who ignore their aged parents 364 days of the year and merely send a card on the 365th do not really care very much about them. There are times, of course, when words do constitute deeds, and the statement of one's moral principles constitutes action in accord with them. Standing up and saying that you care may constitute a convincing demonstration that you really do care at a Gay Pride rally in a conservative small town, for here showing support for one's gay friends involves sharing the risk with them. The same is true of adopting the policy of telling anti-Semites that some of your best friends are Jewish when you know that this will cause them to believe – incorrectly – that you are Jewish, and thus expose you to the same sort of discrimination that your Jewish friends face. But these cases are more the exception than the rule.

When baldly stated, the performative utterance conception of morality is obviously untenable, and it is a view that few people will openly endorse. But as the commercial success of greeting cards (and the electoral success, until 1992, of Republicans) may indicate, it is a view that – at least tacitly – many people accept. What makes the view attractive? Where does the view of morality as performative utterance come from?

In part it may reflect our realization that the planet, and many lives on the planet, are in a truly sorry state, and that something can and should be done to make things better. And – relatedly – it may reflect our recognition that we would be bad and unfeeling individuals if we did not care about other people's plight, or the state of the planet, or do anything to help alleviate them. On the other hand, we recognize that the problems of homelessness, poverty, and pollution are huge, and grow ever huger. The possibility of making a significant personal contribution can thus seem small. Even if I do all that I can to recycle household waste, avoid the use of petrochemical-based packaging, install a fuel-efficient heating system, and give up my car, I will not stop the onslaught of pollution. Even if I feed, clothe, and house a homeless family for a year, I will not appreciably decrease the rising tide of homelessness.

If one thinks of morality as addressed to the individual, as directed at our own actions and their effects, and thinks that the value and importance of our deeds can be measured by how much they materially contribute to the alleviation of the problem, it is easy enough to understand how the greeting card conception of morality might take hold.[4] We see that the plight of the homeless is dreadful, and we think that only a bad person would feel nothing, or do nothing to help. And so we think that we ought to do something. But we are discouraged by the magnitude of the problem and our apparent powerlessness. It may seem to us that we can only hope to effect real, significant change if we devote our life and resources to doing so: the selfless, lifelong dedication of a saint or hero is what is needed to stem the rising tide of homelessness and hunger. And so, while we recognize that we are morally obliged to do something, because we think that we are not obliged to be heroes or saints, and because we think our efforts are wasted unless we can see them as materially and significantly contributing to the alleviation of a problem, we do not think that we are obliged to do much. If nothing I can do can really put an end to homelessness, then why should I waste my energies? When it would involve great sacrifice on our part to effect serious change, we tend to regard a token gesture as sufficient demonstration of our moral commitment. It is sufficient for us to make a contribution to hunger- or homelessness-relief organizations and get on with our lives.

I shall return to the issue of moral sainthood or heroism below. I want first to look more closely at another source of the performative utterance view of morality, its mistaken moral individualism.

The performative utterance view misconstrues the extent to which, and the ways in which, morality is individualistic, and concerned with the goodness of individual agents. This view seems, first of all, to regard people's moral pronouncements as signs or evidence of their virtue. By telling you that I care about the homeless, I show you that I am a good person. But virtue is not simply an inner state, nor can its existence be determined simply by introspection. It is true that we cannot determine whether an act was virtuous simply by observing someone's actions. We must know something about the person's motives and intentions, and we usually regard people's own reports as strong evidence regarding those motives and intentions, and hence as important testimony regarding their virtue. But those reports can be false, and – at least in the area of social policy issues – it is deeds, not just sincerely avowed intentions, that are the measures of a person's goodness (or virtue). Though it is a truism that morality directs us to be concerned with our own virtue, this concern cannot sensibly be thought to be about our purity of heart, independent of its expression in action.

The performative utterance view also misconstrues the extent to which, and the ways in which, individual responsibility is important. It is a truism that each of us is answerable for what he or she does. But this should not be taken as a basis for supposing that morality requires that our actions be (what I will call) aimed directly at accomplishing a goal. It is true that I cannot hope to solve the problem of homelessness (or even significantly alleviate it) by undertaking actions aimed directly at accomplishing that goal, namely, housing and feeding people myself. My house, and my income, are only so large; I cannot comfortably house or feed many people. But I can initiate, or participate in, more indirect collective action that may eventually result in the housing and feeding of many more people. I can urge other people to help put pressure on well-placed individuals to change their policies – for example, persuade local ministers to allow their churches to be used as shelters. Or I can work to elect politicians who treat the plight of the homeless as a priority, or lobby those in office to make it one of their priorities. The view of morality as performative utterance exaggerates both the importance and the difficulty of my doing, by myself, things that effect direct moral change. And it has an overly individualistic conception of what moral efficiency is, and how it is to be accomplished. It both underestimates the value of concerted, committed, collective action and overestimates the helplessness of the individual.

It also treats moral obligations as external and onerous. It exaggerates the extent to which they are seen as unwanted demands on people, and the extent to which our moral obligations should be seen as dischargeable.

Here is a somewhat roundabout explanation of that.

Modern life, as the media frequently remind us, is complicated and stress-filled: there are lots of demands on our time, energy, and resources. Though we have more labor-saving devices than ever before, and the potential for more leisure time, no one seems to have enough time to get everything done. Stress, we are told, is the big disease of the 1980s and 1990s. Women face increased demands as they combine managing the household and raising the children with jobs or careers outside the home; men face increased demands as they respond to social and familial pressure to do more to help run the household and raise the children while they continue to work outside the home.

Demands on our sympathies and concern have increased also. Our mailboxes are full of solicitations from organizations requesting contributions to help alleviate world hunger, stop the destruction of rain forests in Brazil, limit the use of animals in cosmetic and product testing, help the homeless, and stop the erosion of civil rights and liberties (to name just a few). Most of these sound like worthy, and indeed noble, causes, yet few of us believe that we can help them all; and more generally, we feel we cannot meet all the moral demands that are made on us. We are drawn to try to resolve that problem the way we resolve other problems involving too many demands: by increased efficiency and selectivity. We do as little as we decently can on some fronts in order to be able to do things on other fronts. Buying an "I care" button by making a modest contribution to help feed and house the homeless may seem to free us to invest our energies in other causes, to do good elsewhere.

The problems with such a view are many, and I can only touch on a few of them here. One of its dangers is that there may cease to be an elsewhere: we may acquire the habit of doing the minimum, and lose the capacity to really listen and deliberate about what we ought to be doing. Seeing moral demands in this light may also reinforce the adversarial view of morality as something alien that comes along and makes demands on us, demands that we would rather avoid than fulfill. If morality is just one more thing competing for our attention, then it seems both permissible and reasonable for us to do the minimum necessary to keep it at bay.

This view involves a distorted picture of morality, and it misunderstands both the nature of moral motivation, and the role that moral concerns may play in our lives. I will return to that point a bit later. For now I will just note that, in such an atmosphere, it is no wonder that politicians seek to demonstrate their moral commitments merely by announcing that they have them, and ordinary people allow themselves to believe that sending a greeting card or a bunch of flowers amounts to a demonstration of real human concern.

(3) *The sanctification of the morally admirable person*

It is common for people to express moral admiration for Mother Teresa,

Nelson Mandela, or – somewhat less grandly – the person up the street who joins the Peace Corps, or publishes a peace newsletter, or works for a famine relief organization and is paid only a subsistence wage, while at the same time admitting that they themselves cannot or will not do such things. Often, the admiration takes the form of identifying the committed moral conduct of others as saintly or heroic. In so doing, the admirer seems both to accord recognition to the power of the demands of morality and to excuse those individuals who are not saintly or heroic – ourselves, for example – from living up to them.

In some of its incarnations, the moral sanctification view is a variant of the ideal blueprint view: if morality addresses actions in an ideal world, then it may be only saints and heroes (and Dostoyevskian holy fools) who can do its bidding in this imperfect world.

But the moral sanctification view is, more generally, one that combines aspects of both the ideal blueprint and performative utterance views. In expressing their admiration for Mother Teresa, or for the pacifist who publicly refuses to pay taxes that go to weapons research, people take themselves to be acting in accord with their principles and doing something morally worthy. I may not be the person that Mother Teresa is, but I am a good person in so far as I can see and acknowledge that she is an exemplary one.

The obstetrician/gynecologists of the survey mentioned at the beginning of this paper may also exemplify a form of this view. They profess to believe that abortion should be legal and widely available, and they express admiration for those of their pro-choice colleagues who actually perform abortions. But they are unwilling to perform abortions themselves, and they hasten to offer reasons to excuse their refusal: their practice is in a conservative part of the country, and their continued livelihood thus depends on their willingness to identify themselves as mother-and-baby doctors, rather than as doctors who willingly assist women to terminate unwanted pregnancies.[5] They are worried that their practices or their families will suffer if they do what they profess to admire others for doing.

The sanctification view has two components. It treats committed moral action, and morally admirable people, as extraordinary, rather than as things that ordinary people can do or be. And it takes the expression of admiration to be a species of moral action, one that accords with the relevant moral principle, and is itself commendable (when the objects of its admiration are praiseworthy).

It is easy enough to see how such a view may be the source of hypocrisy. I profess to believe that one should help the poor, or that one should not support weapons research, or that drug and cosmetics companies should not test their products on animals, and I act as if, in merely expressing admiration for the people whose deeds actually demonstrate a commitment to these principles, I have done something meaningful to live up to them myself.

Like the ideal blueprint and performative utterance views, the sanctification view may have its roots in certain suppositions about the limits of moral demands and the nature of moral motivation. People often think that they are not obliged to act as those they admire do because they think that the personal sacrifice would be too great: if self-declared pro-choice country doctors performed abortions, their practices or families might suffer; if untenured university professors spoke out against what they perceive as administrative folly, then their jobs might be at risk, and so forth. The view seems to be that one is not obliged to act in accord with one's moral principles if it might involve significant sacrifice (as it frequently will in this non-ideal world). Those who would have to sacrifice too much are excused from meeting the demands of morality – or else, once the sacrifice is too high, then those cease to be moral *demands*. One implication is that those who would not have to sacrifice as much might have a stronger obligation to do the deeds in question: for example, pro-choice city doctors whose patient-base is more liberal might be obliged to perform abortions; tenured professors might be obliged to speak out against administrative folly.

There is something right about the view that the stringency of our obligations may depend (in part) on the gravity of the consequences that would befall us if we fulfilled them: if doing x would involve a major sacrifice on my part, and little or no sacrifice on yours, then – other things being equal – your obligation to do x is stronger than mine, and – unless not doing x has very bad consequences – x may be something that I am not obliged to do at all. If doing x is something that always involves great sacrifice, then, though x may be obligatory in some ideal world, no one in the real world is to be criticized for failing to do it, and those who try, in spite of that, to do x, are to be venerated as saints or heroes.

There are a number of ways to defend the view that the stringency of our moral obligations depends (in part) on the gravity of the consequences that would befall us if we were to try to meet them.[6] It can be seen as an instance of a more general consequentialist view that orders obligations on the basis of the comparison of the projected consequences of alternative actions. Or it can be seen as a view about the nature of morality itself: if demands become too onerous, then – initial appearance to the contrary notwithstanding – they cannot be moral demands. "Ought" is widely supposed to imply "can": and so people cannot be expected to do what they simply cannot do. Or – somewhat more modestly – as Karl Jaspers put it, "No moral law demands a spectacular death."[7]

The problem is that once this view – the view that the stringency of our moral obligations depends in part on the gravity of the consequences that would befall us if we were to act in accord with those putative obligations – is allowed to figure in our own calculations about what to do, it is likely to mislead in one of two ways. We are all more intimately acquainted with, and more interested in, the details of our own case. Focusing on our own circumstances may lead us to overestimate the size of the sacrifice that doing the moral thing would involve – and thus overestimate the degree to which morality itself demands sacrifice – or overestimate the size of the sacrifice that those who do the moral thing have made. Along this route lies the narrowing of the scope of our moral obligations, and the sanctification of the conscientious or committed moral agent: those who undertake active help of the poor and homeless are heroes, for they are doing things that we believe would involve great sacrifice on our part if we were to do them.

Or – since we always know the details of our own situation better than we know the circumstances of others, and are naturally more concerned with our own welfare than that of others – it may lead us to underestimate the size of the sacrifice that others have made. It is easy to suppose that if you are willing to withhold some of your taxes, or willing to speak out against injustice, it must be because it would cost you less than it would cost me.

What lies behind both of these views is a misunderstanding of the nature of morality and the workings of moral motivation. It is common for people to see morality in adversarial terms, as issuing a set of demands that we do things that we do not otherwise wish to do, and as involving our forswearing the doing of things that we would prefer to do. But our penchant for speaking of moral demands should not mislead us into regarding morality as something that must rival, and hence post a threat to, the fulfillment of our own needs and desires. Nor should moral motivation be seen as a species of motivation that is separate and distinct from people's sentiments and sympathies.

Seeing such things as food, shelter, and clean air as human needs involves the recognition that people suffer when they are deprived of them. If we take the needs of other people seriously, then we understand that those others suffer if their needs are not met. And if we care about those other people, then we are moved by their suffering. The improvement of their plight is thus not something to be seen purely as a moral obligation – where obligations are contrasted with desires – but is, rather, something that we want to happen. It becomes one of our own desires or needs. And our own welfare is not something that we should regard as opposed to the welfare of others. It is, rather, something that stands to be affected for the worse by our perception of others' misery, and for the better by the alleviation of that misery. It is thus a mistake to picture morally committed action as something that must be motivated by a cool, abstract determination of rightness, or to see it as something that can win out only if we deny our own "hot" desires and motives. Our perception of others' need and others' suffering can affect the shape of our own desires. Doing the right thing should thus not be viewed purely as a sacrifice, a threat to one's needs and desires; it should also be perceived as a way of expressing our own needs and desires. Those philanthropic individuals who deny that they have sacrificed a great deal in the service of morality may be engaging not in false modesty, but in truthful reporting. In performing their good deeds, they have done what they wanted to do. They are worthy of our admiration – and they are better people – because they take morality seriously, and thus many of their own desires converge with moral demands. They do not (merely) take morality seriously because they just happen to be, in some abstract and unworldly way, better people.

We are now in a better position to understand how the sanctification of the morally good person may be a source of hypocrisy. Being motivated to do good is something that often involves, or is an expression of, caring about the plight of others. When we express admiration for people who do things that we cannot bring ourselves to do, we may often misrepresent just what is involved in acting morally. It is seldom true that we care just as much about the sufferings of others but simply cannot steel ourselves to make what we regard as a large sacrifice. Rather – at least right now – we are confused about what doing good involves, or we simply care less, and pay lip-service to caring more.

I have discussed three types of hypocrisy that have roots in certain conceptions of what morality is. It may seem inevitable that there be a wide gap between our words and our deeds. Morality is demanding, and we want to meet its demands, both because we are moved by the suffering of others and because we want to be decent people. And we think that if more of us did what morality required more often, then we would have a better world, if not a morally perfect world. At the same time, we recognize that our world is not a perfect one: not all evils or sorrows are remediable, and even the most strenuous moral efforts may have unsatisfying results. Moreover, even good and conscientious people have some moral failings, and thus cannot or will not try to act well all the time. Being good is sometimes hard; humans are both finite and fallible, and things happen that are beyond our control.

It is this gap or tension that seems to be the source of hypocrisy, and cynicism. If we believe that morality asks more of us than we can reasonably hope to deliver, then we will learn to live with lowered expectations: not doing what we think we ought to do will be less the exception and more the rule. The realization that even if we tried as hard as we could to do the right thing, there would be evils and sorrows in the world, seems to excuse, if not justify, our trying less hard. For it may lead us to minimize the importance of our doing something, and to devalue the good that we can do by comparing it with the suffering that remains.

There would seem to be two ways to narrow the gap between word and deed: either cure human fallibility and finitude – something that is not likely to be achieved quickly, though we can surely take greater steps to reduce them – or scale down the demands of morality. And there are two obvious ways for us to scale down what we perceive as the excessive demands of morality. We could suppose that we are not, in fact, obliged to do as much as we think we are, and so that we have a mistaken view of what the correct moral principles are. Or we could suppose that, since morality cannot intelligibly be thought to demand more of us than we can provide, its demands must be easier to meet than we supposed. The first response invites us to reconsider the content of our moral principles, and to revise them in the light of careful reflection on our strengths and limitations. The second response allows us to keep our principles lofty – perhaps even ideal blueprintish – and has us (instead) revising our understanding of what sorts of actions those principles demand. Thus – to take a simple example – the first response might have us abandon the principle that enjoins us never to intentionally kill an innocent human being in favor of several less general and more restricted principles,[8] while the second response might have us hold on to the original principle, but reinterpret the notions of "intention," "innocence," "kill," and "human being" to allow for the possibility of justifiable killing in cases of capital punishment, self-defense, and euthanasia.

The second strategy is a familiar one, for it is a variant of one long employed by deontologists, and still favored by contemporary philosophers with deontological sympathies (e.g. Thomas Nagel, Alan Donagan, and Charles Fried.[9] Because I believe that it actually encourages the sort of sophistical thinking and hypocritical conduct that underlie the performative utterance view, it is not a strategy I favor.[10] Unless we think that true moral principles were etched in stone, or have other grounds for thinking that we must continue to espouse the principles enshrined in the Hebrew–Christian tradition, it seems better to revise the principles themselves than to revise our understanding of what it is to act in accord with them.

But the first strategy also has its drawbacks. If we scale down our moral principles to accord with what we believe are our limitations, then we may well set our sights too low. It is always easier for us to know, dwell on, and magnify the sacrifices that we would have to make than it is to empathize with the sufferings of others. Unless we suddenly develop the ability to be amazingly impartial with ourselves, and sympathetically more insightful into the plight of others, adopting the first strategy will result in our setting our moral standards too low. Morality will have lost an important part of its aspirational character.

Happily, there is another way to proceed. I have been suggesting throughout that our understanding of the nature of morality may be the source of various kinds of hypocrisy. Perhaps the problem lies not so much in the tension between a demanding morality and a fallible human nature, but in our seeing morality as external, the source of frustration, rather than fulfillment. The picture that dominates much of our thinking is one of a collection of autonomous agents each struggling to live his or her own good life while simultaneously dodging an increasingly heavy hail of moral demands. And our picture of the virtuous agent is largely that of someone who is either saintly, and thus altogether unmoved by the attractions of our good bourgeois lives, or reactive, willing simply to suspend his or her own concerns whenever the call comes to do good. Like a parent called from sleep by a crying child, doing good is viewed as a deep disturbance of the patterns of our lives. As one can function only if one gets up a maximum of once – or maybe twice – a night, one can break the rhythm of one's life to do good only infrequently if one is to have a good life.

Though it is only a partial solution, I believe that the remedy lies in fostering less reactive and individualistic conceptions of morality, ones that emphasize the fact that doing the right thing need not be a threat to one's needs and desires but can be, instead, a way of expressing them. Morally serious people should not be viewed as holy fools who just happen to be content with less, or as saints who find fulfillment in self-sacrifice. And moral commitments should not be viewed as things whose shape and import are eternal, fixed, and given, or as things that must do battle with our own personal interests and commitments. Rather, they may shape our other commitments and choices.[11]

NOTES

1   See *New York Times*, 8 Jan. 1990.
2   For a powerful discussion of how homelessness affects the lives of children, see Jonathan Kozol, *Rachel and Her Children* (New York: Crown, 1988).
3   One might maintain that this follows only if one does not adopt a consequentialist notion of wrongdoing. On a consequentialist view, we do the right thing (i.e. do not act wrongly) whenever we choose the best of the available options.
    The consequentialists' comparative notion of right and wrong appears to allow for the possibility of our doing the right thing even in the most dreadful of circumstances, in response to the more demented deeds of madmen,

murderers, or evil tyrants. But it seems plausible to suppose that consequentialists would also think that moral education must be increased in its rigor. For it is considerably more difficult to teach someone to do the right thing when that involves choosing the best of whatever options one might happen to face than it is to teach someone just to avoid doing a small number of kinds of things that can be identified in advance as (always) wrongful.

4   For good discussions of some of the common mistakes in moral mathematics, see Jonathan Glover, "It Makes No Difference Whether Or Not I Do It," *Proceedings of the Aristotelian Society*, suppl. vol. 49 (1975), and Derek Parfit, *Reasons and Persons* (Oxford: Oxford University Press, 1984), ch. 3.

5.   See *New York Times*, 8 Jan. 1990, and Jonathan B. Imber, *Abortion and the Private Practice of Medicine* (New Haven: Yale University Press, 1986), p. 68. Says a doctor who chose not to perform anything but therapeutic abortions:

> I hate doing them, but I do them every once in a while. But the real reason we try to avoid them is that I don't want to be known in the community as a local abortionist. I want to be known as a doctor who loves mommies and their babies. I don't care what is said, there is a stigma attached to doing abortions. There are political reasons not to earn the reputation as the local abortionist, I mean, to be known as the physician who will perform abortions whenever asked.

6   Among the things that must be equal: we have not promised to do something, or otherwise undertaken "special obligations" via our jobs, roles, etc.

7   From *The Question of German Guilt*; quoted in Jonathan Glover, *Causing Death and Saving Lives* (New York: Penguin, 1977), p. 92.

8   This is not the only option; one could abandon that principle and other specific ones in favor of a more general principle that generates or orders all obligations, e.g. a consequentialist principle.

9   See Alan Donagan, *The Theory of Morality* (Chicago: University of Chicago Press, 1977); Charles Fried, *Right and Wrong* (Cambridge, Mass.: Harvard University Press, 1978); and Thomas Nagel, *The View From Nowhere* (Oxford: Oxford University Press, 1986).

10   I have tried to explain why at greater length in "The Doctrine of Double Effect: Problems of Interpretation," in *Pacific Philosophical Quarterly*, vol. 65 (1984), and "Contemporary Deontology," in Peter Singer, ed., *A Companion to Ethics* (Oxford: Blackwell, forthcoming).

11   I wish to thank Dale Jamieson for his helpful comments.

Part II
General Issues Related to the Fields of Applied Ethics

Business Ethics

10
How to Think Systematically About Business Ethics

Michael Philips

Philips characterizes current business ethics as dominated by disputes between "minimalists" – those, like Milton Friedman, who insist that the ethics of business should be minimal – and moral philosophers who attempt to restrain minimalism by appeal to higher standards, of social responsibility and so forth. But these efforts at restraint are typically unsystematic and atheoretic because they proceed by importing into the assessment of business practice a variety of precepts and principles that obtain in other domains of social life. This strategy relies on what Philips calls the "constancy assumption," the assumption, roughly, that if a principle applies in one domain of social life, it must apply – with the same force and meaning – in other domains as well. But the constancy assumption leads, inadvertently, to "maximalism," in that no one who criticizes business practices by appeal to principles drawn from the center of our moral tradition has shown how we are to stop short of applying virtually all of them, and with the same force as we do in other spheres. Philips responds to this problem by sketching a theoretical perspective on what moralities are and how they are properly evaluated. He calls this point of view "ethics as social policy" and employs it in the rest of the paper to organize and illuminate our understanding of the whole field of business ethics. The key to his argument is the claim that, contrary to the constancy assumption, the various domains of social life are each in part defined by a set of socially recognized goals or purposes which serve to justify moral standards relative to that domain.

Philips's article should be compared with those of Rachels (chapter 6), Sikora (chapter 5), Winkler (chapter 19), and Hoffmaster (chapter 20), as well as with the others in this section on business ethics. A particular focus of comparison in the case of the papers just named is Philips's account of "ethics as social policy" and its formula for the evaluation of domains of social morality.

The cliché that "business ethics" is an oxymoron sometimes expresses a low opinion of the character of businesspeople: they are ruthless, heartless, crass, deceitful, etc. But it may also reflect the more interesting view that the ethics of business are and should be minimal. Physical force, outright fraud, theft, breach of contract, and, perhaps, violations of the law are and should be prohibited. Otherwise anything goes. In short, many familiar moral standards may be completely ignored; and principles central to our moral and religious tradition may be violated without a second thought. The strong may bully the weak, the cunning may exploit the innocence and goodwill of their trusting neighbors, the environment may be fouled and the fabulously wealthy may further enrich themselves at the expense of the desperately poor. More generally, people may treat others only as means in various ways and everyone is entitled to cause great misery in others for the sake of small personal gain.

Not surprisingly, this barely constrained egoism – this moral minimalism – appalls most moral philosophers. And the discipline of business ethics has emerged largely as a result of their insistence on higher standards. But this insistence has been unsystematic and atheoretic. Philosophers criticize (or defend) various business practices in the name of a variety of precepts or principles that obtain in other domains of life or that are central to our moral tradition. But there is rarely if ever a serious attempt to show that the principles in question are relevant to the business domain. Very roughly, the assumption is that if a principle (precept, rule) applies in one domain it applies – with equal force and the same interpretation – in other domains as well. I call this the constancy assumption and I have argued against it elsewhere. Ethics is not domain-insensitive in this way.[1]

If we accept the constancy assumption, the minimalism of Milton Friedman is rejected in favor of a kind of moral maximalism. No one explicitly endorses maximalism, but no one who criticizes business practices by appealing to precepts from outside business life shows how we can stop short of it. In what follows I propose a principled middle ground between minimalism and maximalism. Sometimes business practices are rightly criticized on the basis of considerations that apply in other domains, sometimes they are not. To think systematically about business ethics we need a method for telling the difference, and that is what I hope to provide.

Any attempt to think systematically about the ethics of a social practice must proceed from some theoretical point of view. Specifically, it must be based on assumptions about what moralities are and how they are properly evaluated. I describe my own perspective in the next section. Obviously I cannot defend it adequately here. But the following account of the way in which this perspective organizes and illuminates the domain of business ethics should testify to its power. And most of that analysis should stand on its own. Readers who are not particularly interested in questions of ethical theory should feel free to skip the following section and move directly to that account.

Ethics as Social Policy

For many centuries, most Europeans identified morality with the law of God. More recently, moral philosophy has turned secular. But much of it retains a central feature of the religious view. Roughly, and most importantly, it retains the view that the term "morality" is a proper name for a code of conduct that is binding on us by virtue of the sorts of beings we are and that is sufficient for the moral life. That code is knowable and every historical code – the morality of any society – is evaluated by reference to it. This secular view differs from most religious views by holding that the code is accessible to us by reason rather than by faith. But both religionists and the relevant secularists share the view that moral standards are discovered, not devised or invented.

Many philosophers – myself included – deny that "morality" is a proper name for a supercode. There is no supercode. The term "morality" stands to moralities as the term "language" stands to languages. Like languages, moralities are human artifacts and are to be evaluated by how well they serve us. These evaluations admit of objectivity. Our choices between standards are not mere matters of taste. But different standards may be justified for different groups and for the same group at different times.[2] The proper terms of evaluation for moral standards are not "true" and "false" but rather "reasonable" or "unreasonable." I call this way of thinking about ethics "instrumentalism."

According to instrumental theories, moral standards are like social policies. The main difference is that policies are established by officially designated bodies, and do not require the allegiance of large numbers of people. Moralities, on the other hand, typically evolve and do require allegiance.[3] If most people in a society do not accept a moral standard, that standard is not an element in that society's morality. When moralities are raised to the level of self-consciousness and evaluated, however, they are evaluated in precisely the same way as policies are.

Given the biological similarities between human beings and the requirements of social life, we can expect certain broad similarities between the reasonable moral codes of various social groups. All such codes will regulate homicide, property exchanges, sexuality, etc. But historically, groups have regulated these activities in very different ways. And given the various conditions of human life, such differences may be reasonable. That is, the specific rules governing homicide, property exchanges, sexuality, etc. may differ from place to place and these differences may be justified.

Moreover, the standards governing these activities may reasonably vary from domain to domain within a given society. Roughly, my own version of instrumentalism differs from other versions by emphasizing this domain sensitivity of ethical standards. It also holds that concrete, domain-specific values play important roles in justifying moral standards. Thus, for example, our standards governing family relations are justified in relation to the concrete goods of family life (intimacy, security, etc.). By virtue of the relative concreteness of this approach, disputes about ethical standards resemble disputes about social policy even more than they do on other versions of instrumentalism. Accordingly, I call this view "ethics as social policy" (EASP).

According to EASP, then, the standards governing homicide, property exchanges, truth-telling, and other such activities differ within a society from domain to domain. Many standards, moreover, are specific to particular domains. This is what is meant by "domain sensitivity." Now is not the time for a rigorous definition of "domain," but the general idea is clear enough. Examples of domains include the family, the educational system, the scientific community, the criminal justice system, the medical system, the economic system, etc.

Roughly, each domain is characterized by a set of socially recognized goals or purposes and by a set of "structures." Among other things, for example, the family is supposed to provide intimacy and love and to nurture children, the scientific community is supposed to deliver truths about nature, and the criminal justice system is supposed to deter crime and otherwise protect our rights as citizens. Unless they can be shown to be unreasonable, these goals count as justificatory values for their respective domains. And moral standards that obtain in a domain are justified in relation to them (as well as in relation to other values).

As suggested, domains are also structured. A domain structure is a set of related roles or positions.[4] Corresponding to any role or position are: (1) some set of qualifying standards (i.e. criteria that govern who or what counts as a role occupant); (2) some set of rights and duties; (3) some system of remuneration and other rewards or penalties; and (4) some set of ideals or virtues and vices (i.e. characteristics that are admired and condemned in role occupants). Taken together, these elements define a role or position. As one can see, various ethical standards are built into roles. Indeed, many of the most important questions of professional ethics are questions about what these elements should be. Most of the standard questions of medical ethics, for example, are questions about what qualifies one to be a patient (i.e. to receive various forms of treatment) or a practitioner; what rights and duties one has as an occupant of these roles; what traits we should encourage in people who occupy them; and on what basis people should be rewarded or penalized for role-related conduct. Assuming that domain-related goods and evils of medicine stand up to rational scrutiny, we answer such questions (in part) by considering whether some particular distribution of rights, powers, ideals, etc. in that domain delivers the goods (constrained by impacts on other domains).[5]

We are now in a position to see how EASP differs from standard versions of rule utilitarianism and contractarianism. These theories begin with very general accounts of goods and evils and try to justify social moralities in relation to them. They move from the top down. EASP moves from the bottom up. We begin with the goods and evils that play justificatory roles in the various domains of social life. We grant these presumptive status, that is, we assume that they are reasonable unless they can be shown to be unreasonable. And, very roughly, we evaluate the moral structure of a domain in relation to reasonable values for that domain (constrained by impacts on other domains).

Before the development of applied ethics, philosophers paid little attention to role-defined moral standards. In so far as they were interested in normative questions at all, as opposed to questions about moral language, they focused their attention on moral considerations that were supposed to be binding on us merely as persons or human beings. It was widely assumed that we could generate role-related standards by applying these "basic" or "core" precepts to specific circumstances (much as we apply basic principles of physics to solve problems of engineering). Few writers in applied and professional ethics now accept this engineering model. But EASP rejects it in a particularly radical way. For it holds that there is no important difference in kind between "core" standards and role-defined standards. Both sorts of standards are domain-sensitive. And, roughly speaking, both are justified in the same way.

"Core" standards like "don't kill" and "don't steal" seem to be more fundamental than role-defined standards like "don't neglect your children" and "pay workers a living wage" in part because they seem to be perfectly general. But few of them apply in every domain. For example, soldiers are expected to kill during war, and active euthanasia is arguably permissible. Moreover, both the importance of and, in some cases, our criteria for applying core standards vary from domain to domain as well. Other things being equal, for example, it is worse to fail to rescue family members than to fail to rescue strangers. And what counts as x's stealing from y often depends on how x and y are related to one another. These domain-related variations in the weight of moral standards explain why the constancy assumption is false.[6]

In more general terms, EASP holds that the purpose of a moral code is to protect and promote a reasonably valued way of life; or, more precisely, a way of life that is reasonably valued from an impartial point of view. And a way of life is reasonably valued from this point of view if – given the historical conditions – it produces an adequate balance of good over evil for all those affected. EASP provides accounts of both "adequate balance" and "goods" and "evils." I cannot review these here, but all these accounts are domain-sensitive. That is, they move from the bottom up by taking as their starting points the goods and evils and distributive criteria that are already in place. Again, EASP grants these domain-specific values and distributive criteria presumptive standing. Unless they can be shown to be unreasonable, we justify moral standards in relation to them. The theory devotes considerable attention to argument strategies for showing that they are unreasonable, but I cannot review these here. I will, however, produce an example of this in what follows.

How to Think Systematically about the Economic Domain

Reflections on the ethics of the economic domain typically occur under two headings: political economy and business ethics. Political economy proceeds at the macro level. To the extent that it is normative, it asks: what set of basic economic institutions serves us best? Here the most basic institution is property. And the question is: what forms or rules of property ownership and exchange serve us best? The traditional candidates are *laissez-faire* capitalism (unregulated private ownership and exchange), regulated capitalism (private ownership with restrictions on ownership and exchange), and various forms of socialism (public ownership, with varying degrees of central planning or control).

Business ethics is a relatively new area in philosophy and its boundaries are not precise. For the most part it addresses questions that arise within the context of capitalism. Many of these questions are wholly or partly about the degree to which private ownership and exchange should be regulated (i.e. about the form of capitalism we should adopt). At a certain point these questions become questions of political economy (the difference is one of degree). But many questions are considerably more specific than that (e.g. those concerning whistleblowing, affirmative action, and corporate responsibility). In any case, however we answer the questions of political economy – even if we are socialists – those of us who live under capitalism will also need to answer the more specific questions of business ethics. This suggests an important theme, namely the fact that a set of basic institutions is flawed does not by itself entail that those institutions impose no obligations.

EASP employs the same basic strategy for questions of both political economy and business ethics. The difference is that in addressing questions of business ethics it takes capitalist institutions as background conditions.

In relation to political economy, the question is, roughly: what general set of economic institutions best promotes the goals of the economic domain? In relation to business ethics, the questions are, roughly: (1) What form of capitalist institutions best promote these goals (i.e. to what degree should private ownership and use of property be regulated)? and (2) given the institutions currently in place, what more specific distribution of rights, duties, virtues, vices, etc. best promotes these goals? These formulations are rough since we also need to take into account the ways in which various answers affect the distribution of goods in other domains. (Some of the most interesting socialist arguments against capitalism contend that capitalism by its nature is corrosive of them.) In any case, EASP holds that disputes about political economy and business ethics are disputes about the ends of economic life and how they are best promoted.

I now want to illustrate how this strategy helps in thinking systematically about business ethics.

As suggested, the strategy is to assess the wisdom of candidate principles in relation to the goods and evils at stake in the economic domain (and, as appropriate, to a more general class of goods and evils as well). What are these goods and evils? That is, what goods do we, collectively and impartially, want from an economy? I will propose a vague but reasonable answer and show that, vague as it is, it enables us to settle certain important points of difference between theorists.

To begin with, other things being equal, we want as much prosperity as we can get, given our resources and technology. Prosperity, of course, is not reducible to the aggregate volume or value of goods and services (e.g. to gross national product). A society that produces an enormous volume of goods that very few people want or need, for example pyramids or jet-powered snowmobiles, is not prosperous in the relevant sense. A society is prosperous to the extent that its members enjoy the material basis for a good life (I will call goods that meet this description "life-enhancing" goods). Very roughly, life-enhancing goods promote "fits." To provide prosperity, then, an economy must produce the right kinds of goods and distribute them to the appropriate people. The variety and magnitude of these goods will vary with cultural values and environmental conditions. What enhances life in New York may ruin life in Eden. I will ignore these complexities here.

Prosperity also has a distributive dimension. A society that produces an enormous volume of goods but makes them available to very few people is not a prosperous one. Here, as above, I am stipulating a particular sense of "prosperity." But it is the sense that captures what interests us when we are giving an account of the reasonable goals of the economic domain from an impartial point of view. We want the best overall pattern

of "fits," impartially considered. Although there is no one rationally compelling abstract principle for deciding this, certain distributions can be
excluded. And this includes most historically actual ones.

Production and distribution are not the only dimensions of prosperity.
We also need to consider certain "externalities." For example, an economy
does less to provide the material basis for a good life to the extent that
it poisons its air, food, and water and destroys the beauty of the land.
Accordingly, these evils must be subtracted from the goods of productive
activity in estimating the life-enhancing value of the whole. This is another
reason that the GNP is a bad measure of social prosperity. Ironically, the
damages in question may lead to increases in the GNP. When water and
air are poisoned, pure water becomes a commodity, and industries devoted
to water and air filtration flourish.

The second goal of the economic domain, maximizing the quality of
working life, also has several dimensions. Most of us spend more than
half our waking time working, so we have a considerable stake in the
quality of our job experience. Other things being equal, we want our jobs
to be safe, socially useful, secure, and interesting. We also want them to
preserve our dignity, that is, we want to eliminate demeaning occupational
statuses and demeaning work relationships. In addition, we want our jobs
to leave us with sufficient time and energy to enjoy our home life and to
develop other interests. Of course, there will be trade-offs among these
goals and between them and the goal of prosperity. But we do not need
to worry about that now.[7]

Suppose one accepts these as basic economic goods. In that case EASP
holds that we can decide basic questions of political economy and business
ethics primarily in relation to them. According to EASP, the best set of
basic economic institutions is (roughly) the one that advances these goals
best while doing the least damage to the goals of other domains. And the
best business ethic is the one that satisfies this description within a
framework of capitalist institutions. Vague as this is, it is enough to show
why minimalism demands too little and those who import principles may
demand too much.

Let us begin with the imported principles approach. Moral criticisms
of business practices take at least three forms. Practices are said to violate
human rights, to violate some principle of commonsense morality, or to
violate some abstract principle central to our tradition (e.g. that persons
should be treated as ends in themselves, or that practices must satisfy
rules that promote utility). According to EASP, these criticisms are valid
only if the precepts on which they are based can be shown to be relevant
to the business domain. And they are only as powerful as those precepts
are in that domain. Both issues are decided by determining to what extent
adopting these precepts promotes the social goals of business activity (and

prevents business activity from undermining other goods). Let us apply this to the kinds of criticisms just sketched.

Consider human rights. According to business ethicist Patricia Werhane, free expression and due process are human rights.[8] Accordingly, businesses violate human rights if they penalize their employees for exercising their right to free expression or if they penalize employees without due process.[9] Unfortunately, however, Werhane does not provide us with a principled basis for fixing the scope or importance of these rights in the domain of business. Clearly they do not have the same scope or force there as they do, for example, in the political realm. What scope and importance should we grant them?

Let us take the example of free expression. The American courts have ruled that our right to free expression *against the state* includes the right to dress more or less as we please. Should we have this right against businesses? If we did we could dress as we pleased on the job, that is, there could be no dress codes or uniforms at all. However, there are obvious economic arguments in favor of dress codes and uniforms in a wide range of occupations, and there are no domain-related arguments against them (although, of course, they should not be stronger than they need to be to realize their objectives). Moreover, restrictions on dress very rarely undermine the goods at issue in other domains and exceptions can be made when these harms are sufficiently strong (as, for example, where religious values are at stake).[10]

Political expression works differently. The political domain is undermined if employers are allowed to prevent employees from making public speeches, participating in political demonstrations, and so forth. Particular companies may have economic reasons for imposing such restrictions, for example, they might lose customers if highly visible employees take politically controversial stands. But it is not clear that this sort of thing will undermine the goods of the economic domain *as a whole*. And it is clear that such restrictions on political expression directly and seriously undermine the goods of the political domain (e.g. the goods of democracy). According to the minimalist, employees have no rights to free expression against businesses (e.g. one can be fired for expressing political views on or off the job); according to the maximalist, they have the same right to free expression against businesses as they have against the state. On Werhane's account, it is not clear on what principled basis the right to free expression against businesses should be delimited. The EASP approach explains how to draw the line.[11]

The same holds for due process. According to the minimalist account, employers have no obligation to provide workers with opportunities to appeal dismissals, demotions, and so forth. According to the maximalist, they are obligated to provide them with the same safeguards they enjoy against the state. Again, EASP allows us to take a principled middle position. There are good job-quality reasons for grievance procedures. Workers are protected against the exercise of arbitrary power, job security is enhanced, etc. However, we can achieve these without instituting the elaborate range of safeguards maximalism would require (lawyers, juries, etc.). So, as Werhane in fact recommends (but without a principled basis), some compromise is in order.

Moreover, there are good reasons for varying both the grounds and the procedures for grievance from one kind of enterprise to another. Thus, for example, other things being equal, corporate managers should not be allowed to make personnel decisions on the basis of personal relationships or likes and dislikes. This is inefficient and creates a low-quality working environment. But personal considerations might be a reasonable basis for hirings, firings, and so forth in small, owner-operated businesses or family businesses. In small businesses, the quality of the work environment and everyone's job performance may depend heavily on goodwill among the employees and between the owner and her workforce. And, of course, it is hard to know how one could have a family business if one could not hire family members preferentially. Obviously, moreover, small businesses cannot afford the time and energy for elaborate courtroom-like grievance procedures that might be appropriate to a large corporation.

We turn now to the second form of importation, namely criticisms that proceed from some standard of commonsense morality.

Such criticisms are common. They appear in sermons, in editorials, and in speeches by business leaders themselves. In his ground-breaking book, *The Moral Foundations of Professional Ethics*, Alan Goldman attempts to provide a theoretical defense of this approach in relation to business (and the professions in general).[12] On Goldman's view, businesspeople (and professionals in general) are sometimes exempt from ordinary moral constraints. But they are exempt only if granting exemptions can be justified in terms of more important *moral* considerations (or, for him, rights). That is, professionals and businesspeople are exempt from a commonsense, *prima facie* duty D in their domains if and only if honoring that precept in that domain violates D', a more important *prima facie* duty. Since Goldman believes that we can make this judgment on a domain-by-domain basis, his view is domain-sensitive. But since he holds that we make these judgments by making trade-offs between a set of (presumably) constantly weighted duties and obligations, it is not domain-sensitive enough.

Consider this account in relation to lying. Goldman would condemn lying in business except in contexts where there is an important moral reason to lie (a reason that outweighs the wrong of lying). But consider lying in business bargaining ("That's my last offer"; "If you don't, I'll take all my business elsewhere," etc.). There seems to be no *moral* reason favoring such lies. But they seem harmless enough. One's "last offer" can always be sweetened if rejected. And the seller can always accept an offer he had (falsely) described as utterly out of the question. Nothing is lost when businesspeople engage in this commonplace strategy. Indeed, the game dimension adds interest to the negotiator's job.[13]

Other lies in business are far more serious, for example, lying about the characteristics of one's products or lying about the terms agreed to in verbal contract agreements. This can be explained in EASP terms. The former lies obviously interfere with getting the right goods to the right people. The latter lies undermine trust in verbal agreements and destroy a useful economic resource. These lies are more serious precisely because they interfere with the goals of economic life.

We now turn to the third form of criticism based on importation: criticism made on the basis of higher-level principles. Consider Kant's principle that we should never treat another person as a means only. Although it is not entirely clear what this means, at the very least it forbids us to disregard the good or interests of those affected by our actions. Yet business life abounds with cases in which we disregard the interests of others. It is difficult to see how a market economy could function otherwise. If we had to treat everyone as an end in himself, we could not win business from a competitor without considering the impact of our decisions on that competitor's life (will she be driven out of business? Will her income be so reduced that she cannot send her children to college? And so on). Nor could we reject offers from prospective house-buyers or renters *merely* because we could get a better price elsewhere (where will they end up living or how much benefit would they get from one's house? etc.). In areas in which a market economy is justified, people must be free to meet as buyers and sellers, considering one another merely as means to each other's financial ends. Of course, charity is permitted. But it cannot be obligatory. Markets could not survive routinized charity-driven decision-making. *If* there are good economic arguments for a market economy, *then* we cannot be required to treat others as ends in themselves in bargaining contexts.[14]

But there are also business contexts where we *should* take the interests of otheres into account. It is wrong to use high-pressure sales techniques to sell people what they neither need nor want, to underproduce some necessary good in order to keep the price high, to pay starvation wages to people who are desperate for work if one can afford more, etc.[15] These particular ways of treating others as means retard prosperity as I have described it.[16] In one way or another they prevent us from getting the right goods to people on a sufficiently large scale. The problem with

Kant's principle is vagueness. We need to know *when* and *how* we are required to take the good of others into account in our actions. EASP provides us with a principled basis for answering that question.

In sum, many well-motivated responses to the minimalism of Milton Friedman and his followers involve importing principles from other areas into the business domain. But no one has yet provided an adequate principled bias for doing this. EASP does. Nonetheless, minimalists will argue that EASP requires too much, so we should also review the EASP case against minimalism.

One theoretical foundation of minimalism is libertarian. Property rights are said to be natural rights; and the exercise of those rights is said to be limited only by a very narrow range of moral side constraints (namely, those mentioned earlier). Any transaction, exchange, or strategy that falls outside the range of these constraints is simply the exercise of a right, and is therefore beyond moral criticism.

The main argument against this natural rights approach is that appeals to natural rights are based on appeals to intuition about principles or cases, or to appeals to the nature of persons, and they have no sound theoretical basis. According to EASP, the rules governing acquisition, use, and exchange may differ reasonably from culture to culture, and from historical period to historical period. These rules delimit recognized property rights (and hence define "property"). And there is no set of "real" or "true" property rights in relation to which they can be evaluated. Rather, other things being equal, they are justified by how well they satisfy the purposes of economic life.

Even if there were natural property rights, minimalism would not follow. Natural rights provide us with protections against certain sorts of interferences by other persons or the state, but they do not provide us with moral carte blanche. Within those protected boundaries, there are plenty of chances to act immorally. Thus, the right to free association does not morally entitle us socially to exclude someone for petty or malicious reasons. The right to free speech does not morally entitle us to gossip maliciously or say hurtful and insulting things for our own entertainment. And the right to property does not morally entitle us to pay our workers starvation wages whenever the market allows.

There is also a second defense of minimalism as well, a defense in the spirit of Adam Smith. According to this defense, private selfishness in the economic realm best promotes the goals of the economic domain. This defense is consistent with the general methodology of EASP. I object to it because I think it is based on an excessively narrow view of the goals of the economic domain and because I disagree with its assessment of the capacity of the free market to realize those goals.

As indicated, I take these goals to include the quality of working life.

A minimalist might reject this goal or he might believe that the invisible hand assures it. If the latter, our dispute is empirical. If the former, he surely needs an argument. Although people are often willing to sacrifice certain dimensions of job quality for higher wages, the quality of working life is obviously important to almost everyone. According to EASP, it is a presumptive good of the economic domain. And the minimalist needs an argument against it.[17]

The minimalist might respond that minimalist business practices so far outstrip morally constrained practices in producing wealth that they provide everyone with a better prosperity/job-quality package even if some job quality is lost. Again, this argument may be empirical, axiological, or some combination of the two. To the degree that it is empirical, the minimalist accepts my account of "prosperity" (and uses "wealth" as a synonym for it). To the extent this is so, we differ on whether minimalist practices do a better job than morally constrained practices at producing and distributing life-enhancing goods, where externalities are taken into account. The arguments are economic but the burden of proof is surely on the minimalist. For the straightforward examples are on the other side. Every time a corporation refuses to produce assault rifles, pollute the air, or lower wages to the minimum it refuses to reduce prosperity as I understand it. The minimalist needs to show that the collective positive impact of unconstrained profit maximization on prosperity is sufficient to compensate for such obvious losses.

Of course, the Adam Smith minimalist might reject my account of prosperity as a goal of economic life.[18] But to reject prosperity from an impartial point of view is (roughly) to oppose getting the right goods to the right people on a wide scale with the least destruction to the environment. Clearly one needs a powerful argument for rejecting this.

It may also be that the minimalist accepts an additional goal, namely the opportunity to become fabulously rich by hard work and intelligence (or simply the opportunity to become fabulously rich). Perhaps he takes this to be more important than one or more of the dimensions of prosperity (or job quality). He acknowledges the value of these presumptive goods, but he believes that they are subordinate to promoting the opportunity for great riches. And he believes that minimalism is necessary to promote that opportunity. Accordingly, he rejects all but the most minimal ethical constraints on property acquisition and use (i.e. all but those required for there to be any orderly system at all).

In evaluating this view we need to consider how much *more* opportunity of this kind there would be in a minimalist economy (if any) and how important these opportunities are (or would be) to how many people (under epistemically ideal conditions). We then need to consider how much prosperity and job quality we would have to give up on average to secure these additional opportunities. In the last analysis we are faced with a choice between packages. The contents of these packages will depend on the economic beliefs we hold. On some factual scenarios, for example my own, the choice between packages will be easy. The switch to a minimalist ethic (and minimalist legal regulations) will provide very little new opportunity for individuals to become fabulously wealthy, and will be very costly in other ways. Like the lottery, it is a bad risk (considered impartially). But some will dispute my version of the facts.

In this section, I have illustrated the use of EASP in the economic domain. The discussion has been highly general. The main point has not been to settle issues, but to show how EASP enables us to stake out a principled middle ground between minimalism and maximalism. Obviously, to defend specific positions on the issues requires additional empirical argument and a further specification of the goals of economic life (for example, we may disagree on the best distributive patterns, on trade-offs between job quality and life-enhancing goods, on the relative importance of wilderness areas, etc.). Some of these differences might be overcome by further argument. Others may not.[19]

NOTES

1   See my paper "Weighing Moral Reasons," *Mind*, vol. 96 (July 1987).
2   In fact, it might be the case that two or more codes are equally reasonable for a given group at a given time.
3   There are societies in which moralities are established by official bodies and imposed on the population. However, if the population resists, the society as a whole does not subscribe to the morality. Subscribing to a morality requires, among other things, holding certain beliefs and having certain affective responses.
4   At a certain level of description, roles may be occupied by institutions as well as by individuals. There are complicated questions about the degree to which institutions can themselves be reduced to sets of roles or positions occupied by individuals. Business ethicists, for example, have a good deal of trouble deciding whether talk about an institution's acts is really shorthand for talk about the actions of role occupants within institutions. The problem is that responsibility for institutional actions is not always easy to assign.
5   There are, of course, disputes about what precisely these goods are. Also, as the parenthetical qualification suggests, no domain can be evaluated exclusively in relation to the goods and evils specific to it. The organization of one domain very often has important impacts on the organization of other domains (e.g., economic structures importantly affect political structures, family life, and so forth). And the fact that the structure of one domain may have adverse impacts on the reasonable values of another counts as an argument against it.

6   For a more detailed discussion of this see "Weighing Moral Reasons." Also, it is worth noting that "core" standards differ from role-defined standards in important ways. To begin with, "core" standards regulate types of action that occur in a wide range of domains. And, although they regulate those activities differently in different domains, many regulations are also the same. We are permitted to kill in self-defense in every domain and we are nowhere permitted to kill other people merely for sport. These identities are not explained in relation to domain-specific goods. They are explained in relation to the more general set of goods on the basis of which domain-specific goods are evaluated. Roughly, the primary objection to killing is that it deprives others of life.

7   Of course we also want our jobs to be high-paying, but that falls under the heading of prosperity. To get goods to the right people on a wide enough basis we must supply people with buying power.

8   Patricia Werhane, "Individual Rights in Business," in Tom Regan, ed., *Just Business*, Random House, New York, 1984, pp. 100–26.

9   Ibid., pp. 107–20.

10 In 1990 the Canadian Sikh community complained that the Royal Canadian Mounted Police violated their rights by requiring that RCMP officers wear the familiar Mountie hat. Sikhs, who often work in law enforcement, are required by their religion to wear turbans. So the RCMP's dress code does undermine an important good. But clearly, the right to free expression does not entitle one to express himself anyway he wants in any circumstance. It is not just that one cannot cry "Fire!" in a crowded theater; one is rightly evicted for talking loudly during a performance as well. Similarly, employers may rightly fire workers who carry on in loud, obnoxious ways that interfere with work, and teachers may penalize students for doing the same. The right to free expression does not trump our competing concerns in these cases, nor should it.

11 Werhane's actual policy suggestions are domain-sensitive and intelligent. But she tries to settle the matter by appealing to general human rights and her account of these rights is universalist and non domain-sensitive at all. She says, for example, that if anyone has them everyone has them and has them equally (even if they are members of different societies with different structures): Werhane, "Individual Rights in Business," esp. pp. 104–5.

12 Alan Goldman, *The Moral Foundations of Professional Ethics*, Rowan and Littlefield, New York, 1980.

13 The fact that people expect lies in such situations does not change the fact that they are lies. One still speaks falsely with the intent to deceive.

14 We can require that people are treated with respect in various ways. We should be polite, we should not lie about our product, and so forth. But when it comes to accepting or rejecting offers from prospective buyers, or offering a competitor's client a better deal, we cannot be required to take as our first priority the impact our decision will have on the lives of those affected. A Kantian might hold that this is sufficient for respect in these circumstances, and argue that respect itself is domain-specific. But short of

appealing to intuitions I do not see how he could do that without appealing to domain-specific goods and evils. If one appeals to domain-specific goods and evils to fix the requirements of respectful treatment, I do not see how one gets anything from respect alone. In that case, respect functions as a kind of summary term for the ways in which people ought to be treated, where that is determined in EASP terms.

15   It is harder to decide whether there should be laws against some or all these activities, and if so, how strong these laws should be. It is clear that there should be a strong moral feeling against them.

16   It might be objected that harsh business practices were necessary to fuel rapid economic development, and that rapid economic development benefits generations to come. Our assessment of this argument depends in part on the degree to which we think the rate of economic development depends on harsh practices. Once we establish the rate, we compare various kinder practice/slower rate scenarios to various crueler practice/faster rate scenarios and see which do the best for all concerned. To do this we need to know to what degree we should discount the interests of future generations.

17   The extent to which we should rely on legislation to protect job quality is a separate question. One could consistently argue that our moral standards should require that employers sustain a certain level of job quality without arguing that they should be legally required to sustain it. However, given the ineffectiveness of merely moral criticism with respect to this matter in the past, this seems an implausible position. Unless it is expressed in law, moral opinion will not do much to protect job quality.

18   The libertarian minimalist, of course, rejects the view that economic life should have goals. Or in any case, she holds that the ethics of economic life are entirely independent of them. The Adam Smith minimalist, on the other hand, agrees that the ethics of economic activity are instrumental. So she could consistently accept the general EASP picture. My difference with her in part concerns the goals in relation to which the instrument is judged.

19   Some disputes that now appear unresolvable may later turn out to have powerful arguments in their favor. There is a developing body of argument to the effect that almost everyone would be better off were people taught to be more appreciative of nature or more connected to living things in general. It is perfectly conceivable that this line of argument will be developed to the point that it becomes compelling. One can imagine studies of various kinds that would greatly strengthen the case.

11
Corporate Roles, Personal Virtues: An Aristotelian Approach to Business Ethics

Robert C. Solomon

Solomon takes issue with business ethicists who attempt to derive guidance for businesspeople from classical ethical theories such as those of Kant, Locke, and Mill. Abstract theories lack applicability, he argues, because they are insensitive to the contexts in which business activity takes place, and to the particular roles played by people in business. He also expresses misgivings about the tendency of many business ethicists to focus exclusively on rather large-scale questions about government policies regarding business or general business practices. Discussions of general policy issues fail to address what Solomon regards as the most important concern of business ethics, namely a consideration of how persons should act in their business roles and in their roles as citizens of a larger community. Given this sort of concern, relevant theory will consist in reflection on the nature of the virtues required by businesspeople and their cultivation.

Although Solomon characterizes his view as "virtue ethics" and traces its lineage to Aristotle, he is careful to distinguish it from several other kinds of virtue ethics theories, including those that see virtues as consisting merely of dispositions to follow moral principles and those that evince nostalgia for a relatively homogeneous community within which virtue can develop. Six ingredients are identified as making up the framework of virtue ethics in business: community, excellence, role identity, holism, integrity, and judgment.

This paper should be compared not only with other papers in the section on business ethics but also with the papers by Winkler (chapter 19) and Hoffmaster (chapter 20), whose main themes involve skepticism about the usefulness of attempting to resolve practical issues by directly applying the abstract principles of classical theories. Jamieson's remarks about the value of a shift in environmental

Portions of this essay were delivered in March 1989 as part of the Ruffin Lectures at the Darden School of Business, University of Virginia, published as R. Edward Freeman, ed., *Business and the Humanities* (Oxford University Press, 1993). Three subsequent versions have also been published, in *Business Ethics Quarterly*, vol. 2, no. 3 (July 1992), in the *Proceedings of the International Association for Business and Society* (with N. Imparato), published as D. Ludwig, K. Paul, eds, *Contemporary Issues in the Business Environment* (Lewiston: Mellen Press, 1992), and in Australia in J. A. C. Coady and C. Sampform, eds, *Proceedings of the Center for Philosophy and Public Issues* (Canberra: Federation Press, 1993). I have greatly expanded the theory in *Ethics and Excellence: Cooperation and Integrity* (New York: Oxford University Press, 1992).

ethics from concentration on specific actions and their consequences to a focus on virtues and dispositions of character (chapter 17) also provide a worthwhile point of comparison.

We are thankfully past that embarrassing period when the very title of a lecture on "business ethics" invited – even required – those malapert responses, "sounds like an oxymoron" or "must be a very short lecture." Today, business ethics is not only well established as part of the standard curriculum in most philosophy departments but, more impressively, is a recommended or required subject in most of the leading business schools in North America, and it is even catching on in Europe (one of the too rare instances of intellectual commerce in that direction). Studies in business ethics have now reached what Tom Donaldson has called "the third wave," having gone beyond the hastily compiled and overly philosophical introductory textbooks and collections of obvious specific case studies to serious engagement in the business world. Conferences filled half-and-half with business executives and academics are common, and in-depth studies based on immersion in the corporate world, such as Robert Jackall's powerful *Moral Mazes*, have replaced more simple-minded and detached glosses on "capitalism" and "social responsibility."[1] Business ethics has moved beyond vulgar "business as poker" arguments into an arena where serious ethical theory is no longer out of place but seriously sought out and much in demand.

The problem with business ethics now is not simple ignorance but a far more sophisticated confusion concerning exactly what the subject is supposed to do and how (to employ a much overworked contrast) the theory applies to the practice of business. Indeed, a large part of the problem is that it is by no means clear what a theory in business ethics is supposed to look like or whether there is, as such, any such theoretical enterprise. It has been standard practice in many business ethics courses and – whether as cause or effect – most standard textbooks, to begin with a survey of ethical theory. This means, inevitably, a brief summary of Kant and deontological ethics, a brief survey of utilitarianism with a note or two about John Stuart Mill, and a distinction or two between act and rule, pleasure versus preference utilitarianism, and some replay of the much-rehearsed contest between the two sorts of theories. Given the business context, libertarianism or some form of contractualism is often included as a third contender. "Justice" is a natural introductory section, and John Locke on natural property rights is an appropriate inclusion too. But is this the theory of business ethics? Not only is the application to concrete business situations in question – and then the message to students is too often an unabashed relativism ("if you are a utilitarian, you'll do this, if you're a Kantian, you'll do that") – but it is not even clear whether there is, then, anything distinctive about *business* ethics. There is just ethics, or rather ethical theory, whatever that may be. Indeed, one is almost tempted to retreat to the tongue-in-cheek advice of Robert Townsend, former chief executive officer of Avis and author of *Up the Organization*, that if a company needs a corporate code of ethics, it should tack up the Ten Commandments. And so, with its success assured, at least for the time being, business ethics faces both a crisis of theory and a pragmatic challenge, that is, what is to count as a theory in business ethics and how is that theory to apply and be used by flesh-and-blood managers in concrete, real-life, ethically charged situations.

One possibility, of course, is that the theory of business ethics is really the philosophy of economics, that is, economics as ethics, social–political philosophy with an emphasis on economic justice. Thus the theoretical questions of business ethics are those raised by John Rawls in his *Theory of Justice* in 1971 and by his colleague Robert Nozick in *Anarchy, State and Utopia* in 1974. The questions of business ethics are those posed repeatedly by Amartya Sen and Jon Elster in their various books and articles and in a more informal way by John Kenneth Galbraith and Lester Thurow in the pages of the *New York Review*.[2] This, of course, is rich and promising territory. The theories are well developed and, though they may take Kant, Locke, and Mill as their precursors, they raise concerns that are particular to economic concerns and ask, with regard to the system as a whole as well as particular practices within it, whether the free market is indeed a just and fair mechanism for the distribution of goods in a grossly inegalitarian world. The theories here are well developed and impressively formalized in the sophisticated techniques of game theory, social choice theory, and all those other accoutrements that make theories look like *theory*, in other words, adequate for publication in the most serious professional journals and conducive to a positive tenure decision.

Such theorizing is, however, utterly inaccessible to the people *for whom* we supposedly do business ethics, our students and the executives and corporations we talk to and write for. Here, especially, the pragmatic problem comes back to haunt us: how do these grand theories of property rights and distribution mechanisms, these visionary pronouncements on the current economy, apply to people on the job? Of course, one could argue that this is the case in any science – and not just in the sciences either: that the hard part of any academic teaching is taking very sophisticated theoretical material and "watering it down" for the *hoi polloi*, or, more modestly, making it accessible in not overly oversimplified terminology. But quite apart from the offensively patronizing attitude embodied in this view – especially in the so-called liberal arts – it is inadequate for a more theoretical reason as well. The grand theories of the philosophy of economics, however intriguing they may be in their own right, are *not adequate* for business ethics, and for many of the same reasons that the classic theories of Kant, Locke, and Mill are inadequate. The theories themselves are incomplete, oblivious to the concrete business context, and indifferent to the very particular roles that people play in business. Their inaccessibility and/or inapplicability to the ordinary manager in the office or on the shop floor is not just a pragmatic problem but a failure of theory as well. At any rate, that is what I wish to argue in this essay. Business ethicists have been looking for theory in the wrong place; and consequently they have been finding and developing the wrong theories.

The Aristotelian Approach to Business Ethics

I once distinguished, in a book entitled *It's Good Business*, between macro and micro ethics, and in terms of this limited dichotomy it should be evident that I am going to argue for the importance of micro business ethics – the concepts and values that define individual responsibilities and role behavior – as opposed to the already well-developed theories of macro business ethics – the principles that govern or should govern our overall system of (re)distribution and reward.[3] (In ethics as a whole, one might argue, the emphasis has been in the opposite direction, ignoring the larger social and anthropological setting in favor of a concentration on individual autonomy and well-being.) The distinction between micro and macro is borrowed from and intended to be parallel to a similar dichotomy in economics. (I have elsewhere argued that economics is a branch of ethics, but that is another story.[4]) That distinction, however, is left over from the ancient days of Lord Keynes and is also inadequate. The integral or "molar" unit of commerce today is neither the individual entrepreneur or consumer nor the all-embracing system that still goes by the antiquated nineteenth-century name "capitalism." It is the *corporation*, a type of entity barely mentioned by Adam Smith in a few dismissive sentences (and of minimal interest even to Keynes). While I will always hold that the existential unit of responsibility and concern is and remains the individual, the individual in today's business world does not operate in a social vacuum. He or she is more likely than not an employee – whether in the stockroom or as chief financial officer – and our basic unit of understanding has to be the company, or rather, the employee in a company, and, in particular, in a company whose perceived primary purpose is "to make money." Theory in business ethics thus becomes the theory of – that is, description of and contemplation about – individuals in (and out of) business roles, as well as of the role of business and businesses in society. People in business are ultimately responsible as individuals, but they are responsible as individuals in a corporate setting where their responsibilities are defined at least in part by their roles and duties in the company and, of course, by "the bottom line." Businesses in turn are defined by their roles and responsibilities in the larger community, where the bottom line is only an internal concern (if the business is to stay in business and the shareholders are to hold on to their shares) and for everyone else may be a minimal consideration.

A different way of putting this central point is to point out that much of business ethics today is focused on questions of *policy* – those large questions about government regulation and the propriety of government intervention (e.g. in failing industries and affirmative action programs) and about very general business practices and problems (e.g. pollution control, opacity and lying in advertising, employee due process, and the social responsibilities of companies to their surrounding communities). All this, of course, is perfectly proper for philosophers and other social observers who have the luxury of standing outside the pressures of the business world to survey the wider scenery. To this end, traditional theories of ethics – especially Kantian deontology and utilitarianism – are called in to support one or another concern beyond or contrary to the bottom line. (Where business profits and public policy agree, of course, there is not much call for debate.[5]) But what gets left out of these well-plumbed studies and arguments is an adequate sense of *personal* values and involvement. Too much of our emphasis in our courses on business ethics is on policy disputes and the grand theories that support one position or another. But the practical problem with such policy disputes is that few people in the business world and even fewer of our students have any real sense of what to do with them, except to argue about them and, perhaps, become aware of the possibility that they may well become the victims of one policy or another. The chairman of the board may have a very real and tangible interest in discussing and resolving policy issues, and so too the members of this or that governmental commission. But policy disputes do not have very much to say to the ordinary manager, or for that matter the ordinary executive, much less the ordinary business student. What is missing from much of business ethics is an adequate account of the *personal* dimension in ethics. Accordingly, I want to defend business ethics as a more personally oriented ethics rather than business ethics as public policy, "applied" abstract philosophy, or a byproduct of the social sciences. But business ethics so conceived is not "personal" in the sense of "private" or "subjective"; it is rather self-awareness writ large, a sense of oneself as an intimate (but not inseparable) part of the business world with a keen sense of the virtues and values of that world, an ethics which might well be called – as I will call it here – an "Aristotelian" approach to business ethics.

Aristotle is the philosopher who is best known for this emphasis on the cultivation of the virtues. But is it not inappropriate – even perverse – to couple Aristotle and business ethics? True, he was the first economist. He had much to say about the ethics of exchange and so might well be called the first (known) business ethicist as well. But Aristotle distinguished two different senses of what we call economics: *oeconomicus* or household trading, which he approved of and thought essential to the working of any even modestly complex society; and *chrematisike*, which is trade for profit. Aristotle declared the latter activity wholly devoid of virtue and called those who engaged in such purely selfish practices "parasites." All trade conducted for profit, he believed, was a kind of exploitation. Such was his view of what we call "business." Indeed, Aristotle's attack on the unsavory and unproductive practice of "usury" and the personal vice of avarice held force virtually until the seventeenth century. Only outsiders at the fringe of society, not respectable citizens, engaged in such practices. (Shakespeare's Shylock, in *The Merchant of Venice*, was such an outsider and a usurer, though his idea of a forfeit was a bit unusual.) It can be argued that Aristotle had too little sense of the importance of production and based his views wholly on the aristocratically proper urge for acquisition, thus introducing an unwarranted zero-sum thinking into his economics.[6] And, of course, it can be charged that Aristotle, like his teacher Plato, was too much the spokesman for the aristocratic class and quite unfair to the commerce and livelihoods of foreigners and commoners.[7] It is Aristotle who initiated so much of the history of business ethics as the wholesale attack on business and its practices. Aristotelian prejudices underlie much of the criticism of business and contempt for finance that preoccupy so much of Christian ethics even to this day, avaricious evangelicals notwithstanding. Even defenders of business often end up presupposing Aristotelian prejudices in such Pyrrhonian arguments as "business is akin to poker and apart from the ethics of everyday life" (Alfred Carr) and "the [only] social responsibility of business is to increase its profits" (Milton Friedman).[8] But if it is just this schism between business and the rest of life that so infuriated Aristotle, for whom life was supposed to fit together in a coherent whole, it is the same holistic idea – that businesspeople and corporations are first of all part of a larger community – that drives business ethics today. We can no longer accept the amoral idea that "business is business" (not really a tautology but an excuse for being an unfeeling bastard). According to Aristotle, one has to think of oneself as a member of the larger community, the *polis*, and strive to excel, to bring out what is best in oneself and in the shared enterprise. What is best in us – our virtues – are in turn defined by that larger community, and there is therefore no ultimate split or antagonism between individual self-interest and the greater public good. Of course, there were no corporations in those days, but Aristotle would certainly know what I mean when I say that most people in business now identify themselves – if tenuously – in terms of their companies, and that corporate policies, much less corporate codes of ethics, are not by themselves enough to constitute an ethics. But corporations are not isolated city-states, not even the biggest and most powerful of the multinationals (contrast the image of "the sovereign state of ITT"). They are part and parcel of a larger global community. The people that work for them are thus citizens of two communities at once, and one might think of business ethics as getting straight about that dual citizenship. What we need to cultivate is a certain way of thinking about ourselves in and out of the corporate context, and this is the aim of ethical theory in business, as I understand it. It is not, let me insist, anti-individualistic in any sense of "individualism" that is worth defending. Rather, the Aristotelian approach to business ethics begins with the idea that it is individual virtue and integrity that count: good corporate and social policy will follow.

With what is this Aristotelian approach to be contrasted? First of all, I want to contrast it with the emphasis on public policy that has preoccupied our subject. In Texas, to take one provincial example, the business school cannot quite give itself over to the idea of a business ethics course, and my own business ethics course in philosophy was (until this year) cross-listed with the management department as a public and social policy course. There is nothing wrong with policy studies, of course, and I do not for a moment suggest that they be replaced or discarded. But policy decisions are not usually made by folks like us. We rarely even get to vote or speak for them. For the ordinary line manager or even most executives policy questions are, for the most part, something to debate over lunch, usually by way of reaction to some *fait accompli*. There is something missing from policy decisions that is absolutely central to ethics on virtually any account: namely, personal responsibility. The ethical problems that the average manager faces on the job are personnel and routine administrative decision-making problems, not policy problems. Some of those problems have to do with temptations – an attractive competing offer, a convenient kick-back, a personal relationship, or a prejudice against an employee. Some have to do with conflicts of duties, mixed messages, crossed loyalties. Business ethics begins, for most of us, in some conflict of roles within an organization, implementing policies or decisions not of our own making and often against our better judgment. Whatever else business ethics may involve and however sophisticated its theories may become, it means knowing that even such decisions (and their consequences) are nevertheless one's own to live with. Ethics is not just a subject for executive boards, planning committees, and government overseers but for all of us, in the details as well as the larger dramas of our everyday lives.

The Aristotelian approach is also to be contrasted with that 200 (or so)-year-old obsession in ethics that takes everything of significance to be a matter of *rational principles*: "morality" as the strict Kantian sense of duty to the moral law. This is not to say, of course, that Aristotelian ethics dispenses with rationality, or for that matter with principles or the notion of duty. But Aristotle is quite clear about the fact that it is cultivation of character that counts, long before we begin to "rationalize" our actions, and the formulation of general principles (in what he famously but confusingly calls his "practical syllogism") is not an explicit step in correct and virtuous behavior as such but rather a philosopher's formulation about what it means to act rationally.[9] And, most important for our purposes here, duties too are defined by our roles in a community, for example a corporation, and not by means of any abstract ratiocination, principle of contradiction, or *a priori* formulations of the categorical imperative. Kant, magnificent as he was as a thinker, has proved to be a kind of disease in ethics.[10] It is all very elegant, even brilliant, until one walks into the seminar room with a dozen or so bright, restless corporate managers, waiting to hear what is new and what is relevant to them on the business ethics scene. And then we tell them: don't lie, don't steal, don't cheat – elaborated and supported by the most gothic non-econometric construction ever allowed in a company training center. But the problem is not just impracticality and the fact that we do not actually do ethics that way; the problem is that the Kantian approach shifts our attention away from just what I would call the "inspirational" matters of business ethics (its "incentives") and the emphasis on "excellence" (a buzz-word for Aristotle as well as Tom Peters and his millions of readers). It shifts the critical focus from oneself as a full-blooded person occupying a significant role in a productive organization to an abstract role-transcendent morality that necessarily finds itself empty-handed when it comes to most of the matters and many of the motives that we hear so much about in any corporate setting.

The Aristotelian approach is also to be contrasted with that rival ethical theory that goes by the name of "utilitarianism." I have considerably more to say about utilitarianism, its continued vulgarization and its forgotten humanistic focus in John Stuart Mill, but not here. For now, I just want to point out that utilitarianism shares with Kant that special appeal to anal compulsives in its doting over principles and rationalization (in crass calculation) and its neglect of individual responsibility and the cultivation of character. (John Stuart Mill exempted himself from much of this charge in the last chapter of *Utilitarianism*, but I promised not to talk about that here.) But I can imagine a good existentialist complaining quite rightly that the point of all such "decision procedures" in ethics is precisely to neutralize the annoyance of personal responsibility altogether, appealing every decision to "the procedure" rather than taking responsibility oneself. Of course, I am not denying the importance of concern for the public good or the centrality of worrying, in any major policy decision, about the number of people helped and hurt. But I take very seriously the problems of mesaurement and incommensurability that have been standard criticisms of utilitarianism ever since Bentham, and there are considerations that often are more basic than public utility – if only because, in most of our actions, the impact on public utility is so small in contrast to the significance for our personal sense of integrity and "doing the right thing" that it becomes a negligible factor in our deliberations.[11]

I would also distinguish the Aristotelian approach to business ethics from all those approaches that primarily emphasize rights, whether the rights of free enterprise as such, the rights of the employee, the customer, or the community and even civil rights. Again, I have no wish to deny the relevance of rights to ethics or the centrality of civil rights, but I think that we should remind ourselves that talk about rights was never intended to eclipse talk about responsibilities and I think the emphasis in business ethics should move from *having* rights oneself to *recognizing* the rights of others; but then, I am not at all sure that all this could not be just as well or better expressed by saying that there are all sorts of things that a virtuous person should or should not ever do to others.[12] Of course, Aristotle's defense of slavery in his *Politics* should be more than enough to convince us that we would still need the language of rights even with a fully developed language of the virtues. The problem with virtue ethics is that it tends to be provincial and ethnocentric. It thereby requires the language of rights and some general sense of utility as a corrective.

It will be evident to most readers that I am arguing – or about to argue – for a version of what has recently been called "virtue ethics," but I do want to distance myself from much of what has been defended recently under that title. First of all, I want to reject those versions of ethics that view the virtues as no more than particular instantiations of the abstract principles of morality. This is an analysis that has been argued at some length, for instance, by William Frankena and Kurt Baier, both distinguished defenders of "the moral point of view."[13] But if, for example, being an honest man or woman is nothing other than obeying the general Kantian-type principle, "do not lie," if being respectful is a conscientious application of the "ends" formulation of the categorical imperative (not even Kant held this), if one's sense of public service is an expression of the utilitarian principle, then this is emphatically not what I have in mind; nor did Aristotle. To be witty or magnificent (two Aristotelian virtues not taken seriously enough by our contemporaries) is surely not to express or apply certain principles, but neither is courage, temperance, nor even justice (contrary to Rawls and many of our finest social thinkers today).

To imagine our good existentialist here again, one can hear him saying, presumably in French, that one's personal judgments precede rather than follow one's abstract ethical pronouncements. Of course, this is not exactly Aristotelian (Aristotle was no existentialist), but modified it makes a good Aristotelian point: choice and character get cultivated first, philosophical ethics – if one is lucky enough to study in the right academy – afterwards. Theory in business ethics consists in part of just such reflection on the cultivation of the right virtues and their nature.

I also want to distance myself from some of the now familiar features of what is being defended as virtue ethics, in particular the rather dangerous nostalgia for "tradition" and "community" that is expressed by Alasdair MacIntyre and Charles Taylor among others.[14] Of course, the Aristotelian approach does presuppose something of sense of community that I particularly want to emphasize. But there is a difference between the more or less singular, seemingly monogeneous, autonomous (and very elite) community that Aristotle simply took for granted and the nostalgic (and I think purely imaginary) communities described or alluded to by recent virtue ethicists, often defined by a naïve religious solidarity and unrealistic expectation of communal consensus. No adequate theory of ethics today can ignore or wish away the pluralistic and culturally diverse populations that make up almost every actual community. Even the smallest corporation will be rent by professional and role-related differences as well as divided by cultural and personal distinctions. Corporate cultures, like the larger culture(s), are defined by their differences and disagreements as well as by any shared purpose or outside antagonist or competition, and no defense of the concept of corporate culture can or should forget that corporations are always part of a larger culture and not whole cultures themselves. And yet, in place of the abstract nostalgia that defines much of the current fascination with "communities," many modern corporations would seem to represent just such community. They enjoy a shared sense of *telos* as many communities do not. They invoke an extraordinary, almost military emphasis on loyalty and, despite the competitive rhetoric, they first of all inspire and require teamwork and cooperation. Corporations are real communities, neither ideal nor idealized, and therefore the perfect place to start understandinig the nature of the virtues.

There has been some suggestion in the literature that virtue ethics is a more "feminine" ethics than Kantian or utilitarian rule-bound ethics. I disagree. I thus want to distance myself from some recent feminist writings – including the work of one of my own best students – who have drawn a sharp contrast between the good, warm, feminine virtues of caring and concern and the oppressive, impersonal, war-mongering masculine principles of justice and duty.[15] I certainly agree with the shift in emphasis, from Kantian justice to compassion and caring, but it is not my intention to supply one more weapon in the perennial war between the sexes, and it seems to me that Aristotle – certainly no feminist – has much to say about the virtues that has little or nothing to do with the (admittedly not unimportant) fact that one is a male or a female. It may be, as some writers have recently argued, that the increasing number of women in significant executive positions will change the dominant ethic of corporate America. I do not yet see much evidence for this promising proposition, but I think the importance of emphasizing the virtues (including the so-called "feminine" virtues) should not be held captive to gender distinctions.

So what is the Aristotelian approach to business ethics? What are its primary ingredients? There is a great deal of ground to be covered, from the general philosophical questions "what is a virtue?" and "what is the role of the virtues in ethics and the good life?" to quite specific questions about virtues and supposed virtues in business, such as loyalty, dependability, integrity, shrewdness, and "toughness." But here I am afraid that I will not get to answer these general questions or speak much of these particular virtues at all. What I will do is very briefly circumscribe the discussion of the virtues in business ethics with a half dozen considerations not usually so highlighted in the more abstract and principle-bound discussions of ethics nor so personalized in the policy discussions that so dominate the field. I want to then talk about a problem that is often overlooked in virtue ethics, indeed, a problem that some authors (e.g. Edmund Pincoffs) think it the virtue of virtue ethics to solve,[16] which I call "the disunity of the virtues," the tendency of virtues to oppose and conflict with one another. Finally, I would like to talk briefly about one of several myths that, in their obtuse single-mindedness, undermine the discussion of the virtues in business. It is the myth of "the profit motive," which in too many corporations manifests itself as a blinding obsession with the bottom line.

Six Ingredients of Virtue Ethics

I would like to outline six ingredients that make up the framework of virtue ethics in business. I call them: community, excellence, role identity, holism, integrity, judgment.

Community

The Aristotelian approach begins with the idea that we are all members of an organized group, with something of a history and established practices governing everything from eating and working to worshipping. To be sure, communities in the contemporary "Western" world are anything but homogeneous or harmonious, but the claim I am making here is more metaphysical than nostalgic, and that is that what we call "the individual" is socially constituted and socially situated. We find our identities and our meanings only within communities, and for most of us that means at work in a company or an institution. The philosophical myth that has grown almost cancerous in many business circles, the neo-Hobbesian view that "it's every man [*sic*] for himself" and the newer Darwinian view that "it's a jungle out there" are direct denials of the Aristotelian view that we are all *first of all* members of a community and our self-interest is for the most part identical to the larger interests of the group. Competition presumes, it does not replace, an underlying assumption of mutual interest and cooperation. Whether we do well, whether we like ourselves, whether we lead happy productive lives, depends to a large extent on the companies we choose. As the Greeks used to say, "to live the good life one must live in a great city." To my busienss students today, who are all too prone to choose a job on the basis of salary and start-up bonus alone, I always say, "to live a decent life choose the right company." In business ethics the corporation is one's community, which is not to say, of course, that the larger community – as diverse as it may be – does not count even more.

Excellence

The Greek *arete* is often translated either "virtue" or, as opposed to the rather modest and self-effacing notion of "virtue" that we inherited from our Victorian ancestors, "excellence" (indeed, even Kant used the term). The dual translation by itself makes a striking point. It is not enough to do no wrong. "Knowingly do no harm" (*primum non nocere*) is *not* the end of business ethics (as Peter Drucker suggests[17]). The hardly original slogan I sometimes use to sell what I do, "ethics and excellence," is not just an echo of Peters and Waterman. Virtue is doing one's best, excelling, and not merely "toeing the line" and "keeping one's nose clean." The virtues that constitute business ethics should not be conceived of as purely ethical or moral virtues, as if (to repeat) business ethics were nothing other than the general application of moral principles to one specific context (among others). Being a "tough negotiator" is a virtue in business but not in babysitting. It does not follow, however, that the virtues of business are therefore opposed to the ordinary virtues of civilized life – as Alfred Carr famously argued in his *Harvard Business Review* polemic of several years ago.[18] The virtues of business ethics are business virtues but they are nonetheless virtues, and the exercise of these virtues is aimed at both "the bottom line" and ethics.

Role Identity

Much has been written, for example by Norman Bowie in his good little book on *Business Ethics*, on the importance of "role morality" and "my position and its duties."[19] It is the situatedness of corporate roles that lends them their particular ethical poignancy, the fact that an employee or an executive is not just a person who happens to be in a place and is constrained by no more than the usual ethical prohibitions. To work for a company is to accept a set of particular obligations, to assume a *prima facie* loyalty to one's employer, to adopt a certain standard of excellence and conscientiousness that is largely defined by the job itself. There may be general ethical rules and guidelines that cut across most positions but as these get more general and more broadly applicable they also become all but useless in concrete ethical dilemmas. Robert Townsend's cute comment that if a company needs an ethical code, it should use the Ten Commandments is thus not only irreverent but irrelevant too.[20] The Aristotelian approach to business ethics presumes concrete situations and particular people and their place in organizations. There is little point to an ethics that tries to transcend all such particularities and embrace the chairman of the board as well as a middle manager, a secretary, and a factory worker. All ethics is contextual, and one of the problems with all those grand theories is that they try to transcend context and end up with vacuity. The problem, of course, is that people in business inevitably play several roles ("wear several hats") at once, and these roles may clash with one another as they may clash with more personal roles based on family, friendship, and personal obligations. This, I will argue, is a pervasive problem in micro business ethics.

Holism

It more or less follows from what I have said above that one of the problems of traditional business thinking is our tendency to isolate our business or professional roles from the rest of our lives, a process that Marx, following Schiller, described as "alienation." The good life may have many facets, but they are facets and not mere components, much less isolated aspects of a fragmented existence. We hear more and more in managerial circles, despite the tiresome emphasis on tasks, techniques, and "objectives," that a manager's primary and ultimate concern is *people.*

It has become trite, but as I watch our more ambitious students and talk with more and more semi-successful but "trapped" middle managers and executives, I am more and more convinced that the tunnel vision of business life encouraged by the too-narrow business curriculum and the daily rhetoric of the corporate community is damaging and counter-productive. Good employees are good people, and to pretend that the virtues of business stand isolated from the virtues of the rest of our lives – and this is not for a moment to deny the particularity of either our business roles or our lives – is to set up that familiar tragedy in which a pressured employee violates his or her "personal values" because, from a purely business point of view, he or she "didn't really have any choice."

Integrity

This is a word, like "honor" – its close kin – that sometimes seems all but archaic in the modern business world. To all too many business executives, it suggests stubbornness and inflexibility, a refusal to be a "team player." But integrity seems to have at least two very different meanings, one of them encouraging conformity, the other urging a belliger-ent independence.[21] The very word suggests "wholeness," but in so far as one's identity is not that of an isolated atom but rather the product of a larger social molecule, that wholeness includes, rather than excludes, other people and one's social roles. A person's integrity on the job typically requires her to follow the rules and practices that define that job, rather than allowing herself to be swayed by distractions and contrary temptations. And yet, critical encounters sometimes require a show of integrity that is indeed antithetical to one's assigned role and duties. This is not the place to work out this complex and central ethical issue, but the point that must be made is that such considerations are a far cry from the sorts of quandary debates that define much of traditional ethics. The question of integrity is not a question of obligation and it is certainly not a matter of utility. It is rather a matter of who one is, coupled with the fact that, on the job, each of us is (at least) two persons at once.

Judgment (*phronesis*)

The fact that our roles conflict and there are often no singular principles to help us decide on an ethical course of action shifts the emphasis away from our calculative and ratiocinative faculties and back toward an older, often ignored faculty called "judgment." Against the view that ethics consists primarily of general principles that get applied to particular situations, Aristotle thought that it was "good judgment" or *phronesis* that was of the greatest importance in ethics. Good judgment (which centered on "perception" rather than the abstract formulation and interpretation of general principles) was the product of a good upbringing, a proper education. It was always situated, perhaps something like Joseph Fletcher's still often cited notion of a "situation ethics," and took into careful account the particularity of the persons and circumstances involved. But I think the real importance of *phronesis* is not just its priority to ethical deliberation and raciocination; it has rather to do with the inevitable conflicts of both concerns and principles that define almost every ethical dilemma. Justice, for example, may sound (especially in some philosophers) as if it were a monolithic or hierarchically layered and almost mechanical process. But, as I have argued elsewhere, there are a dozen or more different considerations that enter into most deliberations about justice, including not only rights, prior obligations, and the public good but questions of merit (which themselves break down into a variety of sometimes conflicting categories), responsibility, and risk.[22] I will not go into this further here, but the point is that there is *no* (non-arbitrary) mechanical decision procedure for resolving most disputes about justice, and what is required, in each and every particular case, is the ability to balance and weigh competing concerns and come to a "fair" conclusion. But what is fair is not the outcome of one or several pre-ordained principles of justice; it is (as they say) a "judgment call," always disputable but nevertheless well or badly made. I have often thought that encouraging abstract ethical theory actually discourages and distracts us from the need to make judgments. I have actually heard one of my colleagues say (without qualms) that, since he has been studying ethical theory, he no longer has any sense of ethics. And if this sounds implausible, I urge you to remember your last department or faculty senate meeting, and the inverse relationship between the high moral tone of the conversation and the ridiculousness of the proposals and decisions that followed.

A Problem for Virtue Ethics: the Disunity of the Virtues

Discussions of the virtues have been hamstrung since Aristotle by a kind of wishful thinking – not itself a virtue, especially in supposedly hard-headed philosophers. The presumption, only sometimes accompanied by argument, has been that there is, at least ideally, a unity of the virtues, a happy harmony that the virtuous man or woman will enjoy. Put crudely, the view is that, if one person (truly) has one virtue, he or she will have all of them. I believe experience proves this to be just plain false, and one of the most obvious discoveries of any empirically minded virtue ethics (and is there another kind?) is that there is often a conflict of virtues, a clash of loyalties, a disharmony of equally valued values. I can readily hear a pressured sales manager arguing that too much dependability and forthright honesty can undermine one's skills in negotiation and, in a sense, the business enterprise itself. (A recent movie, in which an advertising executive decides that his agency will only tell the truth, is instructive in this regard.) It is clear that loyalties often conflict on the job, particularly in a politicized company or institution (does that leave anyone out?). One's duty to superiors may well conflict with one's obligations to subordinates, and in any but the best organized company there is always the possibility of conflicting, even contradictory but equally obliging orders from two different superiors. One's sense of loyalty to an aging and no longer effective manager who provided one's job opportunity in the first place may well clash with a more general sense of obligation to the company. The seriousness of these conflicts and clashes is documented in detail by Jackall in his *Moral Mazes*, though I think he ultimately makes this out to be too straightforward a clash between morality and corporate politics. In any less than perfect organization or society, there is no unity of the virtues and no easy distinction between virtue and the duties of one's job or position. Virtues tend to be context-bound, but contexts overlap and clash with one another. In any organization, there are overlapping and concentric circles of identity and responsibility, and a virtue in one arena may conflict with a virtue – indeed, it may even be a vice – in another. This is a painful realization, and it may even tempt some to declare an Aristotelian ethics to be impossible. Indeed, it is all too easy to retreat in desperation in either direction, to promote a false sense of integrity that is too detached or divorced from the realities of one's role identity in the company (as philosophers, standing on the outside – in their own safe identities – are too prone to do), or to encourage total absorption in one's company role so as to be incapable of seeing beyond it (a favorite strategy of militaristic managers). But there is no such easy answer. We always wear multiple hats and have potentially competing responsibilities. It is simply not true, as an old cartoon used to say, "what's good for General Bullmoose is good for the USA." Thus again we must emphasize the importance of judgment and integrity, which may not mean making the right decision but rather making the decision in the right way, with good judgment and sensitivity.

The Myth of the Profit Motive

Finally, I want to launch a guerrilla attack on a myth that encourages precisely the wrong virtues in business and readily gives rise to what Richard De George has called "the Myth of Amoral Business."[23] It is not as if business life and business talk were devoid of any conception of the virtues. But as has so often been commented and criticized, those virtues most often cited as business virtues belong in a locker room if not in a treatise on Darwinism. Many of the metaphors are macho images of business as a jungle and corporate campaigns as a kind of war in which virtue comes down to "kill or be killed," "eat or be eaten." The most dangerous metaphors, however, are those that present themselves not as metaphors but as straight matter-of-fact description of the ways of the world. Foremost among these is the idea that business at its very essence is defined by and driven by some basic human urge called "the profit motive." It is such talk of the profit motive, I want to suggest, that causes more damage to the virtues – and more emphasis on the wrong virtues – than any amount of sleaziness or dishonest dealings on the part of the business community.

It is often said that businesses and corporations have one and only one end, "the profit motive." This obscures rather than clarifies both the underlying *ethos* that makes business possible and the complex *telos* that business and businesspeople actually pursue. It makes any talk of "virtue" or "integrity" sound merely quaint and naïvely idealistic. But the phrase was invented by the last century's socialists as an *attack* on business and its narrow-minded pursuit of the dollar, the mark, and the pound to the exclusion of all other considerations and obligations. The idea was to criticize and lampoon the vulgar focus and sometimes vicious lack of sensitivity and public spirit of certain ludicrous entrepreneurs, but they took it instead as a compliment and a convenient way not only to describe but to justify their myopia. To be sure, a business does aim to make a profit, but it does so only by supplying quality goods and services, by providing jobs, and by "fitting in" the community. To single out profits rather than productivity or public service as the central aim of business activity is just asking for trouble. And profits are not as such the end or goal of business activity: profits get distributed and reinvested. Profits are a *means* to building the business and rewarding employees, executives, and investors. For some people, profits may be a means of "keeping score," but even in those degenerate cases, it is the status and satisfaction of "winning" that is the goal, not profit as such. It was for good reason, whatever else we might think of his prejudices, that Aristotle scorned the notion of profit for its own sake, and even Adam Smith was clear that it was prosperity, not profit, that constituted the goal of the free market system, whether or not the individual businessman or woman had this in mind.

A more sophisticated but not dissimilar version of the myth acknowledges that employees and executives are not moved by profits as such but insists instead that the managers of a business (and, ultimately, all of its employees) are bound above all by one and only one obligation: to maximize the profits for the owners, their stockholders. We need not inquire whether this is the actual motive behind most upper management decisions in order to point out that, while managers do recognize that their own business roles are defined primarily by obligations rather than by their own profits (unless they happen to be heavy stockholders also), that unflattering image has simply been transferred to the stockholders. But are stockholders in fact the owners of a business, or do we have here another one of those slippery slides between legal and social conceptions that so abound in political philosophy? Is ownership only contractual and without reference to interest, engagement, and, as Locke famously put it, "mixing one's labour with it"? And is it true that investors care *only* about the maximization of their profits? Do they too not think that there are all sorts of values and virtues to be considered along the road to dividends and share value increases? And if some four-month "in and out" investor does indeed care only about increasing his investment by 30 percent or so, why should the managers of the firm have any obligation to him, other than to avoid intentionally frittering away or wasting that money?[24]

Business, *contra* Aristotle, is not about profits but about productivity and prosperity. Business and businesses have a complex *telos* that is only in part making money – and that usually as a means or intermediary, only very rarely as an isolated end in itself. To confuse the need of businesses to make a profit to stay in business or the tendency of businesses to measure their success by their profits with the complex roles and goals of an institution in society is to misunderstand business and lose our Aristotelian orientation: we adopt a too narrow vision of what business is, e.g. the pursuit of profits, and then derive unethical and divisive conclusions. It is this inexcusably limited focus on the "rights of the stockholders," for example, that has been used to defend some of the very destructive and certainly unproductive "hostile takeovers" of major corporations in the last few years, sacrificing in the process whole communities, tens of thousands of employees as well as company morale and, ultimately, financial soundness in favor of a short-term benefit to stockholders who may, in fact, have bought shares only the previous week on a hunch that some power play was already in the offing. To say this is not to deny the rights of stockholders to a fair return, of course; nor is it to deny the "fiduciary responsibility" of the managers of a company. It is only to say that these rights and responsibilities make sense only in a larger social context and that the very idea of "the profit motive" as an end in itself – as opposed to profits as a means of encouraging and rewarding hard work and investment, building a better business, and serving society better – is a serious obstacle to understanding the rich tapestry of motives and activities that make up the business world.

The Bottom Line

The bottom line of the Aristotelian approach to business ethics is that we have to get away from "bottom line" thinking. As John Steinbeck writes in *East of Eden*, "A living, or money ... Money's easy to make if it's money you want. But with a few exceptions people don't want money. They want luxury and they want love and they want admiration." The Aristotelian approach to business ethics ultimately comes down to the idea that, while business life has its specific goals and distinctive practices and people in business have their particular concerns, loyalties, roles, and responsibilities, there is ultimately no "business world" but only people working in business as part of their life in society. The Aristotelian approach to business ethics is, ultimately, just another way of saying that people come before profits, and before a great deal of what is often called "ethics" too.

NOTES

1 Robert Jackall, *Moral Mazes: The World of Corporate Managers* (New York: Oxford University Press, 1988).
2 John Rawls, *A Theory of Justice* (Cambridge, Mass.: Harvard University Press, 1971); Robert Nozick, *Anarchy, State and Utopia* (New York: Basic Books, 1974).
3 Robert C. Solomon and K. R. Hanson, *It's Good Business* (New York: Atheneum, 1985).
4 "The One Minute Moralist," *Business and Society Review*, March 1984.
5 Indeed, the most serious single problem that I find in the teaching of business ethics is the insistence on a false antagonism between profits and social responsibility, perhaps (on the part of philosophers) in order to keep the debate going. A far more productive route would be the search for profit-making solutions, but this would require a major step down from the abstractions of theory into the messy world of details, technology, marketing, and politics. It is the same old problem of egoism in ethics (as in Hobbes and

Butler three centuries ago), now revised on the corporate level. It presupposes an artificial opposition between self-interest and shared interest and then finds it impossible to locate the motivation for mutually interested action.

6   Anthony Flew, "The Profit Motive," *Ethics*, vol. 86 (July 1976), pp. 312–22.
7   Manuel Velasquez, comment on Joanne Ciulla, in Freeman, ed., *Business and the Humanities* (Oxford University Press, 1993).
8   Alfred Carr, "Is Business Bluffing Ethical?" *Harvard Business Review* (Jan.–Feb. 1968); Milton Friedman, "The Social Responsibility of Business is to Increase its Profits," *New York Times Magazine*, Sept. 13, 1970.
9   There is some dispute about this. Cf. G. E. M. Anscombe, *Intention* (Ithaca: Cornell University Press, 1957) and John Cooper, *Aristotle* (Indianapolis: Hackett, 1989).
10 Los Angeles psychologist–philosopher Michael Green has done devastating diagnosis of just this philosophical syndrome, unfortunately unpublished.
11 This is related to, but different from, the point that Bernard Williams makes in his various examples designed to put integrity and utility at direct odds with one another. See, for example, his *Morality* (New York: Harper and Row, 1972), pp. 104ff.
12 Elizabeth Wolgast, "Wrong Rights," in *A Grammar of Justice* (Ithaca: Cornell University Press, 1987).
13 William Frankena, *Ethics*, 2nd edn (Englewood Cliffs, NJ: Prentice-Hall, 1963), pp. 62–70; Kurt Baier, "Radical Virtue Ethics," in P. French et al., eds, *Ethical Theory: Character and Virtue*, Midwest Studies in Philosophy, vol. 13 (Notre Dame: University of Notre Dame Press, 1988), pp. 126–33; also David Braybrooke, "No Virtues without Principles: No Principles without Virtues," unpublished MS presented to a symposium in honor of Edmund Pincoffs, University of Texas, 1990.
14 Alasdair MacIntyre, *After Virtue* (Notre Dame: University of Notre Dame Press, 1979); Charles Taylor, *Philosophical Papers*, vol. 2 (Cambridge: Cambridge University Press, 1985).
15 Cheshire Calhoun, "Justice, Care and Gender Bias," *Journal of Philosophy*, vol. 85, no. 9 (Sept. 1988), pp. 451–63.
16 Edmund Pincoffs, *Quandaries and Virtues* (Lawrence, Kansas: University Press of Kansas, 1986).
17 Peter Drucker, *Management* (New York: Harper and Row, 1973), pp. 366–7.
18 Carr, "Is Business Bluffing Ethical?"
19 Norman Bowie, *Business Ethics* (Englewood Cliffs, NJ: Prentice-Hall, 1982), pp. 1–16.
20 Peter Townsend, *Up the Organization* (New York: Knopf, 1970), p. 129.
21 See Lynn McFall, "Integrity," *Ethics*, vol. 98 (Oct. 1987), pp. 5–20.
22 Robert C. Solomon, *A Passion for Justice* (New York: Addison-Wesley, 1989), ch. 2.
23 Richard De George, *Business Ethics* (New York: Macmillan, 1982).
24 Anthony Flew provides a kind of *reductio ad absurdum* argument, asking why no one speaks of "a rent motive or a wage motive." But then he oddly argues that the attack on the profit motive is a product of Aristotelian prejudices.

To be sure; but he misses the point that, by showing it to be absurd, he certainly should not end by, in effect, defending it (Flew, "The Profit Motive").

12
Moral Philosophy and Business Ethics: The Priority of the Political

Alistair M. Macleod

Aligning himself with the increasing number of moral and political philosophers who have focused their attention on questions about the moral acceptability of institutional arrangements, Macleod argues that business ethicists should also be concerned with such questions. We cannot, he maintains, formulate a satisfactory doctrine of individual morality without tackling questions about the moral acceptability of institutional arrangements. This means that we cannot get a good answer to the question of how persons can maintain their moral integrity while successfully pursuing a business career if we limit out consideration to how business executives should carry out their role-related responsibilities and what personal virtues, such as loyalty and trustworthiness, they should develop. Answers to these "micro" questions are beside the point if we do not also consider macro questions about the moral satisfactoriness of the institutional framework within which business activity takes place. He identifies two clusters of questions needing more adequate answers: (1) How should the distinction between public and private sectors be drawn, and what is its normative significance? (2) What should be the purpose and scope of markets, and what rules should regulate the activities of market participants?

This essay provides an interesting contrast to that by Robert Solomon (chapter 11), who argues for greater attention to what Macleod calls "micro" questions. It should also be compared with the other papers in the section on business ethics, particularly those of Philips (chapter 10) and Goodpaster (chapter 13).

The strong upsurge of interest among philosophers during the past ten or fifteen years in the application of moral principles to practical issues in law, politics, medicine, and – most recently, perhaps – business has been contributing to a transformation, still under way, in our understanding of moral philosophy. Three changes are worthy of note.

The first is an enhanced sense of the importance of questions about the moral acceptability of institutional arrangements. Once institutions are seen, not as relatively unmalleable, quasi-organic structures which it would be perilous to try to modify, but as elaborate human artifacts serving a wide range of human purposes, the question whether they ought to be preserved in something like their present form or changed in some way – radically transformed, even, if they no longer secure the interests, private or public, which provided their *raison d'être* – is bound to win an important place on the moral theorist's agenda. Moreover, serious attention to this question has implications for the handling of questions long thought to be the central ones in moral philosophy – namely, questions about individual conduct and character. When it is appreciated how heavily the alternatives individuals face are constrained by the institutional environment within which they seek to live their lives, it becomes apparent that no satisfactory doctrine of individual morality can be formulated which does not come to grips with questions about the moral acceptability of institutional arrangements. The idea, for example, that the moral life is largely a matter of carrying out the duties which attach to one's "station" in society presupposes an unacceptably conformist attitude toward established social arrangements. F. H. Bradley's 'My Station and Its Duties' strikes the modern reader as a curiously dated piece of moral philosophy at least partly because we find it impossible to share the sanguine view of Victorian society it presupposes.

A second, not unrelated, change has to do with the growing recognition that normative social theory – theory which takes questions about the moral acceptability of social institutions to be of central importance – is unlikely to attach much significance to supposed lines of demarcation between 'social' and 'economic' or between 'legal' and 'political' philosophy. While these distinctions no doubt serve a number of useful purposes, it is antecedently most unlikely that the principles needed for the evaluation of *political* arrangements will be found to be *toto caelo* different, in content and rationale, from the principles which ought to guide us when we attempt to assess such (ostensibly) *non-political* institutions as the market. This is partly a point about the classification of moral principles, but it is also a point about their scope. Attempts to protect what goes on within such demarcated zones as the 'private sector' or 'the market' from unfavorable assessment in the light of principles of distributive justice or the principle which prohibits conduct which is gratuitously harmful to innocent third parties – principles which would be invoked without hesitation in other areas of individual and social life – are plainly in need of rather special justification. The onus is on those who wish to restrict the range of application of such principles to show both that and why the restrictions should be respected.

Around a third interesting feature of recent moral philosophy a consensus has yet to develop, but work in the various parts of applied ethics strongly suggests that it may be methodologically perverse to assume that the principles to be applied – the principles supposedly constitutive of (so-called) *pure* moral theory – can be identified, or articulated, or defended, without careful exploration of their practical implications. The (Rawlsian) view that an 'equilibrium' should be establishable between moral principles and at least the most confident of the judgments reflective moral agents would be disposed to make in particular cases has the considerable virtue of subjecting moral philosophers with an occupational bias in favor of highly general theories to the discipline of a salutary constraint. However, the various parts of applied ethics provide more than a testing ground for the claims of moral theorists. It is not unreasonable to expect that work on the conceptual and normative problems which provide the agenda in these fields will prove indispensable to the task of asking the right kinds of more general questions and of asking them in the right way. How, for example, is the principle that agreements ought to be kept to be interpreted and justified without close attention to the presuppositions and implications of agreements of different kinds? Not all agreements are, or ought to be, legally enforceable, for example. Again, the purposes served by agreements run the gamut from purposes it is arguably morally incumbent upon individuals and groups to pursue, through purposes to the pursuit of which there can be no reasonable objection, to purposes which are uncontroversially objectionable. Without careful exploration of the contexts in which agreements of these very diverse sorts are actually concluded, it is idle to hope that a judiciously formulated rule about the moral propriety of the keeping of agreements can be arrived at. Indeed, the links between the 'pure' and the 'applied' parts of moral philosophy are so close that the risk of failure may be great for moral philosophers with a cultivated distaste for problems of application.

I

When we reflect on the moral significance of business activity in its various forms, we should first set aside the view that business imperatives and the demands of morality are irreconcilably opposed, even though – somewhat ironically – it sometimes seems to provide the only point of agreement between hard-nosed business executives and utopian moralists. We can then move toward an account of the ethical issues to which moral philosophers ought to be particularly attentive in this area by asking about the conditions under which individuals could plausibly hope to be able to combine successful pursuit of a business career with maintenance of moral integrity. Three instructively different answers to this question are worth reviewing.

1   According to one possible account – the least adventurous, but also, as we shall see, the most vulnerable – the key to combining business

success with moral integrity lies in the meticulous discharge of role-related or position-determined responsibilities and in the development of such personal virtues as loyalty to associates, courtesy and consideration to subordinates, and honesty and trustworthiness in all business dealings.

2 Central to a second account is the recognition that tame acceptance of organizational roles, rules, and objectives is inconsistent with imaginative compliance with the demands of morality. On this view ethically responsible business executives must use whatever leeway their positions afford them to go beyond mere conformity to existing institutional rules, but in ways which do not require them to challenge the broader framework – economic, legal, political – within which these rules are normally applied. Thus they may make spontaneous efforts to effect improvements in the working conditions, rates of pay, and fringe benefits of their employees, or to protect the long-term interests of shareholders, or to respond constructively to the concerns of customers and clients, or to deal fairly and generously with their business competitors, or to be solicitous of the interests of the wider community and of the impact of their decisions on its welfare. They will take action along these lines, moreover, in not too calculating a spirit and without waiting for discontent-fueled demands in these areas to be presented.

3 There is a third possible answer, more ambitious than the second, an answer which extends even further the 'reach' of morality in business settings. According to this view, members of the business community can express the firmness of their commitment to the moral point of view by attempting to combine imaginative exploitation of the opportunities afforded by existing arrangements with the playing of a vigorous and enlightened role in the ongoing task of helping to restructure the broader institutional environment – legal, economic, political – within which business activity takes place.

II

For the first of these views the distinguishing characteristic of morally responsible business executives is their recognition of the force even in business settings of the familiar precepts of personal morality. However, important though it no doubt is in most circumstances for such virtues as conscientiousness, trustworthiness, honesty, and thoughtfulness to be displayed on the job no less than in off-duty hours, exclusive emphasis on the development of these qualities does nothing to allay such moral disquiet as there may well be about common business practices and about features of the larger institutional framework presupposed or shaped by business activity.

It is these broader concerns which animate the second and third views.

Thus the second draws attention to the scope there usually is for morally enterprising individuals to effect changes in the structural or operating rules of the organizations to which they belong. As for the third view, it comes into its own once it is observed that even when businesspeople have reasonably extensive opportunities to bring about constructive changes in the structures or the policies of the organizations to which they belong, they may be powerless to do anything about problems which have their source in *society-wide* practices. Competitive pressures, for example, may make it economically impracticable – and ineffectual into the bargain – for a single firm, no matter how morally enlightened its leadership, to attempt *on its own* to reduce environmental pollution, or to improve significantly the economic position or the working conditions of employees, or to abandon morally dubious advertising and marketing strategies. It would no doubt be unfair in such cases to condemn failure on the part of particular businesses to take *independent* action. It is, however, much more difficult to shield business leaders from criticism if they have strenuously opposed public policies aimed at *requiring* private sector organizations to play their part in controlling pollution or in improving working conditions or in phasing out socially objectionable marketing practices. There is of course a conflict between support for government action along these lines and loyalty to the free market ideal (or to the related view that government intervention in economic life must be minimized). However, the existence of this sort of conflict merely serves to underscore the moral dubiousness, in the circumstances supposed, of resolutely anti-interventionist conceptions of the government's role in the economy.

III

It is arguably the second and third views which need special emphasis when attention is directed to the tensions there often are between business imperatives and moral demands. This is partly because the first view is likely to be rejected *in toto* only by those who suppose that the writ of morality does not run during business hours. It is also because an acceptable version of the first view cannot be articulated if the other two views are ignored. Diligence in the execution of job-related responsibilities, for example, is likely to qualify as a morally desirable quality only when the private interests served by such diligence are not too glaringly at odds with the public interest – something which cannot be ascertained without investigation of the objectives pursued by the organizations in question and of the role they play in the wider society.

The second and third views are of course in no way incompatible. They differ merely in focus. The one asks how far imaginative initiatives taken by *individual* business executives or by *individual* firms can contribute to improvement of the moral quality of what is done in business settings, while the other directs attention to the fact that morally necessary change sometimes requires the *concerted* action over time of many different individuals and organizations, generally with the government playing the crucial role of facilitating or orchestrating such action.

Whether the second and third views can be combined with the first view is more difficult to determine. This is because views 2 and 3 require us to question the moral credentials of existing institutional arrangements, while view 1, in at least some of the forms it may take, appears to endorse a rather more conservative, not to say conformist, attitude towards the *status quo*. From the vantage point of those who embrace the second and third views, the personal virtues which are particularly emphasized by the first view – such virtues as loyalty and conscientiousness, for example – deserve only qualified endorsement; they should be endorsed *only if* the organizational rules, roles, and objectives they presuppose have survived moral scrutiny.

If the second and third views I have outlined provide a more adequate framework than the first view does for the handling of questions about the terms on which business success can be sought without sacrifice of moral integrity, it is the "macro" rather than the "micro" questions in the field of "ethics and business" which are most in need of attention. By "macro" questions I mean of course questions about the moral satisfactoriness of the institutional framework within which business activity takes place, by contrast with the ethically toned ("micro") questions which confront individual business executives in the day-to-day exercise of their responsibilities. Since there is perhaps a tendency for the ethical dilemmas dramatized in many business case studies to be "micro" questions, in form at least, it is important not only that cases be considered which highlight the "macro" questions but also that discussion of the "micro" issues proceed in the light of the "macro" questions they too will be found to presuppose.

IV

I conclude by mentioning two clusters of questions to which we lack adequate answers at present but which moral philosophers who take questions about business institutions and practices seriously should place high on their agenda.

First, how is the distinction between the so-called 'public' and 'private' sectors to be understood in societies in which there has been a blurring over time both of the differences and of the boundaries between them? And what is the normative significance of the distinction in the form in which it is worth salvaging? Is it really more important, for example, for the public interest to be served by what is done in the public sector than by what is permitted in the private sector? Are discriminatory hiring practices – those, for example, which give preference to the relatives of employees (or employers) – any more acceptable in the private sector than they would be in the public sector? And if a broadly democratic approach to decision-making in public sector institutions is thought to be desirable, what precisely is the case for resisting moves in the direction of more democratic structures and processes within private sector institutions?

A second cluster of questions have to do with the nature of market arrangements. Both defenders and critics of government intervention in the marketplace sometimes make the mistake of talking as though there were no difference between *market* arrangements and *free market* arrangements. Yet it is surely plausible to suppose that *any* society will have market arrangements of *some* sort, just as a *legal* system of some sort or other is bound to be part of the social set-up in any society. The really interesting question, consequently, is not *whether* we should have markets, but rather what their purpose and scope ought to be and what rules (including legal rules) we ought to put in place to circumscribe the activities of market participants. The free market ideal, in its various formulations, contributes an answer to these questions, but it is by no means the only – or even the most plausible – of the available answers. However, if the debate between the sponsors of competing approaches to the structuring of market arrangements is to be conducted fruitfully, at least the supposition will have to be abandoned that a fateful choice must be made between a 'market economy' and a 'planned economy'. These, it should be clear, are not the interesting alternatives. Neither, indeed, is a single determinate alternative. Both, rather, are classes – overlapping classes – of alternatives, and it is probably no bold conjecture that all the interesting options will be located within the area of overlap.

13
Business Ethics and Stakeholder Analysis

Kenneth Goodpaster

There has been a great deal of attention paid to "stakeholder analysis" in business ethics as a possible means by which to include ethical values associated with social responsibility into management decision-making. In this paper Goodpaster subjects this whole strategy to critical review in an effort to better understand and define ethical management decisions. Goodpaster first distinguishes between "stakeholder analysis" and what he calls "stakeholder synthesis," arguing that only stakeholder synthesis offers a pattern or channel by which to incorporate stakeholder interests into a practical response or resolution. He then distinguishes and discusses two different kinds of stakeholder synthesise which naturally arise: strategic and multi-fiduciary. Paradoxically, the former type of decision-making appears to yield business without ethics and the latter appears to yield ethics without business. Goodpaster concludes by arguing that a third approach to stakeholder thinking needs to be developed, one that avoids the paradox just mentioned and that clarifies for managers and directors the legitimate role of ethical considerations connected with social responsibility in business management.

This paper should be compared with the others in the section on business ethics, most particularly with those of Philips (chapter 10) and Solomon (chapter 11).

> *So we must think through what management should be accountable for: and how and through whom its accountability can be discharged. The stockholders' interest, both short- and long-term, is one of the areas. But it is only one.*
>
> Peter Drucker, *Harvard Business Review*, 1988

What is ethically responsible management? How can a corporation, given its economic mission, be managed with appropriate attention to ethical concerns? These are central questions in the field of business ethics. One approach to answering such questions that has become popular during the last two decades is loosely referred to as "stakeholder analysis."

Ethically responsible management, it is often suggested, is management that includes careful attention not only to stockholders *but to stakeholders generally* in the decision-making process.

This suggestion about the ethical importance of stakeholder analysis contains an important kernel of truth, but it can also be misleading. Comparing the ethical relationship between managers and stockholders with their relationship to other stakeholders is, I will argue, almost as problematic as ignoring stakeholders (ethically) altogether – presenting us with something of a "stakeholder paradox."

Definition

The term "stakeholder" appears to have been invented in the early 1960s as a deliberate play on the word "stockholder" to signify that there are other parties having a "stake" in the decision-making of the modern, publicly held corporation in addition to those holding equity positions. Professor R. Edward Freeman, in his book *Strategic Management: A Stakeholder Approach*, defines the term as follows: "A stakeholder in an organization is (by definition) any group or individual who can affect or is affected by the achievement of the organization's objectives."[1] Examples of stakeholder groups (beyond stockholders) are employees, suppliers, customers, creditors, competitors, governments, and communities. Figure 1 illustrates one way of picturing the conventional stakeholder groups along with the two principal channels through which they often affect the corporation: law and markets.

Another metaphor with which the term "stakeholder" is associated is that of a "player" in a game like poker. One with a "stake" in the game is one who plays and puts some economic value at risk.[2]

Much of what makes responsible decision-making difficult is understanding how there can be an ethical relationship between management and stakeholders that avoids being too weak (making stakeholders mere means to stockholders' ends) or too strong (making stakeholders quasi-stockholders in their own right). To give these issues life, a case example will help. So let us consider the case of General Motors and Poletown.[3]

The Poletown Case

In 1980, GM was facing a net loss in income, the first since 1921, due to intense foreign competition. Management realized that major capital

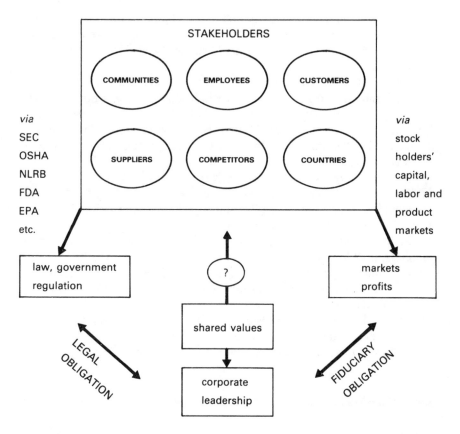

Figure 1 Business decision-making and ethical values

expenditures would be required for the company to regain its competitive position and profitability. A $40 billion five-year capital spending program was announced that included new, state-of-the-art assembly techniques aimed at smaller, fuel-efficient automobiles demanded by the market. Two aging assembly plants in Detroit were among the ones to be replaced. Their closure would eliminate 500 jobs. Detroit in 1980 was a city with a black majority, an unemployment rate of 18 percent overall and 30 percent for blacks, a rising public debt, and a chronic budget deficit, despite high tax rates.

The site requirements for a new assembly plant included 500 acres, access to long-haul railroad and freeways, and proximity to suppliers for "just-in-time" inventory management. It needed to be ready to produce 1983 model year cars beginning in September 1982. The only site in Detroit meeting GM's requirements was heavily settled, covering a section of the Detroit neighborhood of Poletown. Of the 3,500 residents, half were black. The whites were mostly of Polish descent, retired or nearing retirement. An alternative "green field" site was available in another midwestern state.

Using the power of eminent domain, the Poletown area could be acquired and cleared for a new plant within the company's timetable, and the city government was eager to cooperate. Because of job retention in Detroit, the leadership of the United Auto Workers was also in favor of the idea. The Poletown Neighborhood Council strongly opposed the plan, but was willing to work with the city and GM.

The new plant would employ 6,150 workers and would cost GM $500 million wherever it was built. Obtaining and preparing the Poletown site would cost an additional $200 million, whereas alternative sites in the midwest were available for $65–80 million.

The interested parties were many – stockholders, customers, employees, suppliers, the Detroit community, the midwestern alternative, the Poletown neighborhood. The decision was difficult. GM management needed to consider its competitive situation, the extra costs of remaining in Detroit, the consequences to the city of leaving for another part of the midwest, and the implications for the residents of choosing the Poletown site if the decision were made to stay. The decision about whom to talk to and *how* was as puzzling as the decision about *what* to do and *why*.

Stakeholder Analysis and Stakeholder Synthesis

Ethical values enter management decision-making, it is often suggested, through the gate of stakeholder analysis. But the suggestion that introducing "stakeholder analysis" into business decisions is the same as introducing ethics into those decisions is questionable. To make this plain, let me first distinguish between two importantly different ideas: stakeholder analysis and stakeholder synthesis. I will then examine alternative kinds of stakeholder synthesis with attention to ethical content.

The decision-making process of an individual or a company can be seen in terms of a sequence of six steps to be followed after an issue or problem presents itself for resolution.[4] For ease of reference and recall, I will name the sequence PASCAL, after the six letters in the name of the French philosopher–mathematician Blaise Pascal (1623–62), who once remarked in reference to ethical decision-making that "the heart has reasons that reason knows not of."

1 PERCEPTION or fact-gathering about the options available and their short- and long-term implications;

2   ANALYSIS of these implications with specific attention to affected parties and to the decision-maker's goals, objectives, values, responsibilities, etc.;

3   SYNTHESIS of this structured information according to whatever fundamental priorities obtain in the mindset of the decision-maker;

4   CHOICE among the available options based on the synthesis;

5   ACTION or implementation of the chosen option through a series of specific requests to specific individuals or groups, resource allocation, incentives, controls, and feedback;

6   LEARNING from the outcome of the decision, resulting in either reinforcement or modification (for future decisions) of the way in which the above steps have been taken.

We might simplify this analysis, of course, to something like "input," "decision," and "output," but distinguishing interim steps can often be helpful. The main point is that the path from the presentation of a problem to its resolution must somehow involve gathering, processing, and acting on relevant information.

Now, by *stakeholder analysis* I simply mean a process that does not go beyond the first two steps mentioned above. That is, the affected parties caught up in each available option are identified and the positive and negative impacts on each stakeholder are determined. But questions having to do with processing this information into a decision and implementing it are *left unanswered*. These steps are not part of the *analysis* but of the *synthesis, choice* and *action*.

Stakeholder analysis may give the initial appearance of a decision-making process, but in fact is only a *segment* of a decision-making process. It represents the preparatory or opening phase that awaits the crucial application of the moral (or nonmoral) values of the decision-maker. So, to be informed that an individual or an institution regularly makes stakeholder analysis part of decision-making or takes a "stakeholder approach" to management is to learn little or nothing about the ethical character of that individual or institution. It is to learn only that stakeholders are regularly identified – *not why and for what purpose*. To be told that stakeholders are or must be "taken into account" is, so far, to be told very little. Stakeholder analysis is, as a practical matter, morally *neutral*. It is therefore a mistake to see it as a substitute for normative ethical thinking.[5]

What I shall call "stakeholder synthesis" goes further into the sequence of decision-making steps mentioned above to include actual decision-making and implementation (S, C, A). The critical point is that stakeholder synthesis offers *a pattern or channel by which to move from stakeholder identification to a practical response or resolution*. Here we begin to join stakeholder analysis to questions of substance. But we must now ask:

What kind of substance? And how does it relate to *ethics*? The stakeholder idea, remember, is typically offered as a way of integrating *ethical* values into management decision-making. When and how does substance become *ethical* substance?

Strategic Stakeholder Synthesis

We can imagine decision-makers doing "stakeholder analysis" for different underlying reasons, not always having to do with ethics. A management team, for example, might be careful to take positive and (especially) negative stakeholder effects into account for no other reason than that offended stakeholders might resist or retaliate (e.g. through political action or opposition to necessary regulatory clearances). It might not be *ethical* concern for the stakeholders that motivates and guides such analysis, so much as concern about potential impediments to the achievement of strategic objectives. Thus positive and negative effects on relatively powerless stakeholders may be ignored or discounted in the synthesis, choice, and action phases of the decision process.[6]

In the Poletown case, General Motors might have done a stakeholder analysis using the following reasoning: our stockholders are the central stakeholders here, but other key stakeholders include our suppliers, old and new plant employees, the City of Detroit, and the residents of Poletown. These other stakeholders are not our direct concern as a corporation with an economic mission, but since they can influence our short- or long-term strategic interests, they must be taken into account. Public relations costs and benefits, for example, or concerns about union contracts or litigation, might well have influenced the choice between staying in Detroit and going elsewhere.

I refer to this kind of stakeholder synthesis as "strategic" since stakeholders outside the stockholder group are viewed instrumentally, as factors potentially affecting the overarching goal of optimizing stockholder interests. They are taken into account in the decision-making process, but as external environmental forces, as potential sources of either goodwill or retaliation. "We" are the economic principals and management; "they" are significant players whose attitudes and future actions might affect our short-term or long-term success. We must respect them in the way one "respects" the weather – as a set of forces to be reckoned with.[7]

It should be emphasized that managers who adopt the strategic stakeholder approach are not necessarily *personally* indifferent to the plight of stakeholders who are "strategically unimportant." The point is that *in their role as managers*, with a fiduciary relationship that binds them as agents to principals, their basic outlook subordinates other stakeholder concerns to those of stockholders. Market and legal forces are relied upon to secure the interests of those whom strategic considerations might discount. This reliance can and does take different forms, depending on the emphasis given to market forces on the one hand and legal forces on the other. A more conservative, market-oriented view acknowledges the role of legal compliance as an environmental factor affecting strategic choice, but thinks stakeholder interests are best served by minimal interference from the public sector. Adam Smith's "invisible hand" is thought to be the most important guarantor of the common good in a competitive economy. A more liberal view sees the hand of government, through legislation and regulation, as essential for representing stakeholders that might otherwise not achieve "standing" in the strategic decision process.

What both conservatives and liberals have in common is the conviction that the fundamental orientation of management must be toward the interests of stockholders. Other stakeholders (customers, employees, suppliers, neighbors) enter the decision-making equation either directly as instrumental economic factors or indirectly as potential legal claimants (see again figure 1). Both see law and regulation as providing a voice for stakeholders that goes beyond market dynamics. They differ about how much government regulation is socially and economically desirable.

During the Poletown controversy, GM managers as individuals may have cared deeply about the potential lost jobs in Detroit, or about the potential dislocation of Poletown residents. But in their role as agents for the owners (stockholders) they could allow such considerations to "count" only if they served GM's strategic interests (or perhaps as legal constraints on the decision).

Professor Freeman appears to adopt some form of strategic stakeholder synthesis. After presenting his definition of stakeholders, he remarks on its application to any group or individual "who can *affect* or is *affected by*" a company's achievement of its purposes. The "affect" part of the definition is not hard to understand; but Freeman clarifies the "affected by" part:

> The point of strategic management is in some sense to chart a direction for the firm. Groups which can affect that direction and its implementation must be considered in the strategic management process. However, it is less obvious why "those groups who are affected by the corporation" are stakeholders as well . . . I make the definition symmetric because of the changes which the firm has undergone in the past few years. Groups which 20 years ago had no effect on the actions of the firm, can affect it today, largely because of the actions of the firm which ignored the effects on these groups. Thus, by calling those affected groups "stakeholders," the ensuing strategic management model will be sensitive to future change.[8]

Freeman might have said "who can actually or potentially affect" the company, for the mindset appears to be one in which attention to stakeholders is justified in terms of actual or potential impact on the company's achievement of its strategic purposes. Stakeholders (other than stockholders) are actual or potential means/obstacles to corporate objectives. A few pages later, Freeman writes:

> From the standpoint of strategic management, or the achievement of organizational purpose, we need an inclusive definition. We must not leave out any group or individual who can affect or is affected by organizational purpose, *because that group may prevent our accomplishments.*[9]

The essence of a strategic view of stakeholders is not that stakeholders are ignored, but that all but a special group (stockholders) are considered on the basis of their actual or potential influence on management's central mission. The basic normative principle is fiduciary responsibility (organizational prudence), supplemented by legal compliance.

Is the Substance Ethical?

The question we must ask in thinking about a strategic approach to stakeholder synthesis is this: Is it really an adequate rendering of the *ethical* component in managerial judgment? Unlike mere stakeholder analysis, this kind of synthesis does go beyond simply *identifying* stakeholders. It integrates the stakeholder information by using a single interest group (stockholders) as its basic normative touchstone. If this were formulated as an explicit rule or principle, it would have two parts and would read something like this: (1) maximize the benefits and minimize the costs to the stockholder group, short- and long-term, and (2) pay close attention to the interests of other stakeholder groups that might potentially influence the achievement of (1). But while expanding the list of stakeholders may be a way of "enlightening" self-interest for the organization, is it really a way of introducing ethical values into business decision-making?

There are two possible replies here. The first is that as an account of how ethics enters the managerial mindset, the strategic stakeholder approach fails not because it is *im*moral, but because it is *non*moral. By most accounts of the nature of ethics, a strategic stakeholder synthesis would not qualify as an ethical synthesis, even though it does represent a substantive view. The point is simply that while there is nothing necessarily *wrong* with strategic reasoning about the consequences of one's actions for others, the kind of concern exhibited should not be confused with what most people regard as *moral* concern. Moral concern would avoid injury or unfairness to those affected by one's actions because it is wrong, regardless of the retaliatory potential of the aggrieved parties.[10]

The second reply does question the morality (vs immorality) of strategic reasoning as the ultimate principle behind stakeholder analysis. It acknowledges that strategy, when placed in a highly effective legal and regulatory environment and given a time horizon that is relatively long-term, may well avoid significant forms of anti-social behavior. But it asserts that as an operating principle for managers under time pressure in an imperfect legal and regulatory environment, strategic analysis is insufficient. In the Poletown case, certain stakeholders (e.g. the citizens of Detroit or the residents of Poletown) may have merited more *ethical* consideration than the strategic approach would have allowed. Some critics charged that GM only considered these stakeholders *to the extent that* serving their interests also served GM's interests, and that as a result, their interests were undermined.

Many, most notably Nobel Laureate Milton Friedman, believe that market and legal forces are adequate to translate or transmute ethical concerns into straightforward strategic concerns for management. He believes that in our economic and political system (democratic capitalism), direct concern for stakeholders (what Kant might have called "categorical" concern) is unnecessary, redundant, and inefficient, not to mention dishonest:

> In many cases, there is a strong temptation to rationalize actions as an exercise of "social responsibility." In the present climate of opinion, with its widespread aversion to "capitalism," "profits," the "soulless corporation" and so on, this is one way for a corporation to generate good will as a by-product of expenditures that are entirely justified in its own self-interest. If our institutions, and the attitudes of the public make it in their self-interest to cloak their actions in this way, I cannot summon much indignation to denounce them. At the same time, I can express admiration for those individual proprietors or owners of closely held corporations or stockholders of more broadly held corporations who disdain such tactics as approaching fraud.[11]

Critics respond, however, that absent a pre-established harmony or linkage between organizational success and ethical success, some stakeholders, some of the time, will be affected a lot but will be able to affect the interests of the corporation in only a minor way. They add that in an increasingly global business environment, even the protections of law are fragmented by multiple jurisdictions.

At issue, then, are (1) defining ethical behavior partly in terms of the (nonstrategic) decision-making values *behind* it, and (2) recognizing that too much optimism about the correlation between strategic success and virtue runs the risk of tailoring the latter to suit the former.

Thus the move toward substance (from analysis to synthesis) in discussions of the stakeholder concept is not necessarily a move toward ethics. And it is natural to think that the reason has to do with the instrumental status accorded to stakeholder groups other than stockholders. If we were to treat all stakeholders by strict analogy with stockholders, would we have arrived at a more ethically satisfactory form of stakeholder synthesis? Let us now look at this alternative, what I shall call a "multi-fiduciary" approach.

Multi-fiduciary Stakeholder Synthesis

In contrast to a strategic view of stakeholders, one can imagine a management team processing stakeholder information by giving the same care to the interests of, say, employees, customers, and local communities as to the economic interests of stakeholders. This kind of substantive commitment to stakeholders might involve trading off the economic advantages of one group against those of another, e.g. in a decision to close a plant. I shall refer to this way of integrating stakeholder analysis with decision-making as "multi-fiduciary" since all stakeholders are treated by management as having equally important interests, deserving joint "maximization" (or what Herbert Simon might call "satisficing").

Professor Freeman contemplates what I am calling the multi-fiduciary view at the end of his 1984 book under the heading "The Manager As Fiduciary To Stakeholders":

> Perhaps the most important area of future research is the issue of whether or not a theory of management can be constructed that uses the stakeholder concept to enrich "managerial capitalism," that is, can the notion that managers bear a fiduciary relationship to stockholders or the owners of the firm, be replaced by a concept of management whereby the manager *must* act in the interests of the stakeholders in the organization?[12]

As we have seen, the strategic approach pays attention to stakeholders as to factors that might affect economic interests, so many market forces to which companies must pay attention for competitive reasons. They become actual or potential legal challenges to the company's exercise of economic rationality. The multi-fiduciary approach, on the other hand, views stakeholders apart from their instrumental, economic, or legal clout. It does not see them merely as what philosopher John Ladd once called "limiting operating conditions" on management attention.[13] On this view, the word "stakeholder" carries with it, by the deliberate modification of a single phoneme, a dramatic shift in managerial outlook.

In 1954, famed management theorist Adolf Berle conceded a long-standing debate with Harvard law professor E. Merrick Dodd that looks in retrospect very much like a debate between what we are calling strategic and multi-fiduciary interpretations of stakeholder synthesis. Berle wrote:

> Twenty years ago, [I held] that corporate powers were powers in trust for shareholders while Professor Dodd argued that these powers were held in trust for the entire community. The argument has been settled (at least for the time being) squarely in favor of Professor Dodd's contention.[14]

The intuitive idea behind Dodd's view, and behind more recent formulations of it in terms of "multiple constituencies" and "stakeholders, not just stockholders," is that by expanding the list of those in whose trust corporate management must manage, we thereby introduce ethical responsibility into business decision-making.

In the context of the Poletown case, a multi-fiduciary approach by GM management might have identified the same stakeholders. But it would have considered the interests of employees, the city of Detroit, and the Poletown residents *alongside* stockholder interests, not solely in terms of how they might *influence* stockholder interests. This may or may not have entailed a different outcome. But it probably would have meant a different approach to the decision-making process in relation to the residents of Poletown (talking with them, for example).

We must now ask, as we did of the strategic approach: How satisfactory is multi-fiduciary stakeholder synthesis as a way of giving ethical substance to management decision-making? On the face of it, and in stark contrast to the strategic approach, it may seem that we have at last arrived at a truly moral view. But we should be cautious. For no sooner do we think we have found the proper interpretation of ethics in management than a major objection presents itself. And, yes, it appears to be a *moral* objection!

It can be argued that multi-fiduciary stakeholder analysis is simply incompatible with widely held moral convictions about the special fiduciary obligations owed by management to stockholders. At the center of the objection is the belief that the obligations of agents to principals are stronger than or different in kind from those of agents to third parties.

The Stakeholder Paradox

Managers who would pursue a multi-fiduciary stakeholder orientation for their companies must face resistance from those who believe that a strategic orientation is the only *legitimate* one for business to adopt, given the economic mission and legal constitution of the modern corporation. This may be disorienting since the word "illegitimate" has clear negative ethical connotations, and yet the multi-fiduciary approach is often defended on ethical grounds. I will refer to this anomalous situation as the *Stakeholder Paradox*: It seems essential, yet in some ways illegitimate, to orient corporate decisions by ethical values that go beyond strategic stakeholder considerations to multi-fiduciary ones. I call this a paradox because it says there is an ethical problem whichever approach management takes. Ethics seems both to forbid and to demand a strategic, profit-maximizing mindset. The argument behind the paradox focuses on management's *fiduciary* duty to the stockholder, essentially the duty to keep a profit-maximizing promise, and a concern that the "impartiality" of the multi-fiduciary approach simply cuts management loose from certain well-defined bonds of stockholder accountability. On this view, impartiality is thought to be a *betrayal of trust*.

Professor David S. Ruder, a former chairman of the US Securities and Exchange Commission, once summarized the matter this way:

> Traditional fiduciary obligation theory insists that a corporate manager owes an obligation of care and loyalty to shareholders. If a public obligation theory unrelated to profit maximization becomes the law, the corporate manager who is not able to act in his own self interest without violating his fiduciary obligation, may nevertheless act in the public interest without violating that obligation.

He continued:

> Whether induced by government legislation, government pressure, or merely by enlightened attitudes of the corporation regarding its long range potential as a unit in society, corporate activities carried on in satisfaction of public obligations can be consistent with profit maximization objectives. In contrast, justification of public obligations upon bold concepts of public need without corporate benefit will merely serve to reduce further the owner's influence on his corporation and to create additional demands for public participation in corporate management.[15]

Ruder's view appears to be that (a) multi-fiduciary stakeholder synthesis *need not* be used by management because the strategic approach is more accommodating than meets the eye; and (b) multi-fiduciary stakeholder synthesis should not be invoked by management because such a "bold" concept could threaten the private (vs public) status of the corporation.

In response to (a), we saw earlier that there were reasonable questions about the tidy convergence of ethics and economic success. Respecting the interests and rights of the Poletown residents might really have meant incurring higher costs for GM (short-term as well as long-term).

Appeals to corporate self-interest, even long-term, might not always support ethical decisions. But even on those occasions where they will, we must wonder about the disposition to favor economic and legal reasoning "for the record." If Ruder means to suggest that business leaders can often *reformulate* or *re-present* their reasons for certain morally grounded decisions in strategic terms having to do with profit maximization and obedience to law, he is perhaps correct. In the spirit of our earlier quotation from Milton Friedman, we might not summon much indignation to denounce them. But why the fiction? Why not call a moral reason a moral reason?

This issue is not simply of academic interest. Managers must confront it in practice. In one major public company, the chief executive officer put significant resources behind an affirmative action program and included the following explanation in a memo to middle management:

> I am often asked why this is such a high priority at our company. There is, of course, the obvious answer that it is in our best interest to seek out and employ good people in all sectors of our society. And there is the answer that enlightened self-interest tells us that more and more of the younger people, whom we must attract as future employees, choose companies by their social records as much as by their business prospects. *But the one overriding reason for this emphasis is because it is right.* Because this company has always set for itself the objective of assuming social as well as business obligations. Because that's the kind of company we have been. And with your participation, that's the kind of company we'll continue to be.[16]

In this connection, Ruder reminds us of what Professor Berle observed over twenty-five years ago:

> The fact is that boards of directors or corporation executives are often faced with situations in which they quite humanly and simply consider that such and such is the decent thing to do and ought to be done . . . They apply the potential profits or public relations tests later on, a sort of left-handed justification in this curious free-market world where an obviously moral or decent or humane action has to be apologized for on the ground that, conceivably, you may somehow make money by it.[17]

The Problem of Boldness

What appears to lie at the foundation of Ruder's cautious view is a concern about the "boldness" of the multi-fiduciary concept ((b) above).[18] It is not that he thinks the strategic approach is always satisfactory; it is that the multi-fiduciary approach is, in his eyes, much worse. For it questions the special relationship between the manager as agent and the stockholder as principal.

Ruder suggests that what he calls a "public obligation" theory threatens the private status of the corporation. He believes that what we are calling multi-fiduciary stakeholder synthesis *dilutes* the fiduciary obligation to stockholders (by extending it to customers, employees, suppliers, etc.) and he sees this as a threat to the "privacy" of the private sector organization. If public obligations are understood on the model of public sector institutions with their multiple constituencies, Ruder thinks, the stockholder loses status.

There is something profoundly *right* about Ruder's line of argument here, I believe, and something profoundly *wrong*. What is right is his intuition that if we treat other stakeholders on the model of the fiduciary relationship between management and the stockholder, we will, in effect, make them into quasi-stockholders. We can do this, of course, if we choose to as a society. But we should be aware that it is a radical step indeed. For it blurs traditional goals in terms of entrepreneurial risk-taking, pushes decision-making toward paralysis because of the dilemmas posed by divided loyalties, and, in the final analysis, represents nothing less than the conversion of the modern private corporation into a public institution and probably calls for a corresponding restructuring of corporate governance (e.g. representatives of each stakeholder group on the board of directors). Unless we believe that the social utility of a private sector has disappeared, not to mention its value for individual liberty and enterprise, we will be cautious about an interpretation of stakeholder synthesis that transforms the private sector into the public sector.

On the other hand, I believe Ruder is mistaken if he thinks that business ethics requires this kind of either/or: either a private sector with a strategic stakeholder synthesis (business without ethics) or the effective loss of the private sector with a multi-fiduciary stakeholder synthesis (ethics without business).

Recent debates over state laws protecting companies against hostile takeovers may illustrate Ruder's concern as well as the new challenge.

According to journalist Christopher Elias, a recent Pennsylvania anti-takeover law

> does no less than redefine the fiduciary duty of corporate directors, enabling them to base decisions not merely on the interests of shareholders, but on the interests of customers, suppliers, employees and the community at large. Pennsylvania is saying that it is the corporation that directors are responsible to. Shareholders say they always thought they themselves were the corporation.[19]

Echoing Ruder, one legal observer quoted by Elias commented with reference to this law that it "undermines and erodes free markets and property rights. From this perspective, this is an anticapitalist law. The management can take away property from the real owners."

In our terms, the state of Pennsylvania is charged with adopting a multi-fiduciary stakeholder approach in an effort to rectify deficiencies of the strategic approach which (presumably) corporate raiders hold.

The challenge with which we are thus presented is to develop an account of the moral responsibilities of management that (1) avoid surrendering the moral relationship between management and stakeholders as the strategic view does, while (2) not transforming stakeholder obligations into fiduciary obligations (thus protecting the uniqueness of the principal–agent relationship between management and stockholder).

Toward a New Stakeholder Synthesis

We all remember the story of the well-intentioned Doctor Frankenstein. He sought to improve the human condition by designing a powerful, intelligent force for good in the community. Alas, when he flipped the switch, his creation turned out to be a monster rather than a marvel! Is the concept of the ethical corporation like a Frankenstein monster?

Taking business ethics seriously need not mean that management bears *additional* fiduciary relationships to third parties (nonstockholder constituencies) as multi-fiduciary stakeholder synthesis suggests. It may mean that there are morally significant *nonfiduciary* obligations to third parties surrounding any fiduciary relationship (see figure 2). Such moral obligations may be owed by private individuals as well as private sector organizations to those whose freedom and well-being is affected by their economic behavior. It is these very obligations, in fact (the duty not to harm or coerce and duties not to lie, cheat, or steal), that are cited in regulatory, legislative, and judicial arguments for constraining profit-driven

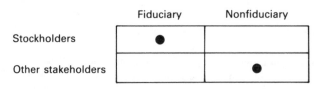

Figure 2   Direct managerial obligations

business activities. These obligations are not "hypothetical" or contingent or indirect, as they would be on the strategic model, wherein they are only subject to the corporation's interests being met. They are "categorical" or direct. They are not rooted in the *fiduciary* relationship, but in other relationships at least as deep.

It must be admitted in fairness to Ruder's argument that the jargon of "stakeholders" in discussions of business ethics can seem to threaten the notion of what corporate law refers to as the "undivided and unselfish loyalty" owed by managers and directors to stockholders. For this way of speaking can suggest a multiplication of management duties *of the same kind* as the duty to stockholders. What we must understand is that the responsibilities of management toward stockholders are of a piece with the obligations that *stockholders themselves* would be expected to honor in their own right. As an old Latin proverb has it, *nemo dat quod non habet*, which literally means "nobody gives what he doesn't have." Freely translating in this context we can say: No one can expect of an *agent* behavior that is ethically less responsible than what he would expect of himself. I cannot (ethically) *hire* done on my behalf what I would not (ethically) *do* myself. We might refer to this as the "Nemo Dat Principle" (NDP) and consider it a formal requirement of consistency in business ethics (and professional ethics generally):

(NDP)   Investors cannot expect of managers (more generally, principals cannot expect of their agents) behavior that would be inconsistent with the reasonable ethical expectations of the community.[20]

The NDP does not, of course, resolve in advance the many ethical challenges that managers must face. It only indicates that these challenges are of a piece with those that face us all. It offers a different kind of test (and so a different kind of stakeholder synthesis) that management (and institutional investors) might apply to policies and decisions.

The foundation of ethics in management – and the way out of the stakeholder paradox – lies in understanding that the conscience of the corporation is a logical and moral extension of the consciences of its principals. It is *not* an expansion of the *list* of principals, but a gloss on the principal–agent relationship itself. Whatever the structure of the principal–agent relationship, neither principal nor agent can ever claim that an agent has "moral immunity" from the basic obligations that would apply to any human being toward other members of the community.

Indeed, consistent with Ruder's belief, the introduction of moral reasoning (distinguished from multi-fiduciary stakeholder reasoning) into the framework of management thinking may *protect* rather than threaten private sector legitimacy. The conscientious corporation can maintain its private economic mission, but in the context of fundamental moral obligations owed by any member of society to others affected by that member's actions. Recognizing such obligations does *not* mean that an institution is a public institution. Private institutions, like private individuals, can be and are bound to respect moral obligations in the pursuit of private purposes.

Conceptually, then, we can make room for a moral posture toward stakeholders that is both *partial* (respecting the fiduciary relationship between managers and stockholders) and *impartial* (respecting the equally important nonfiduciary relationships between management and other stakeholders). As philosopher Thomas Nagel has said, "In the conduct of life, of all places, the rivalry between the view from within and the view from without must be taken seriously."[21]

Whether this conceptual room can be used *effectively* in the face of enormous pressures on contemporary managers and directors is another story, of course. For it is one thing to say that "giving standing to stakeholders" in managerial reasoning is conceptually coherent. It is something else to say that it is practically coherent.

Yet most of us, I submit, believe it. Most of us believe that management at General Motors *owed* it to the people of Detroit and to the people of Poletown to take their (nonfiduciary) interests very seriously, to seek creative solutions to the conflict, to do more than use or manipulate them in accordance with GM's needs only. We understand that managers and directors have a special obligation to provide a financial return to the stockholders, but we also understand that the word "special" in this context needs to be tempered by an appreciation of certain fundamental community norms that go beyond the demands of both laws and markets. There are certain class-action suits that stockholders ought not to win. For there is sometimes a moral defense.

Conclusion

The relationship between management and stockholders is ethically different in kind from the relationship between management and other parties (employees, suppliers, customers, etc.), a fact that seems to go unnoticed by the multi-fiduciary approach. If it were not, the corporation would cease to be a private sector institution – and what is now called business ethics would become a more radical critique of our economic system than is typically thought. On this point, Milton Friedman must be given a fair and serious hearing.

This does not mean, however, that "stakeholders" lack a morally significant relationship to management, as the strategic approach implies. It means only that the relationship in question is different from a fiduciary one. Management may never have promised customers, employees, suppliers, etc. a "return on investment," but management is nevertheless obliged to take seriously its extra-legal obligations not to injure, lie to, or cheat these stakeholders *quite apart from* whether it is in the stockholders' interests.

As we think through the *proper* relationship of management to stakeholders, fundamental features of business life must undoubtedly be reorganized: that corporations have a principally economic mission and competence; that fiduciary obligations to investors and general obligations to comply with the law cannot be set aside; and that abuses of economic power and disregard of corporate stewardship in the name of business ethics are possible.

But these things must be recognized as well: that corporations are not solely financial institutions; that fiduciary obligations go beyond short-term profit and are in any case subject to moral criteria in their execution; and that mere compliance with the law can be unduly limited and even unjust.

The Stakeholder Paradox can be avoided by a more thoughtful understanding of the nature of moral obligation and the limits it imposes on the principal–agent relationship. Once we understand that there is a practical "space" for identifying the ethical values shared by a corporation and its stockholders – a space that goes beyond strategic self-interest but stops short of impartiality – the hard work of filling that space can proceed.

NOTES

1   R. Edward Freeman, *Strategic Management: A Stakeholder Approach* (Pitman, 1984), p. 46.
2   Strictly speaking the historical meaning of "stakeholder" in this context is someone who literally *holds* the stakes during play.
3   See K. Goodpaster and T. Piper, *Managerial Decision Making and Ethical Values*, Harvard Business School Publishing Division, 1989.
4   See K. Goodpaster, "PASCAL: A Framework For Conscientious Decision Making," (1989). Unpublished paper, University of St Thomas.
5   Actually, there are subtle ways in which even the stakeholder identification

or inventory process might have *some* ethical content. The very process of *identifying* affected parties involves the use of the imagination in a way that can lead to a natural empathetic or caring response to those parties in the synthesis, choice, and action phases of decision-making. This is a contingent connection, however, not a necessary one.

6   Note that including powerless stakeholders in the analysis phase may indicate whether the decision-maker cares about "affecting" them or "being affected by" them. Also, the inclusion of what might be called secondary stakeholders as advocates for primary stakeholders (e.g. local governments on behalf of certain citizen groups) may signal the values that will come into play in any synthesis.

7   It should be mentioned that some authors, most notably Kenneth R. Andrews in *The Concept of Corporate Strategy*, 3rd edn (Irwin, 1987) employ a broader and more social definition of "strategic" decision-making than the one implied here.

8   Freeman, *Strategic Management*, p. 46.

9   Ibid., p. 52 (emphasis added).

10   Freeman writes: "Theoretically, 'stakeholder' must be able to capture a broad range of groups and individuals, even though when we put the concept to practical tests we must be willing to ignore certain groups who will have little or no impact on the corporation at this point in time" (ibid., pp. 52–3).

11   Milton Friedman, "The Social Responsibility of Business is to Increase its Profits," New York Times Magazine, Sept. 13, 1970.

12   Freeman, *Strategic Management*, p. 249.

13   Ladd observed in a now-famous essay entitled "Morality and the Ideal of Rationality in Formal Organization (*The Monist*, vol. 54, 1970) that organizational "rationality" was defined solely in terms of economic objectives: "The interests and needs of the individuals concerned, as individuals, must be considered only insofar as they establish limiting operating conditions. Organizational rationality dictates that these interests and needs must not be considered in their own right or on their own merits. If we think of an organization as a machine, it is easy to see why we cannot reasonably expect it to have any moral obligations to people or for them to have any to it" (p. 507).

14   Quoted in David S. Ruder, "Public Obligations of Private Corporations," *University of Pennsylvania Law Review*, vol. 114 (1965).

15   Ibid., pp. 226, 228–9. Ruder recently (in 1989) reaffirmed the views expressed in his 1965 article.

16   "Business Products Corporation – Part 1," Harvard Business School Case Services 9-377-077.

17   Ruder, "Public Obligations of Private Corporations."

18   "The Business Judgement Rule" gives broad latitude to officers and directors of corporations, but calls for reasoning on the basis of the long-term economic interest of the company. And corporate case law ordinarily allows exceptions to profit-maximization criteria only when there are actual or potential *legal* barriers, and limits charitable and humanitarian gifts by the logic of long-term self-interest. The underlying rationale is accountability to investors.

Recent work by the American Law Institute, however, suggests a rethinking of these matters. See appendix.

19   Christopher Elias, "Turning Up the Heat on the Top," *Insight*, July 23, 1990.
20   We might consider the NDP in broader terms that would include the relationship between "client" and "professional" in other contexts, such as law, medicine, education, government, and religion, where normally the community's expectations are embodied in ethical standards.
21   T. Nagel, *The View from Nowhere* (Oxford University Press, 1986), p. 163.

APPENDIX

The American Law Institute

PRINCIPLES OF CORPORATE GOVERNANCE:
ANALYSIS AND RECOMMENDATIONS

Tentative Draft No. 2
(April 13, 1984)

Part II
THE OBJECTIVE AND CONDUCT OF THE
BUSINESS CORPORATION

ANALYSIS AND RECOMMENDATION
§201.   The Objective and Conduct of the Business Corporation

A business corporation should have as its objective the conduct of business activities with a view to enhancing corporate profit and shareholder gain, except that, whether or not corporate profit and shareholder gain are thereby enhanced, the corporation, in the conduct of its business

   (a) is obliged, to the same extent as a natural person, to act within the boundaries set by law,

   (b) may take into account ethical considerations that are reasonably regarded as appropriate to the responsible conduct of business, and

   (c) may devote a reasonable amount of resources to public welfare, humanitarian, educational, and philanthropic purposes.

14
Philosophy and its Host: The Case of Business Ethics

Michael Yeo

Yeo considers different ways in which we might understand the relationship between business ethics – seen primarily as a social phenomenon – and the domain or field of business. At the extremes of a roughly demarcated continuum of different conceptions of this relationship lie the view that business ethics should be subversive in relation to business practice, or much of it, and the view that business ethics inevitably becomes coopted into a kind of apologetics for business interests. Between these extremes is the view of business ethics in a kind of constructively helping relationship to business. Against this background, Yeo goes on to criticize Richard De George's influential account of the nature of business ethics as an "academic field" characterized by practical detachment, ideological neutrality coupled with rational objectivity, and theoretical systematization founded in ethical theory. Yeo takes each of these criteria in turn, arguing, in effect, that they compose an unrealistic and perhaps impossible idea of business ethics and that De George's account fails by its own criteria.

Yeo's paper should be read in connection with those of Wertheimer (chapter 8), Winkler (chapter 19), and Hoffmaster (chapter 20), and compared particularly with those of Philips (chapter 10), Solomon (chapter 11), and Macleod (chapter 12) in the section on business ethics.

> *If you would say to me . . . "Socrates, for now . . . we will let you go, but on this condition: that you no longer spend time in this investigation or philosophize; and if you are caught doing this you will die," . . . I would say to you, "I, men of Athens, salute you and love you, but as long as I breathe and am able to, I will certainly not stop philosophizing."*
>
> Plato, *Apology*

There are a number of angles from which to bring the phenomenon of applied ethics into focus. For example, one might zero in on the word "applied." What gets applied, and how? How does *applied ethics* compare and contrast with *applied mathematics* or *applied science?* Alternatively, one might concentrate on the kinds of problems to which applied ethics *applies* itself, perhaps comparing these with the kinds of problems dealt with in other areas of philosophy.

The focal point of this paper is the fact that most of what gets called applied ethics is in some relationship to a host discipline or profession. Medicine or health care is a sort of host for bioethics; journalism and media for journalism ethics; and business for business ethics. In each case, the host furnishes the problems and issues upon which the applied ethics subdiscipline lives and thrives (or fails to thrive). The subdiscipline, in turn, provides (or at least is expected to provide) some knowledge of interest to the host. This relationship raises a number of important questions. What power, direct or indirect, does (and should) the host exert over the philosophical subdiscipline? To what extent should the subdiscipline be shaped by the host, and to what extent by the tradition of philosophy? Are there any values proper to philosophy and authoritative for those working in philosophy that may be threatened or compromised by the values of the host?

This paper explores these questions with particular reference to business ethics – interpreted broadly and in a loosely sociological sense to encompass ethics centres, ethics committees, ethics consultants, philosophers and theologians, courses, books, and journals.[1] What is the relationship between business ethics and business? How do people working in business ethics understand what they are doing in relation to business? What do people in business think that people in business ethics are doing, and what does business ethics mean to them? How might what people in business ethics are doing (whatever their explicit intentions) be shaped, influenced, or put to use (used or abused) by business?

To fix some reference points for these questions, imagine a continuum along which to situate possible modalities of the relationship between business ethics and business. Points on the continuum would mark different stances or postures business ethics might assume (or be thought to assume) in relation to business. At one extreme of the continuum, business ethics might view itself (or be viewed) as *subversive* in relation to business; at the other extreme, as a kind of *apologetics* or public relations for business and business interests. In the middle, and shading toward either extreme, business ethics might view itself (or be viewed) as a kind of *benign helper* to business. Each of these three basic positions will be elaborated with reference to some exemplary texts in the literature. This continuum, admittedly a crude instrument, will serve as a background against which Richard De George's attempt to delimit business ethics as an "academic field" will be critically analyzed.

Business Ethics as Subversive in Relation to Business

This position (at the extreme left of the continuum, shall we say) conceives business ethics and business as being essentially antagonistic or in opposition to one another. Few philosophers would consciously situate themselves here, and therefore Louis Lombardi is something of a voice in the wilderness in claiming that "the ultimate justification for business ethics" is that "we [philosophers] can wholeheartedly embrace our *subversive role* [italics added]."[2] In his view philosophy, presumably in virtue of its tradition of critical inquiry and relentless questioning even of sacred truths, is by nature subversive. Business, on the other hand, is essentially conservative, and as such threatened by critical inquiry and analysis. "Teaching business ethics is a *subversive activity*," Lombardi claims, because "it threatens longstanding attitudes and practices in business."[3] Moreover, "the standard ideology of business," he continues, "leaves little room for ethical analysis. Even more, on the traditional and still dominant business ideology, ethical analysis is to be avoided in business." Thus viewed, business ethics and business represent competing interests or ideologies: The philosophical commitment to ethical inquiry is at odds with the business commitment to the proverbial bottom line of profit. There seems no possibility of a happy relationship between the two. One must lose to the other.

The story of Socrates and his fate at the hands of the Athenian *polis* may lend some plausibility to this view. At the very least, it underscores a tension between philosophy and its host. One wonders how Socrates would figure in the field of business ethics. It is debatable whether Socrates was or thought of himself as a subversive, but it is significant that he *appeared* so to those who felt threatened by his radical and unsettling questioning. And though few philosophers today would "wholeheartedly embrace a subversive role," the *perception* that business ethics is subversive has currency among many who see things from the point of view of business and who have put business ethics on trial. Milton Friedman, who warns that the doctrine of social responsibility (a favorite theme in business ethics) is a subversive doctrine,[4] represents a familiar line of thinking in business according to which business ethics as represented by professional philosophers and theologians is "anti-business," and its representatives given to "business-bashing."

Along similar lines, business ethics is sometimes portrayed as zealously inspired and inclined toward puritanical moralizing. In a well-known article, Peter Drucker asks: "But what precisely is 'business ethics'? And what could, or should, it be? Is it just another round in the hoary American blood sport of business baiting? Is there more to 'business ethics' than the revivalist preacher's call to the sinner to repent?" The strategy of this line of questioning is to discredit business ethics by identifying it with a style of moralizing Drucker's audience is likely to find unacceptable. "Clearly, one major element of the peculiar stew that goes by the name of 'business ethics,'" he writes, "is plain old-fashioned hostility to business and to economic activity altogether – one of the oldest of American traditions and perhaps the only still-potent ingredient in the Puritan heritage."[5]

There may be an element of truth in these charges, as no doubt there was in the charges brought against Socrates. Nonetheless, there is reason to be concerned that attacks of this sort (and the sympathy behind them is quite common) might put business ethics on the defensive. To be labeled subversive, anti-business, or morally puritanical could be, in any number of ways, damaging for someone or some institution working in business ethics and for business ethics as a whole. Fear of being thus labeled creates a motive to moderate and perhaps even compromise work in business ethics to avoid being tagged with the label. Because the line of influence sketched here is very indirect, and the fear of being labeled may never announce itself as conscious motive, it is difficult to assess this possibility. This is all the more reason to try to become as clear as possible about the lines of force by means of which business ethics might be driven by its host.

Business Ethics as Benign Helper to Business

Here, toward the centre of the continuum, business ethics might represent itself or be represented as a kind of benign helper to business. The relationship is a happy marriage based on mutual trust and support. Business needs (and perhaps genuinely wants) help in negotiating its way through difficult ethical issues, and philosophers, in virtue of a certain expertise in moral reasoning, issue analysis, and the like, seem able and willing to help. In this helping relationship, neither partner need feel threatened by the other. Both retain their integrity in the union. The philosopher and the city at peace. A marriage made in heaven.

Most philosophers working in business ethics would situate themselves somewhere in this middle ground along the continuum. For example, here is how Vincent Barry, to pick one of any number of examples, describes the *raison d'être* of business ethics: "Taken together, the increased ethical content of business decisions and the struggle to reconcile personal values with business decisions have thrown business people into a quandary. They must make decisions, but on what basis?"[6] Enter business ethics to fill the void and make business whole. "The issues that face business people, the decisions they must make, the conflicts they must resolve," Barry says, "all point to the urgent need for the moral principles that a study of business ethics is designed to explore."[7]

Conceived in these terms, what is to be avoided in a good relationship between business ethics and business is not so much subversiveness – although that too – as irrelevance. As one writer, articulating the point of view of business, puts it: "Although the metaphysical question of whether or not a corporation is a person with moral agency is a burning issue with many, it is of little interest to the corporate manager or the entrepreneur. Such discussions only reinforce the view that academics are still debating the issue of how many angels can sit on the head of a pin." He warns philosophers that business ethics "must address the functional needs of the manager or entrepreneur" if it is not to "go the way of the hoola hoop or the cabbage patch doll."[8]

One of the reasons to be concerned about this view, which places so much premium on relevance, is that the label "irrelevant," like the label "subversive," can be damaging, albeit for different reasons. Seduced by the benevolent desire to help, and perhaps bullied by the fear of being or appearing irrelevant, those working in business ethics might buy into narrow standards of relevance, and in the bargain compromise philosophical integrity. What control or influence might the desire or demand to be relevant have over work done in business ethics?

Business Ethics as Apologetics for Business

At the other extreme of the continuum, business ethics might function as a kind of apologetics for business. The boundaries distinguishing this function from the role of "benign helper" blur into confusion at points, but the difference between this and a subversive role for business is unmistakable. There is a symmetry between the two opposite poles in that from each the relationship between business ethics and business is conceived of as a zero-sum game. In the subversive role, business loses. In the apologist role, business ethics loses – that is, it compromises itself or "sells out," the assumption being that business ethics, in virtue of its philosophical genealogy, has some kind of independent essence or *telos* which it might somehow betray in a union with business.

Now, no self-respecting philosopher would self-consciously assume the role of apologist for business, since the label is clearly pejorative. However, he or she might be tagged with this label, as indeed might business ethics as a whole viewed in terms of its social function. Robert Cooke worries that philosophers working in business ethics might be considered "apologists for or pawns of the system."[9] Indeed, this is how Stephen Massey, drawing from Marx, represents business ethics. He argues that

> there are two important class needs with respect to which business ethics might have an important role: (1) to legitimate the system of capitalist production, and thereby to assure those who must work within this system that they do not compromise their integrity by doing so; and (2) to discipline individual members of the bourgeoisie so that they will refrain from pursuing their individual interests when these conflict with the interests of their class.[10]

In a similar vein, Jeffrey Foss argues that the "fear of socialism is the motivation" that has driven business interest in business ethics.[11] Given recent events in the former Soviet Union, there is considerably less basis for such a fear today, and so Foss's claim is somewhat dated. Nevertheless, state intervention in the marketplace remains a concern for North American business, and the incorporation of business ethics is often recommended as an alternative to dreaded government regulation.

An apologist function for business ethics might also be derived from its public relations value in the current climate of public opinion. Whatever lofty things we might think about business ethics, it is important to realize that it has emerged as the social phenomenon it is today – with courses, institutes, chairs, etc. – largely in response to a major public relations problem for business and businesses. A litany of scandals and tales of corruption could be listed which created something of a crisis of public confidence in business. This crisis of public confidence has fueled the demand for business ethics and led to the growth of institutions answering to this demand. Sherwin Klein puts the point clearly, stating that although part of the concern driving the contemporary interest in business ethics "can be traced to the desire of morally conscientious business people for aid in solving business problems that have serious moral implications [the 'benign helper' relationship], the greater part of this concern is related to the widespread belief that amorality, if not immorality, is too prevalent in business."[12] Business ethics, whatever it might be stipulated to mean by philosophers, is viewed by the public as a kind of antidote for wrongdoing or lack of ethical integrity. "The major problem in business ethics," Klein goes on to say, "is the morality, or lack of it, in business."

Yet another apologist function for business ethics, and one we are hearing more and more today, has to do with the marketing of ethics as a means of scoring higher on the bottom line. "Good ethics is good business," or "ethics pays off," are some interesting watchwords here. When the host's interest in ethics is driven by the bottom line, there is reason to be concerned that the ethics that answers the host's needs and demands will bear the imprint of this interest.

De George on the Relation between Business Ethics and Business

In the interest of elucidating business ethics as a social phenomenon, I have until now been using the term very widely to include various meanings assigned it by philosophers, champions of business interests, and more generally the public. De George, however, uses the term in a very specific way, emphasizing the sense in which business ethics is what he calls an "academic field." I will examine in some detail the way he delimits (legislates might be a more precise word) this field, paying particular attention to the criteria by which he excludes certain phenomena that might otherwise get labeled "business ethics" and to how he represents the relation between business ethics and business. De George is especially interesting because he is much more reflective about business ethics as a phenomenon than most philosophers. His view of business ethics as an academic field appears not to fall anywhere along the continuum earlier described – at least, not at first glance.

Three interrelated features stand out in De George's delimitation of the field of business ethics: first, it is said to be marked by a certain *indifference to/detachment from* the practical; second, it is supposed to be *objective or neutral* with regard to ideological differences; third, it is supposed to be *systematic* and to build upon a solid foundation in *ethical theory*. I will examine each of these features in turn.

Business Ethics' Indifference to Practical Application

In delimiting the field of business ethics, De George distinguishes between the pursuit of knowledge for its own sake and the application of that knowledge in the world of practical affairs:

> As an academic discipline those who carry out research follow that research where it leads. They may hope the results they come up with are useful; but their aim is knowledge, enlightenment, clarity, insight. To call the field an academic field means that there is knowledge those in the field pursue. The application of that knowledge is a different task from pursuing it.[13]

The word "application" as here opposed to "knowledge" is somewhat misleading, because there is a sense in which some of the knowledge of which he speaks is "applied" to begin with. For example, he claims that "to the extent that knowledge is developed and tools produced for solving problems, the field is academically defensible, even if businesses are reluctant to adopt the findings or change practices that are shown to be immoral."[14] This implies that the knowledge generated in the field of business ethics is applied enough to be capable of demonstrating certain practices to be immoral. In another place, he is even more direct about this: "In business ethics they [philosophers] have been primarily interested in clarifying issues and determining the rightness or wrongness of actions or practices."[15] Clearly for De George the kind of knowledge business ethics is capable of achieving includes determinant judgments about right and wrong in particular cases, which judgments may arise from the application of some general principles or theory to a given situation.

What De George means by application in contrast with knowledge would better be expressed by the word "implementation." Business ethics, as an academic field, is indifferent to whether its knowledge (including its pronouncements about right and wrong in particular cases) is implemented. It is not out to change the world, or to make business more ethical:

> Academic fields are not judged by their immediate, demonstrable effects in the business world. Clarity, the development of a problematic, and the articulation of alternative approaches to business practices that will enhance morality are worth while even if not directly and immediately adopted by business. The field as an academic field does not depend on producing moral business people, any more than the field of ethics depends on producing moral people.[16]

This is one sense in which business ethics as delimited by De George appears not to fall anywhere along the continuum earlier described. The positions along the continuum are all engaged with business in one way or another and can be assigned some kind of function: subversive, helpful, legitimating. Business ethics, as De George delimits it, appears not to care about changing (or preserving) the world.

It is not clear why De George values indifference as he does. In some places, he comes across as a purist, and links indifference with the integrity of business ethics – its independence from business. "The field of business ethics," he writes, "is an academic field and should not be directed or its concerns determined by business."[17] This declaration of independence is in marked contrast with the following statement from Robert Cooke, who projects a benign helper role for business ethics: "We have a lot to learn from each other, and we must be willing to share such information in a credible and understandable way. *In a real sense, the business community will take a leading role in shaping such an agenda.*"[18] Many philosophers will find the suggestion that the business community will take a leading role in shaping the agenda of business ethics troubling. Thus subordinated to business, it would risk becoming a handmaiden or servant, a form of apologetics perhaps. In stressing the independence of business ethics from practical affairs, De George communicates the message that business ethics ought not to take its marching orders from business. Business ethics is led not by business or business interests but by the search for truth or knowledge, wherever that may lead.

The condition that business ethics be indifferent seems to rule out both the role of benign helper and that of apologist. However, even more frequently in De George's writing, indifference is valued in opposition to a subversive role for business ethics, and the message here is quite different. This becomes apparent in his frequent criticisms of moralizing in business ethics. In this connection it is important to note that, according to De George, the emergence of business ethics as a field began in the 1970s, the decisive point being the entry of philosophers into what hitherto had been the province of theologians.[19] These philosophers, supposedly less interested in changing the world than in securing knowledge, brought with them a more detached and scholarly approach to work in the field. "If one is searching for clarity and is relatively more detached from preaching and teaching people how to act correctly," De George writes, "one is less concerned with what one can teach than with getting a basic position straight."[20] Here indifference ("detachment") is valued not in opposition to apologetics but in opposition to moralizing.

De George's writing is rife with criticisms of preaching and moralizing, but it is not easy to determine exactly what he means by moralizing, and why he finds it objectionable. However, we can piece together three main features he seems to attribute to moralizing and by which he distinguishes it from work in business ethics proper.

In the first place, and paralleling the opposition between theologians and philosophers, De George frequently links moralizing with preaching. Philosophers do not preach: "If we look at the textbooks and journals in the field, we find that although philosophers in business ethics discuss the morality or immorality of practices, they tend to refrain from preaching or moralizing, which is the domain those following the moralistic approach properly take as their province."[21] Note that the difference between the moralistic approach and *bona fide* business ethics is not that the one issues in normative judgments about business practices and the other does not. Both do that. The difference rather, at least from this passage, seems to reside in something like the mood in which such judgments are made and pronounced. The moralizer is intense about these judgments and wants to see them implemented. He or she exhorts. The *bona fide* business ethicist, on the other hand, is relatively detached from the normative judgments he or she makes; is somewhat indifferent as concerns whether they ever get actualized in the world.

However, there is also some suggestion, albeit indirect, that the difference between the moralizing approach and *bona fide* business ethics might have something to do with the content of the normative judgments that issue from each. "The moralistic approach," De George says, "typically places emphasis on the poor, on improving their lot, and on making demands either in justice or in charity for a greater portion of wealth for the poor within a nation or world-wide."[22] Here at least the "moralizing approach" seems less an "approach" than a set of beliefs or an ideology (and, to be precise, the ideology of the political left). This raises questions about the grounds from which De George, the critic of "the moralizing approach," speaks. If substantive beliefs along these lines are indeed a sign of the "moralizing approach," some will wonder why it is taken to be a bad thing, and what other substantive beliefs might be acceptable to *bona fide* business ethics if beliefs such as these are to be ruled inappropriate.

Finally, De George also seems to suggest that the difference between the moralizing approach and *bona fide* business ethics has something to do with the source and grounding of the norms that each applies. He says that "the moralistic approach consists merely of applying general moral prohibitions against stealing, lying, etc. to the realm of business,"[23] the implication being that this is not good enough. Although he does not say it here, it is important to him that whatever norms get applied in business ethics be in some sense "objective," having a pedigree that can be traced back to the oracle of pure reason. This leads to a second defining feature of business ethics as an "academic field," namely, objectivity.

Objectivity

The condition that business ethics be objective does a number of jobs for De George. For one thing, it further distinguishes *bona fide* business ethics from moralizing: "The field is still in the process of definition," he writes, and "will become fully established as a field only to the extent that those within it continue to develop high quality research in an *objective*, scholarly manner."[24] Research conducted in an objective manner is thus to be distinguished from work that is somehow or other moralizing, and this is what will ensure quality in the research.

Related to this, the condition that business ethics be objective is also linked in De George's writing to neutrality with respect to different ideologies or points of view on the status quo in business:

Business ethics is sometimes seen as conservative and is also used as a defense of the status quo. Sometimes it is seen as an attack on the status quo and hence viewed as radical. Ideally it should be neither. It should strive for *objectivity*. When there are immoral practices, structures, and actions occurring, business ethics should be able to show that these actions are immoral and why. But it should also be able to supply the techniques with which the practices and structures that are moral can be defended as such.[25]

Objectivity secures for business ethics a vantage point altogether incommensurate with any of the points that might be located on the continuum described earlier. Any point on the continuum represents a point of view about the status quo in business, a view from somewhere. The objective point of view De George advocates for business ethics, however, although it might superficially resemble points of view somewhere along the middle of the continuum, is not really a point of view at all. It is beyond (or, perhaps better, above) any ideological points of view. It is a view from nowhere. Business ethics as a field inhabits a neutral space beyond the battle of ideologies.

A similar motif is repeated in what De George says about reason, which is that in virtue of which business ethics is able to transcend whatever might otherwise weight it down to some determinate location. "Philosophers can address all people *from the point of view of reason*," De George claims, "on the assumption that all people are rational beings."[26] The philosopher's special relationship to reason is one of the marks that distinguishes him or her from the moralizing theologian: The philosopher, unlike the theologian, "attempts to work on the basis of reason and human experience alone."[27] Part of the work that reason oversees and guarantees for De George has to do with the generation of norms. At least, this is how theologian Paul Camenisch interprets him, offering the following critique:

> Implicit in my position that reason alone, at least as De George seems to understand it, cannot yield normative recommendations is the suggestion that behind even the most carefully "reasoned" normative starting points of philosophical ethics there are prior assumptions not examined by and not verifiable by reason.[28]

Concepts like "objectivity" and "reason" bear a considerable burden in De George's attempt to distinguish the field of business ethics from pretenders to the throne and warrant more careful scrutiny than he gives them. Camenisch is on target in remarking that "compared to the struggling, questioning nature of most seriously and reflectively religious persons' faith in God, De George's faith in reason is almost touching."[29] This would not be so serious a charge where it not that appeals to "objectivity" and "reason" can function rhetorically like weapons, and indeed do function in some such way in De George's attack on theological moralizing. In principle, there is always good reason to be suspicious whenever people appeal to objectivity and pure reason in this way. I do not want to get into the game of unmasking here, and I do not know how De George votes, but I do hear an unmistakable American accent in his own writings that one would not expect to hear in the voice of "objective reason."

Ethical Theory

"Philosophy is not ideology," De George insists. "Philosophical analysis may sometimes undercut and sometimes support traditional moral views."[30] If philosophy (that is, business ethics proper) is not ideology, if it rises above the ideological conflicts that divide left and right, radical and conservative, and so on, one wonders what by contrast it might be, or by what mark it is distinguished from ideology. Although he is not quite explicit about this, De George seems to believe that ethical theory has some significance in this regard. Whereas the moralizing theologians who pioneered the study of ethics in business brought with them ideology, philosophers brought ethical theory, and in so doing paved the way for the development of business ethics proper. The philosophers who entered the field in the 1970s, De George writes, "proved a catalyst for the jelling of previous work and by bringing ethical theory and philosophical analysis to bear, they helped to form the structure of what developed into business ethics."[31] Contrasted with this, "most of the earlier work" by theologians lacked "a theoretical overview of related problems and concepts necessary to constitute a field."[32]

Whatever significance he might attach to ethical theory by way of distinguishing business ethics from ideology, it is clear at least that ethical theory is an essential feature of bona fide business ethics for De George. "Mastery of ethical theory," he asserts, "provides the necessary tools to engage intelligently in personal and social analysis of moral issues."[33] De George is here expressing the party line on ethical theory shared by many philosophers in business ethics, but it is a line that needs to be questioned, and increasingly is being questioned. Why does ethical theory have such an exalted status among philosophers in business ethics?

To address this question, we might begin by asking what philosophers claim ethical theory is supposed to do for business ethics. There are a wide variety of answers to this question in the literature, but one common assumption is that ethical theory, in being applied, is supposed to help yield conclusions about what ought to be done in particular cases or circumstances. Beauchamp and Bowie exemplify the orthodox view. In their introduction to *Ethical Theory in Business*, they write: "Persons actively engaged in normative ethics examine the theoretical basis of a society's morality and, where appropriate, make suggestions for improving it. Their reflection eventuates in systematic ethical theories, which provide rules that help us determine what ought to be done in situations of moral choice."[34] The word "help" bears a considerable burden in this passage, and, unfortunately, is impossibly vague. It begs the question of exactly how ethical theory is supposed to help.

If this question is pushed, one finds in the background of what most ethicists say about ethical theory something very much like what Arthur Caplan calls the engineering model of applied ethics.[35] On this model, the ethicist, instantiating whatever empirical facts and circumstances are relevant to the matter at hand, deduces conclusions about matters of right and wrong from theories. Many philosophers, of course, issue disclaimers to the effect that the application of ethical theory to yield determinate conclusions is not merely a mechanical process, but theory is nevertheless supposed to have deductive force of some sort. Certainly De George is no crass engineer, but he seems to presuppose something very much like the engineering model. Consider the following passage, for example:

> If the basic principle is powerful enough, it should provide the means for deriving the set of consistent norms accepted by a society as well as for making norms explicitly held that were previously held only implicitly. The basic principle should also provide a procedure by which conflicting norms can be adjudicated and *particular cases decided.*[36]

The principles of ethical theory, in other words, are to furnish a method by which we can ultimately decide right and wrong in particular cases.

In my view, the idea that ethical theory has deductive force is based on a questionable understanding of ethical theory to begin with, but even granting this presupposition, serious internal problems can be identified in writing done under its auspices. A recent survey of 25 texts in business ethics, most of which included a substantial treatment of ethical theory, is quite informative in this regard. The authors write: "In the approach typical of the textbooks surveyed, the student must learn (1) the basic arguments of the major ethical theories; (2) how to *apply* the theories in real life situations; (3) how to choose between conflicting theories or resolve their differences."[37] However, the authors found that these texts fell short of the second and third objectives, the ones presupposing the practical usefulness of ethical theory. "Most of these texts provide reasonably thorough explanations for the first task, learning the basics about theories," they observe, "but there is no agreement in the field and a great deal of uncertainty about how to apply theory or how to choose between theories that are in tension with one another ... The result is insufficient guidance to a reader wanting to make careful ethical decisions."[38] This is not surprising.

Vagueness surrounding the application of ethical theory is not unique to business ethics. In bioethics one finds the same pattern. The standard text begins with an introduction to ethical theory in light of some vague promise to the effect that theory will help resolve particular cases. However, when one comes to the discussion of actual cases and issues later in the book, one is at a loss to see how ethical theory is or might be applied. It may be that a careful analysis could take us some distance in the direction of clarifying problems of this sort, but in my view the problems attest not so much to a correctable defect in the literature as to a misguided obsession with ethical theory. At any rate, it is certain at least that there is considerable ambiguity, if not confusion, in the literature about the usefulness of ethical theory in business ethics, and in light of this one wonders how it manages to retain its exalted status. Mark Pastin suggests a cynical answer to this question:

> Ethics is simpler than people with a vested interest in complicating it would have you believe. Ethics racketeers, as well as the academics, theologians, and writers allied with them, want to keep ethics mysterious. If the racket is exposed, it is hard to run it. If ethics is demystified, those who interpret ethics for the uninitiated are out of work.[39]

On this account, ethical theory is a kind of mystifying smoke and mirrors game. Blow away the smokescreen of ethical theory, Pastin implies, and it will be apparent that the philosopher–emperor has no clothes.

If one sifts through his caustic rhetoric, there is some truth in what Pastin says. There is indeed something mystifying about ethical theory in business ethics (and applied ethics as a whole), although perhaps not quite as according to Pastin. Ethical theory (or, more precisely, the claim to mastery of ethical theory) has a kind of political function. It is by mastery of ethical theory that philosophers win authority and recognition. Among other things, ethical theory functions as a symbol of authority in applied ethics, like the doctor's proverbial black bag. A normative judgment that can somehow or other trace its pedigree to ethical theory (such a derivation may already involve some magic) has privileged status compared to the garden variety normative judgment not thus grounded and perhaps "tainted" by ideology. The theory-linked normative judgment gets endowed with the kind of authority that comes with a pronouncement from an oracle. The philosophers who invoke ethical theory to resolve the issue of the day may not believe in magic or oracles, but the uninitiated may be impressed otherwise.[40] My experience with students and non-philosophers generally who have had some minimal exposure to ethical theory is that they tend to have exorbitant expectations about what it can accomplish. Philosophers may not be responsible for how ethical theory is misunderstood by non-philosophers, but I suggest that, especially because philosophers are not very clear about the use of ethical theory among themselves, misunderstandings are only to be expected. In any event, the role of ethical theory being as unclear and uncertain as it is, "mastery of ethical theory" is a highly contentious test by means of which to distinguish those doing work in *bona fide* business ethics from pretenders to the throne. And all the more so given that for De George, and others, it performs a sort of political function by serving as a badge of legitimacy – or, in negative terms, a criterion for exclusion.

Conclusion

I am not sure what the proper relationship between business ethics and business is – or, indeed, that there is *one proper* relationship. Perhaps it is best that there be a plurality of relationships. However, I do have serious concerns about De George's delimitation of the field, and this for several reasons.

In the first place, there is a slippery ambiguity in the approach or methodology by which he delimits the field. Typically, he presents his account of business ethics proper in the context of a narrative recounting of the history of business ethics, giving the impression that he is simply describing what has taken shape, and articulating the features that appear to be essential to the field thus developed. Taken as merely *descriptive*, this may or may not be an accurate account of business ethics today. However, his account is also *prescriptive*: he is recommending what business ethics ought and ought not to be, the role those working in business ethics ought and ought not to adopt.

De George's failure to acknowledge explicitly the normative dimension of his delimitation of the field of business ethics repeats itself at another level within the field thus delimited. Business ethics is supposed to have the resources to yield normative judgments, yet at the same time to be objective and in a sense value-free. Although those in business ethics work with values, they are supposed to do so in such a way that their own values do not taint the objectivity of their analysis. Paradoxically, we are supposed to strive for value-free judgments. Fixing on this point, Dennis McCann charges that the flaw in business ethics as delimited by De George "is not that it has failed to safeguard its ideological virginity, but that it has tended to deny its own ideological involvement as such."[41]

Indeed, the field of business ethics as delimited by De George is circumscribed by or laden with values, most notably, objectivity and a certain detachment from the world. Certainly these values have figured prominently in Western philosophy (although there has by no means been unanimity about them), but the fact is that they are values, albeit quite defensible ones, and ought to be presented and argued for as such.

That the field of business ethics as delimited by De George is value-laden is especially important in so far as, in delimiting the field, he is also restricting it and excluding certain options or possibilities. I find the exclusion of moralizing – and De George seems above all concerned to disassociate business ethics from moralizing – particularly troubling. His attack against moralizing is vague enough that it is hard to say exactly what would count as moralizing, but it seems clear that discourse toward the left extreme of the continuum described earlier would be especially susceptible to being so labeled, and thus to being excluded from the field of business ethics.

De George's attack on moralizing in business ethics gives me pause to wonder about the ideological neutrality of his own stance, and I am intrigued to note how like Peter Drucker he sounds in his attack on moralizing. Whatever his politics, his delimitation of the field – and bear in mind that he is an authoritative and influential figure – would have the effect of suppressing the emergence of radical discourses in business ethics. It is striking how much more radical, in several senses of the word, work in environmental ethics has been than in business ethics. In this regard, it is telling that Louis Lombardi, the philosopher in the wilderness quoted earlier who advocates a subversive role for business ethics, also works in environmental ethics, a field in which it may not be such a bad thing to be a voice in the wilderness.

De George's exclusion of moralizing would not be so troubling, however, were it not that, albeit more subtly, he himself does the thing he excludes. Like Drucker, he moralizes against moralizing in business ethics. No less than the theological moralizers he criticizes, he has his commandments which he delivers to philosophers working in business ethics: Thou shalt not preach; thou shalt not advocate; thou shalt not be passionate (except perhaps for "truth" and "knowledge"); thou shalt not be ideological; and so on. This preaching may or may not be wise, but it is suspect in discourse that explicitly forbids preaching.

With respect to the view that the field of business ethics needs to be restricted, I would prefer rather to see the field shaken up, opened up, and expanded. For example, I know of nothing in business ethics analogous to the distinction between deep and shallow ecology that has been so important in environmental ethics. I think it would be very worthwhile to explore what it might mean to distinguish between something like deep and shallow business ethics. Moreover, this is a job for which theologians – excluded from the field by De George – might be especially well suited.

But how one feels about these matters will be to some extent a function of how one feels about the status quo in business ethics, and the fact of the matter is that De George is an admirer and defender of the status quo. He quite clearly likes the paradigm that has emerged, which is not surprising since he played a major role in defining it. In my view this paradigm, although certainly impressive in many ways, can and should be questioned regarding fundamentals – such things as the place and purpose of ethical theory, for example. Furthermore, I think there needs to be more radical questioning around the task, function, role, use, and abuse of philosophers in business ethics, or in the moral domain more generally. What are the uses and abuses of moral philosophy? What tensions and temptations might arise for the moral philosopher regarding such matters as relevance and irrelevance, cooption, compromise, confrontation, subversion? What ought the moral philosopher in the public domain to strive for – and perhaps against?

In exploring these questions, I think it more helpful to think along the lines of integrity than of objectivity. To be sure, integrity is a slippery concept, but no less so than other possible guiding concepts like "objectivity." In any event, we can say at least that integrity involves being self-conscious about where one stands and the values in light of which one speaks, and being willing to acknowledge and defend those values wherever they may come into play. In whatever role philosophers find themselves, integrity requires an awareness that one's philosophizing can always be brought under some kind of socio-political description, and a mindfulness of the influences and forces extrinsic to philosophy that shape or may shape one's philosophizing. In addition to being true to oneself, integrity also means being true to one's calling in philosophy. But what does philosophy call us to, or call upon us to do, such that in answering other calls, from various hosts, we might be untrue to our calling as philosophers?

NOTES

1   In what follows, I will not limit myself to what business ethics might mean as defined by philosophers. As concerns the different meanings of the term "business ethics," the following conceptual elucidation is useful:

> "Business ethics" can mean, first, an activity, the process of reflecting and deciding what it is that one should do. Second, the term can be used to refer to the results or object of such reflection, to the set of principles which state what one should do. And third, it can refer to behavior – someone might mean by the claim "There is no such thing as business ethics" that business people

do not in fact behave ethically.

See Eric H. Beversluis, "Is there no such thing as Business Ethics?" *Journal of Business Ethics* 6, no. 4 (1987): 84.

2   Louis G. Lombardi, "A Quick Justification for Business Ethics," *Journal of Business Ethics* 4, no. 4 (1985): 356.

3   Ibid.: 353 (emphasis added).

4   Milton Friedman, *Capitalism and Freedom* (Chicago: University of Chicago Press, 1962): 133.

5   Peter Drucker, "What is 'Business Ethics'?" *The Public Interest* 63 (Spring 1981): 18, 34.

6   Vincent Barry, *Moral Issues in Business* (Belmont, Ca.: Wadsworth, 1979): 9.

7   Ibid.: 13.

8   Robert Allan Cooke, "Business Ethics at the Crossroads," *Journal of Business Ethics* 5, no. 3 (1986): 262, 260.

9   Ibid.: 259.

10   Stephen J. Massey, "Marxism and Business Ethics," *Journal of Business Ethics* 1, no. 4 (1982): 302. One need not be a card-carrying party member to appreciate this analysis. De George, for example, who is not at all sympathetic with the ideology that informs Massey's analysis, acknowledges that business ethics has some such legitimizing function as Massey describes. Speaking against liberation theologians who write on ethics in business, he queries: "Why should they try to make moral or appear moral what is basically and ultimately immoral? Why help preserve the business system? Why mitigate its ills and help make it plausibly respectable and acceptable?" "Theological Ethics and Business Ethics," *Journal of Business Ethics* 5, no. 6 (1986): 429.

11   Jeffrey Foss, review of *Discourses on Ethics and Business*, by Jack Behrman, in *Journal of Business Ethics* 2, no. 4 (1983): 306.

12   Sherwin Klein, "Two Views of Business Ethics: A Popular Philosophical Approach and a Value Based Interdisciplinary One," *Journal of Business Ethics* 4, no. 1 (1985): 71.

13   Richard T. De George, "Replies and Reflections on Theology and Business Ethics," *Journal of Business Ethics* 5, no. 6 (1986): 524.

14   Richard T. De George, "The Status of Business Ethics: Past and Future," *Journal of Business Ethics* 6, no. 3 (1987): 205.

15   De George, "Theological Ethics and Business Ethics": 430.

16   De George, "The Status of Business Ethics": 205.

17   Ibid.: 208.

18   Cooke, "Business Ethics at the Crossroads": 262, emphasis added.

19   De George, "The Status of Business Ethics": 202. According to De George, it was not until some time later that business ethics proper was born out of these developments: "By 1985 business ethics had become an academic *field*, albeit still in the process of definition" (ibid.: 203).

20   De George, "Replies and Reflections on Theology and Business Ethics": 522.

21   De George, "Theological Ethics and Business Ethics": 426.

22   Ibid.: 425. Later, he links this moralizing with the moral majority, which is

puzzling since the moral majority have never had much use for the so-called social gospel.

23 De George, "Theological Ethics and Business Ethics": 425. Curiously, De George himself endorses the application of such norms in another place: "the morality which is to be *applied* to business in our society is the morality which is generally held by the members of our society" ("Moral Issues in Business," in *Ethics, Free Enterprise, and Public Policy: Original Essays on Moral Issues in Business*, eds Richard T. De George and Joseph A. Pichler (New York: Oxford University Press, 1978): 6 (emphasis added).

24 De George, "Theological Ethics and Business Ethics": 421 (emphasis added).

25 Richard T. De George, *Business Ethics* (New York: Macmillan, 1982): 18 (emphasis added).

26 De George, "Replies and Reflections on Theology and Business Ethics": 522 (emphasis added).

27 De George, "Theological Ethics and Business Ethics": 424.

28 Paul F. Camenisch, "On Monopoly in Business Ethics: Can Philosophy Do It All?" *Journal of Business Ethics* 5, no. 6 (1986): 435.

29 Ibid.: 434.

30 De George, "Replies and Reflections on Theology and Business Ethics": 522.

31 De George, "The Status of Business Ethics": 202.

32 De George, "Theological Ethics and Business Ethics": 422.

33 De George, *Business Ethics*: 14.

34 Tom L. Beauchamp and Norman E. Bowie, eds, *Ethical Theory in Business* (New Jersey: Prentice-Hall, 1979): 2.

35 Arthur Caplan coined this expression in his analysis of theory in the field of biomedical ethics: "Can Applied Ethics be Effective in Health Care and Should it Strive to Be?" *Ethics* 93 (Jan. 1983): 311–19.

36 De George, *Business Ethics*: 13 (emphasis added).

37 Robbin Derry and Ronald M. Green, "Ethical Theory in Business: A Critical Assessment," *Journal of Business Ethics* 8, no. 7 (1987): 531–2.

38 Ibid.: 532.

39 Mark Pastin, *The Hard Problems of Management: Gaining the Ethics Edge* (San Francisco: Jossey-Bass, 1988): 23.

40 It is revealing to read the account of ethical theory given by Renate Mai-Dalton, one of twelve faculty members from the School of Business at the University of Kentucky who participated in a two-week seminar on ethics organized by De George (the first week was devoted to ethical theory). Mai-Dalton reports that he came away from the course disillusioned of the belief that "one theory of ethics could lead to the one correct answer to a given question" but appears nonetheless to hold to the belief that ethical theory has some kind of deductive force analogous to that of theory in the natural sciences. Summarizing what he learned about theory from the seminar, he writes:

> Theories can be useful in suggesting research questions and in arriving at predictions of future events. However, confirmation of the correctness of the

hypothesis or the future postulated conduct of an individual can be had only after the hypothesis has been tested or the behavior has been observed. Thus, no 'truth' could be determined beforehand. ("The Experience of One Faculty Member in a Business Ethics Seminar: What Can We Take Back to the Classroom?", *Journal of Business Ethics* 6, no. 7 (1987): 510)

The notion of ethical theory operative here is quite bizarre, and no doubt based on some misunderstanding of what was taught. Nevertheless, it is telling that this is what ethical theory meant to a professor of business who was taught ethical theory for a week.

41   Dennis P. McCann, "Umpire and Batsman: Is it Cricket to Both?" *Journal of Business Ethics* 5, no. 6 (1986): 446.

Environmental Ethics

15
Environmental Ethics: Values in and Duties to the Natural World

Holmes Rolston III

Philosophical writings in environmental ethics reveal two basic approaches to the subject. One is traditional moral expansionism which tries to expand outward from human-centred ethics toward fuller moral recognition of and protection for future generations, non-human animals, and perhaps sentient life generally. Moral expansionism relies powerfully on principles of consistency – particularly as deployed in relation to the idea that equivalent "interests" are of equal moral importance – and is typically committed to the idea that there is no value except in relation to an evaluator.

Rolston is a champion of an opposing, nonanthropocentric approach, one which bases itself in the science of ecology. Moving from consideration of higher animals to individual organisms, to species, to ecosystems, Rolston argues for an ecologically informed moral outlook that discovers objective "intrinsic value" in all of life and in nature as a whole. At the heart of this outlook are generalizations concerning basic organizational similarities common to all life forms (including remarkably close connections between plant and animal life), generalizations about the relation of individuals to species, and generalizations about the interconnectedness of all life, particularly with regard to fundamental aspects of ecosystemic homeostasis. The ideas about intrinsic value and its objects, which Rolston explains and defends, entail radical alterations in traditional moral attitudes and beliefs.

This paper has no close comparisons nor direct contrasts in this volume, but it can be usefully compared with Sikora's paper on the question of the moral status of animals (chapter 5) and, more generally, with Gruen (chapter 16), Rachels (chapter 6) and others in terms of methodology in the construction of ethical theory.

Environmental ethics stretches classical ethics to the breaking point. All ethics seeks an appropriate respect for life. But we do not need just a humanistic ethic applied to the environment as we have needed one for

Holmes Rolston III, "Environmental Ethics: Values in and Duties to the National World," from F. Herbert Bormann and Stephen R. Kellert, *The Broken Circle: Ecology, Economics, Ethics* (Yale University Press, 1991), copyright ©1991, Yale University Press. Reprinted with permission of author and publisher.

business, law, medicine, technology, international development, or nuclear disarmament. Respect for life does demand an ethic concerned about human welfare, an ethic like the others and now applied to the environment. But environmental ethics in a deeper sense stands on a frontier, as radically theoretical as it is applied. It alone asks whether there can be nonhuman objects of duty.

Neither theory nor practice elsewhere needs values outside of human subjects, but environmental ethics must be more biologically objective – nonanthropocentric. It challenges the separation of science and ethics, trying to reform a science that finds nature value-free and an ethics that assumes that only humans count morally. Environmental ethics seeks to escape relativism in ethics, to discover a way past culturally based ethics. However much our worldviews, ethics included, are embedded in our cultural heritages, and thereby theory-laden and value-laden, all of us know that a natural world exists apart from human cultures. Humans interact with nature. Environmental ethics is the only ethics that breaks out of culture. It has to evaluate nature, both wild nature and the nature that mixes with culture, and to judge duty thereby. After accepting environmental ethics, you will no longer be the humanist you once were.

Environmental ethics requires risk. It explores poorly charted terrain, where one can easily get lost. One must hazard the kind of insight that first looks like foolishness. Some people approach environmental ethics with a smile – expecting chicken liberation and rights for rocks, misplaced concern for chipmunks and daisies. Elsewhere, they think, ethicists deal with sober concerns: medical ethics, business ethics, justice in public affairs, questions of life and death and of peace and war. But the questions here are no less serious: The degradation of the environment poses as great a threat to life as nuclear war, and a more probable tragedy.

Higher Animals

Logically and psychologically, the best and easiest breakthrough past the traditional boundaries of interhuman ethics is made when confronting higher animals. Animals defend their lives; they have a good of their own and suffer pains and pleasures like ourselves. Human moral concern should at least cross over into the domain of animal experience. Yet this boundary crossing is also dangerous because if made only psychologically and not biologically, the would-be environmental ethicist may be too disoriented to travel further. The promised environmental ethics will degenerate into a mammalian ethics. We certainly need an ethic for animals, but that is only one level of concern in a comprehensive environmental ethics.

One might expect classical ethics to have sifted well an ethics for animals. Our ancestors did not think about endangered species, ecosystems, acid rain, or the ozone layer, but they lived in closer association with wild and domestic animals than we do. Hunters track wounded deer; ranchers who let their horses starve are prosecuted. Still, until recently, the scientific, humanistic centuries since the so-called Enlightenment have not been sensitive ones for animals, owing to the Cartesian legacy. Animals were mindless, living matter; biology has been mechanistic. Even psychology, rather than defending animal experience, has been behaviorist. Philosophy has protested little, concerned instead with locating values in human experiences at the same time that it dis-spirited and devalued nature. Across several centuries of hard science and humanistic ethics there has been little compassion for animals.

The progress of science itself blurred the human–nonhuman boundary line. Animal anatomy, biochemistry, cognition, perception, experience, behavior, and evolutionary history are kin to our own. Animals have no immortal souls, but then persons may not either; or beings with souls may not be the only kind that count morally. Ethical progress further blurred the boundary. Sensual pleasures are a good thing; ethics should be egalitarian, nonarbitrary, nondiscriminatory. There are ample scientific grounds that animals enjoy pleasures and suffer pains; and ethically there are no grounds to value these sensations in humans and not in animals. So there has been a vigorous reassessment of human duties to sentient life. The world cheered in the fall of 1988 when humans rescued two whales from winter ice.

"Respect their right to life": A sign in Rocky Mountain National Park enjoins humans not to harass bighorn sheep. "The question is not, Can they reason, nor Can they talk? but, Can they suffer?" wrote Jeremy Bentham, insisting that animal welfare counts too. The Park Service sign and Bentham's question increase sensitivity by extending rights and hedonist goods to animals. The gain is a vital breakthrough past humans, and the first lesson in environmental ethics has been learned. But the risk is a moral extension that expands rights as far as mammals and not much further, a psychologically based ethic that counts only felt experience. We respect life in our nonhuman but near-human animal cousins, a semianthropic and still quite subjective ethics. Justice remains a concern for just-us subjects. There has, in fact, not been much of a theoretical breakthrough: there has been no paradigm shift.

Lacking that, we are left with anomaly and conceptual strain. When we try to use culturally extended rights and psychologically based utilities to protect the flora or even the insentient fauna, to protect endangered species or ecosystems, we can only stammer. Indeed, we get lost trying to protect bighorns, because, in the wild, cougars are not respecting the rights or utilities of the sheep they slay, and, in culture, humans slay sheep and eat them regularly, while humans have every right not to be eaten by either humans or cougars. There are no rights in the wild, and nature is indifferent to the welfare of particular animals. A bison fell through the ice into a river in Yellowstone Park; the environmental ethic there, letting nature take its course, forbade would-be rescuers from either saving or killing the suffering animal to put it out of its misery. A drowning human would have been saved at once. Perhaps it was a mistake to save those whales.

The ethics by extension now seems too nondiscriminating; we are unable to spearate an ethics for humans from an ethics for wildlife. To treat wild animals with compassion learned in culture does not appreciate their wildness. Man, said Socrates, is the political animal; humans maximally are what they are in culture, where the natural selection pressures (impressively productive in ecosystems) are relaxed without detriment to the species *Homo sapiens*, and indeed with great benefit to its member persons. Wild animals cannot enter culture; they do not have that capacity. They cannot acquire language at sufficient levels to take part in culture; they cannot make their clothing or build fires, much less read books or receive an education. Animals can, by human adoption, receive some of the protections of culture, which happens when we domesticate them, but neither pets nor food animals enter the culture that shelters them.

Worse, such cultural protection can work to their detriment; their wildness is made over into a human artifact as food or pet animal. A cow does not have the integrity of a deer, or a poodle that of a wolf. Culture is a good thing for humans but often a bad thing for animals. Their biology and ecology – neither justice nor charity, nor rights nor welfare – provide the benchmark for an ethics.

Culture does make a relevant ethical difference, and environmental ethics has different criteria from interhuman ethics. Can they talk? and Can they reason? – indicating cultural capacities – are relevant questions as well as Can they suffer? *Equality* is a positive word in ethics, *discriminatory* a pejorative one. On the other hand, simplistic reduction is a failing in the philosophy of science and epistemology; to be "discriminating" is desirable in logic and value theory. Something about treating humans as equals with bighorns and cougars seems to "reduce" humans to merely animal levels of value, a "no more than" counterpart in ethics of the "nothing but" fallacy often met in science. Humans are "nothing but" naked apes. Something about treating sheep and cougars as the equals of humans seems to elevate them unnaturally and not to value them for what they are. There is something insufficiently discriminating in such judgements;

they are species-blind in a bad sense, blind to the real differences between species, valuational differences that do count morally. To the contrary, a discriminating ethicist will insist on preserving the differing richness of valuational complexity, wherever found. Compassionate respect for life in its suffering is only part of the analysis.

Two tests of discrimination are pains and diet. It might be thought that pain is a bad thing, whether in nature or culture. Perhaps when dealing with humans in culture, additional levels of value and utility must be protected by conferring rights that do not exist in the wild, but meanwhile we should at least minimize animal suffering. That is indeed a worthy imperative in culture where animals are removed from nature and bred, but it may be misguided where animals remain in ecosystems. When the bighorn sheep of Yellowstone caught pinkeye, they were blinded, injured, and starving as a result, and 300 of them, more than half the herd, perished. Wildlife veterinarians wanted to treat the disease, as they would have in any domestic herd, and as they did with Colorado bighorns infected with an introduced lungworm, but the Yellowstone ethicists left the animals to suffer, seemingly not respecting their life.

Had those ethicists no mercy? They knew rather that, although intrinsic pain is a bad thing whether in humans or in sheep, pain in ecosystems is instrumental pain, through which the sheep are naturally selected for a more satisfactory adaptive fit. Pain in a medically skilled culture is pointless, once the alarm to health is sounded, but pain operates functionally in bighorns in their niche, even after it is no longer in the interests of the pained individual. To have interfered in the interests of the blinded sheep would have weakened the species. Even the question Can they suffer? is not as simple as Bentham thought. What we ought to *do* depends on what *is*. The *is* of nature differs significantly from the *is* of culture, even when similar suffering is present in both.

At this point some ethicists will insist that at least in culture we can minimize animal pain, and that will constrain our diet. There is predation in nature; humans evolved as omnivores. But humans, the only moral animals, should refuse to participate in the meat-eating phase of their ecology, just as they refuse to play the game merely by the rules of natural selection. Humans do not look to the behaviour of wild animals as an ethical guide in other matters (marriage, truth-telling, promise-keeping, justice, charity). Why should they justify their dietary habits by watching what animals do?

But the difference is that these other matters are affairs of culture; these are person-to person events, not events at all in spontaneous nature. By contrast, eating is omnipresent in wild nature; humans eat because they are in nature, not because they are in culture. Eating animals is not an event between persons but a human-to-animal event; and the rules for this act come from the ecosystems in which humans evolved and have no duty to remake. Humans, then, can model their dietary habits on their ecosystems, though they cannot and should not so model their interpersonal justice or charity. When eating, they ought to minimize animal suffering, but they have no duty to revise trophic pyramids whether in nature or culture. The boundary between animals and humans has not been rubbed out after all; only what was a boundary line has been blurred into a boundary zone.We have discovered that animals count morally, though we have not yet solved the challenge of how to count them.

Animals enjoy psychological lives, subjective experiences, the satisfaction of felt interests – intrinsic values that count morally when humans encounter them. But the pains, pleasures, interests, and welfare of individual animals make up only one of the considerations in a more complex environmental ethics that cannot be reached by conferring rights on them or by a hedonist calculus, however far extended. We have to travel further into a more biologically based ethics.

Organisms

If we are to respect all life, we have still another boundary to cross, from zoology to botany, from sentient to insentient life. In Yosemite National Park for almost a century humans entertained themselves by driving through a tunnel cut in a giant sequoia. Two decades ago the Wawona tree, weakened by the cut, blew down in a storm. People said "Cut us another drive-through sequoia." The Yosemite environmental ethic, deepening over the years, answered. "No. You ought not to mutilate majestic sequoias for amusement. Respect their life." Indeed, some ethicists count the value of redwoods so highly that they will spike redwoods, lest they be cut. In the Rawah Wilderness in alpine Colorado, old signs read, "Please leave the flowers for others to enjoy." When the signs rotted out, new signs urged a less humanist ethic: "Let the flowers live!"

But trees and flowers cannot care, so why should we? We are not considering animals that are close kin, nor can they suffer or experience anything. Plants are not valuers with preferences that can be satisfied or frustrated. It seems odd to assert that plants need our sympathy, odd to ask that we should consider their point of view. They have no subjective life, only objective life.

Perhaps the questions are wrong, because they are coming out of the old paradigm. We are at a critical divide. That is why I earlier warned that environmenal ethicists who seek only to extend a humanistic ethic to mammalian cousins will get lost. Seeing no moral landmarks, those ethicists may turn back to more familiar terrain. Afraid of the naturalistic fallacy, they will say that people should enjoy letting flowers live or that it is silly to cut drive-through sequoias, that it is aesthetically more excellent for humans to appreciate both for what they are. But these ethically conservative reasons really do not understand what biological conservation is in the deepest sense.

It takes ethical courage to go on, to move past a hedonistic, humanistic logic to a bio-logic. Pains, pleasures, and psychological experience will no further be useful categories, but – lest some think that from here on I as a philosopher become illogical and lose all ethical sense – let us orient ourselves by extending logical, propositional, cognitive, and normative categories into biology. Nothing matters to a tree, but much is vital to it.

An organism is a spontaneous, self-maintaining system, sustaining and reproducing itself, executing its program, making a way through the world, checking against performance by means of responsive capacities with which to measure success. It can reckon with vicissitudes, opportunities, and adversities that the world presents. Something more than physical causes, even when less than sentience, is operating within every organism. There is information superintending the causes; without it, the organism would collapse into a sand heap. This information is a modern equivalent of what Aristotle called formal and final causes; it gives the organism a telos, or end, a kind of (nonfelt) goal. Organisms have ends, although not always ends in view.

All this cargo is carried by the DNA, essentially a linguistic molecule. By a serial reading of the DNA, a polypeptide chain is synthesized, such that its sequential structure determines the bioform into which it will fold. Ever-lengthening chains are organized into genes, as ever-longer sentences are organized into paragraphs and chapters. Diverse proteins, lipids, carbohydrates, enzymes – all the life structures – are written into the genetic library. The DNA is thus a logical set, not less than a biological set, and is informed as well as formed. Organisms use a sort of symbolic logic, using these molecular shapes as symbols of life. The novel resourcefulness lies in the epistemic content conserved, developed, and thrown forward to make biological resources out of the physicochemical sources. This executive steering core is cybernetic – partly a special kind of cause-and-effect system and partly something more. It is partly a historical information system discovering and evaluating ends so as to map and make a way through the world, and partly a system of significances attached to operations, pursuits, and resources. In this sense, the genome is a set of conservation molecules.

The genetic set is really a propositional set – to choose a provocative term – recalling that the Latin *propositum* is an assertion, a set task, a theme, a plan, a proposal, a project, as well as a cognitive statement. From this, it is also a motivational set, unlike human books, because these life motifs are set to drive the movement from genotypic potential to phenotypic expression. Given a chance, these molecules seek organic self-expression. They thus proclaim a lifeway; and with this an organism, unlike an inert rock, claims the environment as source and sink, from which to abstract energy and materials and into which to excrete them. It takes advantage of its environment. Life thus arises out of earthen sources (as do rocks), but life (unlike rocks) turns back on its sources to make resources out of them. An acorn becomes an oak; the oak stands on its own.

So far we have only description. We begin to pass to value when we recognize that the genetic set is a normative set; it distinguishes between what is and what ought to be. This does not mean that the organism is a moral system, for there are no moral agents in nature; but the organism is an axiological, evaluative system. So the oak grows, reproduces, repairs its wounds, and resists death. The physical state that the organism seeks, idealized in its programmatic form, is a valued state. Value is present in this achievement. *Vital* seems a better word here than *biological*. We are dealing not simply with another individual defending its solitary life but with an individual having situated fitness in an ecosystem. Still, we want to affirm that the living individual, taken as a point-experience in the web of interconnected life, is *per se* an intrinsic value.

A life is defended for what it is in itself, without necessary further contributory reference, although, given the structure of all ecosystems, such lives necessarily do have further contributory reference. The organism has something it is conserving, something for which it is standing: its life. Though organisms must fit into their niche, they have their own standards. They promote their own realization, at the same time that they track an environment. They have a technique, a know-how. Every organism has a good of its kind; it defends its own kind as a good kind. In that sense, as soon as one knows what a giant sequoia tree is, one knows the biological identity that is sought and conserved.

There seems no reason why such own-standing normative organisms are not morally significant. A moral agent deciding his or her behavior ought to take account of the consequences for other evaluative systems. Within the community of moral agents, one has not merely to ask whether *x* is a normative system but also, because the norms are at personal option, to judge the norm. But within the biotic community, organisms are amoral normative systems, and there are no cases in which an organism seeks a good of its own that is morally reprehensible. The distinction between having a good of its kind and being a good kind vanishes, so far as any faulting of the organism is concerned. To this extent, everything with a good of its kind is a good kind and thereby has intrinsic value.

One might say that an organism is a bad organism if, during the course of pressing its normative expression, it upsets the ecosystem or causes widespread disease. Remember, though, that an organism cannot be a good kind without situated environmental fitness. By natural selection the kind of goods to which it is genetically programmed must mesh with its ecosystemic role. In spite of the ecosystem as a perpetual contest of goods in dialectic and exchange, it is diffuclt to say that any organism is a bad kind in this instrumental sense either. The misfits are extinct, or soon will be. In spontaneous nature any species that preys upon, parasitizes, competes with, or crowds another will be a bad kind from the narrow perspective of its victim or competitor.

But if we enlarge that perspective, we typically have difficulty in saying that any species is a bad kind overall in the ecosystem. An "enemy" may even be good for the "victimized" species, though harmful to individual members of it, as when predation keeps the deer herd healthy. Beyond this, the "bad kinds" typically play useful roles in population control, in symbiotic relationships, or in providing opportunities for other species. The *Chlamydia* microbe is a bad kind from the perspective of the bighorns, but when one thing dies, something else lives. After the pinkeye outbreak among the bighorns, the golden eagle population in Yellowstone flourished, preying on the bighorn carcasses. For the eagles, *Chlamydia* is a good kind instrumentally.

Some biologist–philosophers will say that even though an organism evolves to have a situated environmental fitness, not all such situations are good arrangements; some can be clumsy or bad. True, the vicissitudes of historical evolution do sometimes result in ecological webs that are suboptimal solutions, within the biologically limited possibilities and powers of interacting organisms. Still, such systems have been selected over millennia for functional stability, and at least the burden of proof is on a human evaluator to say why any natural kind is a bad kind and ought not to call forth admiring respect. Something may be a good kind intrinsically but a bad kind instrumentally in the system; such cases will be anomalous however, with selection pressures against them. These assertions about good kinds do not say that things are perfect kinds or that there can be no better ones, only that natural kinds are good kinds until proven otherwise.

In fact, what is almost invariably meant by a bad kind is an organism that is instrumentally bad when judged from the viewpoint of human interests, often with the further complication that human interests have disrupted natural systems. *Bad* as so used is an anthropocentric word; there is nothing at all biological or ecological about it, and so it has no force in evaluating objective nature, however much humanistic force it may sometimes have.

A vital ethic respects all life, not just animal pains and pleasures, much less just human preferences. The old signs in the Rawah Wilderness – "Please leave the flowers for others to enjoy" – were application signs using an old, ethically conservative, humanistic ethic. The new ones invite a change of reference frame – a wilder ethic that is more logical because it is more biological, a radical ethic that goes down to the roots of life, that really is conservative because it understands biological conservation at depths. What the injunction "Let the flowers live!" means is this: "Daisies, marsh marigolds, geraniums, and larkspurs are evaluative systems that conserve goods of their kind and, in the absence of evidence to the contrary, are good kinds. There are trails here by which you may enjoy these flowers. Is there any reason why your human interests should not also conserve these good kinds?" A drive-through sequoia causes no suffering; it is not cruel. But it is callous and insensitive to the wonder of life.

Species

Sensitivity to the wonder of life, however, can sometimes make an environmental ethicist seem callous. On San Clemente Island, the US Fish and Wildlife Service planned to shoot two thousand feral goats to save three endangered plant species (*Malacothamnus clementinus*, *Castilleja grisea*, and *Delphinium kinkiense*), of which the surviving individuals numbered only a few dozen. After a protest, some goats were trapped and relocated. But trapping all of them was impossible, and thousands were killed. In this instance, the survival of plant species was counted more than the lives of individual mammals; a few plants counted more than many goats.

Those who wish to restore rare species of big cats to the wild have asked about killing genetically inbred, inferior cats presently held in zoos, in order to make space available for the cats needed to reconstruct and maintain a population that is genetically more likely to survive upon release. All the Siberian tigers in zoos in North America are descendants of seven animals; if these tigers were replaced by others nearer to the wild type and with more genetic variability, the species might be saved in the wild. When we move to the level of species, sometimes we decide to kill individuals for the good of their kind.

Or we might now refuse to let nature take its course. The Yellowstone ethicists let the bison drown, in spite of its suffering; they let the blinded bighorns die. But in the spring of 1984 a sow grizzly and her three cubs walked across the ice of Yellowstone Lake to Frank Island, two miles from shore. They stayed several days to feast on two elk carcasses, and the ice bridge melted. Soon afterward, they were starving on an island too small to support them. This time the Yellowstone ethicists promptly rescued the grizzlies and released them on the mainland, in order to protect an endangered species. They were not rescuing individual bears so much as saving the species.

Coloradans have declined to build the Two Forks Dam to supply urban Denver with water. Building the dam would require destroying a canyon and altering the Platte River flow, with many negative environmental consequences, including further endangering the whooping crane and endangering a butterfly, the Pawnee montane skipper. Elsewhere in the state, water development threatens several fish species, including the humpback chub, which requires the turbulent spring runoff stopped by dams. Environmental ethics doubts whether the good of humans who wish more water for development, both for industry and for bluegrass lawns, warrants endangering species of cranes, butterflies, and fish.

A species exists; a species ought to exist. An environmental ethics must make these assertions and move from biology to ethics with care. Species exist only instantiated in individuals, yet they are as real as individual plants or animals. The assertion that there are specific forms of life historically maintained in their environments over time seems as certain as anything else we believe about the empirical world. At times biologists revise the theories and taxa with which they map these forms, but species are not so much like lines of latitude and longitude as like mountains and rivers, phenomena objectively there to be mapped. The edges of these natural kinds will sometimes be fuzzy, to some extent discretionary. One species will slide into another over evolutionary time. But it does not follow from the fact that speciation is sometimes in progress that species are merely made up and not found as evolutionary lines with identity in time as well as space.

A consideration of species is revealing and challenging because it offers a biologically based counterexample to the focus on individuals – typically sentient and usually persons – so characteristic in classical ethics. In an evolutionary ecosystem, it is not mere individuality that counts; the species is also significant because it is a dynamic life-form maintained over time. The individual represents (re-presents) a species in each new generation. It is a token of a type, and the type is more important than the token.

A species lacks moral agency, reflective self-awareness, sentience, or organic individuality. The older, conservative ethic will be tempted to say that specific-level processes cannot count morally. Duties must attach to singular lives, most evidently those with a self, or some analogue to self. In an individual organism, the organs report to a center; the good of a whole is defended. The members of a ːpecies report to no center. A species has no self. It is not a bounded singular. There is no analogue to the nervous hookups or circulatory flows that characterize the organism.

But singularity, centeredness, selfhood, and individuality are not the only processes to which duty attaches. A more radically conservative ethic knows that having a biological identity reasserted genetically over time is as true of the species as of the individual. Identity need not attach solely to the centered organism; it can persist as a discrete pattern over time. From this way of thinking, it follows that the life the individual has is something passing through the individual as much as something it intrinsically possesses. The individual is subordinate to the species, not the other way around. The genetic set, in which is coded the telos, is as evidently the property of the species as of the individual through which it passes. A consideration of species strains any ethic fixed on individual organisms, much less on sentience or persons. But the result can be biologically sounder, though it revises what was formerly thought logically permissible or ethically binding.When ethics is informed by this kind of biology, it is appropriate to attach duty dynamically to the specific form of life.

The species line is the vital living system, the whole, of which individual organisms are the essential parts. The species too has its integrity, its individuality, its right to life (if we must use the rhetoric of rights); and it is more important to protect this vitality than to protect individual integrity. The right to life, biologically speaking, is an adaptive fit that is right for life, that survives over millennia. This idea generates at least a presumption that species in a niche are good right where they are, and therefore that it is right for humans to let them be, to let them evolve.

Processes of value that we earlier found in an organic individual reappear at the specific level: defending a particular form of life, pursuing a pathway through the world, resisting death (extinction), regenerating, maintaining a normative identity over time, expressing creative resilience by discovering survival skills. It is as logical to say that the individual is the species' way of propagating itself as to say that the embryo or egg is the individual's way of propagating itself. The dignity resides in the dynamic form; the individual inherits this form, exemplifies it, and passes it on. If, at the specific level, these processes are just as evident, or even more so, what prevents duties from arising at that level? The appropriate survival unit is the appropriate level of moral concern.

A shutdown of the life stream is the most destructive event possible. The wrong that humans are doing, or allowing to happen through carelessness, is stopping the historical vitality of life, the flow of natural kinds. Every extinction is an incremental decay in this stopping of life, no small thing. Every extinction is a kind of superkilling. It kills forms (species) beyond individuals. It kills essences beyond existences, the soul as well as the body. It kills collectively, not just distributively. It kills birth as well as death. Afterward nothing of that kind either lives or dies.

The question: Ought species x to exist? is a distributive increment in the collective question, ought life on earth to exist? Life on earth cannot exist without its individuals, but a lost individual is always reproducible; a lost species is never reproducible. The answer to the species question is not always the same as the answer to the collective question, but because life on earth is an aggregate of many species, the two are sufficiently related that the burden of proof lies with those who wish to deliberately extinguish a species and simultaneously to care for life on earth.

One form of life has never endangered so many others. Never before has this level of question – superkilling by a superkiller – been deliberately faced. Humans have more understanding than ever of the natural world they inhabit and of the speciating processes, more predictive power to foresee the intended and unintended results of their actions, and more power to reverse the undesirable consequences. The duties that such power and vision generate no longer attach simply to individuals or persons but are emerging duties to specific forms of life. What is ethically callous is the maelstrom of killing and insensitivity to forms of life and the sources producing them. What is required is principled responsibility to the biospheric earth.

Human activities seem misfit in the system. Although humans are maximizing their own species interests, and in this respect behaving as does each of the other species, they do not have any adaptive fitness. They are not really fitting into the evolutionary processes of ongoing biological conservation and elaboration. Their cultures are not really dynamically stable in their ecosystems. Such behavior is therefore not right. Yet humanistic ethical systems limp when they try to prescribe right conduct here. They seem misfits in the roles most recently demanded of them.

If, in this world of uncertain moral convictions, it makes any sense to assert that one ought not to kill individuals without justification, it makes more sense to assert that one ought not to superkill the species without superjustification. Several billion years' worth of creative toil, several million species of teeming life, have been handed over to the care of this late-coming species in which mind has flowered and morals have emerged. Ought not this sole moral species to do something less self-interested than count all the produce of an evolutionary ecosystem as nothing but human resources? Such an attitude hardly seems biologically informed, much less ethically adequate. It is too provincial for intelligent humanity. Life on earth is a many-splendored thing; extinction dims its luster. An ethics of respect for life is urgent at the level of species.

Ecosystems

A species is what it is where it is. No environmental ethics has found its way on earth until it finds an ethic for the biotic communities in which all destinies are entwined. "A thing is right," urged Aldo Leopold, "when it tends to preserve the integrity, stability, and beauty of the biotic community. It is wrong when it tends otherwise."[1] Again, we have two parts to the ethic: first, that ecosystems exist, both in the wild and in support of culture; second, that ecosystems ought to exist, both for what they are in themselves and as modified by culture. Again, we must move with care from the biological assertions to the ethical assertions.

Giant forest fires raged over Yellowstone National Park in the summer of 1988, consuming nearly a million acres despite the efforts of a thousand fire fighters. By far the largest ever known in the park, the fires seemed a disaster. But the Yellowstone land ethic enjoined: "Let nature take its course; let it burn." So the fires were not fought at first; but in midsummer, national authorities overrode that policy and ordered the fires to be put out. Even then, weeks later, fires continued to burn, partly because they were too big to control but partly too because Yellowstone personnel did not really want the fires put out. Despite the evident destruction of trees, shrubs, and wildlife, they believe that fires are a good thing – even when the elk and bison leave the park in search of food and are shot by hunters. Fires reset succession, release nutrients, recycle materials, and renew the biotic community. (Nearby, in the Teton wilderness, a storm blew down 15,000 acres of trees, and some people proposed that the area be declassified from wilderness to allow commerical salvage of the timber. But a similar environmental ethic said, "No, let it rot.")

Aspen are important in the Yellowstone ecosystem. Although some aspen stands are climax and self-renewing, many are seral and give way to conifers. Aspen groves support many birds and much wildlife, especially beavers, whose activities maintain the riparian zones. Aspen are rejuvenated after fires, and the Yellowstone land ethic wants the aspen for their critical role in the biotic community. Elk browse the young aspen stems. To a degree this is a good thing, because it provides the elk with critical nitrogen, but in excess it is a bad thing. The elk have no predators, because the wolves are gone, and as a result the elk overpopulate. Excess elk also destroy the willows, and that destruction in turn destroys the beavers. So, in addition to letting fires burn, rejuvenating the aspen might require park managers to cull hundreds of elk – all for the sake of a healthy ecosystem.

The Yellowstone ethic wishes to restore wolves to the greater Yellowstone ecosystem. At the level of species, this change is desired because of what the wolf is in itself, but it is also desired because the greater Yellowstone ecosystem does not have its full integrity, stability, and beauty without this majestic animal at the top of the trophic pyramid. Restoring the wolf as a top predator would mean suffering and death for many elk, but that would be a good thing for the aspen and willows, the beavers, and the riparian habitat, and would have mixed benefits for the bighorns and mule deer (the overpopulating elk consume their food, but the sheep and deer would also be consumed by the wolves). Restoration of wolves would be done over the protests of ranchers who worry about wolves eating their cattle; many of them also believe that the wolf is a bloodthirsty killer, a bad kind. Nevertheless, the Yellowstone ethic demands wolves, as it does fires, in appropriate respect for life in its ecosystem.

Letting nature take its ecosystemic course is why the Yellowstone ethic forbade rescuing the drowning bison but required rescuing the sow grizzly and her cubs, the latter case to insure that the big predators remain. After the bison drowned, coyotes, foxes, magpies, and ravens fed on the carcass. Later, even a grizzly bear fed on it. All this is a good thing because the system cycles on. On that account, rescuing the whales trapped in the winter ice seems less of a good thing, when we note that rescuers had to drive away polar bears that attempted to eat the dying whales.

Classical, humanistic ethics finds ecosystems to be unfamiliar territory. It is difficult to get the biology right and, superimposed on the biology, to get the ethics right. Fortunately, it is often evident that human welfare depends on ecosystemic support, and in this sense all our legislation about clean air, clean water, soil conservation, national and state forest policies, pollution controls, renewable resources, and so forth is concerned about ecosystem-level processes. Furthermore, humans find much of value in preserving wild ecosystems, and our wilderness and park system is impressive.

Still, a comprehensive environmental ethics needs the best, naturalistic reasons, as well as the good, humanistic ones, for respecting ecosystems. Ecosystems generate and support life, keep selection pressures high, enrich situated fitness, and allow congruent kinds to evolve in their places with sufficient containment. The ecologist finds that ecosystems are objectively satisfactory communities in the sense that organismic needs are sufficiently met for species to survive and flourish, and the critical ethicist finds (in a subjective judgment matching the objective process) that such ecosystems are satisfactory communities to which to attach duty. Our concern must be for the fundamental unit of survival.

An ecosystem, the conservative ethicist will say, is too low a level of organization to be respected intrinsically. Ecosystems can seem little more than random, statistical processes. A forest can seem a loose collection of externally related parts, the collction of fauna and flora a jumble, hardly a community. The plants and animals within an ecosystem have needs, but their interplay can seem simply a matter of distribution and abundance, birth rates and death rates, population densities, parasitism and predation, dispersion, checks and balances, and stochastic process. Much is not organic at all (rain, groundwater, rocks, soil particles, air), and some organic material is dead and decaying debris (fallen trees, scat, humus). These things have no organized needs. There is only catch-as-catch-can scrimmage for nutrients and energy, not really enough of an integrated process to call the whole a community.

Unlike higher animals, ecosystems have no experiences; they do not and cannot care. Unlike plants, an ecosystem has no organized center, no genome. It does not defend itself against injury or death. Unlike a species, there is no ongoing telos, no biological identity reinstantiated over time. The organismic parts are more complex than the community whole. More troublesome still, an ecosystem can seem a jungle where the fittest survive, a place of contest and conflict, beside which the organism is a model of cooperation. In animals the heart, liver, muscles, and brain are tightly integrated, as are the leaves, cambium, and roots in plants. But the so-called ecosystem community is pushing and shoving between rivals, each aggrandizing itself, or else seems to be all indifference and haphazard juxtaposition – nothing to call forth our admiration.

Environmental ethics must break through the boundary posted by disoriented ontological conservatives, who hold that the only organisms are real, actually existing as entities, whereas ecosystems are nominal – just interacting individuals. Oak trees are real, but forests are nothing but collections of trees. But any level is real if it shapes behavior on the level below it. Thus the cell is real because that pattern shapes the behavior of amino acids; the organism, because that pattern coordinates the behavior of hearts and lungs. The biotic community is real because the niche shapes the morphology of the oak trees within it. Being real at the level of community requires only an organization that shapes the behavior of its members.

The challenge is to find a clear model of community and to discover an ethics for it: better biology for better ethics. Even before the rise of ecology, biologists began to conclude that the combative survival of the fittest distorts the truth. The more perceptive model is coaction in adapted fit. Predator and prey, parasite and host, grazer and grazed, are contending forces in dynamic process in which the well-being of each is bound up with the other – coordinated as much as heart and liver are coordinated organically. The ecoystem supplies the coordinates through which each organism moves, outside which the species cannot really be located.

The community connections are looser than the organism's internal interconnections but are not less significant. Admiring organic unity in organisms and stumbling over environmental looseness is like valuing mountains and despising valleys. The matrix that the organism requires to survive is the open, pluralistic ecological system. Internal complexity – heart, liver, muscles, brain – arises as a way of dealing with a complex, tricky environment. The skin-out processes are not just the support; they are the subtle source of the skin-in processes. In the complete picture, the outside is as vital as the inside. Had there been either simplicity or lockstep concentrated unity in the environment, no organismic unity could have evolved. Nor would it remain. There would be less elegance in life.

To look at one level for what is appropriate at another makes a mistake in categories. One should not look for a single center or program in ecosystems, much less for subjective experiences. Instead, one should look for a matrix, for interconnections between centers (individual plants and animals, dynamic lines of speciation), for creative stimulus and open-ended potential. Everything will be connected to many other things, sometimes by obligate associations but more often by partial and pliable dependencies, and, among other things, there will be no significant interactions. There will be functions in a communal sense: shunts and crisscrossing pathways, cybernetic subsystems and feedback loops. An order arises spontaneously and systematically when many self-concerned units jostle and seek to fulfill their own programs, each doing its own thing and forced into informed interaction.

An ecocystem is a productive, projective system. Organisms defend only their selves, with individuals defending their continuing survival and with species increasing the numbers of kinds. But the evolutionary ecosystem spins a bigger story, limiting each kind, locking it into the welfare of others, promoting new arrivals, increasing kinds and the integration of kinds. Species increase their kind, but ecosystems increase kinds, super-posing the latter increase onto the former. Ecosystems are selective systems, as surely as organisms are selective systems. The natural selection comes out of the system and is imposed on the individual. The individual is programmed to make more of its kind, but more is going on systemically than that; the system is making more kinds.

Communal processes – the competition between organisms, statistically probable interactions, plant and animal successions, speciation over histori-cal time – generate an ever-richer community. Hence the evolutionary toil, elaborating and diversifying the biota, that once began with no species and results today in five million species, increasing over time the quality of lives in the upper rungs of the trophic pyramids. One-celled organisms evolved into many-celled, highly integrated organisms. Photosynthesis evolved and came to support locomotion – swimming, walking, running, flight. Stimulus – response mechanisms became complex instinctive acts.

Warm-blooded animals followed cold-blooded ones. Complex nervous systems, conditioned behavior, and learning emerged. Sentience appeared – sight, hearing, smell, taste, pleasure, pain. Brains coupled with hands. Consciousness and self-consciousness arose. Culture was superposed on nature.

These developments do not take place in all ecosystems or at every level. Microbes, plants, and lower animals remain, good of their kinds and, serving continuing roles, good for other kinds. The understories remain occupied. As a result, the quantity of life and its diverse qualities continue – from protozoans to primates to people. There is a push-up, lock-up ratchet effect that conserves the upstrokes and the outreaches. The later we go in time, the more accelerated are the forms at the top of the trophic pyramids, the more elaborated are the multiple trophic pyramids of earth. There are upward arrows over evolutionary time.

The system is a game with loaded dice, but the loading is a pro-life tendency, not mere stochastic process. Though there is no Nature in the singular, the system has a nature, a loading that pluralizes, putting natures into diverse kinds: $nature_1$, $nature_2$, $nature_3$ . . . $nature_n$. It does so using random elements (in both organisms and communities), but this is a secret of its fertility, producing steadily intensified interdependencies and options. An ecosystem has no head, but it heads toward species diversification, support, and richness. Though not a superorganism, it is a kind of vital field.

Instrumental value uses something as a means to an end; intrinsic value is worthwhile in itself. No warbler eats insects to become food for a falcon; the warbler defends its own life as an end in itself and makes more warblers as it can. A life is defended intrinsically, without further contributory reference. But neither of these traditional terms is satisfactory at the level of the ecosystem. Though it has value *in* itself, the system does not have any value *for* itself. Though it is a value producer, it is not a value owner. We are no longer confronting instrumental value, as though the system were of value instrumentally as a fountain of life. Nor is the question one of intrinsic value, as though the system defended some unified form of life for itself. We have reached something for which we need a third term: systemic value. Duties arise in encounters with the system that projects and protects these member components in biotic community.

Ethical conservatives, in the humanistic sense, will say that ecosystems are of value only because they contribute to human experiences. But that mistakes the last chapter for the whole story, one fruit for the whole plant. Humans count enough to have the right to flourish in ecosystems, but not so much that they have the right to degrade or shut down ecosystems, not at least without a burden of proof that there is an overriding cultural gain. Those who have traveled partway into environmental ethics will say that ecosystems are of value because they contribute to animal experiences or to organismic life. But the really conservative, radical view sees that the stability, integrity, and beauty of biotic communities are what are most fundamentally to be conserved. In a comprehensive ethics of respect for life, we ought to set ethics at the level of ecosystems alongside classical, humanistic ethics.

Value Theory

In practice the ultimate challenge of environmental ethics is the conservation of life on earth. In principle the ultimate challenge is a value theory profound enough to support that ethics. In nature there is negentropic construction in dialectic with entropic teardown, a process for which we hardly yet have an adequate scientific theory, much less a valuational theory. Yet this is nature's most striking feature, one that ultimately must be valued and of value. In one sense, nature is indifferent to mountains, rivers, fauna, flora, forests, and grasslands. But in another sense, nature has bent toward making and remaking these projcts, millions of kinds, for several billion years.

These performances are worth noticing, are remarkable and memorable – and not just because of their tendencies to produce something else, certainly not merely because of their tendency to produce this noticing in certain recent subjects, our human selves. These events are loci of value as products of systemic nature in its formative processes. The splendors of earth do not simply lie in their roles as human resources, supports of culture, or stimulators of experince. The most plausible account will find some programmatic evolution toward value, and not because it ignores Darwin but because it heeds his principle of natural selection and deploys it into a selection exploring new niches and elaborating kinds, even a selection upslope toward higher values, at least along some trends within some ecosystems. How do we humans come to be charged up with values, if there was and is nothing in nature charging us up so? A systematic environmental ethics does not wish to believe in the special creation of values or in their dumbfounding epigenesis. Let them evolve. Let nature carry value.

The notion that nature is a value carrier is ambiguous. Much depends on a thing's being more or less structurally congenial for the carriage. We value a thing and discover that we are under the sway of its valence, inducing our behavior. It has among its strengths (Latin: *valeo*, "be strong") this capacity to carry value. This potential cannot always be of the empty sort that a glass has for carrying water. It is often pregnant fullness. Some of the values that nature carries are up to us, our assignment. But fundamentally there are powers in nature that move to us and through us.

No value exists without an evaluator. So runs a well-entrenched dogma. Humans clearly evaluate their world; sentient animals may also. But plants cannot evaluate their environment; they have no options and make no choices. *A fortiori*, species and ecosystems, earth and Nature, cannot be bona fide evaluators. One can always hang on to the assertion that value, like a tickle or remorse, must be felt to be there. Its *esse* is *percipi*. To be, it must be perceived. Nonsensed value is nonsense. There are no thoughts without a thinker, no percepts without a perceiver, no deeds without a doer, no targets without an aimer.

Such resolute subjectivists cannot be defeated by argument, although they can be driven toward analyticity. That theirs is a retreat to definition is difficult to expose, because they seem to cling so closely to inner experience. They are reporting, on this hand, how values always excite us. They are giving, on that hand, a stipulative definition. That is how they choose to use the word *value*.

If value arrives only with consciousness, experiences in which humans find value have to be dealt with as appearances of various sorts. The value has to be relocated in the valuing subject's creativity as a person meets a valueless world, or even a valuable one – one able to be valued but one that before the human bringing of valuableness contains only possibility and not any actual value. Value can only be extrinsic to nature, never intrinsic to it.

But the valuing subject in an otherwise valueless world is an insufficient premise for the experienced conclusions of those who respect all life. Conversion to a biological view seems truer to world experience and more logically compelling. Something from a world beyond the human mind, beyond human experience, is received into our mind, our experience, and the value of that something does not always arise with our evaluation of it. Here the order of knowing reverses, and also enhances, the order of being. This too is a perspective but is ecologically better informed. Science has been steadily showing how the consequents (life, mind) are built on their precedents (energy, matter), however much they overleap them. Life and mind appear where they did not before exist, and with them levels of value emerge that did not before exist. But that gives no reason to say that all value is an irreducible emergent at the human (or upper-animal) level. A comprehensive environmental ethics reallocates value across the whole continuum. Value increases in the emergent climax but is continuously present in the composing precedents. The system is value-able, able to produce value. Human evaluatiors are among its products.

Some value depends on subjectivity, yet all value is generated within the geosystemic and ecosystemic pyramid. Systemically, value fades from subjective to objective value but also fans out from the individual to its role and matrix. Things do not have their separate natures merely in and for themselves, but they face outward and co-fit into broader natures. Value-in-itself is smeared out to become value-in-togetherness. Value seeps out into the system, and we lose our capacity to identify the individual as the sole locus of value.

Intrinsic value, the value of an individual for what it is in itself, becomes problematic in a holistic web. True, the system produces such values more and more with its evolution of individuality and freedom. Yet to decouple this value from the biotic, communal system is to make value too internal and elementary; this decoupling forgets relatedness and externality. Every intrinsic value has leading and trailing *ands*. Such value is coupled with value from which it comes and toward which it moves. Adapted fitness makes individualistic value too system-independent. Intrinsic value is a part in a whole and is not to be fragmented by valuing it in isolation.

Everything is good in a role, in a whole, although we can speak of objective intrinsic goodness wherever a point-event – a trillium, for example – defends a good (its life) in itself. We can speak of subjective intrinsic goodness when such an event registers as a point-experience, at which point human pronounce both their experience and what it is to be good without need to enlarge their focus. Neither the trillium nor the human judges of it require for their respective valuings any further contributory reference.

When eaten by foragers or in death resorbed into humus, the trillium has its value destroyed, transformed into instrumentality. The system is a value transformer where form and being, process and reality, fact and value, are inseparably joined. Intrinsic and instrumental values shuttle back and forth, parts-in-wholes and wholes-in-parts, local details of value embedded in global structures, gems in their settings, and their setting-situation a corporation where value cannot stand alone. Every good is in community.

In environmental ethics one's beliefs about nature, which are based upon but exceed science, have everything to do with beliefs about duty. The way the world is informs the way it ought to be. We always shape our values in significant measure in accord with our notion of the kind of universe that we live in, and this process drives our sense of duty. Our model of reality implies a model of conduct. Differing models sometimes imply similar conduct, but often they do not. A model in which nature has no value apart from human preferences will imply different conduct from one in which nature projects fundamental values, some objective and others that further require human subjectivity superimposed on objective nature.

This evaluation is not scientific description; hence it is not ecology *per se* but meta-ecology. No amount of research can verify that, environmentally, the right is the optimum biotic community. Yet ecological description generates this valuing of nature, endorsing the systemic rightness. The transition from *is* to *good* and thence to *ought* occurs here; we leave science to enter the domain of evalation, from which an ethics follows.

What is ethically puzzling and exciting is that an *ought* is not so much derived from an *is* as discovered simultaneously with it. As we progress from descriptions of fauna and flora, of cycles and pyramids, of autotrophs coordinated with heterotrophs, of stability and dynamism, on to intricacy, planetary opulence and interdependence, unity and harmony with oppositions in counterpoint and synthesis, organisms evolved within and satisfactorily fitting their communities, and we arrive at length at beauty and goodness, we find that it is difficult to say where the natural facts leave off and where the natural values appear. For some people at least, the sharp *is–ought* dichotomy is gone; the values seem to be there a: soon as the facts are fully in, and both values and facts seem to be alike properties of the system.

There is something overspecialized about an ethic, held by the dominant class of *Homo sapiens*, that regards the welfare of only one of several million species as an object and beneficiary of duty. If the remedy requires a paradigm change about the sorts of things to which duty can attach, so much the worse for those humanistic ethics no longer functioning in, or suited to, their changing environment. The anthropocentrism associated with them was fiction anyway. There is something Newtonian, not yet Einsteinian, besides something morally naïve, about living in a reference frame in which one species takes itself as absolute and values everything else relative to its utility. If true to its specific epithet, which means wise, ought not *Homo sapiens* value this host of life as something that lays on us a claim to care for life in its own right?

Only the human species contains moral agents, but perhaps conscience on such an Earth ought not to be used to exempt every other form of life from consideration, with the resulting paradox that the sole moral species acts only in its collective self-interest toward all the rest. Is not the ultimate philosophical task the discovery of a whole great ethic that knows the human place under the sun?

NOTE

1   Aldo Leopold, *A Sand County Almanac* (New York: Ballantine Books, 1970): 262.

16
Re-valuing Nature

Lori Gruen

In this paper Gruen attempts to extend feminist communitarian philosophy so as to properly include basic ecological and environmental concerns. Communitarian philosophy has certain roots in modern pragmatism of the sort advanced prominently by Richard Rorty and partially reflected in the work of Alasdair MacIntyre, both of whom give central place to the idea of the social construction of knowledge and value. Accordingly, Gruen begins by rejecting the common philosophical approach to environmental ethics which seeks to ground itself in objectivist notions of the intrinsic value of nature and of living things. Expanding on feminist communitarian ideas, she outlines her own constructive position on ecofeminist moral theory, offering, at the same time, general reassurances intended to counter fears of relativism. What emerges is an account of the way that the concepts of voluntariness, inclusivity, and direct experience might combine to provide a dialogic process by which intersubjective agreement on environmental value can be reached.

This paper contrasts sharply with that of Rolston (chapter 15) on the question of intrinsic value. On the other hand, it has various affinities with the papers of Baier (chapter 7) and Jaggar (chapter 4), and with that of Kettner (chapter 2) regarding discourse ethics.

As our knowledge of environmental devastation and the global conse-quences of this devastation grows, so do questions about how we ought to think about and act toward the natural world.[1] Initially such questions were left to economists and policy-makers; more recently these questions have been addressed, although not answered, by politicians and government bureaucrats. Philosophers, too, have played an important role in the global environmental debate. Philosophical reflection has done a great deal to clarify and illuminate useful strategies for dealing with our global ecological crises. In this paper, I will examine some basic themes in environmental ethics through an ecofeminist lens. Specifically, I will look at how we might answer the questions: (1) How do we justify our moral claims about human interactions with nature? and (2) Does this justification provide motivating reasons for acting morally toward nature?

Intrinsic Value and Ecological Moral Ontologies

In so far as there is something that can be called a philosophical tradition in environmental ethics, it is a tradition which often attempts to answer questions of justification by drawing on the notion of intrinsic value. An examination of two prominent strains of thinking about the construction of an environmental ethic, namely social ecology and deep ecology, illustrates the central role intrinsic value plays. While there are significant differences between these two positions,[2] I want to suggest that they both attempt to justify moral claims about the environment by appealing to the notion of intrinsic value.

When I talk about intrinsic value I am speaking of those theories that adhere to an ontological doctrine of objectivism about value. That is to say, those theorists who justify moral claims by appealing to intrinsic value as part of the fabric of the universe are moral realists. They maintain that there are values that exist independently of our conceptual schemes and linguistic frameworks and that these values can be determined not only independently of the usefulness of a particular entity but also independently of our feelings or attitudes about it. On this view, minds discover values, they do not create them. The intrinsic value that I will be discussing is what Holmes Rolston has called "non-instrumental, non-anthropogenic" value.[3]

I will look first at what is called "social ecology," a theory most commonly associated with the work of Murray Bookchin and which finds some of its roots in the writing of the early Frankfurt School.[4] Simply put, social ecology sees the problem of environmental destruction as emerging from a number of social structures, most fundamentally capitalism and the centralized state. In order to address global environmental problems, social ecologists argue that we must engage in complete analyses of advanced capitalist societies, and ultimately recognize how the social structures within these societies are antithetical to both humans' and non-humans' free nature or *telos*.[5]

According to social ecologists "values are implicit in the natural world."[6] Bookchin claims that "mutualism is an intrinsic good by virtue of its function in fostering the evolution of natural variety and complexity ... similarly freedom is an intrinsic good."[7] They are not, he suggests, simply human values but they are apparent "in larger cosmic or organic processes."[8] Social ecologists adhere to a type of naturalistic moral realism which suggests that values can be located in "the latent potentialities" and "essences" inherent in the natural world. This naturalistic theory is characterized by a strict objectivism. For example, Beihl claims that "the ecology question thus raises once again the need for an objective ethics ... We must once again find an ethics somehow grounded in objectivity." [9] She, following Bookchin, maintains that there is an inherent logic in nature that can serve as the foundation for a "dialectically naturalist ethic." [10] Such an approach is important and necessary, according to the social ecologists, because "obviously, the ground of an ecological ethic must be ontological: it cannot be grounded on the vagaries of social constructions, public opinion, or tradition." [11] While the ontological complexities that these assertions involve require more analysis, for present purposes suffice it to say that social ecologists believe that our moral claims about the environment can be grounded by appeals to natural properties. For this sort of theorist, to say that "x is intrinsically valuable" is to say "x has some particular natural property y instantiated in it."

A problem which has always plagued naturalist views is that of determining which natural properties make a thing "good" or "intrinsically valuable" and what the relationship is between the two. Bookchin and others talk of latent potentialities, but what are these? It seems that defining inherent value in terms of such intangible natural properties does not help much. Social ecologists talk about self-organization and natural evolution, but this too leads to problems. If, as Bookchin and many others suggest, humans are part of nature, then their destruction of nature can be seen as a function of natural evolution. If what accords with natural evolution is right, then the destruction of the environment is right. A social ecologist would undoubtedly respond that it is the social institutions in capitalist societies which have thwarted natural evolution, that humans are thus separated from their true self-organization which they must regain in order to fulfill their natural ethical mandate. While it is difficult to dispute the claim that humans are influenced by the social conditions in which they find themselves, it is harder to substantiate the claim that there is some objective mutualist human nature that lies beneath the social conditioning. However, even if such an argument were available, there is the difficulty of determining how these moral facts would motivate moral behavior. If the motivation is thought to be natural or unavoidable, then it is hard to figure out how we as a species have gotten ourselves into the current ecological predicament. Unsurprisingly, naturalistic environmental ethical theories, though initially attractive, run into the same problems that naturalistic ethical theories do.

Perhaps the justification can be found in a non-naturalistic theory of value. This is the approach that the deep ecologists have embraced. When these theorists suggest that nature has intrinsic value, which is the first basic principle of deep ecology, they adopt a realist moral ontology that suggests there are knower-independent non-natural values that exist in the world. Tom Regan claims that "presence of inherent value in a natural object is independent of any awareness, interest or appreciation of it by a conscious being."[12] One is forced to ask: "How do we discover this value?", a question that many have posed for non-naturalist theories. Pathetically, Regan's only response is "I wish I knew." Braver souls have answered the question by suggesting that objective non-natural moral values are discovered by some special faculty or by intuition. This answer, however, seems to imply that only those specially trained or gifted can know what is intrinsically valuable, and thus they may be the only ones motivated to act accordingly.[13] In addition, some have suggested that such odd values and such utterly unique ways of knowing them make a mockery of moral thinking. Others have argued that such questionable ontological commitments cut certain kinds of values off from others and from the very process of valuing itself.[14]

The objectivist ontologies that ground these approaches to environmental ethics are problematic in a number of ways. They do not appear to provide particularly defensible or coherent ways of justifying moral claims about our environmental concerns. Moreover, even if such claims could be justified by appeals to objective, non-anthropogenic intrinsic value, it is not at all clear that such claims provide compelling reasons for acting morally. Yet, if we reject such a foundation for environmental value we may be left unable to justify our moral claims. I want to suggest that there is a way to justify such claims without appeals to an objectivist moral ontology and that such justification could provide direct motivation for acting morally.[15]

Valuing in Community

In recent years there has been a resurgence of communitarian philosophy which includes a range of views which all maintain that moral claims can be justified in community.[16] The growing popularity of communitarian views can in part be attributed to the problems associated with objectivist approaches to justifying values, and perhaps to a rejection of the underlying presuppositions of liberalism as well.[17] For communitarian theorists, the values arrived at in community serve as the foundations for our moral knowledge. But here too there are problems.

Specifically, the concern with communitarianism in its standard formulation has to do with its focus on tradition and its potential legitimation of a merely conventional morality. Most communitarian notions of community are based on national identities and/or the family and neighborhood into which one is born. These communities are non-voluntary; they are communities in which we simply find ourselves and discover relationships rather than ones in which we create ourselves and our relationships. And, as Marilyn Friedman has suggested in a feminist analysis of communitarianism, "communities of origin, may harbor ambiguities, ambivalences, contradictions, and oppressions."[18] One need only think of the inferior status of women in virtually all countries in the world, or of conventional attitudes toward animals, in order to recognize how values originating in these communities will be problematic.

In order to avoid these dangers, a theory of community must be developed that is considerably richer than that of the traditional communitarian philosophers. The meaning of community must be more than simply a place where intersubjective agreement determines value. In order for a community-based justification of value to be defensible and to motivate moral behavior, the proper conditions of dialogic communication and evaluation must be clarified.

Friedman recommends that the focus be placed on communities of choice and uses the example of modern friendships to illustrate the importance of this enhanced notion of community. Friendship, as we commonly understand it, can serve as a model for communities of choice as it is within friendships that support, respect, and mutual growth most readily occur. However, while friendship is indeed a central feature of building community and may be a necessary relationship for building a respectful appreciation of difference,[19] friendship itself is not enough. Often our friendships are strained by political affiliations and motivations. Consider how friendships can be destroyed when one person becomes a vegetarian while the other continues to eat meat; or when the lesbian one came out with begins sleeping with a man; or when a pacifist's friend joins the military; or when a friend's racism becomes overt. Communities of choice based on friendship may serve as one model, but contemporary individuals are rarely, if ever, constituted (or reconstituted) by a single community. Chosen political affiliations must also play a significant role.

Ann Ferguson's notion of "oppositional communities" is particularly appropriate in this regard. "An oppositional community involves a network of actual and imagined others which one voluntarily commits oneself to, and in so doing, re-defines one's personal identity."[20] These oppositional communities move beyond friendship in that they provide a central place from which to challenge racist, sexist, classist, heterosexist, and other biases our friends have. Communities of opposition, while created on the basis of certain shared interests, allow for the important recognition of differences between members of the community. Such communities are committed to "revolutionary love or caring that requires that those feminists with race, class and national privilege accept an ethic of radical justice which continually challenges and attempts to dismantle the effects of such privilege, particularly in our relations with others in our intentional communities."[21] Thus, oppositional communities provide room not only for challenging our friends, but also for challenging ourselves.

Chosen oppositional communities are places in which status quo interests can be reconstituted. The process of reconstituting our interests may come about as a result of concerns expressed by community members about one's status quo interests or through the recognition and reconciliation of particular contradictions in one's self, contradictions which are made clear because of the way the self is situated. It is important to note that the contradictions that exist within a self are not contradictions that stem from a clash between essential components and something outside of the self, but rather from the self in different aspects.[22] "Each aspect of self is defined by its relation to a different set of social practices with different built in norms and expectations, and therefore different meaning-relations with others. The self is a multi-faceted conscious and unconscious process."[23] A central feature of the process of defining self in community is experience.

In her recent work, Alison Jaggar highlights the importance of experience, not only for self-construction but as a way of knowing and valuing in community. Her work, drawing on the practice of feminist dialogue, provides a starting point for a feminist moral epistemology.

> Feminist practical dialogue continues to assume that personal experience is indispensable to moral and political knowledge and that every woman's experience is equally important, both morally and epistemically. It also continues to assume that the ideal context for revealing personal experience is a nurturing and supportive environment.[24]

The practice of feminist dialogue is more than just a way of reaching knowledge, it is also an important moral experience in itself. It cultivates not only the values of mutual equality and respect but also virtues such as courage, caring, trust, sensitivity, self-discipline, and so on. Jaggar, like Ferguson, recognizes the crucial role that challenges within community play in creating better knowledge and value claims and to that end suggests that the dialogic community be made up of people with very different lives and experiences. Both suggest that we should always seek to make our chosen communities as inclusive as possible.

Clearly, the central role that experience plays in the process of generating moral claims is an advantage to this approach. Community becomes more than just a place where values are created; it also encourages participants to take seriously the moral imperatives that are reached. In this way, the generation of moral claims and the motivations to act according to them are inseperable. An answer to the question "why should I do X?" is simply that "you were part of the evaluative process that arrived at X as the right thing to do."

The process of generating values in community can only occur between those willing to engage in a self-reflective way. Valuing in community is predicated upon the desire to communicate, not the desire to talk at or dictate to other members of the community. Those people who are unable or unwilling to enter into the democratic process that leads to value claims – people who hate, for example – can legitimately be excluded from the community. As concentration camp survivor Elie Wiesel wrote,

> I believe in dialogue, even when the dialogue is difficult. But I would never dialogue with one who hates. I would never dialogue with a Nazi ... A hater doesn't listen. You may speak to the hater, but you will never convince him because he doesn't listen. A hater doesn't remember. A hater doesn't live except with the framework of his or her hatred.[25]

But in a world that seems hopelessly incapable of engaging in such a process, will not those who do be marginalized and their value claims be invalidated if not ignored? While this may be the case among those people who refuse to evaluate their own perspectives, I would suggest that the simple moral subjectivism of these very people can be revealed and challenged. Because of their refusal to engage honestly in the process of value generation, the values that they represent, values based on unchallenged subjective beliefs, can rightly be rejected.

The process of generating value in chosen communities requires that individuals and communities themselves always seek to expand their moral experience by including those who may not initially be friends but who nonetheless deserve respect. In this way we can begin building a community of communities and avoid the parochialism that plagues traditional communitarian notions. This inclusive process allows for a broader base on which to build knowledge and at the same time allows those in the community to reconstitute themselves. In addition, the process of feminist dialogue which encourages the cultivation of values of care, courage, and cooperation also strengthens the community. Valuing in community allows for the creation of more self-reflective individuals and more complete, fulfilling, and just communities.

While I believe these insights are tremendously important for the creation of a feminist moral epistemology, how do they help with the creation of an *ecofeminist* theory of moral justification and motivation? Jaggar, for example, suggests that feminist community be based on actual dialogue, which "presupposes that the speakers are members at least of a linguistic community."[26] Ferguson notes that community must be a "group of real or imagined humans through which an individual identifies an aspect of self."[27] Other feminist theorists, like Marilyn Friedman and Iris Young, look to urban cities as possible models for community.[28] All of these feminist theories, like all constructivist or contractual approaches to valuing, are human-centered and thus run into the problem of exclusion. Even when communities are committed to including as many individuals and other communities as possible, how can nature fit in?

Community with Nature

I believe the feminist articulation of valuing in community can provide some insight into building community with nature. Including nature in community is not inconsistent with at least some of the views expressed by feminist theorists as there are a number of common features of feminist theory which can be used to justify a place in community for the natural world. The concern for empathic identification with the oppressed and the focus on direct experience and actual dialogue are good places to start.

Empathy with non-human animals is not only possible, but widely practiced. Moreover, our ability to empathize with other beings need not be based solely on anthropomorphic projection.[29] That is to say, an empathetic response does not rest solely on a being's likeness to us. This way of understanding empathy has two important implications. It suggests that we can empathize with animals that are not close to us either in their physical makeup or in their relational proximity. An aardvark, for example, with whom I have no proximal relationship and from whom I consider myself very different, may nonetheless be a being with which I can empathize.

An additional possibility for building community with nature may be found in Alison Jaggar's work, albeit indirectly. One of the adequacy conditions of her theory of feminist practical dialogue is that such dialogue be actual. This requirement is emphasized because it is only through the actual experience of others in community (and the process of dialogue that ensues) that strong value claims can be generated. Talking about the lives and experiences of women in the third world, for example, will generate a different sort of knowledge from talking with women who have lived experiences in the third world. The former is apt to carry a certain amount of imperialist bias as well as being prone to ethnocentric distortion. Direct experience in conversations with these women will serve to eliminate (or at least mitigate) these problems. Clearly it is not possible for the non-human world to engage directly in the process of practical dialogue, but the underlying motivation for actual dialogue – direct experience – can serve as a guide for including nature in community.

For example, just as it is better to talk with women from other cultures about their lives rather than guess at what their lives might be like, so too is it better to directly experience nature, rather than guess at what such an experience might be like. Much of the problem with the attitudes many have toward animals and the rest of the non-human world stems from a removal from them. Our experience of the consequencs of these attitudes have been mediated. Consider how most Western people obtain the meat they eat. Most do not think to ask "Who are these animals who suffer and die so that I can eat pot roast?" I do not deprive them of movement and comfort; I do not take their young from them; I do not have to look into their eyes as I cut their throats.[30] Similarly, few people from the industrialized world have experienced the barrenness of a cleared forest and thus are not compelled to think about the vast destructiveness that accompanies the consumption of large quantities of paper, overpackaged products, redwood decks, and the like. Direct experiences of the non-human world will create better knowledge of nature and can only help us make more informed judgments about our relation to it.

In addition, direct experiences of nature can proviude us with challenges that provide significant opportunities for the reconstitution of our selves. Valuing in community requires both diversity of lives and of experiences. Such diversity allows for significant moral challenges. A community which includes the natural world can be challenging in a variety of ways. In addition to the aforementioned experiences and the challenges these experiences evoke, one can look to the positive experiences people have in the natural world and the effect they have on different aspects of ourselves. For example, I found living in an intentional rural community designed to create more harmonious relations between humans and nature radically altered the way I think of myself in the world. The series of experiences I had in this community posed difficult questions – How were we humans to coexist with the woodchucks who persistently ate the bean crop? How could we ensure the growth of the corn stalks in a drought? If we rescued the crippled duck whose wing was frozen to the river, would it be possible to preserve her "wildness" while at the same time protecting her from predators? – and the process of answering them reshaped my knowledge and values. Hiking among thousand-year-old trees, revitalizing a polluted lake, rock climbing,[31] any such encounter with the natural world or those people for whom nature is an integral part of their community[32] can only add to a reconstitution of self and increase the diversity of experience that makes community-based values solid.

At this point, it might be suggested that it is precisely this ability to work nature into community-based valuing that is objectionable. This objection may be raised by some feminists or by some environmentalists. Some feminists have devoted much energy to arguments insisting that women are just as much a part of culture as men and therefore should be accorded the respect that they deserve as full participants in human cultural activities.[33] For too long, these theorists argue, women have been relegated to the undervalued realm of non-culture, or at best thought to be the bridge between culture and nature. Some might suggest that if we allow nature into the moral community, if, that is, we start valuing nature seriously and start seeing the non-human world as providing us with challenges that can influence not only our selves but our values, are we not thereby devaluing what is distinctly human?[34] Would this inclusion of nature, and the arguements for such an inclusion made by women, not legitimate the subservient position reserved for women, a position that feminists have struggled so hard to leave behind? Is this expansion of community to include nature not just regressive and ultimately harmful for women?

I think not. As many feminists, ecofeminists, and others have suggested, the distinction between culture and nature, or between the social and the biological, is problematic not only because it is conceptually difficult to maintain[35] but also because it provides the groundwork for a system of domination. "Nature" and "culture" are categories that humans have created to help us understand and order the world. Like all categories, one is not better than the other until humans make it so. Because it is thought that reason, culture, and all that is distinctively human emerges from nature and then transcends it, the two categories are indelibly cast in opposition to one another. As long as this model of distinction and transcendence shapes our understanding of nature and our human place in it, the relationship between humans and the non-human world will be shaped by what Karen Warren has called the logic of domination.[36] In working to eliminate domination, whether it be the domination of women, people of color, working-class people, lesbians, bisexuals, gays, or the non-human world, the logic that separates and subjugates must be exposed and rejected. The division between nature and culture is based on such logic. It seems that some feminists' objection to the inclusion of nature in communities is based on a dangerous dichotomy. As some have suggested, feminist thinking, rather than being antithetical to nature, is in fact continuous with ecological perspectives.[37]

The environmentalists' objection to my argument may take different forms. The first may be that we cannot base our commitment to nature on our subjective experiences of it. There must be some other reason for including the non-human world into our communities; because positive experiences of nature may not be had by everyone. Eric Katz argues in this way and suggests that we must have an ethical obligation to protect nature that is not based on experience. He writes:

some people do not care at all about the experience of nature ... The ethical obligation to tell the truth is not based on the subjective experience of truth telling, nor on the avoidance of the experience of lying. One need not experience adultery to know that it is ethically incorrect . . . If some people do not respond to nature in a "positive" environmentalist way, that is no excuse for them to violate the obligation to protect the environment.[38]

There are a number of responses to this sort of concern. As I suggested earlier, the views that maintain that there are intrinsic values to which we can appeal in order to ground an environmental ethic are seriously flawed. In so far as this is what Katz is advocating, I believe the burden of proof lies with him, and those like him, to show how the problems associated with intrinsic value can be overcome. However, if the concern is rather that even within the framework of communitarian valuing it is not going to be possible to have every community include nature because certain communities may consist entirely of people who do not have positive experience of nature, then there is something to say.

First, it is not only positive experiences that are going to provide the challenges to selves, communities, and the knowledge claims they generate. Direct experience is what is important. And the direct experience need not exactly correspond to any particular moral dilemma. For example, if a community is entrusted with making a decision about whether to dam a river, it may be enough if one member of that community has experienced a canyon before and after the river that ran through it was dammed. The crucial thing is to recognize that direct experience is important and its voice should be sought. It cannot be thought of as always necessary, nor as normally sufficient for the determination of defensible values.

Second, given that more inclusive, more diverse communities will tend to generate more complete knowledge claims, it seems that a community that has no experiences of nature will strive to incorporate such experiences. For this reason, I believe it will not be possible for such a community to arrive at the conclusion that there is no basis for valuing, and thus protecting, nature. It might be suggested that it is mere optimism that leads me to believe that such a conclusion would not be reached. However, given that community-based knowing and valuing is understood as a process, and that the community of knowers and valuers will be shifting to include more people and experiences over time, it seems a well-supported optimism.

The objection that Katz raises is partially directed at the underlying fear that community-based valuing condemns us "to the swamp of subjective relativism."[39] I would argue that to accept community-based valuing does not commit one to accepting arbitrariness, chaos, emotionalism, or any relativistic notion. To conceptualize in this fashion is to reduce and oversimplify an issue that is far more complex than many believe. The problem is not between objectivism and what Sandra Harding calls its "mirror-linked twin, judgmental relativism."[40] Indeed, many have argued that the issue is not strictly polar.[41] As the early Frankfurt School theorists argued, this sort of false dichotomization is often characteristic of the sickness that results when

> even the best-intentioned reformer who uses an impoverished and debased language to recommend renewal, by his adoption of the insidious mode of categorization and the bad philosophy it conceals, strengthens the very power of the established order he is trying to break.[42]

For many, relativism only makes sense "from the biased assumption of a static ontology."[43] When we recognize the dialectical nature of the process of valuing in the world the concerns that are generated by the oversimplified conception of relativism should be minimized. The choices that we seem to be presented with presuppose an illusory structure. If we recognize that values are central features of our conceptual schemes and theoretical frameworks we can begin to feel less worried that there is no order. In structuring our beliefs we can do better or worse. As Nelson Goodman suggests:

> Willingness to accept countless alternative true or right world-versions does not mean that everything goes, that tall stories are as good as short ones, that truths are no longer distinguished from falsehoods ... Though we make worlds by making versions, we no more make a world by putting symbols together at random than a carpenter makes a chair by putting pieces of wood together at random.[44]

Positing objective, non-anthropogenic intrinsic value is but one way of ordering the world; it is neither the best nor the only way.

Furthermore, by accepting community-based valuing we are not forced to choose between rationalism and emotionalism. The very distinction that is made between reason and emotion must be challenged.[45] Morwenna Griffiths suggests that:

> In effect, feelings are a route to truth: they both provide us with our beliefs about the world and also provide a basis for assessing beliefs ... it appears that the place of feelings in human conduct has not been properly understood. Attention to its significance is important because any proper running of private and public life depends on it.[46]

I would suggest that just as we can alter and critically reflect on our commonly held beliefs and "cultivate" tastes, so we can be reasonable about creating our versions of reality. The interactive process of reason and emotion, of feeling and contemplation, allows us to set limits on what is acceptable. Ruth Anna Putnam argues that

(1) we are constrained by the actual sensory inputs we receive; (2) we are constrained by what we have made of our sensory inputs in the past, the conceptual framework embodied in our prior beliefs, what we have taken to be facts so far; (3) we are constrained by the insistent demand for coherence and consistency.[47]

Far too often the concern about relativism stems from the belief that without objective values we will have no way to resolve disagreement. Once we start recognizing that reason and desire are not entirely separate and can be the objects of critical reflection then we have at least one way to approach resolutions. However, it is important to note that this particular concern presupposes that there is a great deal of fundamental disagreement and I want to suggest that such a focus comes from a fixed and negative conception of human nature. When living in a society which is structured in an atomistic and competitive fashion it is not surprising that individuals find it difficult to recognize the widespread agreement and fundamental similarity in belief that structures a common world. If relativism were as troublesome as people often make it out to be then we should find virtually complete epistemic disorder in areas that one might call "common space."[48] Consider the experiences of travellers who come together from various cultures and find themselves in another culture with which they are unfamiliar. Even when language and custom are not shared it is often the case that individuals from very different backgrounds can successfully engage in activities that require considerable negotiating. I am not suggesting that problems do not arise or that conflicts and disagreements do not exist, but rather that the problem of value relativism is not as severe as some would make it.

If we view valuing as a communitarian process, then we must also recognize and learn to be comfortable with the trial and error that any such process entails. A commitment to the process is a sure way to avoid most of the pitfalls associated with relativism, and that commitment must come from a blend of reason and emotion. As Adorno said, seemingly anticipating the work of recent feminist philosophers of science:

I have never really understood the so-called problem of relativism. My experience was that whoever gave himself over in earnest to the discipline of a particular subject learned to distinguish very precisely between true and false, and that in contrast to such experience the assertion of general insecurity as to what is known had something abstract and unconvincing about it.[49]

This process can work particularly well when the concept of community is taken seriously.

Another environmentalist objection is that valuing based on community is basically human-centered and thus anthropocentric. The debate about anthropocentrism has permeated the environmental ethics literature for years.[50] As the debate became more sophisticated, distinctions started to be made between what we might call pernicious anthropocentrism, the view that humans are all that matter, and inevitable anthropocentrism,[51] the view that while values are created by humans, nature nonetheless has a place in this process. It should be clear that it is the latter view to which I have been appealing. Without getting too far into the debate, as that would be beyond the scope of this discussion, there are two arguments in favour of inevitable anthropocentrism that must be mentioned.

If we are to accept somethign like the framework provided by community valuing, then a rejection of inevitable anthropocentrism would generally imply one of two views. First, it could mean the acceptance of pernicious anthropocentrism, which is unacceptable in itself, but which, in combination with the justificatory framework being suggested here, becomes inconsistent. As I have briefly suggested, the community that provides the most compelling value claims will be one which seeks diversity of experience. A disregard for the natual world would deny relevance and value to all such experiences.

The second view that a rejection of inevitable anthropocentrism might imply is one in which nature is itself seen as possessing a kind of subjectivity. This approach requires positing some consciousness or intentionality within the natural world. Some theorists have attempted to develop the notion of nature as a knowing, speaking subject. Linda Holler, for example, suggests that the world is always part of the evaluative dialogue. While I appreciate the notion that we all need air to breathe in order to even engage in community activities, I worry about the idea that "we can find support in the voice of the earth, long silenced but now crying loudly and tragically in its refusal to absorb the by-products of our denial of beiug in the world."[52] Similarly I do not know how to understand questions such as those Elizabeth Dodson Gray asks: "What language do mountains speak to tell of the grandeurs of time so vast we can scarcely imagine it? Do you begin to sense the nonverbal language of the Earth as a living organism? ... Can we hear the plant calling out to us just before the bulldozers reach it?"[53] While it may be useful in certain instances to speak metaphorically of the subjectivity of nature, the literal suggestion to "think like a mountain" only serves to obfuscate and confuse.[54]

While feminist practical dialogue stresses the importance of trying to take another's point of view, it is difficult to imagine what point of view nature might have. Even with non-human animals, who possess consciousness, what is assumed to be their points of view is actually, but nontrivially, the animals' point of view from a human point of view.[55] It is presumptuous and misleading to think that we can actually achieve the particular perspective of another. We are always restricted by the resources of our own minds and the experiences that we have had. These resources and experiences may be inadequate for understanding those that are significantly different from us, whether in ethnicity, sexual orientation, gender, or species. This position does not imply, however, that the perspective of another does not count. Quite the contrary. But when it is unclear whether or not an entity has a perspective, that is, when the entity in question does not have at least the minimal characteristics needed for the formulation of a perspective, a different approach is necessary.

Inevitable anthropocentrism avoids the unintelligible suggestion that nature is intentional, yet when combined with an inclusive conception of dialogic communities can provide a meaningful way to know and value the non-human world. The approach I am suggesting, rather than stretching the notions of consciousness and volition, stretches human imagination and perception in ways that provide challenges not only to ourselves, but to our very ways of living on the planet. It is consistent with the suggestion made by Patrick Murphy, that "the point is not to speak for nature but to work to render the signification presented us by nature into a verbal depiction by means of speaking subjects, whether this is through characterization in the arts or through discursive prose."[56] Including nature in community requires that we learn to comprehend nature's signs. Some of these are relatively obvious, for example, the "jelly-fish babies" born of Bikini Island women, the mass death of dolphins in the North Sea, the contamination of Southern California groundwater that has caused deformities in animals and congenital diseases in humans, and the thinning of the ozone layer. In communities that are voluntary, empathetic, inclusive, and actual, we can give these signs meaning and act accordingly; we can thus value the natural world.

Conclusion

I have suggested that an ecofeminist theory of moral justification and motivation – an ecofeminist answer to the question "How can we justify our moral claims about human interactions with nature, and can this justification provide motivation for acting morally toward nature?" should not be grounded on traditional objectivist notions of intrinsic value. A rejection of this sort of foundation for valuing does not, however, leave one in a relativist abyss. I have tried to show that a conceptualization of values which focuses on chosen communities, direct experience, and inclusivity is a starting point from which to construct an ecofeminist moral theory. Further, I have suggested that the inclusion of nature is not only possible but desirable also, in terms of the criteria of adequacy for communitarian philosophy itself. What I have not done is address the practical difficulties that must be overcome in order to make this kind of theory a reality. Obviously, progress toward the ideals of feminist communitarian philosophy depends upon progress in the conditions of democracy itself.[57]

NOTES

1 When I speak of "nature" I am not necessarily speaking of "wilderness," "wild areas," etc. Rather I am speaking of all that is non-human. This way of undrstanding the term "nature" is meant to include non-human animals, ecosystems (urban and otherwise), and non-sentient natural things. The distinction between human and nature is not meant to be the same as the distinction between culture and nature, it is not meant to imply that humans are not a part of nature, nor is it meant to capture any normative dualism. It is a constructed distinction which I hope will allow for clarity; nothing beyond clarity is intended.

2 For an interesting, albeit at times ideological, look at the differences see Murray Bookchin and Dave Foreman, *Defending the Earth* (Boston: South End Press, 1991).

3 There has been some interesting discussion about the meaning of intrinsic value. See e.g. J. B. Callicott, "Intrinsic Value, Quantum Theory, and Environmental Ethics," *Environmental Ethics*, 7 (1985), and Robin Attfield, *The Ethics of Environmental Concern* (New York: Columbia University Press, 1983). Some philosophers use the term intrinsic value to mean something other than instrumental value. Others have made distinctions between inherent value and intrinsic value. Here "intrinsic value" is objective value – value that a being or thing has in and of itself, independent of human valuation.

4 Particularly the work of Max Horkheimer and Theodore Adorno, e.g. *Dialectic of Englightenment* (New York: Continuum, 1987) and Horkheimer, *The Eclipse of Reason* (New York: Columbia University Press, 1947).

5 Janet Beihl, *Rethinking Ecofeminist Politics* (Boston: South End, 1991): 127.

6 Murray Bookchin "Recovering Evolution: A Reply to Eckersley and Fox," *Environmental Ethics*, 12 (Fall 1990): 255.

7 Murray Bookchin, *The Philosophy of Ecology* (Montreal: Black Rose Books, 1990): 83.

8 Ibid.: 85.

9 Beihl, *Rethinking Ecofeminist Politics*: 21.

10 She writes, "Education, writes Bookchin, is directed 'toward an exploration

of [a potentiality's] latent and implicit possibilities.' It aims to understand the inherent logic of a thing's development" (ibid.: 123).

11 Ibid.: 124.

12 Tom Regan, *Deep Ecology* (Salt Lake City: Pergrine Smith Books, 1985): 71. In Appendix D, George Sessions develops the deep ecologist's non-naturalistic intuitionism by drawing on such traditional philosphers as Spinoza.

13 Or, worse, the only motivation left for those that do not share the intuition might be coercion or fear of retribution from those who do see the flashing light of intrinsic value, assuming those specially trained or gifted are in a position of power over those who are not.

14 See, for example, J. L. Mackie, *Ethics: Inventing Right and Wrong* (New York: Penguin Books 1977), ch. 1, and Anthony Weston, "Beyond Intrinsic Value: Pragmatism in Environmental Ethics," *Environmentnal Ethics*, 7 (1985).

15 To avoid appealing to an objectivist moral ontology for the justification of moral value is not to deny the possibility that there may be objective moral values. This sort of claim would require further argument and is beyond the scope of the present discussion. Having given reasons for doubt, I want to assume a certain agnosticism about objective value and proceed from there.

16 See, for example, Alisdair MacIntyre, *After Virtue* (Notre Dame: Notre Dame University Press, 1981); Michael Sandel, *Liberalism and the Limits of Justice* (New York: Cambridge University Press, 1982); and Michael Walzer, *Spheres of Justice* (New York: Basic Books, 1983).

17 Communitarians are apt to note that the liberal notion of the "abstract individual" whose identity can be understood apart from her place in community is flawed. For a review essay of the communitarian critiques of liberalism, see Amy Gutmann, "Communitarian Critics of Liberalism," *Philosophy and Public Affairs*, 14 (1985). Gutmann suggests that Sandel's criticism, for example, is that "liberalism rests on a series of mistaken metaphysical and metaethical views: for example, that the claims of justice are absolute and universal; that we cannot know each other well enough to share common ends; and that we can define our personal identity independently of socially given ends" (p. 310).

18 Marilyn Friedman, "Feminism and Modern Friendship: Dislocating the Community," *Ethics* 99 (1989): 285.

19 Maria Lugones and Vicki Spelman argue that it is only through friendship that women of privilege can begin to respect and understand the experiences of non-privileged women and that this understanding is essential in order to build a non-imperialistic, non-ethnocentric, and respectful feminist theory. See "Have We Got a Theory For You! Feminist Theory, Cultural Imperialism and the Demand for 'The Woman's Voice'" in Marilyn Pearsall, ed., *Women and Values* (Belmont, Ca.: Wadsworth, 1986). While I agree that friendship is an important first step for bridging gaps and working across differences, I believe, as I shall argue, that it must not be the last step.

20 References to Ann Ferguson's work on oppositional communities come from her manuscript, "Constructing Ourselves Through Community: Feminism

and Moral Revolution," presented at the Morris Colloquium on Feminist Ethics held in Boulder, November 1991 (hereafter AF manuscript): 6

21 AF manuscript: 9.

22 See Ann Ferguson, "Feminist Aspect Theory of the Self,", in Marsha Hansen and Kai Nielsen, eds, *Science, Morality, and Feminist Theory* (Calgary: University of Calgary Press, 1987).

23 AF manuscript: 15.

24 References to Alison Jaggar's theory of feminist practical dialogue are from her work in progress, "Telling Right from Wrong: Feminism and Moral Epistemology" (hereafter AJ manuscript). This citation is from p. 19.

25 "Education Against Hatred: A Conversation with Elie Wiesel," *American Association of Higher Education Bulletin* (June 1991): 10

26 AJ manuscript: 32.

27 AF manuscript: 17.

28 Friedman, "Feminism and Modern Friendship", *Ethics* 99 (1989); and Iris Young, *Justice and the Politics of Difference* (Princeton: Princeton University Press, 1990).

29 John Fisher notes two features of our ability to empathize with other creatures:

> The first is that our lives are part of a larger biological life full of common characteristics and needs. Animals have needs for nourishment, water, air; they have life cycles, a sort of family life, a sort of social life with other members of their species; they suffer and flourish; many of them engage in exploratory and playful behavior ... the second mitigating feature [is that] we frequently feel sympathy for a creature when we believe it to be suffering ... although I may have it wrong when I think that a penguin suffers to hatch its egg, I plausibly have it right when I think that a young ape is suffering if it appears to pine over its mother's death and dies a few days later. ("Taking Sympathy Seriously," *Environmental Ethics*, 9 (1987): 203)

30 I briefly discuss this problem in my piece "Animals," in Peter Singer, ed., *A Companion to Ethics* (Oxford: Basil Blackwell, 1991): 350–2.

31 For a discussion of the latter see Karen Warren, "The Power and the Promise of Ecological Feminism," *Environmental Ethics*, 12 (Summer 1990): 134–8.

32 For discussion of how Western views about nature differ from indigenous peoples' see e.g. J. Baird Callicott, "Traditional American Indian and Western European Attitudes Toward Nature: An Overview," and the citations therein; in *In Defense of the Land Ethic* (Albany: State University of New York Press, 1989): 177–202.

33 See e.g. Simone de Beauvoir, *The Second Sex* (New York: Bantam, 1953) or Sherry Ortner, "Is Female to Male as Nature is to Culture?" reprinted in Pearsall, *Women and Values*.

34 Virginia Held, for example, argues this way in her article "Birth and Death," *Ethics*, 99 (1989): 362–89.

35 Alison Jaggar suggests that "We cannot identify a clear, nonsocial sense of 'biology', nor a clear, nonbiological sense of 'society'" cited in Held, "Birth and Death": 374.

36 Warren, "The Power and the Promise of Ecological Feminism."

37 See Lorraine Code's discussion of community and ecology in "Second Persons," in Hansen and Nielsen, *Science, Morality, and Feminist Theory*: 371–4. See also Karen Warren and Jim Cheney, "Ecological Feminism and Ecosystem Ecology," *Hypatia* 6(1), 1991.

38 Eric Katz, "Searching for Intrinsic Value," *Environmental Ethics*, 9 (Fall 1987): 238–9.

39   This ironic and ill-chosen phrase seems to represent not just fear, but terror. Subjectiv-
     ism is, of course, quite different from relativism and it should be clear that it is not
     really the problem with community valuing, given the emphasis on community. Simple
     relativism, however, is a concern. (It is ironic because while arguing for the value of
     nature, even for what we find unpleasant, Katz ends up devaluing swamps.) "Searching
     for Intrinsic Value": 239.
40   Sandra Harding, *Whose Science? Whose Knowledge?* (Ithaca: Cornell University Press,
     1991): 142.
41   Donna Haraway, "Situated Knowledges," *Feminist Studies*, 14 (1988) also argues against
     viewing the problem in polar extremes.
42   Horkheimer and Adorno, *Dialectic of Enlightenment*: xiv. Adorno also writes, "The
     problem of relativism exists only so long as one discusses the relation of a supposed
     'consciousness in general' to a supposed 'object in general.' It disappears in the
     concrete process in which subject and object mutually determine and alter each other"
     (quoted in Susan Buck-Morss, *The Origin of Negative Dialectics* (New York: The Free
     Press, 1977): 53). It has always been interesting to me that these theorists (most of
     whom were assimilated Jews) rejected relativism as a problem while they were actually
     living through the paradigm example used to refute relativism, namely Nazi Germany.
43   Buck-Morss, *Negative Dialectics*: 225.
44   Nelson Goodman, *Ways of Worldmaking* (Indianapolis: Hacket Publishers Co., 1978):
     94.
45   See Alison Jaggar, "Love and Knowledge," in A. Jagger, and S. Bordo, eds, *Gender/-
     Body/Knowledge* (New Brunswick: Rutgers University Press, 1989).
46   Morwenna Griffiths, "Feminism, Feeling and Philosophy," in M. Griffiths and M.
     Whitford, eds, *Feminist Perspectives in Philosophy* (Bloomington: Indiana University Press,
     1988): 148–9.
47   Ruth Anna Putnam, "Creating Facts and Values", *Philosophy* 60 (1985): 198.
48   I owe this insight to Nancy (Ann) Davis.
49   Buck-Morss, *Negative Dialectics*: 53.
50   These are just a few of the many discussions: Donald Scherer,
     "Anthropocentrism, Atomism, and Environmental Ethics," *Environmental Ethics*, 4
     (Summer 1982): 115–24; W. H. Murdy, "Anthropocentrism: A Modern Version," in
     Donald Scherer and Thomas Attig, eds, *Ethics and the Environment* (Englewood Cliffs:
     Prentice-Hall, 1983): 12–21; Richard Watson, "A Critique of Anti-anthropocentric
     Biocentrism," *Environmental Ethics*, 5 (Fall 1983): 245–56; Bryan Norton, "Environmen-
     tal Ethics and Weak Anthropocentrism," *Environmental Ethics*, 6 (Summer 1984):
     131–48; and Warwick Fox, *Toward a Transpersonal Ecology* (Boston: Shambhala, 1990):
     3–40.
51   Inevitable anthropocentrism should not be confused with inevitable human chauvinism,
     which Richard and Val Routley argue against: "Against the Inevitability of Human
     Chauvinism," in Kenneth Goodpaster and K. Sayre, eds, *Ethics and Problems of the
     21st Century* (Notre Dame: University of Notre Dame Press, 1979): 36–59. Inevitable
     anthropocentrism is rather like the view articulated by J. Baird Callicott: "there can
     be no value apart from an evaluator, that all value is as it were in the eye of the
     beholder. The value that is attributed to the ecosystem, therefore, is humanly dependent
     or at least dependent upon some variety of morally and aesthetically sensitive conscious-
     ness" (*In Defense of the Land Ethic*: 26).
52   Linda Holler, "Thinking with the Weight of the Earth: Feminist Contributions to an
     Epistemology of Concreteness," *Hypatia*, 5 (Spring 1990): 19.
53   Elizabeth Dodson Gray, "Seeing and Hearing the Living Earth," *Woman of Power*, 20
     (Spring 1991): 21.

54 There is a trend among feminist theorists to reappropriate terms, and this may be what is going on with the suggestion that nature is intentional. Many feminist theorists, for example, are disinclined to give up terms such as "autonomy" and "objectivity" and choose instead to redefine them. I tend to think that coining new terms such as "autokeonony," created by Sarah Hoagland (*Lesbian Ethics: Toward New Value* (Palo Alto: Institute for Lesbian Ethics, 1988) is not only a clearer strategy, but also marks the significant differences from traditional usage that such theories suggest. That is not to say, however, that the reappropriation of certain normative terms, such as "dyke," with a corresponding shift in value, is not appropriate or liberatory.

55 For a discussion of this claim see my work with Marc Bekoff et al., "Animals in Science: Some Areas Revisited," *Animal Behaviour* 44 (1992): 473–84.

56 Patrick Murphy, "Ground, Pivot, Motion; Ecofeminist Theory, Dialogics, and Literary Practice," *Hypatia*, 6 (Spring 1991): 152.

57 I would like to express my gratitude to the following people who read or heard versions of this paper and provided useful commentary: Ann Ferguson, Alison Jaggar, Ken Knowles, Earl Winkler, and participants in the Center for Values and Social Policy discussion, March 1992.

17
Ethics, Public Policy, and Global Warming

Dale Jamieson

In his introduction Jamieson describes the 1990 backlash to the consensus of serious concern that had been established in relation to the problem of global warming. While acknowledging a range of differences in scientific opinion and emphasis – concerning, for example, degrees of certainty or uncertainty attaching to predictions in this area – he sees the main force driving this backlash to be the realization that efforts to slow global warming may involve large economic costs and radical revisions in lifestyle. Accordingly, the central burden of the paper is to argue that the problem of global warming is not primarily a scientific problem. It is an ethical and political problem concerning our values. Jamieson examines the "policy management" approach to the problem of climate change which derives from neo-classical economic theory. This approach so dominates current public discussion that its assumptions and biases are hardly visible. Jamieson questions these basic assumptions but goes on to argue that, in any case, this approach cannot succeed on its own terms because its analytic techniques are simply inadequate to the complexities of the problem of anthropogenic climate change. Next he explores the dimensions of this problem that make it fundamentally an ethical one requiring re-examination and reform in our system of values. In his conclusion Jamieson speculates about the sort of changes in our values that will be needed if humans and other animals are to survive current threats to the global environment.

Jamieson's speculations about desirable directions of change in our values and dispositions of moral thought, relative to environmental degradation, parallel Solomon's rejection of principle-based

This essay is an overview of material that I hope to develop in greater detail elsewhere. It is presented in this form in the hope that some may find these ideas suggestive and stimulating. This material has been discussed with an audience at the 1989 meetings of the American Association for the Advancement of Science in New Orleans; at a conference on "Global Warming and the Future: Science Policy, and Society" at Michigan Technological University; and with the philosophy departments at the University of Redlands and the University of California at Riverside. I have benefited greatly from each of these discussions. In addition, Michael H. Glantz (National Center for Atmospheric Research) made many helpful comments on an earlier draft, and Karen Borza (George Washington University) has contributed to this research in many ways. I also gratefully acknowledge the support of the Ethics and Values Studies Program of the National Science Foundation for making this research possible.

theories in favor of virtue ethics in relation to business practice (chapter 11). Other papers with which this essay may be usefully compared are those of Winner (chapter 3), Flyvbjerg (chapter 1), and Danielson (chapter 18), as well as others in the section on environmental ethics.

There has been speculation about the possibility of anthropogenic global warming since at least the late nineteenth century (Arrhenius 1896, 1908). At times the prospect of such a warming has been welcomed, for it has been thought that it would increase agricultural productivity and delay the onset of the next ice age (Callendar 1938). At other times, and more recently, the prospect of global warming has been the stuff of "doomsday narratives," as various writers have focused on the possibility of widespread drought, flood, famine, and the economic and political dislocations that might result from a "greenhouse warming"-induced climate change (Flavin 1989).

Although high-level meetings have been convened to discuss the greenhouse effect since at least 1963 (see Conservation Foundation 1963), the emergence of an approximate international consensus about the likelihood and extent of anthropogenic global warming began with a National Academy Report in 1983 (NAS/NRC 1983) and meetings in Villach, Austria in 1985 (World Climate Program 1985) and Toronto in 1988 (Conference Statement 1988). The consensus holds that, although there are uncertainties, a doubling of atmospheric carbon dioxide from its preindustrial baseline is likely to lead to an increase in the Earth's mean surface temperature of between 1.5 and 4 degrees Centigrade by the middle of the next century. (Interestingly, this estimate is only slightly lower than that of Arrhenius 1896.) This increase is expected to have a profound impact on climate, and therefore on plants, animals, and human activities of all kinds. Moreover, there is no reason to suppose that, without policy interventions, atmospheric carbon dioxide will stabilize at twice preindustrial levels, and we can only speculate about what impacts may lie beyond a carbon dioxide doubling.

These predictions were brought home to the American public on June 23, 1988, a sweltering day in Washington in the middle of a severe national drought, when James Hansen testified to the US Senate Committee on Energy and Natural Resources that it was 99 percent probable that global warming had begun. Hansen's testimony was front-page news in the *New York Times*, and was extensively covered by other media as well. By the end of the summer of 1988 the greenhouse effect had become an important public issue. According to a June 1989 Gallup poll, 35 percent of the American public worried "a great deal" about the greenhouse effect while 28 percent worried about it "a fair amount" (Gallup 1989).

Recently, however, there has been a media "backlash" against the "hawkish" views of Hansen and others (for the typology of "hawks," "doves," and "owls" see Glantz 1988b). In 1989 the *Washington Post* (February 8), the *Wall Street Journal* (April 10), and the *New York Times* (December 13) all published major articles expressing skepticism about the predictions of global warming, or minimizing its potential impacts. These themes were picked up by other media, including such mass circulation periodicals as *Reader's Digest* (February 1990). In its December, 1989 issue *Forbes* published a hard-hitting cover story entitled "The Global Warming Panic," and has since taken out a full-page advertisement in the *New York Times* (February 7, 1990) congratulating itself for its courage in "risking some heat from this growing group of alarmists."

The Bush administration seemed to have been influenced by this backlash. The April, 1990 White House conference on global warming concluded with a ringing call for more research, disappointing several European countries who were hoping for concerted action. In July at the Houston Economic Summit the Bush administration reiterated its position, warning against precipitous action.

It is a fact that there are a number of different hypotheses about the future development of the global climate and its impact on human and other biological activities; and several of these are dramatically at variance with the consensus. For example, Budyko (1988) and Idso (1989) think that global warming is good for us, and Ephron (1988) argues that the injection of greenhouse gases will trigger a new ice age. Others, influenced by the "Gaia hypothesis" (see Lovelock 1988), believe that there are self-regulating planetary mechanisms that may preserve climate stability even in the face of anthropogenic forcings of greenhouse gases.

Most of the differences of opinion within the scientific community are differences of emphasis rather than differences of kind. Rather than highlighting the degree of certainty that attaches to predictions of global warming, as does Schneider (1989) for example, some emphasize the degree of uncertainty that attaches to such predictions (for example Abelson 1990).

Another force driving the backlash, in my view the most important one, is the realization that slowing global warming or responding to its effects may involve large economic costs and redistributions, as well as radical revisions in lifestyle. Special interests have begun to argue that they are already doing enough to forestall global warming. Some economists have begun to express doubt whether it is worth trying to prevent substantial warming (*New York Times*, November 11, 1989; White House Council of Economic Advisors 1990). What seems to be emerging as the dominant view among economists is that chlorofluorocarbons (CFCs) should be eliminated, but emissions of carbon dioxide or other trace gases should be reduced only slightly if at all (for discussion see Nordhaus 1990).

There are many uncertainties concerning anthropogenic climate change, yet we cannot wait until all the facts are in before we respond. All the facts may never be in. New knowledge may resolve old uncertainties, but it may bring with it new uncertainties. And it is an important dimension of this problem that our insults to the biosphere outrun our ability to understand them. We may suffer the worst effects of the greenhouse before we can prove to everyone's satisfaction that they will occur.

The most important point I wish to make, however, is that the problem we face is not a scientific problem that can be solved by the accumulation of scientific information. Science has alerted us to a problem, but the problem concerns our values. It is about how we ought to live, and how humans should relate to each other and to the rest of nature. These are problems of ethics and politics rather than problems of science.

In the first section that follows I will examine what I call the "management" approach to assessing the impacts of, and our responses to, climate change. I will argue that this approach cannot succeed, for it does not have the resources to answer the most fundamental question that we face. In the second section I will explain why the problem of anthropogenic global change is primarily an ethical problem. In the final section I will speculate about the sort of value system that I think we need if humans and other animals are to survive anthropogenic threats to the global environment.

1 Why Management Approaches Must Fail

From the perspective of conventional policy studies, the possibility of anthropogenic climate change and its attendant consequences are problems to be "managed." Management techniques mainly are drawn from neo-classical economic theory, and are directed toward manipulating behavior by controlling economic incentives through taxes, regulations, and subsidies.

In recent years economic vocabularies and ways of reasoning have dominated the discussion of social issues. Participants in the public dialogue have internalized the neo-classical economic perspective to such an extent that its assumptions and biases have become almost invisible. It is only a mild exaggeration to say that in recent years debates over policies have largely become debates over economics.

The EPA draft report on *Policy Options for Stabilizing Global Climate* (United States Environmental Protection Agency 1989) is a good example. Despite its title, only one of its nine chapters is specifically devoted to policy options, and in that chapter only "internalizing the cost of climate change risks" and "regulations and standards" are considered. For many people questions of regulation are not distinct from questions about internalizing costs. According to one influential view, the role of regulations and standards just is to internalize costs, thus (to echo a parody of our forefathers) "creating a more perfect market." For people with this view, political questions about regulation are really disguised economic questions (for discussion see Sagoff 1988).

It would be both wrong and foolish to deny the importance of economic information. Such information is important when making policy decisions, for some policies or programs that would otherwise appear to be attractive may be economically prohibitive. Or in some cases there may be alternative policies that would achieve the same ends and also conserve resources.

These days it is common for people to make more grandiose claims on behalf of economics. As philosophers and clergymen have become increasingly modest and reluctant to tell people what to do, economists have become bolder. Some economists or their champions believe not only that economics provides important information for making policy decisions, but that it provides the most important information. Some even appear to believe that economics provides the only relevant information. On this view, when faced with a policy decision, what we need to do is assess the benefits and costs of various alternatives. The alternative which maximizes the benefits less the costs is the one we should prefer. This alternative is "efficient," and choosing it is "rational."

Unfortunately, too often we lose sight of the fact that economic efficiency is only one value, and not necessarily the most important one. Consider, for example, the idea of imposing a carbon tax as one policy response to the prospect of global warming (Moomaw 1988/1989). What we think of this proposal may depend to some extent on how it affects other concerns that are important to us. Equity is sometimes mentioned as one other such concern, but most of us have very little idea about what equity means, or exactly what role it should play in policy considerations.

One reason for the hegemony of economic analysis and prescriptions is that many people have come to think that neo-classical economics provides the only social theory we have that accurately represents human motivation. According to the neo-classical paradigm, welfare can be defined in terms of preference satisfaction, and preferences are defined in terms of choice behavior. From this, many (illicitly) infer that the perception of self-interest is the only motivator for human beings. This view suggests the following "management technique": if you want people to do something, give them a carrot; if you want them to desist, give them a stick.

As Parfit (1984) and other philosophers have shown, it is far from clear that we have any coherent notion of self-interest. And many times the claim that people do what they believe is in their interests is understood in such a way as to be circular, therefore unfalsifiable and trivial. We know that something is perceived as being in a person's interest because the person pursues it; and if the person pursues it then we know that the person must perceive it as being in his or her interests.

On the other hand, if we take it as an empirical claim that people always do what they believe is in their interests, it appears to be false. If we look around the world we see people risking or even sacrificing their own interests in attempts to overthrow oppressive governments, or to realize ideals to which they are committed. It is implausible to suppose that a cost–benefit analysis (even one that appeals to the "selfish gene") can reveal the motivations of a revolutionary, a radical environmentalist, or a friend or lover. It seems plain that people are motivated by a broad range of concerns, including concern for family and friends, and religious, moral, and political ideals. And it seems just as obvious that people sometimes sacrifice their own interests for what they regard as a greater, sometimes impersonal, good. (It is worth considering that many more people die in wars fighting for some perceived collective good than die in attempts to further their own individual interests by committing crimes.) These facts puzzle some researchers in rational choice theory, who do not understand why people often systematically behave in ways that are contrary to the dictates of their theories. (Opp 1989 defends a version of rational choice theory that he claims is not committed to the idea that people always do what they consider to be in their interests. His views cannot be considered here.)

People often act in ways that are contrary to what we might predict on economic grounds, and moreover they sometimes believe that it would be wrong or inappropriate even to take economic considerations into account. Many people would say that choosing spouses, lovers, friends, or religious or political commitments on economic grounds is simply wrong. People who behave in this way are often seen as manipulative, not to be trusted, without character or virtue. One way of understanding some environmentalists is to see them as wanting us to think about nature in the way that many of us think of friends and lovers – to see nature not as a resource to be exploited, but as a partner with whom to share our lives.

What I have been suggesting in this section is that it is not always rational to make decisions solely on economic grounds. Although economic efficiency may be a value, there are other values as well, and in many areas of life values other than economic efficiency should take precedence. I have also suggested that people's motivational patterns are complex, and that preying on people's perceptions of their self-interest is not the only way to move them. This amounts to a general critique of viewing all social issues as "management" problems to be solved by the application of economic techniques.

There is a further reason why economic considerations should take a back seat in our thinking about global climate change: there is no way to accurately assess all the possible impacts, and assign economic values to alternative courses of action. Global warming, if it occurs, will have impacts that are so broad, diverse, and uncertain that conventional economic analysis is practically useless. (Our inability to perform reliably the economic calculations also counts against the "insurance" view favored by many "hawks.")

Consider first the uncertainty of the potential impacts. Some uncertainties about the global effects of loading the atmosphere with carbon dioxide and other greenhouse gases have already been noted. But even if the consensus is correct, that global mean surface temperatures will increase by 1.5–4 degrees Centigrade some time in the next century due to a doubling of atmospheric carbon dioxide, there is still great uncertainty about the impact of this warming on regional climate. One thing is certain: the impacts will not be homogeneous. Some areas will become warmer, some will probably become colder, and overall variability is likely to increase. Precipitation patterns will also change, and there is much less confidence in the projections about precipitation than in those about temperature. These uncertainties about regional effects make estimates of the economic consequences of climate change radically uncertain.

There is also another source of uncertainty regarding these estimates. In general, predicting human behavior is difficult, as recent events in Central and Eastern Europe have demonstrated. These difficulties are especially acute in the case we are considering because climate change, if it occurs, will affect a wide range of social, economic, and political activities. Changes in these sectors will affect emissions of "greenhouse gases" which will in turn affect climate, and around we go again (Jamieson, 1990). Climate change is itself uncertain, and its human effects are even more radically so. It is for reasons such as these that in general the area of environment and energy has been full of surprises.

A second reason why the benefits and costs of the impacts of global climate change cannot reliably be assessed concerns the breadth of the impacts. Global climate change will affect all regions of the globe. About many of these regions – those in which most of the world's population live – we know very little. Some of these regions do not even have monetarized markets. It is ludicrous to suppose that we could assess the economic impacts of global climate change when we have such little understanding of the global economy in the first place. (Nordhaus 1990, for example, implausibly extrapolates the sectorial analysis of the American economy to the world economy for the purposes of his study.)

Finally, consider the diversity of the potential impacts. Global climate change will affect agriculture, fishing, forestry, and tourism. It will affect "unmanaged" ecosystems and patterns of urbanization. International trade and relations will be affected. Some nations and sectors may benefit at the expense of others. There will be complex interactions between these effects. For this reason we cannot reliably aggregate the effects by evaluating each impact and combining them by simple addition. But since the interactions are so complex we have no idea what the proper mathematical function would be for aggregating them (if the idea of aggregation even makes sense in this context). It is difficult enough to assess the economic benefits and costs of small-scale, local activities. It is almost beyond belief to suppose that we could aggregate the diverse impacts of global climate change in such a way as to dictate policy responses.

In response to skeptical arguments like the one that I have given it is sometimes admitted that our present ability to provide reliable economic analyses is limited, but then it is asserted that any analysis is better than none. I think that this is incorrect, and that one way to see this is by considering an example.

Imagine a century ago a government doing an economic analysis in order to decide whether to build its national transportation system around the private automobile. No one could have imagined the secondary effects: the expanding road network, the loss of life, the effects on wildlife, on communities, on noise; the impact on air quality, travel time, and quality of life. Given our inability to reliably predict and evaluate the effects of even small-scale technology (e.g. the artificial heart; see Jamieson 1988), the idea that we could predict the impact of global climate change reliably enough to permit meaningful economic analysis seems fatuous indeed.

When our ignorance is so extreme, it is a leap of faith to say that some analysis is better than none. A bad analysis can be so wrong that it can lead us to do bad things, outrageous things – things that are much worse than what we would have done had we not tried to assess the costs and benefits at all. (This is the wisdom in the old adage "a little learning is a dangerous thing.")

What I have been arguing here is that the idea of "managing" global climate change is a dangerous conceit. The tools of economic evaluation are not up to the task. However, the most fundamental reason why management approaches are doomed to failure is that the questions they can answer are not the ones that are most important and profound. The problems posed by anthropogenic global climate change are ethical as well as economic and scientific. I will explain this claim in the next section.

2   Ethics and Global Change

Since the end of World War II, humans have attained a kind of power that is unprecedented in history. While in the past entire peoples could be destroyed, now all people are vulnerable. While once particular human societies had the power to upset the natural processes that made their lives and cultures possible, now people have the power to alter the fundamental global conditions that permitted human life to evolve and continue to sustain it. While our species dances with the devil, the rest of nature is held hostage. Even if we step back from the precipice now, it will be too late for many or even perhaps most of the plant and animal life with which we share the planet (Borza and Jamieson 1990). Even if global climate can be stabilized, the future may be one without wild nature (McKibben 1989). Humans will live in a humanized world with a few domestic plants and animals that can survive or thrive on their relationships with humans.

The questions that such possibilities pose are fundamental questions of morality. They concern how we ought to live, what kinds of societies we want, and how we should relate to nature and other forms of life. Seen from this perspective it is not surprising that economics cannot tell us everything we want to know about how we should respond to global warming and global change. Economics may be able to tell us how to reach our goals efficiently, but it cannot tell us what our goals should be or even whether we should be concerned to reach them efficiently.

It is a striking fact about modern intellectual life that we often seek to evade the value dimensions of fundamental social questions. Social scientists tend to eschew talk about values, and this is part of the reason why we have so little understanding of how value change occurs in individuals and societies. Policy professionals are also often reluctant to talk about values. Many think that rational reflection on values and value change is impossible, unnecessary, impractical, or dangerous. Others see it as a professional, political, or bureaucratic threat (Amy 1984). Generally, in the political process value language tends to function as code words for policies and attitudes that cannot be discussed directly.

A system of values, in the sense in which I will use this notion, specifies permissions, norms, duties, and obligations; it assigns blame, praise, and responsibility; and it provides an account of what is valuable and what is not. A system of values provides a standard for assessing our behavior and that of others. Perhaps indirectly it also provides a measure of the acceptability of government action and regulation.

Values are more objective than mere preferences (Andrews and Waits

1978). A value has force for a range of people who are similarly situated. A preference may have force only for the individual whose preference it is. Whether or not someone should have a particular value depends on reasons and arguments. About values we can have rational discussion. Preferences may be rooted simply in desire, without supporting reasons. They may be whimsical or eccentric.

A system of values may govern someone's behavior without these values being fully explicit. They may figure in people's motivations and in their attempts to justify or criticize their own actions or those of others. Yet it may require a theorist or a therapist to make these values explicit. In this respect a system of values may be like an iceberg – most of what is important may be submerged and invisible even to the person whose values they are. Because values are often opaque to the person who holds them, there can be inconsistencies and incoherencies in a system of values. Indeed, much debate and dialogue about values involves attempts to resolve inconsistencies and incoherencies in one direction or another.

A system of values is generally a cultural construction rather than an individual one (Weiskel 1990). It makes sense to speak of contemporary American values, or those of eighteenth-century England or tenth-century India. Our individual differences tend to occur around the edges of our value system. The vast areas of agreement often seem invisible because they are presupposed or assumed without argument.

I believe that our dominant value system is inadequate and inappropriate for guiding our thinking about global environmental problems, such as those entailed by climate change caused by human activity. This value system, as it impinges on the environment, can be thought of as a relatively recent construction, coincident with the rise of capitalism and modern science, and expressed in the writings of such philosophers as Francis Bacon (1620/1870), John Locke (1690/1952) and Bernard Mandeville (1714/1970; see also Hirschman 1977). It evolved in low-population-density and low-technology societies, with seemingly unlimited access to land and other resources. This value system is reflected in attitudes toward population, consumption, technology, and social justice, as well as toward the environment.

The feature of this value system on which I wish to focus is its conception of responsibility. Our current value system presupposes that harms and their causes are individual, that they can readily be identified, and that they are local in space and time. Consider an example of the sort of case with which our value system deals best. Jones breaks into Smith's house and steals Smith's television set. Jones's intent is clear: she wants Smith's TV set. Smith suffers a clear harm; he is made worse off by having lost the television set. Jones is responsible for Smith's loss, for she was the cause of the harm and no one else was involved. What we have in this case is a clear, self-contained story about Smith's loss. We know how to identify the harms and how to assign responsibility. We respond to this breech of our norms by punishing Jones in order to prevent her from doing it again and to deter others from such acts; or we require compensation from Jones so that Smith may be restored to his former position.

It is my contention that this paradigm collapses when we try to apply it to global environmental problems such as those associated with human-induced global climate change. It is for this reason that we are often left feeling confused about how to think about these problems.

There are three important dimensions along which global environmental problems, such as those involved with climate change, vary from the paradigm: apparently innocent acts can have devastating consequences; causes and harms may be diffuse; and causes and harms may be remote in space and time (other important dimensions may concern nonlinear causation, threshold effects, and the relative unimportance of political boundaries, but I cannot discuss these here; see Lee 1989).

Consider an example. Some projections suggest that one effect of global warming may be to shift the southern hemisphere cyclone belt to the south. If this occurs the frequency of cyclones in Sydney, Australia will increase enormously, resulting in death and destruction on a large scale. The causes of this death and destruction will be diffuse. There is no one whom we can identify as the cause of destruction in the way in which we can identify Jones as the cause of Smith's loss. Instead of there being a single cause of harm, millions of people will have made tiny, almost imperceptible causal contributions – by driving cars, cutting trees, using electricity, and so on. They will have made these contributions in the course of their daily lives performing apparently "innocent" acts, without intending to bring about this harm. Moreover, most of these people will be geographically remote from Sydney, Australia. (Many of them will have no idea where Sydney, Australia is.) Further, some people who are harmed will be remote in time from those who have harmed them. Sydney may suffer in the twenty-first century in part because of people's behavior in the nineteenth and twentieth centuries. Many small people doing small things over a long period of time together will cause unimaginable harms. Yet despite the fact that serious, clearly identifiable harms will have occurred due to human agency, conventional morality would have trouble finding anyone to blame. For no one intended the bad outcome, nor brought it about, nor even was able to foresee it.

Today we face the possibility that the global environment may be destroyed, yet no one will be responsible. This is a new problem. It takes a great many people and a high level of consumption to change the earth's climate. It could not have been done in low-density, low-technology societies. Nor could it have been done in societies like ours until recently.

London could be polluted by its inhabitants in the eighteenth century, but its reach was limited. Today no part of the planet is safe. Unless we develop new values and conceptions of responsibility we will have enormous difficulty in motivating people to respond to this problem. In the next section I will gesture toward the values that I believe are needed in order to cope with the problem of global climate change.

3 Ethics for the Twenty-First Century

One of the most important benefits of viewing global environmental problems as moral problems is that this brings them into the domain of dialogue, discussion, and participation. Rather than being "management" problems that governments or experts can solve for us, when seen as ethical problems they become problems for all of us, both as political actors and as everyday moral agents. Some who seek quick fixes may find this frustrating. A moral argument will not change the world overnight. Collective moral change is fundamentally cooperative rather than coercive. No one will fall over, mortally wounded, in the face of an argument.

Some may think that discussion about new values is idealistic. They will say that human nature cannot be changed. But as anyone who takes anthropology or history seriously will know, our current values are at least in part historical constructions, rooted in the conditions of life in which they developed. What we need are new values that reflect the interconnectedness of life on a dense, high-technology planet.

Others may think that a search for new values is excessively individualistic, and that what is needed are collective and institutional solutions. This overlooks the fact that our values permeate our institutions and practices. Reforming our values is part of constructing new moral, political, and legal concepts, and eventually a new world order. In my view, the new values that are needed to cope with global environmental problems should incorporate at least three elements. Some of these elements may sound like platitudes or cliches, but I believe that if taken seriously they could have profound effects.

First, we need to become more holistic in our thinking along at least two different dimensions. One aspect of a holistic view involves integrating environmental concerns with other concerns. As several international reports have pointed out (e.g. World Commission on Environment and Development, 1987; see also Simonis et al. 1989), environmental problems are inextricably bound up with issues of economic development. This is especially clear with respect to the greenhouse effect. The emissions that may be changing our climate are not incidental pollutants. Some of them, at least, are part of the lifeblood of industrial society. We will have a difficult time understanding the problems that we face and developing solutions until we recognize that "pollution" is often just the apparently inconsequential byproduct of everyday life. Seen from this perspective, concern for the environment is not a desideratum that is additional to others such as economic development, but should permeate the way we view all our activities.

A second aspect of a holistic view involves seeing ourselves as part of a single moral community that is global in scope and extended in time. What we do here and now can deeply affect people who are remote from us in both time and space. When it comes to waste disposal, for example, we often think "out of sight, out of mind." But waste disposal does not make waste disappear; at best it transforms the problem, and often it transfers it to someone else. If we were to see the problem of "waste disposal" as a problem of "waste distribution" with both geographical and temporal dimensions, it would appear to us in a very different light.

I believe that we are beginning to evolve a global consciousness, but at this point we are awkwardly positioned between the local consciousness traditionally characteristic of our culture and a larger vision. We have come to see the Brazilian rain forests as part of the global environment, and therefore "ours" as well as "theirs." However, we do not see the "old growth" forests of the Pacific north-west as "theirs" as well as "ours." And all too often we see the economic problems of the developing world that are inextricably linked to global environmental problems as being "their" problems, due to their ignorance, profligacy, or mismanagement, rather than as structural problems of the global community. And as I write this sentence we are experiencing military intervention in the Middle East to defend "our" oil which happens inconveniently to be located in someone else's country.

A second element of a new ethic concerns mindfulness. While the first element expands our vision in space and time, this element concentrates it on the mundane details of everyday life. One of the lessons of the greenhouse effect is that "innocent" acts done in concert are not innocent. We must be mindful about everything we do because in a highly interconnected world almost nothing is done without effect.

It has sometimes been objected that such a vision of morality is unacceptable because it is too strenuous (for discussion see Kagan 1989). Such a vision conflicts with common sense, it is argued, and may even be debilitating because there are too many ways in which we can go wrong. It is true that on this conception we can and often do behave wrongly in the ordinary conduct of our everyday lives. But it is also true that on this conception we can and do behave well when doing ordinary things. Driving when one could bicycle may be wrong, but bicycling when one could drive is morally praiseworthy behavior. The mindfulness that I recommend is indeed part of a strenuous morality, one that sees moral content in many activities that have been seen traditionally as morally neutral. However, such a morality can be empowering as well as debilitating. It gives us enormous opportunity to make a moral difference.

Finally, we should focus more on character than on calculation. Focusing on outcomes has made us cynical calculators and has institutionalized hypocrisy. We can each reason: since my contribution is small, outcomes are likely to be determined by the behavior of others. Reasoning in this way I can justify driving my car while advocating bicycles, or enjoy using my fireplace while favoring regulations against them. In such a climate we do not condemn, or even find it surprising that Congress exempts itself from civil rights laws. Even David Brower, the "archdruid" of the environmental movement, owns two cars, four color televisions, two video cameras, three video recorders, and a dozen tape recorders, and he justifies this by saying that "it will help him in his work to save the Earth" (*San Diego Union*, April 1, 1990).

Calculating leads to unraveling the patterns of collective behavior that we need in order to save the earth. When we "economize" our behavior in the way that is required for calculating, we systematically neglect the subtle and indirect effects of our actions, and for this reason we see individual action as inefficacious. It is useful to consider the revolutions of 1989, which are the most dramatic examples of peaceful social change in our time. They were not made by people who calculated the effects of individual action, but by people of integrity and character who acted on the basis of principles and ideals. It matters, of course, what our principles and ideals are. We need to nurture and give new content to some old virtues such as humility, courage, and moderation, and perhaps develop some new ones such as simplicity and conservatism.

The search for new values, as I conceive it, is not a quest for moral purity. Globally conscious, individually mindful behavior that issues from character and ideals rather than calculation is most likely to bring about the best consequences. In recommending these new values my focus is on the collective good, not on individual virtue. Ultimately we should live virtuous lives not because they are virtuous, but because this will have the effect of saving the earth.

Science has alerted us to the impact of humankind on the planet, each other, and all life. This dramatically confronts us with questions about who we are, our relations to nature, and what we are willing to sacrifice for various possible futures. We should confront this as a fundamental challenge to our values, and not treat it as if it were simply another technical problem to be managed.

REFERENCES

Abelson, Philip, 1990: "Uncertainties About Global Warming," *Science* 247 (30 March), p. 1529.
Amy, Douglas R., 1984: "Why Policy Analysis and Ethics are Incompatible," *Journal of Policy Analysis and Management* 3, 4, pp. 573–91.
Andrews, Richard, and Waits, Mary Jo, 1978: *Environmental Values in Public Decisions: A Research Agenda* (Ann Arbor: School of Natural Resources, University of Michigan).
Arrhenius, S., 1896: "On the Influence of Carbonic Acid in the Air upon the Temperature of the Ground," *Philosophical Magazine* 41, p. 237.
Arrhenius, S., 1908: *Worlds in the Making* (New York: Harper and Brothers).
Bacon, F., 1620/1870: *Works*, ed. James Spedding, Robert Leslie Ellis, and Douglas Devon Heath (London: Longmans Green).
Bolin, B., R. D. Doos, J. Jager, and R. Warrick, eds, 1986: *The Greenhouse Effect, Climatic Change, and Ecosystems*, SCOPE 29 (New York: Wiley).
Borza, K., and Jamieson, D., 1990: *Global Change and Biodiversity Loss: Some Impediments to Response* (Boulder: University of Colorado, Center for Space and Geoscience Policy).
Budyko, M. I., 1988: "Anthropogenic Climate Change," paper presented at the World Congress on Climate and Development, Hamburg, Federal Republic of Germany.
Callendar, G. S., 1938: "The Artificial Production of Carbon Dioxide and its Influence on Temperature," *Quarterly Journal of the Royal Meteorological Society* 64, pp. 223–240.
Conference Statement, 1988: *The Changing Atmosphere: Implications for Global Security*, conference held June 27–30, 1988, Toronto, Canada.
Conservation Foundation, 1963: *Implications of Rising Carbon Dioxide Content of the Atmosphere* (New York: Conservation Foundation).
Ephron, L., 1988: *The End: The Imminent Ice Age and how We can Stop it* (Berkeley, CA: Celestial Arts).
Flavin, C., 1989: *Slowing Global Warming: A Worldwide Strategy*, Worldwatch Paper 91 (Washington DC: Worldwatch Institute).
Gallup 1989: *The Gallup Report #285: Concern About the Environment* (Washington DC: The Gallup Organization).
Glantz, M., 1988a: *Societal Responses to Regional Climate Change: Forecasting by Analogy* (Boulder: Westview Press).
Glantz, M., 1988b: "Politics and the Air Around Us: International Policy Action on Atmospheric Pollution by Trace Gases," in Glantz 1988a, pp. 41–72.
Hirschman, Albert, 1977: *The Passions and the Interests* (Princeton: Princeton University Press).
Idso, Sherwood B., 1989: *Carbon Dioxide and Global Change: The Earth in Transition* (Tempe, Arizona: IBR Press).
Jamieson, Dale, 1990: "Managing the Future: Public Policy, Scientific Uncertainty, and Global Warming," in D. Scherer, ed., *Upstream/Downstream: New Essays in Environmental Ethics* (Philadelphia: Temple University Press).

Jamieson, Dale, 1988: "The Artificial Heart: Reevaluating the Investment," in D. Mathieu, ed., *Organ Substitution Technology* (Boulder: Westview Press).

Kagan, Shelly, 1989: *The Limits of Morality* (New York: Oxford University Press).

Lave, Lester, 1982: "Mitigating Strategies for Carbon Dioxide Problems," *American Economic Review* 72, 2, pp. 257–61.

Lee, Keekok, 1989: *Social Philosophy and Ecological Scarcity* (New York: Routledge).

Locke, John, 1690/1952: *The Second Treatise of Government* (Indianapolis: Bobbs-Merrill).

J. E. Lovelock, 1988: *The Ages of Gaia: A Biography of Our Living Earth* (New York: Norton).

McKibben, W., 1989: *The End of Nature* (New York: Knopf).

Mandeville, B., 1714/1970: *The Fable of the Bees*, trans. P. Harth (Harmondsworth, England: Penguin).

Moomaw, William R., 1988/1989: "Near-term Congressional Options for Responding to Global Climate Change," repr. in Dean Edwin Abrahamson, ed., *The Challenge of Global Warming* (Washington DC: Island Press), pp. 305–26.

NAS/NRC 1983: *Changing Climate* (Washington DC: National Academy Press).

Nordhaus, W., 1990: "To Slow or Not to Slow: The Economics of the Greenhouse Effect," paper presented at the American Association for the Advancement of Science, New Orleans.

Opp, Karl-Dieter, 1989: *The Rationality of Political Protest* (Boulder: Westview Press).

Parfit, Derek, 1984: *Reasons and Persons* (Oxford: Oxford University Press).

Sagoff, Mark, 1988: *The Economy of the Earth* (New York: Cambridge University Press).

Schneider, Stephen H. 1989: *Global Warming: Are We Entering the Greenhouse Century?* (San Francisco: Sierra Club Books).

von Simonis, Udo E., von Weizsacker, Ernst, U., Hauchler, Ingomar, and Boll, Winfried, 1989: *Globale Umweltprobleme, Globale Umweltpolitik* (Bonn: Foundation for Development and Peace).

United States Environmental Protection Agency, 1988: *The Potential Effects of Global Climate Change in the United States, Draft Report to Congress*, ed. J. B. Smith and D. A. Tirpak (Washington DC: US Government Printing Office).

United States Environmental Protection Agency, 1989: *Policy Options for Stabilizing Global Climate, Draft Report to Congress*, ed. D. Lashof and D. Tirpak (Washington DC: US Government Printing Office).

Weiskel, Timothy, 1990: "Cultural Values and Their Environmental Implications: An Essay on Knowledge, Belief and Global Survival," paper presented at the American Association for the Advancement of Science, New Orleans.

White House Council of Economic Advisors, 1990: *The Economic Report of the President* (Washington DC: Executive Office of the President, Publications Services).

World Climate Program, 1985: *Report of the International Conference on the Assessment of the Role of Carbon Dioxide and of Other Greenhouse Gases in Climate Variations and Associated Impacts*, Report of an International Conference held at Villach, Austria, October 9–15, 1985 (Geneva: World Meteorological Organization).

World Commission on Environment and Development, 1987: *Our Common Future* (Oxford: Oxford University Press).

18
Morality, Rationality, and Politics: The Greenhouse Dilemma

Peter Danielson

Analyzing the problem of global warming from the point of view of rational decision theory, Danielson concludes that it represents a fundamental dilemma. Although everyone would be better off if all of us were to change our practices to reduce the amount of greenhouse gases we produce, it is rational for individuals to continue to produce such gases so long as they have no assurance of compliance on the part of a significantly large number of other people. Moreover, attempting to induce others to cooperate by threatening to continue practices which produce greenhouse gases oneself is an unacceptable strategy, because the values at stake are too important to put at risk in this way. Attempting to solve the problem by morally reproving those who do not comply is rejected on the grounds that such sanctioning has costs that make it unattractive.

Since moral sanctioning does not have the same costs when performed by children, Daniels suggests we attempt to solve the problem by teaching children to monitor and register their moral disapproval of practices that needlessly increase greenhouse gases. This strategy is defended as not being inconsistent with democratic ideals on the grounds that the children would have no power to coerce compliance.

This paper represents an interesting contrast to that by Jamieson (chapter 17). Although both concern the problem of global warming and the ethics of cooperation in regard to this problem, their views about what is required to increase cooperation are interestingly different in kind. Danielson, in effect, is looking for ways to increase individuals' rational assurance of compliance by others. In recommending more virtue-oriented moral thinking regarding environmentally sensitive behavior, Jamieson wants to de-emphasize individual calculation of probable effectiveness in doing one's own part.

In the late 1970s a colleague from the faculty of environmental studies contrasted his low enrolment with my oversubscribed introduction to

This paper was presented at the conference on Moral Philosophy in the Public Domain, University of British Columbia, June 1990. Thanks to the programme committee for comments on an earlier version and to the many participants who made helpful suggestions.

personal computing. Why, he wondered, had he so few takers for his tutorial on The Conserver Society? I applied my favourite strategic categories and the answer seemed plain. Computer literacy is a private good; environmental constraint generates public goods. It was rational for students to improve their own lot; irrational to improve everyone else's.

Of course, times have changed. Now we have green supermarkets and right-leaning provincial governments tax disposable diapers. Evidently it is rational, in the narrowest sense, for someone to look after the environment. Furthermore, I now believe that it is rational to be moral in some situations. Nonetheless, when we understand the strategic structure of environmental problems like global warming, we shall see that even a moralized rationality is unlikely to solve them. In this paper I shall argue that we need a strictly speaking *moral* solution. I will sketch such a solution and distinguish it from the more popular political approach.

1   Rationality and Public Goods

In this section I focus on the strategic structure of social situations to indicate the task for morality. I shall argue that a central problem for moral philosophy occurs when what is individually rational conflicts with what is best for all.

1.1   The Greenhouse Dilemma

The conflict between the common good and individual advantage is central to environmental questions. Hardin (1968) captures this conflict in his model of the "Tragedy of the Commons." We all do better by moderate use of a common resource but each does best by unilateral heavier use, regardless of what the others do. It is rational in such situations for each to act to undermine the common good, by over-fishing, private driving, or burning more fossil fuels. Since it is puzzling how these seemingly irrational behaviors could be rational, we should look more carefully at the structure these situations share. The problem is clearest in the abstract form of a two-player game, the Greenhouse Dilemma, depicted in figure 1.[1]

The matrix depicts the situation of two agents, you and I. Each of us has two alternatives: to burn less or more cheap fuel.[2] Why call this situation a *dilemma*? Because there are two plausible lines of argument supporting a decision. First, I consider what I can do independently of

	You burn	
	less	more
I burn less	good for both	my worst, your best
I burn more	my best, your worst	bad for both

Figure 1   The two-player greenhouse dilemma

your decision. We shall see that this is particularly easy in this case, as the same action is best for me regardless of what you do. If you burn less, I do better (best is better than good) by burning more as I gain the advantage of cheap dirty fuel. Alternatively, should you burn more, I also should burn more (bad is better than worst; mutual profligacy is better than one-sided conservation). Since you must either burn more or less, we have what appears to be a conclusive logical argument for the rationality of my choosing to burn more. This is the first horn of the dilemma. The other horn considers the symmetry of our situation, which makes it rational for you to do what I do. It would be better for us both to burn less, if we could act together. But so long as we act independently, the first argument is conclusive, and rational individual agents end up with their third best outcome. It is important to feel the force of this practical dilemma.[3] There is wide recognition that global warming has this strategic structure.[4]

1.2 Rational and Moral Failure

In a Greenhouse Dilemma the invisible hand fails to direct individually rational agents to optimal outcomes.[5] This goes some way toward explaining why people contribute to the greenhouse effect even when they know that their behavior is harmful. Although global warming is a bad outcome, the actions producing it form a stable equilibrium; burning more is best for each of us regardless of what we expect others to do. This also explains why the problem resists some simple moral appeals. First, note that we do not face a coordination problem, where pointing out the better alternative allows us better to choose among several agreeable outcomes.[6] This is not to say that our interests purely conflict. It is obvious to everyone that mutual cooperation (in this case, universal reduction in emissions) is good for all. It is certainly uncontroversially better, by each agent's values, than joint defection. One challenge for moral philosophy is to show us how to act in order to achieve the good of joint cooperation, given the strategic temptations and dangers that partially conflicting interests present.[7] This is more difficult than is commonly realized, which brings us to the second criticism of simple moral appeals. For example, many claim that either utilitarianism or Kantian universalization provides the morally correct basis for action. In the Greenhouse Dilemma, both agree that moral agents ought unconditionally to cooperate.[8] But unconditional cooperation encourages others to exploit the morally constrained agent. From a strategic point of view, both of these widely recommended moral principles are utopian.

I conclude that social problems like the Greenhouse Dilemma reveal the failure of widely accepted theories of rationality and morality; the former is cynical and the later naïve. Moral agents face a compliance problem: how to achieve joint cooperation without being taken advantage of. There is much to say about how we might improve moral principles so that they pass this strategic test. In my own work I have emphasized two features of rationally successful principles:

1 They must be responsive to the other agents. Unconditional cooperation is foolish; a moral agent needs, at the same time, to protect herself from exploitation and to encourage others to respond to her by adopting moral constraint.
2 The best way to achieve mutual, responsive cooperation is to communicate one's commitment by transparent principles.

Following Gauthier (1986), I argue that properly designed moral principles can solve some Prisoner's Dilemmas. In the two-agent Greenhouse Dilemma, I ought to burn less if and only if you are similarly publicly committed to burning less. In cases like this, it is rational to be moral.

1.3 The Need for Sanctions

Unfortunately, the two-player Greenhouse Dilemma is not a good model of the problem of global warming. When more decision-makers are added to the situation, conditional moral principles (of the sort just sketched) cease to be rational. To see why, consider our own situation. Suppose some countries refuse to constrain themselves and continue freely to burn cheap fossil fuel. Still the rest of us are better off with less than universal restraint than with universal licence. Therefore it would be foolish to commit ourselves to the generalized conditional principle: cooperate if but only if *all* others will. However, if we allow some to freeload, then it becomes rational to join the free riders. Alternatively, we could try to make free-riding more costly, by *sanctioning* those who burn more. But sanctioning others is itself costly. In the global Greenhouse Dilemma, we cannot induce others to cooperate by threatening to withhold our own cooperation.[9] The threat (to cook the world for the sake of a fairer distribution of ecological restraint) is simply not credible; it risks values too important to all of us. We must look to other ways to sanction the non-compliant. But these sanctions are also costly. (When was the last time you scolded a stranger for a minor traffic offense, or littering, or smoking where banned?) Sanctioners make themselves worse off for the sake of a global benefit. In some situations, morality requires sanctions; but it is difficult to show that sanctioning is rational.[10]

2   A Moralizing Proposal

The need for sanctions marks a limit on instrumentally rational morality. Fortunately, we are not merely instrumentally rational agents. It would be foolish to assume, for any but theoretical philosophical purposes, that actual human beings are so narrowly motivated. To the contrary, it is a remarkable fact about people that they are so often motivated by moral considerations.[11] In this section, I start from the middle, assuming that some people are capable of moral motivation, and ask how insights gained from a strategic understanding of the greenhouse problem might be applied to solve it.

Reviewing our conclusions so far, strategically effective moralizing should have two features. First, we need a clear understanding of what we want to achieve given our situation. Second, moral agents need to be discriminating. Moral principles should distinguish more and less moral agents and treat them differently. In particular, principled private compliance is not sufficient. We must discover and develop motivations to sanction non-compliers. I propose a two-pronged assault on the greenhouse problem. First, we should create public awareness of an ecological accounting system; and second, we should encourage children to become moralistic around this issue.

2.1   How Green Are You?

We have been assuming that moral principles direct each of us to what we all want. What do we want in the greenhouse case?[12] Roughly, we want a fair distribution of emissions. This is already a complex goal, as it must take into account both production and absorption of several green-house gases (GHG). It is also an interesting goal, as it reveals much about our ignorance and motivation on the issue of global warming. Consider a simple question: are you – and I mean *you* – part of the problem or part of the solution? How would you find out? If, like everyone that I have asked so far,[13] you don't know, this shows us something significant. Ironically, it seems that most of us take the problem of global warming *too globally*. But it is obviously true that each of us is accountable for some share of the effect; each of us is either part of the problem or part of the solution.[14] Therefore we need to do some *moral accounting*. Much of our ignorance is factual: Canada ranks second in per capita energy consumption but exports some of this and also has much forest. How do these balance in terms of greenhouse gases? More locally, how much GHG does my tiny Honda produce? How much CO_2 does my family's woodlot (in Pennsylvania) sequester? There are accounting questions as well: Does that woodlot count for me? How about my share of Canada's national forests? What about the manufacturing effluent at Honda's plants? It would be presumptuous to answer any of these questions at this point. Evidently much work needs to be done; individual moral accountancy (casuistry?) is neither a profession (for reasons related to my opening story) nor well studied. I note some leading problems. Does moral accountability follow ownership or use? (I recommend the former; one reason comes out below.) Do we consider historical or only present activity?[15] Finally, I do not mean to imply that this is a black and white issue. Since the question is not whether we shall cooperate or not with a particular agent, drawing a definite moral/immoral line is less important in the global greenhouse dilemma.[16] Indeed, sharp line-drawing may be counterproductive (why reinvent ecological *sin?*). I suggest a continuum of shades from dead grey (bad) through brown, yucky yellow, and green (good) as a way to know where you and others stand.

2.2 A Moral Reformation

Most of those concerned with global warming look to governments for the solution. Before I consider their reasons (in section 3.2), I want to suggest an alternative institutional instrument, namely moralizing. I am suggesting that we try to start – to seed, as it were – a new moral norm instead. I take morality to be an informal institution that works by means of personal principle, example, discussion, and informal, non-coercive sanctions. For example, such an institution has been responsible for the decline of nose-picking among my four-year-old's friends; it may help us grown-ups with our emission problem. I am suggesting that we make it publicly acceptable to flaunt one's grey/green stand and to ask others about theirs. I would like to see a fad for moralizing buttons (in a continuum of shades) and similarly coloured meaningful tee-shirts.

Talk of 'making' something acceptable does not make it so. We are back to the question of sanctions. Who is going to make this happen? Whence cometh the motivation, the manpower, to power this institution? Here I suggest that we take advantage of forces most of us only lament, namely the power of fads and fashion over children. I propose that we seed a Let's Get Greener movement among the young. When I propose buttons and tee-shirts, I hope to interest Benetton in contributing to the ecological cause. And I envision squads of little green hornets with infra-red detectors bugging residents about their leaky doors, windows, and dryer-vents, with companies like Sony and Fisher-Price supplying the needed devices.

Why involve children? Three reasons stand out. First, children like to sanction people; indeed, they *love* to sanction adults. Second, children may make an end-run around the motivational problem of adults' counter-suggestivity to sanctioning. We typically react adversely to moral criticism from our peers (*a fortiori*, to moralistic sanctioning that goes beyond criticism). I suggest, on the basis of my experience as a parent, that we grown-ups react much better when morally questioned or criticized by children.[17] Third, making people's green position public is morally edu-cational. Too much of the lives that we offer our children is morally inane. The greenhouse problem is initially so simple, so easy to talk about and apply, and the buck is difficult to pass. Indeed, the problem is so tempting as an exercise in moral education ("Daddy, we really ought to shop by bike, you know") that I would be tempted to invent it. Unfortunately I do not have to.

3 Two Objections

3.1 The Green Guard and Original Ecological Sin

I should address two objections to using children. First, I am aware of the dangers; I have heard of the children's crusade, Hitler Youth and Red Guard. Children's moral fervor is a force to be reckoned with.[18] Still, global warming is a serious problem and it may require a powerful force to budge us from our comfortable habits and entrenched position of power.[19] Second, may it not be harmful to moral development to start with such a gloomy beginning? Am I not proposing the ecological analogue of *original* sin? Fortunately, no. Recall my suggestion to let accountability follow ownership. This has the consequence that our children start green (they each own some Canadian national trees and not much on the downside of their personal ecological moral ledger). Thus I recapture – derive from my green principle – the important thesis of original innocence.[20]

3.2 Politics and Morality

Another objection to my proposal is more sweeping. I have considered whether children should be encouraged morally to judge and sanction people. The prior question is whether any private individuals should undertake such invasive actions. For example, in "The Tragedy of the Commons," Hardin proposed the solution of "mutual coercion mutually agreed upon."[21] This brings into focus the *political* alternative to my moral proposal. In particular, two aspects of the political solution stand out: democracy (mutual agreement) and fairness/coercion. My proposal is undemocratic because it is not addressed to the democratic organs of the country, our elected representatives. Moral sanctions may be unfair because some – those least sensitive to childish pestering – may escape it. Contrast a legally imposed policy such as a carbon tax. It must pass democratic tests and it is fairly imposed on all.

These are powerful arguments for legally protecting many morally important matters. But no liberal democratic state tries to enforce all of everyone's morality. Indeed, precisely the virtues of political solutions count against this. They demand national attention and require wide consensus. Much of my radical proposal would be unlikely to survive this scrutiny. Witness the great watering-down of the Canadian government's environmental proposals. I can put this rejoinder more forcefully. Precisely because my green cohorts *cannot* coerce anyone, my proposal need not.be vetted democratically. Unlike a prohibition or a tax, and like a proposal to picket or rally, we moral enthusiasts should be free to organize non-coercively.

Nonetheless, states are traditionally seen as particularly well placed to deal with public goods problems. A government can *internalize* local environmental issues. What is an external benefit or cost to each of us is internal to Ontario or Canada. But this justification of the state suggests two limiting factors. First, states are local actors in *global* environmental conflicts.[22] Second, states are not abstract protectors of even local interests; they are real institutions with their own dynamics. This is most troubling when governments have a large stake in dirty production processes, as when provincial governments burn coal to generate electricity or have large stakes in oil production. For example, recently we have discovered how ecologically bad governments in Eastern Europe can be; how green (if at all) is Ontario or Alberta?[23]

Conclusion

Let me summarize my themes. First, a central problem of moral philosophy is the fact that moral constraint creates *public goods*. This gives rise to the problem of rational compliance. Second, large-scale problems like the Greenhouse Dilemma require public action to sanction non-compliers. Principled private compliance is not sufficient; moral philosophy must "go public" and try to change the way people behave. Third, moral philosophers in the public domain face the challenge of competing institutions such as churches and governments. Here competition is to be welcomed. My own view is that the division of moral labor merits further study to determine how different institutions best perform various morally desirable tasks.[24]

NOTES

1   The Greenhouse Dilemma is an instance of the mixed motive game usually called 'the Prisoner's Dilemma' for reasons that need not concern us here.
2   These are conventionally labelled C (for cooperate) and D (for defect) respectively. The interaction of this pair of individual choices results in four possible social outcomes: both burn more, one burns less, etc. which each agent ranks from best through good and bad to worst asccording to her own values. For example, we agree that both conserving is better than both continuing to burn much but we disagree about whether it is better that only I or only you shall continue burning cheap fuel.
3   Pause for a moment and consider one of these concrete instances of the dilemma. (Different pedagogic strategies work for different people.) (1) You are responsible for deciding the crucial development policy for a large, poor country such as India or China. Should you (C) restrain development, at a cost to your own people, or (D) develop using cheap and dirty coal and freon-11? (2) You are given this exercise in a course for which the grade is important to you:

		Others choose	
		C	D
You choose	C	You get B	You get D
	D	You get A	You get C

Would you choose C or D? (3) You are choosing a car in which your children will be the primary passengers. C = buy tiny efficient but easily crushed car; D = buy huge inefficient but relatively uncrushable car.

4 This example comes from a letter to the *New York Times*:

> Every ton of carbon dioxide removed from the atmosphere by photosynthesis is a gain in controlling the greenhouse effect. But it is clearly in the interest of nations, businesses and individuals to cut down forests and absorb agricultural and open land into urban employment and community benefits. The oxygen gained and carbon dioxide disposed of are gone with the wind. The benefits are so widely dispersed and uncapturable that, although beneficial to humanity, they are not worth producing for any ... decision-making body. Haller (1988)

5 It fails because no one *owns* the atmosphere, which indicates that this failure is a deep problem based on the existence of a shared public world.

6 An example of a coordination problem is the question how each should write their pronouns in sentences like this very one. We could coordinate on the conventionally correct 'his' or the sexually neutral 'their.' The observation that the latter is better for anti-sexist moral reasons can be a reason to coordinate on it.

7 Another challenge, perhaps more difficult, is to address the questions of distributive justice that arise when there are several different ways to cooperate. Although this problem is important for global warming, I ignore it in this paper.

8 Distinctively strong utilitarianism generates its recommendations by summing benefits across parties; cooperation leads to higher sums (cf. the Student's Dilemma in note 2 above, where $(2B + D + A) > (2C + D + A)$). Universalization considers what happens if all do the same, excluding the possibility of asymmetrical action and recommending that one choose C.

9 The availability of this conditional strategy made morality rational in the two agent case.

10 Cf. Danielson (1992, 1989b); the non-rationality of social norms is a theme in Elster (1989). Note the regress; one cannot make sanctions rational by means of further sanctioning. As Elster puts it, an unmoved mover is needed at the beginning of the chain.

11 For example, see Kahneman et al. (1986) for empirical studies of the motivating power of fairness.

12 Often it is clear what we want morally to encourage. For example, the paradigm civic virtues of refraining from force and fraud are evident and invite no vice of excess. It is less clear what is fair and reasonable to demand in terms of environmental restraint.

13 That is everyone I have met in the last few days, around my neighborhood and university department.

14 In part, this ignorance reflects a lack of motivation. It is not easy to find out next season's fashions, yet we have – because we give each other, by sanctioning social norms – much more reason to think about what we wear than to think about our car's emissions or our leaky windows. But we could easily change this. Smoky exhaust could be as embarrassing as an open fly; leaky windows as unattractive as a snotty nose. I take up the question of sanctions in section 2.2 below. However, motivation is only part of the problem. In addition, I now see that we may need new institutions to generate the relevant information. See Danielson (1991).

15 Most of the extra CO_2 up there is the product of *our* development, so a distributively fair solution would not make newly developing areas pay equally with those who caused the problem.

16 Even in the two-agent Prisoner's Dilemma, drawing the moral/immoral line is not always easily done; cf. Danielson (1989a).

17 I realize that these claims are psychologically naïve and need to be related to wider empirical study of the phenomena noted. Furthermore, it would be strategically naïve to ignore that our reaction to sanctioning may not be a psychological peculiarity but a rational response to another game of Chicken played at the level of sanctioner and would-be sanctioned. But this would take us far beyond our present subject.

18 After I wrote this, children were influential in the campaign that led McDonald's restaurants to switch from foam to paper packaging. Corcoran (1991) and Guillet (1990) raise important objections to the role children played in this controversy.

19 Moreover, note that the children's power is the only *force* my proposal involves. The counter-examples are objectionable in part because they made children into unwitting agents of harmful and coercive institutions.

20 Of course, I need to say much more about the moral complexities of involving children. An interesting contrast is the recent campaign against smoking conducted by the Canadian Lung Association in Toronto's schools, both in terms of impact on moral education and its use of moralizing. First, children were encouraged to make commitments ("I'll never smoke" buttons) at an age which mocks this morally important idea. Second, the campaign arguably misused the tactic of moralizing sanctions, since smoking falls mainly on the protected individual liberty side of the line drawn by John Stuart Mill's Harm Principle. Burning fossil fuels, in contrast, harms others (via the greenhouse effect) and thus is a more appropriate target for sanctioning.

21 However Hardin (1968) has an additional reason to support this conclusion. He is discussing population control and he believes that moral

constraint ("conscience") is self-eliminating for reasons of individual selection.

22 Cf. McInnes (1990) for the example of China and India as actors in a Greenhouse Dilemma.

23 Although it is a long way from the Polish and Czech ecological monsters, my government-owned electric utility (Ontario Hydro) sells me hot water only at a flat rate ("Gee, it's free at the margin!") from a primitive poorly insulated heater without the alternative of an off-prime rate intelligent heater controller (which my sister's private utility offers). And the government of Canada seems committed to helping the Roumanians produce 'Chernobyl II: What Slavelabour Candu.'

24 I continue the study of alternative institutional solutions to the problem of global warming in Danielson (1991).

REFERENCES

Corcoran, T., 1991: "Keep Politicians off the Tax Revolt Ark," *Toronto Globe and Mail*, B6, March 22.
Danielson, Peter, 1989a: "Artificial Morality: New Problems for Old," Paper presented at Ontario Philosophical Society.
Danielson, Peter, 1989b: "The Rights of Chickens: A Rational Foundation for Libertarianism?" Paper presented at the American Association for the Philosophic Study of Society meeting with the APA Eastern Division.
Danielson, Peter, 1991: "The Atmospheric Trust: A Proposal for Global Warming," position paper prepared for first team meeting, SSHRC project on Ethics and Climate Change: Greenhouse Effect, Kananaskis, Alberta.
Danielson, Peter, 1992: *Artificial Morality*. Routledge, London.
Elster, Jon, 1989: *The Cement of Society: A Study of Social Order*. Cambridge University Press, Cambridge.
Gauthier, David P., 1986: *Morals by Agreement*. Oxford University Press, Oxford.
Guillet, James, 1990: "Kid's Crusades Bad Idea," letter, *Toronto Globe and Mail*, D7, December 1.
Haller, William, 1988: Letter, *New York Times*, F13, September 18.
Hardin, Garrett, 1968: "The Tragedy of Commons," *Science*, 162: 1243–8.
Kahneman, Daniel, Knetsch, Jack L., and Thaler, Richard H., 1986: "Fairness and the Assumptions of Economics," *Journal of Business*, 59: S285–S300.
McInnes, Craig, 1990: "Worlds Apart over the Environment," *Toronto Globe and Mail*, D1, D8, January 6.

Biomedical Ethics

19
From Kantianism to Contextualism: The Rise and Fall of the Paradigm Theory in Bioethics

Earl R. Winkler

Briefly reviewing the history of bioethics, Winkler describes how a traditional "applied ethics" model of moral reasoning gave rise to a "paradigm theory" of bioethics consisting of three main principles – those of autonomy, beneficence, and justice. After criticizing the methodological shortcomings of the paradigm theory in relation to a variety of biomedical cases, Winkler goes on to challenge the adequacy of the whole "applied ethics" model of moral reasoning. Against this model he counterposes "contextualism," a dominantly case-driven model of actual moral reasoning which disallows any decisive role for principle in the resolution of genuinely problematic moral issues. In the course of developing his argument against the traditional philosophical account of the relations between ethical theory and moral practice, Winkler discusses wide reflective equilibrium theory and the importance of interpretation in moral reasoning. He suggests that ethical theory and moral philosophy can serve positive functions in practical moral reasoning, but defers consideration of these matters to future work.

The view of practical reasoning presented in this paper may be usefully compared with those of Hoffmaster (chapter 20), Sikora (chapter 5), Rachels (chapter 6), Flyvbjerg (chapter 1), and Wertheimer (chapter 8), and with Philips's general sketch of what social moralities are and how they are properly evaluated (chapter 10).

It is a familiar observation that moral philosophy in the twentieth century has been dominated by meta-ethical concerns, at least until fairly recently. Nevertheless, there have been many notable efforts at systematic normative theory in this period and, in general, faith in the possibility and power of such theory has persisted. Within applied ethics, however, doubt about the relevance and applicability of general ethical theory has not been uncommon, although skepticism has tended to be both poorly articulated and extremely perplexed about alternatives. But aversion to normative theory, and to traditional ideas about its applicability, has become increasingly well defined in the last few years. Also, a general methodological rival to the "applied ethics" model of moral reasoning is emerging. "Contextualism," as I will term this rival, is the idea, roughly, that moral problems must be resolved within concrete circumstances, in all their interpretive complexity, by appeal to relevant historical and cultural traditions, with reference to critical institutional and professional norms and virtues, and by utilizing the primary method of comparative case analysis. Applicable moral principles will derive mainly from these sources, rather than from ethical theory on the grand scale. Current distrust and rejection of theory, which is gathering momentum, has been profoundly influenced by the experience, as well as by the writings, of many philosophers and others working in applied ethics. What is ultimately at stake is our understanding of the nature of moral reasoning and justification.

In this paper I want to explore the way in which this conflict over methodology in moral reasoning has taken shape in biomedical ethics. Because the ongoing conversion in methodological allegiance, from an applied ethics model to contextualism, has typically been conditioned by the experience of working in the field of bioethics, it is important to consider the history that gave rise to what I will call its "paradigm theory." I provide a narrative sketch of this history in section I, touching as I go on such topics as moral expertise and the conflict over biomedical ethics vs clinical ethics. Part II offers a critical account of the main complaints against the methodology of the paradigm theory. Following a discussion of wide reflective equilibrium, I place special emphasis on the importance of interpretation and comparative case analysis in actual moral reasoning. It is the interconnected force of these operations, in real, practical decision-making, that subverts the applied ethics model in general, and the paradigm theory in particular; or so I claim.

I Relevant History

As the familiar story goes, the field of bioethics arose and developed over the last twenty years mainly in response to the moral crisis created by technology. In the years between the close of World War II and the early 1970s the power and potential of medical science expanded exponentially. Key elements of this radical alteration in the powers and the realistic possibilities of medicine include the development of antibiotics; the introduction of the birth control pill; the discovery of powerful psychotropic drugs; new resuscitative and life supportive techniques, such as artificial respiration and dialysis; organ transplantation, including the current prospect of cross-species transplantation; novel reproductive procedures; and the possibility of direct manipulation of the human genome.

These technologies have created situations of choice in the face of which traditional values and principles have been inadequate. A classic illustration relates to the Karen Quinlan case. (This famous case occurred in New Jersey in 1976 and involved the question whether Karen's father could legitimately decide, on Karen's behalf, to have an artificial respirator removed. Karen's parents believed that her life was being artificially sustained beyond all prospects of her deriving any meaning from life.) Through the influence of Christianity, the ancient commitment of medicine to the primacy of patient welfare came to be understood to involve the idea of the sanctity of each individual life. For centuries this idea, or principle, of the sanctity of life was taken, broadly, to require that doctors make every effort to preserve the life of every patient. Ironically, as we can see in retrospect, this worked reasonably well only so long as there were fairly fixed limits to what doctors were actually able to do. The Quinlan case, and others like it, forced upon us the difficult issue of the quality of the life that is preserved, as distinct from its mere biological extension. Ensuing debate has eventually led to a reinterpretation of the sanctity of life principle, requiring not the provision of every treatment that might prolong life, but the provision only of treatments that genuinely serve the patient's best interests.

Besides the rapid growth of medical technology – itself promoted by massive infusions of government monies made possible by the general economic prosperity of the period – there were other important factors influencing the emergence of bioethics. New conceptions of social justice that developed as part of the dominant political ideology of the liberal welfare state also played a role. The power of medicine would provide the means for realizing a much higher standard of human well-being; and liberal ideals of entitlement would legitimize a broad extension of these benefits through the operations of the state. Beyond this, there was, in those days, a pervasive sense of moral liberation. A new moral order was in the making, one that would free individual choice from outmoded and dysfunctional social restrictions and psychological repressions. Many movements and enthusiasms of the time manifest this spirit, such as the free speech movement and the so-called sexual revolution. Certainly the general emphasis on personal freedom and human rights, as exemplified in the civil rights movement and the women's movement, exerted a powerful influence on the direction and emphasis of bioethics in its formative phase.

Hare's Hope and Moral Expertise

Much of the literature surrounding the development of bioethics reveals a fairly common conception of medical ethics as a form of *applied ethics*, to which philosophy can make a special and significant contribution. Speaking at a major conference on Medical Ethics and Philosophy in 1975, Richard Hare boldly expressed this view:

> I should like to say at once that if the moral philosopher *cannot* help with the problems of medical ethics, he ought to shut up shop. The problems of medical ethics are so typical of the moral problems that moral philosophy is supposed to be able to help with, that a failure here would be a sign either of the uselessness of the discipline or of the incompetence of the particular practitioner. (Hare 1977, p. 49)

Hare went on to insist, in the fashion of the times, that the philosopher's contribution is technical and morally neutral, centered in methods of conceptual analysis and the assessment of argument, rather than in any special moral insight or wisdom. Moral philosophy provides rigorous training in classical theories of ethics and in the logic of moral discourse and reasoning. The knowledge and analytical skills thus developed can help to order our understanding of practical issues and to overcome various confusions and fallacies. About the results of this, in relation to the moral problems in medicine, Hare is optimistic: "It is my belief that, once the issues are thoroughly clarified in this way, the problems will not seem so perplexing as they did at first and, the philosophical difficulties having been removed, we can get on with discussing the practical difficulties" (Hare 1977, p. 52). Reference to systematic understanding and analytic technique has prevailed as the standard kind of account of the special contribution that philosophy can make in its interaction with the medical profession and its moral quandaries. In a 1982 issue of the *Hastings Centre Report*, Cheryl Noble offers a rather scattered and, in my opinion, a confused critique of philosophy's role, or pretensions, in applied ethics (Noble 1982, pp. 7–9). Noble's principal complaint against philosophy's claim to have some special competence to offer in the world of practice seems to be that the philosophers' concern with method and argument is indifferent to history, sociology, and psychology and that this inevitably produces a kind of moral criticism that is conventional, comfortable, and tame.

What is of interest here, however, is the nature of the responses to Noble's article contained in the same journal issue. There are four respondents: one physician, Jerry Avorn, and three philosophers, Peter Singer, Daniel Wikler, and Tom Beauchamp. All four respondents stress the power of philosophy in clarifying our thinking about moral issues through the analysis of important concepts and by organizing and rectifying arguments and points of view. Beauchamp's view is typical. He forcefully rejects the idea that the resolution of moral problems is in any way the special province of philosophy. Rather, philosophy can contribute to moral decision-making in four ways, ways that are characteristic of philosophy though not unique to it. First, philosophers can straighten out needlessly tangled disputes by making appropriate distinctions and by analyzing concepts. Secondly, they can expose inconsistencies, inadequacies, and unacceptable or unexpected consequences of various arguments and positions. Thirdly, working with professionals and researchers from other fields, on joint projects or commissions for example, they can contribute to the evaluation and development of policy and thus assist in institutional reform. And, fourthly, by participating within certain institutional settings, such as hospitals or particular government agencies, philosophers "can assist in various ways with policy decisions" and the resolutions of particular cases (Beauchamp 1982, p. 14).

Of the four respondents to Noble, only Peter Singer goes so far as to suggest that philosophers may typically have a certain advantage in actually resolving or settling moral problems. He does not say exactly this, instead commenting that he sees "four advantages that moral philosophers may have over others when it comes to *discussing* difficult moral issues" (my italics). But he goes on to disavow any suggestion "that *only* philosophers are capable of settling moral problems" (my italics), which implies that philosophers, at least sometimes, are capable of this (Singer 1982, p. 10). And, of course, he repudiates Noble's insinuation that philosophers want to have moral problems of all kinds handed over to them as the appropriate experts in applied ethics.

Singer's attitude concerning the advantages of moral philosophy is probably the most honest and, in any case, it can seem fairly plausible. For suppose, merely, that there are often better and worse answers to important moral problems, even if there are seldom uniquely correct answers. This difference among answers to moral questions must be a function of differences in adequacy and sensitivity in factual understanding, together with differences in quality and depth of reasoning and justification. Suppose further that training in philosophy does advance powers of analysis and clarification, and that it increases skill in moral reasoning and argument. This is the main burden of Singer's claims for the prolonged study of moral philosophy. If we now add Singer's final point, that the philosopher has the time to study and ponder practical issues in depth, drawing on the researches and considered positions of others, why should we not conclude that there is, in general, an increased likelihood of "better answers" to moral issues when philosophy is consulted? In fact, to deny this, at this point, would seem to imply that conceptual clarity, power in reasoning, and familiarity with our moral traditions are of no particular value in moral affairs. Rather than simple denial, better to emphasize that it is the *skills* in question that are the important thing and that not only philosophers can acquire them. But beyond this, there is the larger possibility, which lies further down our path, that philosophy has radically misconceived the real nature of moral reasoning and justification, with consequent distortions of its own powers.

Even accepting Singer's point, however, its effect may be very modest. It is consistent with the possibility that on many, or most, or all difficult and complex moral issues, factual understanding together with philosophical analysis and moral argument, carried to a practical limit – and perhaps even to a theoretical limit – can at best only partially reduce the range of what survives as defensible or justifiable moral options. Within this range we would be left with no decision procedure, except that of personal commitment or individual conscience.

The Rise of the Paradigm Theory

What actually occurred, in the early interaction of moral philosophy with clinical medicine, was a result that was often *felt* by participants to have exactly the structure of the situation just described. Richard Zaner provides an instructive summary history of the various strains and difficulties, rooted often in misapprehension and professional defensiveness, that frequently attended efforts at interdisciplinary cooperation in bioethics (Zaner 1988, ch. 1). But beyond all this, and even as these tensions were overcome, the figure of the ethicist as "moral options broker" began to emerge. As we have seen, philosophers and other ethicists were at pains to represent themselves, in their dealings with doctors and nurses, as other professionals with their own particular brand of expertise to offer – powers of conceptual analysis, clarification of argument, and theoretical organization. But our traditions of moral theory, after all, are various, divided, and extremely abstract. It was therefore typical of these early interprofessional encounters that, after problematic cases were trotted out, initial positions taken, facts and values clarified, and positions rectified and systematized, everyone tended to wind up with more elaborate versions of the views they had started with. Optimism like Hare's, that with philosophical clarification the problems would not seem so perplexing, rapidly faded. The frustrations of this sort of situation were remarked by Alasdair MacIntyre:

> It is, I believe, a common experience for doctors, nurses, and others to become very excited when discussion of these problems is first opened up and past silences are broken. There follows a short period of increasing clarity during which disagreements and divisions are formulated. And then nothing or almost nothing. Where everyone had hoped to move towards a constructive resolution of these disagreements, instead they find themselves merely restating them. (MacIntyre 1977, p. 197)

It was in these circumstances, then, that the role of the ethicist in the clinical setting acquired the form of a "moral options broker" who functioned to clarify alternative positions and relate them to central aspects of moral theory.

As these developments took place in the early encounter between ethicists and clinicians, theory construction aimed at medicine and its problems was underway in a variety of forms and venues. Bioethics became a growth industry. Professional journals representing the field multiplied, books poured forth, conferences abounded, centres and institutes were created, usually in support of interdisciplinary work in the field, and government commissions and research groups were formed. By the late 1970s there emerged from this concentration of activity a mainline philosophical theory of biomedical ethics. This theory has by now achieved the status of a standard or genuine paradigm of the field. I am referring to the familiar theory that comprises three main principles, those of autonomy, beneficence (including non-maleficence), and justice.

In 1979 two members of the Kennedy Institute of Ethics, Tom Beauchamp and James Childress, published their seminal work, *Principles of Bioethics*, which is a thorough and systematic development of this theory (Beauchamp and Childress 1979). More synoptic presentations are the usual fare of introductory chapters in many of the most widely used anthologies in bioethics. An earlier expression of the same set of basic principles appears in the Belmont Report, commissioned as a study of the protection of human subjects of research (Belmont Report 1978, p. 4). And The President's Commission for the Study of Ethical Problems in Medicine and Biomedical and Behavioral Research gave central place to these principles in its several influential publications appearing between 1980 and 1983 (President's Commission 1983a, b).

The paradigm theory of bioethics is, of course, articulated and filled out by giving extensive explanations of its basic principles; by making connections with subsidiary principles, or rules, such as those of informed consent, truth-telling, and confidentiality; and by drawing distinctions that are crucial in applying the theory, such as between active and passive euthanasia and the like. That this paradigm theory has, for almost ten years, dominated the field of bioethics cannot be doubted. Nor should it be denied that general assent to it was won mainly because the theory provides the basic framework for a coherent perspective on virtually the whole range of moral issues in medicine. General acceptance of this theoretical framework brought with it a sense of unification and definition for a disparate and adolescent field struggling to identify itself. And this unification of theoretical vision and moral vocabulary served to gain credibility and legitimacy for the field as a whole. But the ascendancy of this theoretical model has still deeper sources in an ideal of comprehensive moral understanding, and in its promise of overcoming the impasse of undecidability that was bedeviling the encounter between philosopher and physician at the clinic.

The Theory of Applied Ethics

As is already suggested in the foregoing, the basic philosophical idea of applied ethics has been that it is continuous with general ethical theory. Biomedical ethics is not a special kind of ethics; it does not include any special principles or methods that are specific to the field of medicine and not derivable from more general considerations. The practical field of medicine is governed by the same general normative principles and rules as hold good in other spheres of human life. If there are any special prerogatives, or requirements of a moral kind that go with the practice of medicine, these will be explained and justified from the perspective of general moral theory. In their introduction to *Principles of Biomedical Ethics*, Beauchamp and Childress declare themselves as follows: "We understand 'biomedical ethics' as one type of *applied ethics* – the application of general ethical theories, principles and rules to problems of therapeutic practice, health care delivery, medical and biological research" (Beauchamp and Childress 1983, p. x). The holy grail of moral philosophy is a single, comprehensive, and coherent theory that is based in universal, basic principles, which, in their turn, yield more particular principles and rules that are capable of deciding concrete issues of practice. Accordingly, the ideal of moral justification is essentially deductivist, involving different levels of generalization. One justifies a particular judgment by showing that it falls under a rule, and the rule by showing that it is a specification of a principle, and the principle by showing that it is grounded in the most abstract levels of normative theory.

Shifting from ideal to reality, recall the impasse at the clinic. The problem was that the logical chasm between the abstractions of normative theory – principally utilitarianism and Kantianism – and the complexities of actual situations left the ethicist with nothing to do but "broker" moral options defined in relation to this or that theory. But as John Arras remarks, the discovery that a Kantian would do this, a Millian that, and a Rawlsian something else was not terribly helpful for those who had to make a decision without the leisure to sort out where they stood in these debates (Arras 1986, p. 18). The paradigm theory offered the prospect of rescuing this situation by bridging the logical space between abstract theory and the world of particulars. On the one hand, the combination of its three mid-level principles appears to provide enough substance to guide practice. On the other hand, it keeps faith with the ideal of comprehensive justification because each of its principles is linked with one or another of our central traditions in normative theory. The principle of autonomy, for example, is an expression of the rights and dignity of the person that forms the foundation of Kantianism and modern forms of deontological theory generally. The principle of beneficence, obviously, has its heritage in classical utilitarianism. And the principle of justice is most naturally connected with contractarian traditions in moral theory. The faith that is thus kept with normative theory is, of course, not perfect. The paradigm theory draws upon very different and conflicting forms of general theory. But each of these traditions is centuries-old and vital today; each, therefore, is likely to have some share of the truth. So the question of the *ultimate* derivation of the paradigm theory's three principles can be left to future resolutions and reconciliations of normative theory, following perhaps upon further developments in meta-ethics.

Two Ironies

Work in bioethics has constituted an important instrument of change in medicine, law, and social attitudes. For example, bioethics has contributed to the reduction of traditional forms of paternalism in medicine, to a general strengthening of the rights of patients and research subjects, and to improved conceptions of the appropriate use of medical technology and of the proper goals of medicine. Having assumed the status of a paradigm of bioethics, particularly after validation by the President's Commission, the standard theory stands today as a powerful counterpoint to the precious conceit of the *ancien régime* that "philosophy boils no cabbages."

As bioethics has grown and developed in form and influence the predominance of theoreticians in the field has led to a backlash from certain quarters in medicine. This stems from the concern of some physicians that bioethics is essentially a theoretical and intellectual discipline and that too many of its representatives have too little knowledge or appreciation of actual clinical work. There is the feeling, moreover, that only the physician is in a position to really understand and address moral problems in medicine. Mark Siegler is a principal advocate of this view (Siegler 1979). He believes that, because the physician is the one who must actually decide moral issues in medical practice, and who must be accountable for these decisions, physicians must become immersed in *clinical ethics* as opposed to biomedical ethics. Clinical ethics will be dominated by people from the medical scientific community, its main activities will be centred in the clinic and its counsels will be informed by the realities of actual professional practice.

Zaner reports at some length on the results of these efforts by Siegler and others to replace the standard theory with a more clinically informed style of moral reasoning. What one finds, according to Zaner, is an increase in clinical detail, a decrease in philosophical jargon, and final counsels or recommendations that are otherwise indistinguishable from what one would expect from "the biomedical ethics establishment" that has been criticized as too remote from actual practice (Zaner 1988, pp. 14–16). In short, these efforts to repudiate the standard model seem, in the end, to attest to its power. Zaner himself believes that this is because Siegler and his cohorts come at moral problems with essentially the same conception of the nature of ethics as the philosophers they criticize. The real problem lies in an inadequate and oversimplified conception of moral reasoning as the application of principles to concrete issues of practice.

There is another irony which one finds in the current practice of bioethics that is related to that of "clinical ethics" largely retaining what it attempts to repudiate. As mentioned in the introduction, increasing numbers of theoretically trained, philosophically minded bioethicists, who are actually working in the clinical setting, are becoming skeptical of the adequacy of the paradigm theory and, consequently, of the entire "applied ethics" model of moral reasoning. At the same time, because of its attractiveness and teachability, and because so many health care professionals by now have attended bioethics conferences, classes, workshops, and programs in which the paradigm theory reigns supreme, the skeptical bioethicist now confronts whole armies of converted clinicians. The skeptical bioethicist in the clinic is working and thinking along contextualist lines, while all around him or her there is heard nothing but invocations of autonomy, beneficence, and justice.

We turn, then, to a consideration of the main difficulties with the paradigm theory in bioethics and, more generally, to questions about the relation between ethical theory and moral practice.

II Theory and Practice

As we have seen, the paradigm theory of bioethics exemplifies the applied ethics model of moral reasoning oriented to the field of medicine. My principal concern in this part of the paper is the methodological conflict between this model and contextualism. However, before turning in this direction, we should for completeness' sake consider the prior question of the moral scope of the paradigm theory.

Scope and Content

The essential content of the paradigm theory is made up of its three basic principles concerning autonomy, beneficence, and justice. But to whom, exactly, do these principles apply, and on what basis? This is the question of scope. It is a request for some account of what constitutes moral status, of what gives something this sort of standing. Unfortunately, the paradigm theory in bioethics is silent on the question of moral standing itself – what must something be like in order to qualify as a subject of serious moral concern in its own right? The abortion issue, for instance, has tended to formulate the question of fetal moral status as the question whether a fetus has a right to life. And perhaps it has been the abortion issue, more than any other, that has dramatized the need for a general account of the conditions for moral standing. But the general issue itself has, by now, cropped up all over the field of bioethics: in connection, for example, with the use of anencephalic babies as organ donors; in regard to the therapeutic transfer of fetal tissue; in respect of research with embryos and their use in some of the new reproductive technologies; and in the treatment of the most severely impaired infants and adults. We should note, also, that moral status, as a fundamental issue, has become a dominant preoccupation of the developing field of environmental ethics.

This omission is a serious limitation of the standard theory. It means that the theory is more or less useless in those many areas of bioethical decision-making where the crucial issue precisely is that of moral status. Although this point is obvious, it is nonetheless important to remind ourselves how critically dependent the standard theory is on some supplementary account of moral standing. Our philosophical heritage, moreover, is not particularly helpful on this matter. Anything one is able to infer about moral status from our central traditions in moral theory seems either to be too restrictive, as is the case with Kant, or too vague and indeterminate to guide the discriminations that are called for today.

Wide Reflective Equilibrium

We come at last to issues of method. A common charge against the paradigm theory of bioethics is that, even though it is an improvement over straight Kantianism or utilitarianism, its principles are still too abstract to yield definite results. Moral reasoning, even when one is directly seeking principled solutions, is simply not a matter of applying principles in any straightforward way. The whole deductivist approach that characterizes the applied ethics model, and hence the paradigm theory, is simply too unidirectional and "top–down" in its basic conception. It does not take adequate account of the complexities of interplay between our understanding of practical issues and our understanding of principles.

This criticism of the paradigm theory may have had considerable validity in earlier phases of the history I sketched above. At this point, however, there are very few strict deductivists left in bioethics, and probably none at all who have had any experience with moral problems in clinical settings. In contrast to the unidirectional application of principles in a deductivist fashion, most current work in bioethics appears sensitive to the need for a Rawlsian kind of "reflective equilibrium" between principles and concrete judgments.[1] The method of wide reflective equilibrium (WRE) seeks coherence among three divisions of moral thought: our considered moral judgments, a set of principles designed to rationalize and order these judgments, and a set of relevant background theories or understandings about such things as human nature and psychology, the workings of the law and procedural justice, conditions for social stability and change, and the socio-economic structure of society (Daniels 1979).

The process of theory building can be said to begin with our most secure considered judgments, which may be either general or particular. Next we develop a set of principles which rationally orders and explains these judgments. This is the first criterion for judging the acceptability of a set of principles, their ability to bring the whole array of our considered judgments into coherent order. Secondly, principles must be judged against the general theories we hold about human psychology, social practicability, the functioning of various institutions, and so forth. This constraint, concerning fit with our background theoretical commitments, is especially important because it is this level of assessment that provides a check against the distortions of self-interest, class bias, and ideology. Equally important, there is no point of definitive, epistemological priority or foundationalism in wide reflective equilibrium theory. Principles may be modified or rejected under the pressure of considered moral judgments. Considered moral judgments remain open to revision under the pressure of theory-based principles. The most we ever achieve is "provisional fixed points" among our considered moral judgments (Daniels 1979, p. 267). The method consists, then, in a process of dialectical interchange between the three main elements of moral thought, adjusting and revising our considered judgments, our principles, and our background theories in an effort to achieve overall congruence or reflective equilibrium. As will become clear below, a critical implication of WRE for our purposes is that the principles of the paradigm theory can normatively override contextually derived considered moral judgment.

The Unbearable Lightness of Principle

Even including the sophistication of reflective equilibrium theory, the applied ethics model in bioethics remains open to the charge of being seriously mistaken. It can be said to leave out of account the very complex processes of *interpretation* that constitute our moral understanding both of cases and of principles.[2] Most importantly, within the complex realities of practice, it is dominantly the interpretation of cases that informs our understanding of principles rather than principles guiding the resolution of difficult cases. All or most of the real work in actual moral reasoning and decision making is case-driven rather than theory-driven. Therefore, the criticism would continue, the applied ethics model, even when amended by the methodology of reflective equilibrium, sustains the illusion that bioethics is essentially or primarily a matter of constructing and applying principles when in fact it is almost anything but this. I will attempt to develop this argument in the remainder of this section and the next one. Without any pretence of doing justice to this topic I will simply try to illustrate, in a variety of ways, how thoroughly the problems of interpretation dominate much of the work in bioethics.

Consider, then, the case of a 74-year-old woman with a cardiac condition residing in a retirement home. An avid baseball fan who has many friends, she enjoys a very full life. Having witnessed what has happened to one or two of her acquaintances who have been resuscitated following cardiac arrest – brain-damaged and surviving on machines – she makes it clear to her doctor that she does not want to be resuscitated if she suffers such an arrest. Suppose, now, that she experiences a fairly mild arrythmia and is consequently moved to the infirmary in order to try some different medications. Owing to an allergic reaction, a trial medication causes her heart to go into fibrillation and then full-scale arrest. We know that the adverse reaction to the drug can be reversed if she is resuscitated. Moreover, because the arrest was caused by the allergic reaction, and because the code team is immediately available, we shall say that her chances of a full recovery, following resuscitation, are about 75–80 percent. The downside, of course, is the still significant chance of a permanently weakened heart and brain damage – exactly what she most dreads.

The principle of autonomy bids us do what our patient would want for herself. But her desires have now become quite ambiguous. Did she have *this* sort of thing in mind? Would not a rational person want resuscitation with these odds, especially in light of the quality of the life that she will most likely recover? Or does none of this matter? In short, how are we to morally interpret this situation? Some of the most important recent work in bioethics has dealt with this matter of the interpretation of the particular case. Eric Cassell, for example, has focused extensively on the importance of an increased sensitivity to the language of the clinical encounter between physician and patient (Cassell 1985). A recognition of the need for interpretation, and of the subtleties involved in this, also helps explain the value of current programs in medical humanities that emphasize psychology and literary studies.

Beyond the particular case, there are also problems in interpreting *kinds* of cases, especially regarding novel issues that are generated by rapidly changing technology. As Arras says, in these areas of bioethical concern – such as the new reproductive techniques, the foregoing of life-sustaining treatments, and genetic engineering – moral progress often depends as much on fashioning the right understandings as on applying the right principles (Arras 1986, p. 29). For example, much of the debate over the morality of withdrawing food and fluid has stemmed from disagreement over how to interpret such action. Can such action avoid classification as intentional killing? Even if it can, is the usual comparison with the withdrawal of a respirator a proper or decisive comparison? What are we to make of the claim that there are institutionally important expressive and symbolic functions connected with providing food and fluid which require us to assess their value in terms that go beyond the benefit to an individual patient? (Winkler 1988, pp. 155–72).

Many writers in bioethics, perhaps even a strong majority, do not find anything seriously wrong with relatively early abortion. At various centers around the world research continues on the therapeutic use of fetal tissue transfers – infusions of brain cells to ameliorate certain nervous disorders like Parkinson's disease, and infusions of bone marrow cells to overcome various cancers, and so forth. Fetal tissues, in these instances, are obtained from elective abortions. The commercial value of fetal tissues, however, is definitely on the rise. There have already been rumours that some clinics in other parts of the world have offered payment to women for their aborted fetuses. Suppose that some women were to supplement their income by repeatedly taking advantage of this commercial opportunity. Most bioethicists, as well as most others, find this whole prospect extremely repugnant. Yet the abortions in question would occur quite early and the research efforts are not usually objected to as being offensive in themselves. So why is this enterprising behavior not to be seen as merely making an honest buck?

If the repugnance is to be rendered consistent with the attitudes that accommodate abortion and fetal tissue transfer *per se*, it will be hard to avoid the admission that there is *something* wrong with deliberately getting pregnant with the full intention of aborting the fetus. One cannot say, for example, that it is just the profit motive itself that makes it wrong, as if, like donating blood, everything would be fine if the woman was only wanting to get pregnant repeatedly so she could simply donate her fetuses. And, *ex hypothesi*, it is not wrong because of any wrongness that is inherent in the program for which the fetal tissues are destined. But, then, to repeat the same point in other words, if early abortion is itself morally weightless, hardly different from a form of birth control, then how can planned pregnancy with abortion for profit be a problem? How can it be even unseemly or indecent? After all, we do not normally object to people being paid for unobjectionable work.

I raise this issue, of course, not to take any stand on it but to illustrate the general problem of interpreting types of moral issue that confront us in bioethics. In the same vein, consider the following case. A woman with a 12-year-old diabetic daughter proposes to practitioners in fetal tissue transfer that she will get pregnant and abort the fetus so that islet cells from its pancreas can be used to correct her daughter's diabetes. Again, how are we to understand and interpret the moral dimensions of this case? Cases involving emotional ties of this kind usually elicit much more sympathy than planned abortion for profit. Also, there is often the clinical advantage in these cases of achieving an optimal tissue match. Nevertheless, most people object. Informing intuitions generally reflect a particular aversion to a calculated exploitation of nascent human life for someone else's benefit. The thought seems to be that it is one thing to take advantage of an unfortunate situation in which an abortion is going to be performed anyway, but quite another thing to plan for and create the life that is to be thus exploited. But what does "exploitation" even *mean* in this situation? Does it have primarily to do with misuse or victimization of the *particular* fetus or is it the more general idea of creating human life, in any form, simply to be used in this way?

We have just seen how much of the real work of bioethics centers on the interpretation of individual cases and kinds of cases. This work goes on with scant attention to principles or to processes of applying principles. We have to know what is going on and how to understand the moral dimensions of situations before we can intelligently relate cases to principles. But principles do not interpret themselves either. Often our problem is precisely one of trying to figure out exactly what some abstract formulation of principle might mean in a given situation. And it is a significant fact that, within actual processes of moral reasoning concerning genuine problems, it is more often that the resolution of case analysis informs our understanding of principles than that principles serve in the resolution of cases. It is largely from a close comparison of relevant cases that we discover, or invent, more determinate meanings for the often conflicting values and principles which merely give situated moral problems their basic shape.

We can exemplify this important point more fully by considering another case. A man with multiple sclerosis is admitted to the hospital for treatment of spinal meningitis with a bacterial origin. His past history indicates a very satisfactory adjustment to MS. He has taken an active part in family life, he has had various interests, hobbies, and so forth. Despite all of this, and despite the fact that his MS has not worsened, the man refuses antibiotic therapy to treat his meningitis, saying only that he wants to be left alone and allowed to die with dignity. Suppose consultation with the family reveals that the patient has been very withdrawn and depressed lately. It is also learned that the patient has been deprived for some time of the usual attentions and support of other family members because of a prolonged crisis elsewhere in the family. More evidence of the same kind makes it fairly probable that the patient's decision is a product of a sense of self-pity and worthlessness accompanying feelings of isolation and depression. Physicians explain to the patient what they think is happening with him, they inform him decisively that they intend to give him antibiotics to save his life and that family counseling will be provided in due course. The patient is silent. Antibiotics are administered, the man recovers completely, counseling reveals to the family the importance of this patients' being informed and involved in family affairs, and everything turns out fine.

What of the principle of autonomy? It was, in fact, cases of this kind that persuaded many people in bioethics that the conditions for the kind of autonomous choice that must be respected in medicine are more complex than they had realized. Particularly when the stakes are high, it is not enough merely to be competent and rational in a legal sense. It can also be critical whether the choice is *authentic*, in the sense of being consonant with one's own most important values and commitments (Miller 1981, pp. 22–8). We are all liable to make distorted, uncharacteristic, and inauthentic decisions under the strain of severe depression, fear, or grief. As a kind of insurance against this liability, therefore, we all benefit from an interpretation of autonomy that includes something like an authenticity condition, especially within an institutional setting like that of medicine. The very nature of serious illness accentuates the liability in question, and the seriousness of the circumstances make the cost of honoring inauthenticity very high. Whether one agrees with this sketch of an argument or not, the pattern of reasoning, which has in fact been very influential, illustrates the way in which moral interpretation of cases informs the understanding of principles rather than principles determining the morality of cases.

But can we now go confidently forth with applications of the principle of autonomy under this new, more complex understanding of its essential force in the clinical setting? We cannot. I recently became aware of a case concerning a patient who is paraplegic as a result of a motorcycle accident.

The psychological dimensions of this case are endlessly complicated, but, on the patient's part, turn critically on a deep, pervasive sense of victimization, coupled with extreme, generalized anger and resentment. After years in hospital, effectively refusing all rehabilitative programs, the patient's present condition makes discharge unthinkable. Most recently the patient has adamantly refused to eat, resisting all offers and efforts of help and counseling, while continually abusing health care staff. What makes this situation most disturbing is the way the patient's confused tendency to blame everyone and everything for his condition prevents him from genuinely "owning" and taking responsibility for his decision not to eat. Yet he is fully competent. Arguably, therefore, we confront here a thoroughly embittered and essentially *inauthentic* refusal of food, threatening the life of the patient. Yet everything indicates that attempting to force-feed this patient would be perfectly brutal and without foreseeable end. If force-feeding were attempted, the situation would likely be even worse than what Annas reports – and, in my judgment, rightfully condemns – about certain phases of a somewhat similar case in California, the Bouvia case (Annas 1984, pp. 20–2; 1986, pp. 24–5).

What are we to say now about our previous conclusions concerning the interpretation of autonomy in the clinical setting? What we have to realize, I think, is that it is not an insignificant feature of the former case that, even in the absence of consent and cooperation, it was possible to provide effective therapy, quickly and easily, and without great physical invasiveness or brutalization. Although it is not my purpose to pursue the point at length, I would argue, therefore, that we need to further revise our understanding of the principle of autonomy along the lines that are suggested by this comparison of cases.

Contrary to the applied ethics model of moral reasoning, an enormous amount of the real work in bioethics is composed of interpretation and the lateral comparison of cases. Even when principles do come into the picture they seem to come, so to speak, from the wrong direction relative to the applied ethics model. True, a developed sense of relatively fundamental values or principles may initially shape the moral contours of cases. Apart from this framing function, however, what we have found to be characteristic of bioethical reasoning so far is a "bottom–up" illumination of principle, through interpretive comparison of cases, rather than a "top–down" resolution of cases by principles.

It is, of course, perfectly consistent with wide reflective equilibrium theory that one should find considered moral judgment forcing modifications and adjustments in our commitments to principle. Nevertheless, what is damaging to WRE, and to the applied ethics model generally, is the apparent dominance and hegemony of case-driven methodology in the moral confrontation with real problems. Even so, it might be said, moral reasoning may still critically require the appeal to normative theory and general principle. A crucial question, therefore, is whether the methodological arrow decisively moves in the other direction as well. Put more sharply, to what extent does direct appeal to normative principle play a determining role in actual moral practice?

My remarks in the final section will bear on this question. Within the context of the present debate, this is not simply a matter of the relative frequency of inductive and deductive processes in moral reasoning. As has become clear in the foregoing, it is as much a question of the relative *importance* of these different movements in moral decision-making. Besides coming to grips with this issue, the last section will summarize and round out the entire argument of this paper.

Contextualism vs Applied Ethics

The dispute between defenders of the applied ethics model and contextualists is a disagreement over the essential nature of moral reasoning and justification. Important conclusions have already been reached about the greater sensitivity and realism of contextualism's general conception of the processes of actual moral practice. Our discussion of moral reasoning can be related to the issue of justification in the following terms.

Applied ethics, in the classical sense, views systematic, normative theory as aspiring to a rational reconstruction of the basic principles informing the whole of the moral life. Perfect justification, therefore, must ultimately be a matter of subsuming a particular case under a principle that either has, or shares, supreme normative scope and power. Naturally, compromise is necessary in practice, but the ideal of complete justification remains.

Contextualism, by contrast, is deeply skeptical about the possibility of any complete, universally valid ethical theory that is even remotely adequate to the moral life. This skepticism springs from the sense that the very idea of such a theory is inconsistent with the conception of morality as a social instrument, serving certain very general ends, within the context of real time, pervasive uncertainty, and continually evolving historical circumstance. In any case, this skepticism informs a far more realistic and limited account of justification. Contextualism holds that, in the real encounter with genuine moral problems, considered moral judgments are justified by defending themselves against objections and rivals. The process of justification is essentially continuous with the case-driven, inductive process of seeking the *most reasonable* solution to a problem, carried out within a framework of central cultural values and guiding norms, professional functions, obligations, and virtues, legal precepts, and so forth.

As discussed in section I, however, the applied ethics model has tended to accommodate itself to a less complete notion of justification than it projects as an ideal. In light of seemingly endless conflicts at the level of abstractive normative theory, and in light of the remoteness of such theory from practice, the applied ethics model hitches its wagon to mid-level theories, such as the paradigm theory in bioethics. Within bioethics, subsumption under its principles will go proxy for the kind of complete justification that will follow upon the hoped-for eventual working out of ultimate foundations. Nevertheless, as argued in the section on interpretation and general principle, the basic problems of uncertain relevance and abstraction remain acute even at this level of theory. The paradigm theory's most explicit principle is that of autonomy, yet we saw how this principle continues to undergo case-driven refinement and qualification. The principle of beneficence is, in itself, very vague, although it has received greater determinateness through subsidiary elaboration of principles employing the concept of "best interests." But again, for problematic cases, which still abound, one can never simply rely on the force and applicability of any current formulation of a "best interests" standard. Concerning the principle of justice matters are even worse, as the meaning of this principle remains mostly a mystery.

In consequence of these general difficulties with application, it becomes extremely difficult to conceive of realistic circumstances in which the principles of the paradigm theory could be supposed to have the morally decisive power, over contextually justified considered judgments, that the applied ethics model seems to require of them. In my judgment, even the refinements of WRE theory do not help the applied ethics model because reference to principle seems to have no tendency to override considered judgment in genuinely difficult moral situations. This is the essential thrust of our earlier reflections on the role of interpretation and comparative case analysis in actual moral reasoning in bioethics. Still, it might be said in defense of the applied ethics model, that all of this concentrates too exclusively on problematic and difficult cases. There are easy cases too; in sum total, indefinitely many more of them than hard cases. When we reach new refinements of principle these understandings must carry forward so as to yield moral guidance for many relevantly similar cases. Since such instances are numerous, moral reasoning involves a great deal of more or less deductive application of principle, in bioethics as elsewhere – just as the applied ethics model says it does.

Here we have to remind ourselves that what is at issue is the relative importance of inductive and deductive phases in moral reasoning, not their relative frequency. It is true, of course, that provisionally fixed understandings of principle will carry over so as to normatively determine relevantly similar cases. But it is equally true, and more relevant to the present debate, that the less obvious is the similarity in question the more analogical and interpretive reasoning must precede "application" – thus confirming contextualism's claim about what is most important. Alternatively, the more obvious is the similarity in question, the less important the new application of principle is for the purpose of understanding what moral reasoning is like in its interesting and progressive phases. Presumably, it is moral reasoning in its practically significant modes that we want to understand and accurately model. In any case, this is a guiding assumption of contextualism.

At this point, the applied ethics model can altogether retreat from its classical form, including its modifications in connection with the paradigm theory or the like, and rest content with a much weaker claim about the nature of principle in moral reasoning. The claim would be that, whatever their provenance and scope, and however their application is conditioned by inductive processes, principles in moral reasoning must be seen to have *normative force*. To better understand what this proposition means it will be helpful to consider it in direct contrast with a central claim of Jonson and Toulmin's "new casuistry" (Jonson 1986; Toulmin 1981; Jonson and Toulmin 1988).

Although sympathetic to much of Jonson and Toulmin's work, John Arras questions what may be the most distinctive aspect of their new casuistry, namely their novel account of the nature and function of moral principles. According to this account, just as common law legal principles are developed in and through judicial decisions concerning individual cases, so moral principles emerge gradually from reflection on particular cases. Moreover, the *meaning* of the principles which thus emerge is closely tied to the factual contexts forming the ground and need for the moral responses producing them. Accordingly, and most crucially, principles turn out to be nothing more than generalizations, or summaries of what we have decided so far within certain kinds of moral contexts or domains (Arras 1986, pp. 33–4, 41–5).

Arras rejects this understanding of principles on the grounds that it deprives them of any normative force and therefore deprives the casuistical method of any critical edge or reformative power. In short, it reduces the entire methodology to an elaborate working out of our varied, and sometimes mutually conflicting, intuitions about cases (Arras 1986, pp. 50–6). In order to effectively criticize moral judgments and practices, and in order to work toward collective uniformity among our judgments, moral principle must be capable of shaping and reforming our moral deliberations and judgments. I will close by commenting on the implications of this for contextualism.

Contextualism does not altogether deny the normative force of moral principle. In the first place, as we have seen, many situations of moral choice are clear and straightforward. We sometimes virtually "read off" from the situation the morally most reasonable thing to do. Here certain values or principles can be seen to apply normatively without difficulty or hesitation. Secondly, concerning the kind of cases that are methodologically interesting – the genuinely problematic cases – it will still be the tensional structure of values and principles that shape and contour the basic nature of the problem itself. This also reveals the normative force of principle.

Finally, after interpretation, comparative case analysis, further general reasoning about consequences, and so forth, have all done their work, and we come to rest in a reasonable, well-justified, considered judgment, we can always construct a deductive, or quasi-deductive, syllogism that derives our moral conclusion from the principle we then see it as upholding. Relative to such a construction, we will say that it is conformity with the major premise of the syllogism that *makes* the particular case, described in the minor premise, right or wrong. This gives the *reason* why it, and all relevantly similar cases, have the moral quality they have. In this same vein, we can say that conformity with the stated principle *explains* the morality of the case. On this basis we can say, if we like, that the relation between the principle and the facts of the case, revealed in the syllogism, *justifies* the moral conclusion. In fact, how can we resist saying any of these things? All this certainly upholds the normative force of moral principle. It is also easy to see, in outline anyway, how such provisional fixed points in the moral landscape (as justified considered judgment permits) could be interconnected in various ways, both inductive and deductive, to chart critically potent moral campaigns. This, too, is altogether consistent with contextualism.

All that contextualism need insist upon is our recognizing that, in the practical confrontation with real moral problems, the deductive construction of moral explanation and justification is irredeemably *ex post facto* and retrospective. In a far more important, essential, and primary sense, justification is a *process*. It is the process, in all its interpretive and analogical complexity, of arriving at a considered moral judgment and defending it as a fully reasonable alternative within the full context of the problem.

Leaving aside the question of the general conception of normative theory that lies behind it, the critical difficulties with the applied ethics model are twofold. In the final analysis, it tends to confuse the deductive explanatory pattern that is a product of difficult moral reasoning with the inductive process that is its essential method. And, to the extent that it acknowledges inductive processes in moral reasoning, it ignores their greater relative importance, over procedures of deductive application, in connection with moral progress.

A final disclaimer: my target in this paper has been the "applied ethics" model of moral reasoning and justification as defined herein. Certain appearances notwithstanding, it is no part of my view of things that moral philosophy or ethical theory is irrelevant or unimportant to moral practice. On the contrary, I believe that certain kinds of ethical theory make indispensable contributions to our understanding of morality and, more directly, to many of the practical resolutions that morality seeks. Although I have included some positive suggestions above, my account of these constructive functions of moral philosophy must wait for another occasion.[3]

NOTES

1 Rawls's original idea of reflective equilibrium in theory construction is further developed and defended by Norman Daniels (1979). My sketch of wide reflective equilibrium owes a lot to Daniels' article and to John Arras's discussion of the way this method is reflected in work in bioethics (see Arras 1986, pp. 21–6).
2 Arras also provides a discussion of the role of interpretation in moral reasoning. Although the basic points that I attempt to make here were fully worked out before I read his paper, my exposition of these points has benefited in several places from Arras's work and I indicate this in the text (see Arras 1986, pp. 227–32).
3 I want to thank my colleagues Howard Jackson, Peter Remnant, and Andrew Irvine for their help and critical advice in the final preparation of this paper.

REFERENCES

Annas, G., 1984, "When Suicide Prevention Becomes Brutality: The Case of Elizabeth Bouvia," *Hastings Center Report*, vol. 14, no. 2, pp. 20–2.
Annas, G., 1986, "Elizabeth Bouvia: Whose Space is this Anyway?" *Hastings Center Report*, vol. 16, no. 2, pp. 24–5.
Arras, J., 1986, "Methodology in Bio-ethics: Applied Ethics Versus the New Casuistry," paper presented at a conference on "Bioethics as an Intellectual Field," the Institute for The Medical Humanities, Galveston, Texas.
Beauchamp, T. L., 1982, "What Philosophers Can Offer," *Hastings Centre Report*, vol. 12, no. 3, pp. 13–14.
Beauchamp, T. L., and Childress, J. F., 1979 (2nd edn 1983), *Principles of Biomedical Ethics* (Oxford University Press, New York).
Belmont Report, 1978, The National Commission for the Protection of Human Subjects of Biomedical and Behavioral Research, *The Belmont Report: Ethical Principles and Guidelines for the Protection of Human Subjects of Research* (US Government Printing Office, Washington DC).
Cassell, E. J., 1985, *Talking With Patients* (MIT Press, Boston).
Daniels, N., 1979, "Wide Reflective Equilibrium and Theory Acceptance in Ethics," *Journal of Philosophy*, pp. 256–82.
Hare, R. M., 1977, "Medical Ethics: Can the Philosopher Help?" in Spicker, S. F., and Englehardt, H. T., eds, *Philosophical Medical Ethics: Its Nature and Significance* (D. Reidel, Boston), pp. 49–62.

Jonson, A., 1986, "Casuistry and Clinical Ethics," *Theoretical Medicine*, vol. 7, pp. 65–74.

Jonson, A., and Toulmin, S., 1988, *The Abuse of Casuistry* (University of California Press, Berkeley).

MacIntyre, A., 1977, "Patients as Agents," in Spicker, S. F., and Englehardt, H. T., eds, *Philosophical Medical Ethics: Its Nature and Significance* (D. Reidel, Boston), pp. 192–212.

Miller, B., 1981, "Autonomy and Refusing Life Saving Treatment," *Hastings Centre Report*, vol. 11, no. 4, pp. 22–8.

Noble, C., 1982, "Ethics and Experts," *Hastings Centre Report*, vol. 12, no. 3, pp. 7–9.

President's Commission, 1983a, President's Commission for the Study of Ethical Problems in Medicine and Biomedical and Behavioral Research, *Deciding to Forgo Life Sustaining Treatment: Ethical, Medical and Legal Issues in Treatment Decision* (US Government Printing Office, Washington DC).

President's Commission, President's Commission for the Study of Ethical Problems in Medicine and Biomedical and Behavioral Research, *Summing Up: Final Report on Studies of the Ethical and Legal Problems in Medicine and Behavioral Research* (US Government Printing Office, Washington DC).

Siegler, M., 1979, "Clinical Ethics and Clinical Medicine," *Archives of Internal Medicine*, vol. 139, pp. 914–15.

Singer, P., 1982, "How Do We Decide?" *Hastings Centre Report*, vol. 12, no. 3, pp. 9–10.

Toulmin, S., 1981, "The Tyranny of Principles," *Hastings Centre Report*, vol. 11, no. 6, pp. 31–9.

Winkler, E., 1988, "Forgoing Treatment: Killing vs Letting Die and the Issue of Non-Feeding," in J. Thornton and E. Winkler eds, *Ethics and Aging: The Right to Live, the Right to Die* (University of British Columbia Press, Vancouver).

Zaner, R. M., 1988, *Ethics and the Clinical Encounter* (Prentice-Hall, Englewood Cliffs).

20
Can Ethnography Save the Life of Medical Ethics?

Barry Hoffmaster

Since its inception, contemporary biomedical ethics has been seen by many of its practitioners to consist in the application of ethical theories to the moral problems that arise in health care. Hoffmaster opposes this "applied ethics" model of medical ethics in terms of both internal and external criticisms. Internal criticisms aim to show that this model cannot succeed in its own terms. Here Hoffmaster concentrates on the inevitable generality and vagueness of the central principles of the standard theory of medical ethics, which make application indeterminate; on the problem of conflict between principles in the absence of any method for resolution; and on the issue of moral standing itself. External criticisms point out the ways in which the applied ethics model fails to account for certain important aspects of morality, such as the phenomenon of moral change. He claims that the applied ethics model lacks the resources even to approach this and similar phenomena. Arguing for a shift away from theory-driven applied ethics, Hoffmaster turns to a subtle demonstration of how ethnographic studies can make important critical and constructive contributions to our understanding of morality. Critically, the results of ethnographic studies serve to further undermine the orthodox applied ethics approach; constructively, they reveal that morality must be understood contextually. This contextualized understanding requires ethicists to pay more attention to the psychological, institutional, and cultural aspects of the circumstances that generate and structure moral problems within medicine.

Hoffmaster's paper should be compared with those by Winkler (chapter 19), Sikora (chapter 5), Rachels (chapter 6), Keyserlingk (chapter 21), and Flyvbjerg (chapter 1).

A decade ago Stephen Toulmin published his now well-known article,

This paper appeared in *Social Science and Medicine*, vol. 35, no. 12, 1992, pp. 1421–31. It began as a presentation to the Medical Sociology Section of the American Sociological Association. Later versions were read to the Canadian Humanities Association and the Canadian Philosophical Association and at a conference on "Moral Philosophy in the Public Domain" sponsored by the University of British Columbia. I would like to thank all those who reacted to it on these occasions. I am particularly grateful for the comments I received from Valerie Alia, John Arras, Paula Chidwick, Peter Conrad, Sharon Kaufman, Judith Swazey, Michael Yeo, and anonymous referees for the Canadian Philosophical Association.

"How Medicine Saved the Life of Ethics," in which he claimed that renewed attention to moral problems in medicine had rejuvenated the moribund discipline of ethics.[1] Even if the correctness of Toulmin's analysis is granted, the salvaging of ethics by medicine has been short-lived because the patient has, regrettably, had a relapse. Two symptoms of the patient's critical condition have been recorded. First, Peterson, in reviewing a recent textbook in medical ethics, tellingly captures the barren-ness of its theoretical approach. He describes articles intended to impart an "understanding of underlying ethical principles" and "skill in critical analysis" as lacking "substance" and observes that the introductory section on ethical foundations is "insufficiently related to the rest of the book."[2] These defects do not reflect a lack of expertise or diligence on the part of the editors; rather, they are unavoidable because they are endemic to the prevailing "applied ethics" approach to moral problems in medicine.

Second, Baron has observed that "practising clinicians often feel let down by bioethics." The enchantment cast by exposure to the concepts and jargon of a new field has dissipated. Yet although the spell of the philosophical incantations has worn off, the problems that confront clin-icians stubbornly persist. Baron attributes the disappointment of clinicians in part to their own unrealistic expectations, but adds that it is also a function of

> the extent to which bioethics as a discipline doesn't seem to be in possession of the realities of practice. Bioethicists tend to leave the "facts" of clinical medicine to the doctors; their task is then to apply elegant and compelling arguments drawn from first principles of ethics . . . to these undisputed and indisputable facts. Unfortuantely, when the relationship between clinical medicine and bioethics is conceived . . . [in this way], the result is a very sterile discourse.[3]

The culprit here, too, is the regnant conception of medical ethics as applied moral philosophy. In moral philosophy factual matters are prescinded in favor of constructing rational defenses of general principles and organizing these principles into a consistent theoretical system. The assumption behind the view that medical ethics is applied ethics is that the resulting moral system can yield determinate solutions for real moral problems. The failure of this assumption is largely responsible for the parlous state of orthodox medical ethics.

The uncritical manner in which applied ethics has been adopted as *the* way of approaching moral problems in medicine and the emerging discomfiture with applied ethics reflect an underlying ambivalence about the function of moral philosophy. On one side is the view that moral philosophy should have something productive to say about actual moral

issues. Sidgwick, for example, held the aim of a moral philosopher to be .
"to do somewhat more than define and formulate the common moral
opinions of mankind. His function is to tell men what they ought to think,
rather than what they do think."[4] Confidence that moral philosophy can
in fact provide this kind of practical direction animates the enterprise of
applied ethics.

On the other side, though, are those who do not see practical guidance
as a proper task for moral philosophy. Why, it can be asked, should moral
philosophy be different from any other branch of philosophy? Epistemology
does not tell us which of our particular beliefs are true and justified;
aesthetics does not tell us how to paint a beautiful landscape;[5] and philosophy of science does not discover new laws of physics. Why, then, should
moral philosophy be unique in having putative practical import?

A number of philosophers explicitly disclaim any such function for moral
theory. Broad, for example, says: "We can no more learn to act rightly
by appealing to the ethical theory of right action than we can play golf
well by appealing to the mathematical theory of the flight of the golf-ball.
The interest of ethics is . . . almost wholly theoretical, as is the interest
of the mathematical theory of golf or of billards."[6] Bradley describes as
"a strangely erroneous preconception" the view that moral philosophy can
answer the question, "How do I get to know in particular what is right
and wrong?" In Bradley's view, "there cannot be a moral philosophy which
will tell us what in particular we are to do, and . . . it is not the business
of philosophy to do so. All philosophy has to do is 'to understand what
is,' and moral philosophy has to understand morals which exist, not to
make them or give directions for making them."[7] G. E. Moore agrees:
"The direct object of Ethics is knowledge and not practice."[8] The weight
of philosophical opinion, if anything, seems to be against regarding moral
theory as a source or repository of practical directives.[9] But why is it that
providing practical guidance is not a proper task for moral philosophy?

Problems with Applied Ethics

Before enumerating its shortcomings, what is meant by "applied ethics"
needs to be clarified. The object of these criticisms is not applied ethics
when that term is used in a catch-all way to refer to activities such as
ethics rounds and consultations, the workings of ethics committees, and
policy formation with respect to moral issues in health care such as the
development of guidelines for "do not resuscitate" orders. The target is
not, in other words, all the morally charged activities that occur on. the
front lines of health care delivery. Rather, the target is "applied ethics"

in the sense of a philosophically based and motivated theory about how that front-line activity ought to be analyzed and conducted and how medical ethics ought to be taught. Yet to put it this way is misleading, because it makes it appear as if there is a gulf between the practice of applied ethics and the theory of applied ethics, and it suggests that only the theory of applied ethics is awry.[10] The real culprit, however, is a philosophical approach that creates and sustains the impression that moral theory and moral practice are discrete.

An additional qualification is necessary. Work described as applied ethics is not homogeneous in nature or quality. Many philosophers have made valuable contributions to our understanding of practical moral problems in health care as well as to the moral improvement of front-line activities in the delivery of health care. Those contributions are the result of highly nuanced, particularized analyses of cases and problems and an appreciation of the settings in which these cases and problems arise. So it is important to recognize that not everyone who does medical ethics adopts an applied ethics approach and, indeed, that there has been a gradual, but progressive shift away from an applied ethics model. Yet a more situational, contextual approach has not yet displaced the theory-driven conception of what medical ethics is and, more importantly, of how medical ethics is taught. Nor has it yet made medical ethics a more hospitable venue for social scientists. The criticisms that follow consequently should not be construed as an indiscriminate exercise in "bioethics bashing." But the movement away from a theory-driven approach to medical ethics needs a further push, one that opens the field to contributions from an even broader array of disciplines.

There are two kinds of criticism that can be levelled against "applied" moral philosophy – internal criticism and external criticism. Internal criticism aims to show that a moral theory cannot succeed on its own terms.[11] External criticism points out that a moral theory cannot account for the phenomena of morality. Several familiar internal criticisms will be presented briefly before turning to external criticisms.[12]

First of all, the principles standardly regarded as constituting the core of theoretical medical ethics – principles of autonomy, beneficence, nonmaleficence, and justice, for example[13] – are too general and vague to apply determinately to concrete situations. In any moral controversy the question of whether, and, if so, how, a principle is to be brought to bear upon that dispute is itself contentious. As Frohock observes in his study of treatment decisions in neonatal intensive care units: "The cases themselves – their complexity, the severity of the problems – allow reasonable people to apply the same principles in different ways. This discretionary power, rather than disagreement on principle, is the main source of disputes over therapy in the gray zone . . . of treatment."[14] The substantive moral work occurs in determining how a principle might impinge upon a particular problem, but the resources for addressing that issue are external to the principles themselves.

Disparity between the abstract semantic formulations of principles and the particular empirical circumstances they supposedly govern is a consequence of the inherently general nature of language.[15] One manifestation of this disparity is the existence of "essentially contested" concepts, that is, concepts "the proper use of which inevitably involves endless disputes about their proper uses on the part of their users."[16] Applied ethics might be rescued if it had some way of dealing with the "essentially contested" concepts at its core, such as the notion of autonomy, but all it has to offer in this regard is the technique of conceptual analysis. Analysis can distinguish a number of different senses that a concept can have, and by exposing ambiguity and equivocation it can make an important, albeit limited, contribution to practical morality. It cannot, however, resolve substantive issues because it cannot establish that one of these senses is what the concept "really" means. In other words, although conceptual analysis can elevate a concept from the status of being "radically confused" to the status of being "essentially contested,"[17] it cannot go on to resolve the dispute in which that concept figures.

Take, for example, the controversy about whether a market in transplantable human tissues and organs should be permitted. Are bodily tissues and organs the kinds of things that can be owned and therefore bought and sold? Honoré, a legal commentator, points out that an analysis of the concept of "things" is, in general, an inviting strategy for trying to decide questions of ownership: "There is, clearly, a close connexion between the idea of ownership and the idea of things owned, as is shown by the use of word such as 'property' to designate both. We ought, apparently, to be able to throw some light on ownership by investigating 'things'."[18] This strategy is ultimately fruitless, though, as Honoré recognizes, because what lies behind the doctrine that one does not own one's body is not a more perspicuous understanding of what "thing" means but a substantive moral judgment: "It has been thought undesirable that a person should alienate his body, skill or reputation, as this would be to interfere with human freedom." And, as Honoré also recognizes, conceptual analysis can neither produce nor defend such substantive judgments: "It is clear that to stare at the meaning of the word 'thing' will not tell us which protected interests are conceived in terms of ownership."[19]

Now, it might be objected that this example undermines a critique of applied ethics because Honoré's judgment about no ownership of the body rests on an appeal to human freedom, and that is simply to invoke one of the bedrock principles of applied ethics, namely, the principle of autonomy. But rather than undermining the critique, the example strengthens it because autonomy is itself an "essentially contested" concept. Four senses of autonomy have been distinguished in medical ethics: autonomy as free action, autonomy as authenticity, autonomy as effective deliberation, and autonomy as moral reflection.[20] Given the complexity of the concept, how does one decide which senses are appropriate in given situations? Suppose that a patient's decision to refuse life-saving treatment is autonomous in two of the senses – it is, say, free and the result of effective deliberation – but not autonomous in the senses of being authentic and the product of moral reflection. What conclusion follows about whether the patient's decision should be respected? The answer to that question must turn on an assessment of underlying substantive considerations, not further refinement of the concept of autonomy.

Another internal difficulty with applied ethics is that a multiplicity of principles are taken to be relevant to moral problems in medicine, but when two or more of these principles conflict, as they inevitably do in any serious moral quandary, applied ethics offers no way of resolving the conflict. When the principle of autonomy is at odds with the principle of beneficence, say, how does one decide which principle prevails? Theoretical applied ethics contains no hierarchical ordering of its principles and no procedure for weighing or balancing these principles against one another. A standard response is to retreat to even more rarefied theoretical air and contend that moral theories, such as utilitarianism or Kantianism, should be invoked when principles "run out." But even if such theories could provide determinate outcomes for moral problems, the same difficulty emerges at this level. When "doing the greatest good for the greatest number" conflicts with "not treating persons as means alone," how does one decide which theory prevails? Moral philosophy has yet to produce an accepted way of appraising rival moral theories.[21]

A third internal difficulty is that applied ethics is not helpful in addressing some crucial moral issues because these issues challenge assumptions upon which the theoretical edifice of applied ethics is erected. Perhaps the most obvious examples are debates about the domain of morality. What moral status, and therefore what moral protection, do entities such as fetuses, anencephalic infants, animals, and the environment have?[22] The fundamentally rationalistic program of philosophical ethics embodies an answer to this question, namely, that morality protects all and only those beings capable of acting as rational agents, which in turn means all and only those beings capable of rational deliberation. This answer is not obviously correct, however. In response to a question about what makes life worth living, for example, one neonatologist interviewed by Frohock cites simply the ability of a child to smile at his or her parents.[23] Thus the rationalist position needs to be defended; but there is a problem here, because whatever practical bite moral philosophy has in this regard is inadvertent – it is the result of how the overall project of doing moral philosophy proceeds, not of attending to the particular moral controversy in question. Inadvertent answers are not, of course, necessarily wrong, but their relevance needs to be established and their plausibility needs to be supported. Yet moral philosophy seems to have no way of mounting such a defense on its own terms. Because the rationalist answer emerges from the assumptions that ground moral theory, any attempt to defend it in terms of that theory would be circular. Some of the most troublesome questions in medical ethics consequently remain "up for grabs" within the program of rationalist moral philosophy.

Turning to the external criticisms, there are a number of respects in which moral theory is blind to actual moral phenomena. To begin, applied ethics does not appreciate the dynamic character of morality. Because applied ethics takes morality to be an autonomous theoretical system under which the flotsam of human experience is subsumed, it cannot account for the flux in that experience. It therefore cannot answer three questions that are central to our understanding of morality: why only certain issues come to be recognized as moral problems; how moral problems get categorized or labeled; and how and why moral change occurs.

With respect to the first, why, for example, is *in vitro* fertilization a hot moral topic but not expensive microsurgery to reconstruct Fallopian tubes? How is it that some issues but not others come to be dubbed "moral," and what is the upshot of conferring this appellation upon them? Inattention to this matter contributes to the almost indiscriminate way in which the rubric of morality is now being used. Fox has noted "a certain inflation in the public and professional notice being given to bioethical questions," which has produced "a kind of 'everything is ethics' syndrome."[24] But when everything becomes ethics, the danger is that ethics becomes nothing.

Second, how is the phenomenon of moral labeling to be understood? The new reproductive technologies, for instance, can be regarded as either therapies for infertility or alternative means of reproduction, and those labels are not neutral because they carry different implications for who should have access to these technologies. Similarly, medically administered hydration and nutrition can be categorized as either basic human care or medical treatment, with different ramifications for the obligatoriness of providing artificial sustenance.[25] But how is the appropriateness of such labels ascertained?

Finally, what induces and precipitates moral change? The salient moral issues of today are different from those of a decade ago, let alone a century ago. Applied ethics nevertheless remains impervious to moral change; it will deal with whatever moral problems are brought before it, assuming that the identification and characterization of moral problems themselves raise no difficulties and that moral problems can be dealt with independently of the contexts in which they arise. Yet what issues become "moral," and how and when they do so, are vitally important questions. Disputes about the moral status of infants and animals, for example, are not new. To cite only one instance, consider Whewell's reaction in 1852 to Bentham's hedonistic theory of value:

> I say nothing further of Mr Bentham's assumption . . . that because a child cannot *yet* take care of itself, and cannot converse with us, its pleasures are therefore of no more import to the moralist than those of a kitten or a puppy. We hold that there is a tie which binds together all human beings, quite different from that which binds them to cats and dogs;—and that a man, at any stage of his being, is to be treated according to his human capacity, not according to his mere animal condition.[26]

Now why is it that the animal rights movement, and the charge of species-ism against those who believe in "a tie which binds together all human beings, quite different from that which binds them to cats and dogs," has recently gained such currency? The kinds of arguments upon which proponents of animal rights rely have been around for a long time, so what explains their newfound popularity? Answering that question requires a broader conception of morality than its identification with philosophical moral theory, a conception that situates morality in social, cultural, and historical milieux. Even the abortion controversy – perhaps the most intractable of moral disputes – can be illuminated by locating it culturally and historically, as Ginsburg's ethnographic study of abortion activists in Fargo, North Dakota, admirably does.[27] In sum, charting the ebbs and flows of morality in action would provide important insights into what morality, as it is actually lived, is all about.

In addition, taking medical ethics to be applied moral philosophy simply does not fit the experience of those who have spent time in clinical settings. The reports of moral problem-solving by philosophers who have clinical experience (in particular, Caplan's conclusion about two cases he relates – that "ethical theory would have been the wrong place to turn for a solution to the issues under consideration") raise a daunting challenge to defenders of applied ethics.[28] To skeptics who continue to maintain that reading and thought experiments are adequate substitutes for experience, one can merely reply, "Go and see for yourself." But until they have done that, deference ought to be given to those who have done the reading and acquired the experience.

The only surprise about these criticisms is the steadfastness with which they are ignored. Two factors contribute to that resistance. One is the centrality of the orthodox theoretical conception of morality to the concerns of contemporary analytic philosophy. The motivation for conceiving of morality as an independent, consistent system of theoretical norms is, as G. E. Moore recognized, the allure of moral knowledge. As long as epistemology continues to dominate philosophy, moral philosophers will pay obeisance to it. Unfortunately, the philosophical project of generating moral knowledge ultimately displaces morality from the experience in which it is grounded. Moreover, how the transformation of practice into theory is supposed to occur and why it is necessary remain mysterious. Theoretical systematization supposedly transubstantiates the water of moral experience into the wine of moral knowledge. Although this ritual may continue to play a role in the cathedral of academia, it remains peripheral to the outside world. There moral experience retains its primacy, and it is in appreciating the primacy of experience and in providing ways of understanding and guiding that experience that ethnography can be useful.

The other factor is that there remains no enticing alternative to conventional philosophical moral theory and thus to applied ethics. What is needed is a different brand of moral theory, one that is more closely allied with and faithful to real-life moral phenomena. Ethnography has a vital role to play in developing a more empirically grounded theory of morality.

How Can Ethnography Help?

Ethnographic studies can make important critical and constructive contributions to our understanding of morality.[29] On the critical side, the results of ethnographic investigations challenge both the dogmas that pervade the received view of medical ethics and the underlying philosophical model upon which "applied ethics" is predicated. On the constructive side, ethnographic work reveals that morality must be understood contextually, and once that broader, more realistic perspective is adopted, it provides a sobering appreciation of the prospects for moral reform. Examples of ethnography's critical contributions will be provided first.

Perhaps the most prominent tenet of orthodox medical ethics is its individualism, manifested by the field's conspicuous preoccupation with the notion of autonomy.[30] Both Bosk's study of the training of surgeons and Frohock's study of treatment decisions in neonatal intensive care units suggest that an individualistic orientation does not capture the realities of clinical practice. Frohock, for example, observes, "Humanness is not assigned to the individual baby but to the family of the baby," and Bosk, in commenting on a case presentation by a pediatric surgeon, notes, "Interesting here is the surgeon's definition of his client as the entire family network."[31]

In the same vein, Frohock contends that the language of rights, the rhetoric of individualism, does not fit a neonatal care unit: "Contemporary moral terms like rights are inappropriate in a neonatal nursery. The new and, in many cases, unique medical events require a different moral vocabulary. The introduction of harm in place of rights is a reconstruction of the language of medical staffs."[32] Not only does the language of harm more accurately portray the moral ethos of neonatal intensive care units, it is also superior because it is responsive to situational particularities:

> The proposition that harm is to be avoided whenever possible can constrain actions, and because of its contextual qualities it can do so more credibly than a right-to-life shield. Not claiming the identity of all life forms when none can be established, a harm constraint can instead be concerned to disclose how particular forms of life are harmed and to draw constraints on action that are sensitive to differences among life forms.[33]

"Life forms" does not refer to aliens from outer space, but to embryos, fetuses, anencephalic newborns, and infants who are profoundly neurologically impaired – entities whose moral status remains problematic. What is objectionable about a rights-based approach is that it crudely assimilates these various life forms to a single moral category and treats them uniformly regardless of significant differences that might exist.[34] A harm-based approach, in contrast, can respond to relevant differences among these life forms, differences that, moreover, cannot be exhaustively stipulated in advance or identified theoretically (as proposed definitions of "humanhood" try to do[35]), but can only be discovered through experience.

In addition to disputing some of the substantive claims of applied ethics, social science investigations challenge its underlying philosophical model in two ways. On the one hand, they call into question the existence of a rational method for moral decision-making, and on the other hand, they raise doubts about the independence of morality.

The assumption that there is a rational method of moral decision-making is, for example, belied by the research of Lippman-Hand and Fraser on the decision-making of women after genetic counseling.[36] Lippman-Hand and Fraser set out believing that women would make decisions about whether to run the risk of conceiving a defective child by being good utility-maximizers. Women would, that is, meld the probabilities communicated to them by genetic counselors with their own assessments of the value of likely consequences and then adopt the course of action that maximized expected utility. The work of Lippman-Hand and Fraser was, in other words, designed to assess the adequacy of genetic counseling in terms of an influential philosophical method of moral decision-making. What they discovered, to their surprise, is that women uniformly ignore the probabilities of alternative outcomes. They reduce the problem to two results – either I will have a defective child or I will not have a defective child. They then construct scenarios of what it would be like to live with a defective child, and if they think they could cope with the worst of these scenarios, they run the risk of conceiving a child who might be handicapped. Women who think they could not cope do not undertake that risk, and women who cannot make up their minds engage in "reproductive roulette," that is, they have sexual intercourse using methods of contraception they know are insufficient.

What this research reveals is that actual moral decision-making is situational: it is tailored to the demands of particular circumstances as well as the capacities and limitations of the persons enmeshed in those circumstances. Yet the decision-making of these women appears to be an eminently reasonable way of responding to the pervasive uncertainties that confront them, even if it does not conform to the dictates of an influential philosophical model.[37]

Another example of the adaptability and flexibility of moral practice occurs in neonatal intensive care units when a seriously ill baby is allowed to "declare itself": "The child declares himself one way or the other (makes the decision for the doctor by taking a dramatic turn for the worse and dying, or by showing signs of improvement that clearly justify aggressive therapy)."[38] Here health care professionals and parents defer to the baby, who, of course, is in no position whatsoever to "decide." But again, such temporizing seems perfectly reasonable in the necessitous and uncertain circumstances in which it is used.

Frohock's study also provides examples of how the momentous decision of whether to treat aggressively or allow to die can be replaced by smaller, incremental decisions. A physician might decide not to increase the settings on a ventilator, to use a more "gentle" antibiotic, or not to check some laboratory values, for instance.[39] A theoretically oriented applied ethics, though, tends to focus on "big" decisions and portray them in binary terms. By doing so, it ignores pragmatic strategies for responding to moral problems such as biding time, compromising, or cycling through competing values.[40]

What these examples suggest is that moral decision-making is a search for a feasible, appropriate response to a particular situation, not the application of a method that in virtue of its extreme generality is insensitive to the particularities that structure the situation. There is no homogeneous, unifying conception of rationality in morality – or anywhere else for that matter, including that veritable paragon of rationality: science. The theoretical disposition of applied ethics renders it insensitive to the flexible ways in which human beings actually handle moral problems. Moral decision-making is more a matter of coming up with creative, responsive solutions than it is trying to apply a philosophical formula. Moral rationality consequently assumes diverse, sometimes protean forms. By investigating how moral problems are perceived and constructed by those whom they affect and how these individuals handle those problems, and by assessing these attempted resolutions, ethnographic studies can discover the disparate forms of moral rationality and stake out, in at least a provisional way, the limits of those forms.

Ethnographic studies also suggest that the widespread concern to demarcate morality – to provide criteria that will distinguish morality from, say, prudence, etiquette, and law – is misplaced. Positivist philosophers of science have thought it important to distinguish "genuine" science from pseudo-science – alchemy, for instance – in the hope that the resulting criteria would have something of consequence to say about dubious pretenders to the mantle of science such as psychoanalysis. This concern with demarcation has infected philosophical morality and impels the repeated and persistent, but ultimately futile, attempts to define morality.[41] It is a concern that also pervades applied ethics, surfacing every time someone insists on addressing only the ethical issues and not the associated economic, legal, social, or policy issues in an area.

The attempt to delimit morality assumes that morality can be isolated in two ways. One is that morality can be detached from practice and exhaustively represented in a consistent theoretical system. The other is that the discrete theoretical system of morality is independent of other discrete theoretical systems such as the law. The work of Bosk and Frohock casts doubt on both assumptions. Bosk concludes, with respect to the inculcation of norms in young surgeons, "The moral and ethical dimensions of training are not bracketed from all other concerns but are instead built into everyday clinical life."[42] In a hospital or out of a hospital, morality is part and parcel of everyday life. Even if the thread of morality could be extracted intact from the fabric of experience, examining that naked thread would produce an incomplete and distorted impression of morality. What needs to be understood is how morality is woven into the experiences and the lives it helps to constitute.

Frohock's comment about the impact of difficult moral decisions is equally telling: "Pain and guilt, rather than immorality and irrationality, plague therapy decisions."[43] Parents of a seriously impaired newborn, in other words, do not see the problems they have to wrestle with as paradigmatically moral, or search for distinctive moral reasons to support their decisions. They know they have a hard, perhaps tragic, decision to make, and they want to do the best or the right thing (not the *morally* right thing). They agonize over these decisions, but they do not ask themselves whether a proposed course of action would be immoral or irrational, or whether a reason that appears persuasive to them is really a valid *moral* reason. The philosophical desire to portray such decisions as exclusively and prototypically moral is not faithful to the phenomena. Rather than trying to impose an *a priori* conception of morality on these decisions, theorists should pay more careful attention to how parents themselves perceive the problem and work their way through it. Recognizing the artificiality of the borders of applied ethics leads to worries about the separation of the moral, on the one hand, from the social, the cultural, and the political, on the other. As Fox points out, the circumscription of the moral is most evident in discussions of neonatal intensive care units:

> Bioethical attention has been riveted on the justifiability of nontreatment decisions. Relatively little attention has been paid to the fact that a disproportionately high number of the extremely premature, very low birth weight infants, many with severe congenital abnormalities, cared for in NICUs are babies born to poor, disadvantaged mothers, many of whom are single nonwhite teenagers. Bioethics has been disinclined to regard the deprived conditions out of which such infants and mothers come as falling within its purview. These are defined as *social* rather than ethical problems.[44]

But why is it that ethics stops at the door of the neonatal intensive care unit? What, other than a concern for the theoretical purity of the discipline or an ideological commitment to the individual, prevents a genuine moral questioning of the conditions that contribute to the need for neonatal intensive care units?

Ethnographic studies thus reveal *prima facie* tensions between the realities of clinical practice and the dictates of philosophical medical ethics. On which side does the burden of proof reside? The burden, it seems to me, falls to philosophers, who themselves acknowledge it in their recognition that moral theory begins in and ultimately must be tested by practice. It is hard to find a philosopher for whom practice does not remain the touchstone of the adequacy of moral theory. Aristotle provides the clearest statement of this position, but it is prominent in many others, including Sidgwick, the arch-proponent of philosophical moral theory.[45] The Kantian stream in moral philosphy might be regarded as an exception, but even Kant insisted that his view merely elaborated common moral opinions. The methodology of moral philosophy itself recognizes a presumption in favor of the legitimacy of moral practice; departures from moral practice, therefore, need to be vindicated on more than the *a priori* grounds provided by applied ethics.

Another advantage of paying attention to moral practice is the appreciation of context that results. Moral philosophy and its adjunct applied ethics movement run into trouble because they remain stubbornly acontextual. To borrow an example from Toulmin, who in turn borrows it from John Wisdom, the question, "Is a flying boat a ship or an airplane?" is, in the abstract, hopelessly sterile.[46] When a context is supplied – ought the captain of a flying boat to have an airline pilot's licence, a master mariner's certificate, or both? – the issue comes into focus and pertinent arguments can be advanced. Reading books and engaging in armchair speculation do not supply contexts, however. The contexts in which the moral problems of medicine arise can be appreciated only by becoming immersed in clinical settings, as ethnographers do.

In fact, the most important constructive contribution of ethnographic studies is that they give content to the vague notion of "putting moral problems into context." One of the best illustrations is Anspach's study of a neonatal intensive care unit.[47] Anspach found that consensus around moral principles does not remove controversy about the treatment of seriously ill newborns because doctors and nurses frequently disagree about the prognoses for these infants. Her work is an investigation of the forces that shape these discrepant prognostic judgments. Anspach shows that prognostic conflicts result from the different "modes of knowing" of doctors and nurses respectively. Doctors, who spend relatively little time with these infants, base their conclusions on physical findings, the results of diagnostic tests, and the literature of medical research. Nurses, who spend concentrated and extended periods of time with these infants, rely on their personal and social interactions with the infants. There is, as a result, a clash between what Anspach calls "the perspectives of engagement and detachment."[48]

What comes out of Anspach's study for our purposes is the recognition that a contextual understanding of morality has at least three facets. One facet concerns individual particularities. A decision about treatment must take into account, obviously, the idiosyncrasies of an infant's condition – factors such as this specific infant's diagnosis, medical history, and family situation. Institutional structure is a second facet. Institutional structure has two main impacts in a neonatal intensive care unit. On the one hand, decisions about treatment can be affected by considerations such as how long an infant has been in the unit and whether infants with similar problems have been in the unit recently, and if so, what the outcomes for them were. On the other hand, as Anspach discovered, how work is divided and organized within a neonatal intensive care unit can influence how issues are perceived and how judgments are made. Because, for instance, attending physicians visit the unit for short periods of time, because house staff rotate through the unit on short cycles, and because physicians in tertiary care institutions often have research interests, doctors are both organizationally and personally detached from these infants and their parents. The information they rely on to formulate a problem and resolve it is the technical and, in the case of research findings, general information they possess and value. Because nurses, in contrast, are intimately and continuously involved with these infants, they are organizationally and personally attached to them. Their perceptions of problems and their responses to them consequently are a function of their social interactions with the infants for whom they care.

A third facet emerges when it is pointed out, as Anspach does, that the "technological cues" of the doctors and the "interactive cues" of the nurses are not valued equally: "The interactive cues noted by the nurses are *devalued data*."[49] Why is that? There are several components to the answer, but the point for our purposes is that all the answers are embedded in the social and cultural background that structures the definition and delivery of health care. One obvious answer ties the devaluation of the nurses' data to prevailing gender roles in society. Another answer, given by Anspach, does not roam quite so far. It appeals to the history of diagnostic technology and locates intensive care of newborns in a "post-clinical" medical culture, that is, a culture in which the science of medicine has displaced the art of medicine. In such a scientific culture, the "subjective" information of the nurses is no match for the hard, "objective," technical data of the doctors.

Understanding the problem posed by life-and-death decision-making in neonatal intensive care units requires an appreciation of all three facets. Morality cannot be severed from the social, cultural, and historical milieux in which this decision-making occurs; nor can morality be identified with any single facet.[50] Morality suffuses this context, and the philosophical attempt to isolate it and treat it as an autonomous, independent theoretical system simply fosters a picture of morality that is artificial, distorted, and ultimately desiccated.

A contextual understanding of morality does not mean that there is no room for moral theory or philosophizing about morality: simply that the nature of that theory must be different. Anspach's research poses obvious and difficult epistemological questions, in particular, the question of whether it is possible to integrate or synthesize the "partial and selective visions of reality" possessed by the nurses and doctors.[51] Moral theory needs to take a new turn, however, and be responsive to the issues posed by morality in context.

One of these issues is that, once morality is understood contextually, impediments to moral reform loom large. As Anspach recognizes, any attempt to improve the quality of life-and-death decisions about seriously ill newborns must recognize that "to the extent that decisions cannot be extricated from the social organization of the intensive care nursery, broader changes in that organization may be necessary."[52] Jennings, commenting on the relationship between ethics and ethnography, explains why a recognition of the institutional and structural constraints on behavior should make one less sanguine about the prospects for reform:

Bioethics generally has a simple, not to say simpleminded, notion of what can be done to bring about social change – in most cases to reform professional practice to bring it more into line with established ethical obligations and principled responsibilities. The strategy is: argument, agreement through rational persuasion, and education. The commitment to this polis model runs very deeply in philosophy, and the applied ethics movement of the past twenty years has been premised on the belief that it can be brought out of the confines of the academy and introduced into the conduct of public and professional life ... But what social scientific studies have done, and neonatal ethnography is particularly insistent in this regard, is to force ethicists to pay more attention to the cultural, institutional, and psychological preconditions for social and behavioral change.[53]

If moral theory is to be truly practical, it must come to grips with realities that its theoretical preoccupation has so far caused it to steadfastly ignore.

Objections

Philosophers have, in the past, been tempted by ethnography but have not succumbed to it. Toulmin cites Descartes' repudiation of his own fascination with history and ethnography on the ground that "history is like foreign travel. It broadens the mind, but it does not deepen it."[54] Whereas ethnographers and historians collect facts that fascinate and titillate, philosophers, in Descartes' view, do the real work of extracting the general principles behind these facts. This sharp division of labor that consigns ethnographers and historians to the menial task of assembling raw material for philosophers begs the question, however, because it assumes the correctness of the philosophical model of morality that drives applied ethics.

Understood differently, though, there is something to Descartes' objection. Bosk appreciates the danger it points to: "Ethnography ... runs the risk of being dismissed as 'merely description' ... [but] doing ethnography is always both a theoretic and a theoretically motivated activity."[55] The challenge this objection raises is to account for the theoretical side of ethnography. If one sees theory in purely formal, *a priori* terms, that, of course, is a hopeless task, and it is no surprise that "merely" empirical enquiries are deprecated. But once such a narrow conception of rational inquiry is abandoned, the way is open for alternative understandings of theory.

One aim of a critique of applied ethics is precisely to clear the field for new understandings of theory and practice, in particular, understandings that locate theories *in* our practices rather than *underlying* them.[56] What might this involve? A review of a recent study of crime notes the author's ethnographic approach of "turn[ing] away from enquiry after alleged 'background' causes to look at the surface, the 'foreground,' 'the lived experience' of crime," focusing on "many individual human beings," and "cast[ing] doubt on reconstructions of aggregates." The reviewer points out that the author "sets out to ask not, 'Why did you do it?' but 'How?' As he says, 'The social science contains only scattered evidence of what it means, feels, sounds, tastes, or looks like to commit a particular crime.' The evidence he has gathered gives some of the answers, after all, to the question 'Why?'"[57] Accounting for the theoretical side of ethnography requires an understanding of this transition from 'How?' to 'Why?' That understanding will not be arrived at in global, *a priori* terms. Rather, it will be embedded in and relative to particular domains of inquiry and particular contexts. The task that ethnography poses for philosophers and social scientists, therefore, is twofold: to do moral ethnography and thereby to make more productive contributions to practical ethics; and to develop the moral theory implicit in ethnographic studies.

But, it might be objected, there are daunting practical barriers to that kind of genuinely interdisciplinary work. Just as one must be cognizant of the structural and institutional constraints within neonatal intensive care units, so one must be cognizant of the structural and institutional factors that separate ethnography and ethics. Even if ethnography could save the life of medical ethics, ethnographers have little incentive to do so, particularly if they work in research-oriented universities that prize mainstream contributions to their disciplines. Matters such as degree and licensing requirements, employment prospects, research funding opportunities, tenure and promotion criteria, and formal and informal reward systems militate against research that is non-traditional, innovative, and risky. Ethnography is already marginal enough in sociology, although it is less so in anthropology. An ethnography that contributed to ethics or bioethics rather than sociology would most likely be ignored, if not resisted. On the philosophical side, the opportunities and incentives for rigorous, empirically informed research are equally meager. So who actually would do this work?

In addition, it could be argued that there is a fundamental, and ultimately fruitful, opposition between the humanities and the social sciences. To train philosophers to be good ethnographers could make them bad philosophers; to train ethnographers to be good philosophers could, in turn, make them bad ethnographers. This worry assumes the legitimacy of the disciplinary boundaries, as well as the exaggerated demarcation between facts and values that helps to sustain those boundaries, and is being challenged here. Once philosophy is disabused of its preoccupation with the *a priori* and the pristinely rational, there is no reason to regard philosophy and ethnography as incompatible. And once ethnography finally sheds its vestigial pretension to "positivist" science, it can become comfortable with investigating the values and the moralities that inform and guide so much of human experience and that make life meaningful. As they exist today, ethics and ethnography probably are at odds. But reconceived in ways that are responsive to the lives and problems they study, ethics and ethnography are not only complementary, they are indispensable to one another.

The practical impediments to this kind of work are, nevertheless, real and should not be underestimated. The way to begin removing them, though, is to make a case for the importance of the work and to recognize its practical value. How to do the research will have to be learned through experience. Bosk describes himself as "a medical sociologist, an ethnographer of medical action," and he admits, "As such, my primary research techniques in this highly technological world are primitive."[58] That might be all that can be expected now, but approaches will mature as this kind of work evolves and develops. As well, it might be prudent at present for only those with security to embark on such risky research ventures. But a caution appropriate to individuals should not be extended to a general domain of inquiry. What must be offered are support for and recognition of the work that has been done, and encouragement to continue and develop this line of research. The need for and the merits of the results ultimately will dismantle the barriers. To expect deeply ingrained, long-entrenched obstacles to disappear before the work is undertaken is no more than the counsel of despair.

Conclusion

It is time to admit the terminal condition of "applied ethics." As Hare has conceded,

> if the moral philosopher *cannot* help with the problems of medical ethics, he ought to shut up shop. The problems of medical ethics are so typical of the moral problems that moral philosophy is supposed to be able to help with, that a failure here would be a sign either of the uselessness of the discipline or of the incompetence of the particular practitioner.[59]

It would be rash to suggest that all practitioners of applied ethics are incompetent. So what is a moral philosopher with practical leanings to do? If ethnography is simply incorporated into the prevailing "theory-centered" approach to philosophy, that is, the concentration on "abstract, timeless methods of deriving general solutions to universal problems," the attempt to rescue medical ethics with ethnography will be futile.[60] Ethnography needs to be integrated into a revivified practical philosophy that, in the words of Toulmin, is interested in the "oral," the "particular," the "local," and the "timely."[61]

In a union of ethnography and "theory-centered" philosophy, social scientists could continue to be no more than servants to philosophers – collectors of the facts that philosophers need to "apply" their theories. And as long as medical ethics remains "theory-centered," philosophers working in the field will continue to do what the Chinese, in a marvelously apt phrase, call "playing with emptiness."[62] A more viable approach to medical ethics, and a more robust and productive role for both social scientists and philosophers, depends upon the alignment of ethnography with a "recovered" practical philosophy, that is, a conception of the discipline that recognizes that contributions to "the reflective resolution of quandaries that face us in enterprises with high stakes" are not "applied philosophy" but philosophy itself.[63] But unless that happens, moral philosophers should heed the advice of Hare and shut up their clinical shops.

NOTES

1 S. Toulmin, "How Medicine Saved the Life of Ethics," *Perspectives in Biology and Medicine* 25 (1982), 740.
2 L. Peterson, review of Rem B. Edwards and Glenn C. Graber, eds, *Bioethics*, *New England Journal of Medicine* 318 (1988), 1546–7.
3 R. J. Baron, "Dogmatics, Empirics, and Moral Medicine," *Hastings Center Report*, 19 (1) (1989), 41.
4 H. Sidgwick, *The Methods of Ethics* (7th edn, originally published 1907), Dover Publications, New York, 1966, p. 373.
5 Philosophers have, however, recently begun talking about "applied aesthetics." The assumption apparently is that philosophers of art can have, *qua* philosophers of art, something meaningful to say about issues such as what works of art should be purchased with public funds or what parts of the environment should be preserved for distinctly aesthetic reasons. See e.g. M. Eaton, *Basic Issues in Aesthetics*, Wadsworth, Belmont, Ca., 1988.
6 C. D. Broad, *Five Types of Ethical Theory*, Routledge & Kegan Paul, London, 1930, p. 285. Broad does concede, however, that moral theory may have "a certain slight practical application" in so far as "it may lead us to look out for certain systematic faults which we should not otherwise have suspected."
7 F. H. Bradley, "My Station and its Duties," in *Ethical Studies*, Liberal Arts Press, New York, 1951, p. 128.
8 G. E. Moore, *Principia Ethica*, Cambridge University Press, Cambridge, 1903, p. 20.

9 William James falls into this camp, too. Of the choice between life and good, on the one hand, and death and evil, on the other, James says, "From this unsparing practical ordeal no professor's lectures and no array of books can save us." In James's view, a moral philosopher has no advantage in making practical decisions: "The ethical philosopher . . . whenever he ventures to say which course of action is the best, is on no essentially different level from the common man": W. James, "The Moral Philosopher and the Moral Life," in *The Writings of William James* (ed. J. J. McDermott): The Modern Library, New York, 1967, p. 629. Melden's comment that "it would be a mistake . . . to identify the moralist with the moral philosopher" likewise separates the moralist's practical task of giving advice from the philosopher's theoretical interest in exploring the question of what counts as a good moral reason: A. Melden, "On the Nature and Problems of Ethics," in *Ethical Theories* (2nd edn), Prentice-Hall, Englewood Cliffs, NJ, 1967, p. 2.

10 A distinction between theory and practice and the concomitant gulf that emerges when theory is understood as it has been in medical ethics exist in other "applied ethics" bailiwicks as well. A review of a recent book in environmental ethics, for example, distinguishes between "mainline" environmental ethics and "nonprofessional" environmental ethics and says that elements of the latter, the deep ecology movement and the Earth First! movement, for instance, "are playing a major role at the practical level, where professional writing in the field is currently having little or no impact": E. C. Hargrove, review of Roderick Frazier Nash, *The Rights of Nature: A History of Environmental Ethics*, Can. Phil. Rev. 9 (1989), 457. And a recent article on the role of theory in business ethics surveys the plethora of theoretical approaches in that discipline and concludes that "there is a serious lack of clarity about how to apply the theories to cases and a persistent unwillingness to grapple with tensions between theories of ethical reasoning"; R. Derry and R. M. Green, "Ethical Theory in Business Ethics: A Critical Assessment," *Journal of Business Ethics* 8 (1989), 521.

11 The notion of "internal criticism" is borrowed from the critical legal studies movement. Singer describes it as follows: "Internal criticism – criticism that uses a paradigm's criteria against the paradigm itself – merely shows that a certain theory does not do what it purports to do": J. W. Singer, "The Player and the Cards: Nihilism and Legal Theory," *Yale Law Journal* 94 (1984), 60.

12 For a more extended criticism of the philosophical underpinnings of applied ethics, see B. Hoffmaster, "Morality and the Social Sciences," in *Social Science Perspectives on Medical Ethics* (ed. G. Weisz, Kluwer Academic, Boston, 1990, pp. 241–60.

13 See e.g. T. L. Beauchamp and J. F. Childress, *Principles of Biomedical Ethics* (2nd edn), Oxford University Press, New York, 1983.

14 F. M. Frohock, *Special Care*, University of Chicago Press, Chicago, 1986, p. 51.

15 For a beautiful example of the limited and crude capacity of language to

capture particular objects and experiences, see the discussion of Libanius' description of a picture in the Council House at Antioch in M. Baxandall, *Patterns of Intention*, Yale University Press, New Haven, 1985, pp. 2–5.

16 W. B. Gallie, "Essentially Contested Concepts," *Proceedings of the Aristotelian Society* 56 (1955–6), p. 169.

17 Ibid., p. 180.

18 A. M. Honoré, "Ownership," in *Oxford Essays in Jurisprudence*, 1st ser. (ed. A. G. Guest), Clarendon Press, Oxford, 1961, p. 128.

19 Ibid., p. 130.

20 B. L. Miller, "Autonomy and the Refusal of Lifesaving Treatment," *Hastings Center Report* 11 (4) (1981), 22.

21 The most recent and most influential candidate for such a method is Rawls's notion of reflective equilibrium: J. Rawls, *A Theory of Justice*, Harvard University Press, Cambridge, Mass., 1971. The attraction of reflective equilibrium is easy to understand because it seemingly allows moral philosophers to have their cake and eat it, too. In theory, principles are revised in light of "considered judgments" and "considered judgments" are amended in light of principles until an equilibrium is attained. But close examination reveals, I think, that principles are an idle cog in this justificatory process. Elsewhere I have tried to show that it is the considered judgments, not the principles, that do the work in reflective equilibrium: see Hoffmaster, "Morality and the Social Sciences."

22 For a discussion of this issue with respect to the environment, see C. D. Stone, *Earth and Other Ethics*, Harper and Row, New York, 1987.

23 Frohock, *Special Care*, p. 13.

24 R. C. Fox, *The Sociology of Medicine*, Prentice-Hall, Englewood Cliffs, NJ, 1989, p. 229.

25 E. D. Mirale, "Withholding Nutrition from Seriously Ill Newborn Infants: A Parent's Perspective," *Journal of Pediatrics* 113 (1988), 262.

26 W. Whewell, *Lectures on the History of Moral Philosophy in England*, John W. Parker and Son, London, 1852, p. 226 (emphasis in original).

27 F. D. Ginsburg, *Contested Lives*, University of California Press, Berkeley, 1989.

28 A. L. Caplan, Can Applied Ethics be Effective in Health Care and Should it Strive to Be?" *Ethics* 93 (1983), 312. See also E. H. Morreim, "Philosophy Lessons from the Clinical Setting: Seven Sayings that Used to Annoy Me," *Theoretical Medicine* 7 (1986), 47.

29 Ethnography is not easy to define, but the following characterization fits the studies discussed in this paper:

> The data of cultural anthropology derive ultimately from the direct observation of customary behavior in particular societies. Making, reporting, and evaluating such observations are the tasks of ethnography ... An ethnographer is an anthropologist who attempts ... to record and describe the culturally significant behaviors of a particular society. Ideally, this description ... requires a long period of intimate study and residence in a small, well defined community, knowledge of the spoken language, and the employment of a wide range of observational techniques including prolonged face-to-face contacts with mem-

bers of the local group, direct participation in some of the group's activities, and a greater emphasis on intensive work with informants than on the use of documentary or survey data. (H. C. Conklin, "Ethnography," *International Encyclopedia of Social Science* (1968), 172.

The term "ethnography" is, as this account makes clear, closely allied·with anthropology. Comparable research in sociology goes by many names, including "fieldwork" and "qualitative social research." See J. Lofland and L. H. Lofland, *Analyzing Social Settings* (2nd edn), Wadsworth, Belmont, Ca., 1984, p. 3.

30 For a powerful criticism of this preoccupation with individualism and autonomy, see R. C. Fox and J. P. Swazey, "Medical Morality is not Bioethics – Medical Ethics in China and the United States," *Perspectives in Biology and Medicine* 27 (1984), 336.

31 Frohock, *Special Care*, p. 98; C. L. Bosk, *Forgive and Remember*, University of Chicago Press, Chicago, 1979, p. 134.

32 Frohock, *Special Care*, p. x.

33 Ibid., p. 205.

34 One is reminded here of the lawyers' refrain that "the law is a blunt instrument." One important difference between law and morality is that morality should escape this objection.

35 For one notorious attempt, see J. Fletcher, "Indicators of Humanhood: A Tentative Profile of Man," *Hastings Center Report* 2 (5) (1972), 1.

36 A. Lippman-Hand and F. C. Fraser, "Genetic Counseling: Parents' Responses to Uncertainty." *Birth Defects: Original Article Series* 15 (5C) (1979), 325. This is an interview study. Lofland and Lofland include "intensive interviewing" of the sort used by Lippman-Hand and Fraser as one of the methods of qualitative social research. They define "intensive interviewing" as "a guided conversation whose goal is to elicit from the interviewee rich, detailed materials that can be used in qualitative analysis" (Lofland and Lofland, *Analyzing Social Settings*, p. 12). Those are the kinds of materials Lippman-Hand and Fraser obtained, and their analysis of them was qualitative. For a longer discussion of the moral implications of the work of Lippman-Hand and Fraser, see B. Hoffmaster, "The Theory and Practice of Applied Ethics," *Dialogue* 30 (1991), 213.

37 Lippman-Hand and Fraser would, I think, agree with this claim despite their repeated description of the decision-making of these couples as non-rational or arational. They say: "[the couples'] behavior and their ways of formulating the other issues relevant to childbearing do follow logically when viewed as an attempt to limit or neutralize ... uncertainty": "Genetic Counseling," p. 333.

38 Frohock, *Special Care*, p. 62. For another description of this phenomenon, see W. Carlton, *"In Our Professional Opinion ... " The Primacy of Clinical Judgment Over Moral Choice*, University of Notre Dame Press, Notre Dame, 1978, p. 68.

39 Frohock, *Special Care*, pp. 48–9.

40 For a discussion of the cycling strategy, see G. Calabresi and P. Bobbitt, *Tragic Choices*, W. W. Norton, New York, 1978.

41 G. Wallace and A. D. M. Walker, eds, *The Definition of Morality*, Methuen, London, 1970.

42 Bosk, *Forgive and Remember*, p. 190.

43 Frohock, *Special Care*, p. 115.

44 Fox, *Sociology of Medicine*, p. 231 (emphasis in original).

45 Sidgwick says: "I should . . . rely less confidently on the conclusions set forth in the preceding section, if they did not appear to me to be in substantial agreement – .in spite of superficial differences – with the doctrines of those moralists who have been most in earnest in seeking among commonly received moral rules for genuine intuitions of the Practical Reason": *The Methods of Ethics*, p. 384.

46 S. Toulmin, "The Recovery of Practical Philosophy," *American Scholar* 57 (1988), 349.

47 R. R. Anspach, "Prognostic Conflict in Life-and-Death Decisions: The Organization as an Ecology of Knowledge," *Journal of Health and Social Behavior* 28 (1987), 215.

48 Ibid., p. 227.

49 Ibid., p. 229 (emphasis in original).

50 The danger of a case-oriented approach to "applied ethics" is that it becomes absorbed with the particularities of individual situations and thus never gets beyond the first facet. This danger is, for the most part, realized in the discussions of cases in A. R. Jonsen and S. Toulmin, *The Abuse of Casuistry*, University of California Press, Berkeley, 1988. Broader background considerations are introduced in only their analysis of usury.

51 Anspach, "Prognostic Conflict in Life-and-death Decisions," p. 230.

52 Ibid.

53 B. Jennings, "Ethics and Ethnography in Neonatal Intensive Care," in *Social Science Perspectives on Medical Ethics* (ed. G. Weisz), Kluwer Academic, Boston, 1990, pp. 270–1.

54 Toulmin, "The Recovery of Practical Philosophy," p. 340; S. Toulmin, *Cosmopolis*, Free Press, New York, 1990, p. 33.

55 Bosk, *Forgive and Remember*, p. 17.

56 Levinson makes this point with respect to theories of constitutional law. See S. Levinson, "Law as Literature," *Texas Law Review* 60 (1982), 391.

57 G. Owen, "The Pleasures of Crime," *The Idler* 23 (1989), 52, reviewing J. Katz, *Seductions of Crime*, Basic Books, New York, 1988.

58 C. Bosk, "The Fieldworker as Watcher and Witness," *Hastings Center Report* 15 (3) (1985), 10.

59 R. M. Hare, "Medical Ethics: Can the Moral Philosopher Help?" in *Philosophical Medical Ethics: Its Nature and Significance* (ed. S. F. Spicker and H. T. Engelhardt, Jr.), Reidel, Dordrecht, 1977, p. 49 (emphasis in original).

60 Toulmin, "The Recovery of Practical Philosophy," pp. 338–41; Toulmin, *Cosmopolis*, p. 11.

61 Toulmin, "The Recovery of Practical Philosophy," pp. 338–41; Toulmin,

Cosmopolis, pp. 186–92. See also J. Dewey, *Reconstruction in Philosophy*, Henry Holt, New York, 1920.
62 Fox and Swazey, "Medical Morality is not Bioethics," p. 339.
63 Toulmin, "The Recovery of Practical Philosophy," pp. 352, 345; Toulmin, *Cosmopolis*, p. 190.

21
Ethics Codes and Guidelines for Health Care and Research: Can Respect for Autonomy be a Multi-cultural Principle?

Edward W. Keyserlingk

Keyserlingk accepts the standard theory of Western bioethics based on three principles: autonomy, beneficence, and justice. His central concern is to defend the principle of "respect for autonomy" as a viable multi-cultural ethical principle that is suitable for incorporation into international codes of biomedical ethics. Keyserlingk briefly explores the question of the function of international codes of ethics in the area of health care and medicine, arguing that they can and should aspire to a universal normative validity. He than asks which interpretation of the meaning of "respect for autonomy" has the best chance of preserving multi-cultural validity and applicability for the principle. Here his main point is to protect the principle from excessively individualistic interpretations related to peculiarly Western ideas of the rational self. The main burden of the rest of Keyserlingk's paper is to argue first that, in the preferred sense, non-Western cultures do already value and respect autonomy to some degree; and second, that various cultural practices which appear to involve flagrant disrespect for persons – such as the favouring of male over female children regarding scarce nutritional resources in times of famine in Bangladesh – are often better explained in terms of natural exigencies and social factors.

Keyserlingk's paper should be compared with those of Winkler (chapter 19) ahd Hoffmaster (chapter 20) regarding the viability of the paradigm theory of bioethics; with Philips's section on "ethics as social policy" (chapter 10); with Wertheimer's discussion of "moral expertise" (chapter 8); and with Sikora's discussion of Kantian autonomy (chapter 5).

Most Western, principle-based ethical systems have long tended to consider respect for persons a central and indispensable normative principle in moral reasoning. Under the umbrella of that principle are typically placed these derived obligations: respect for autonomy, the protection of nonautonomous persons and those with diminished autonomy, informed consent, privacy, and confidentiality.

Moral philosophers and ethicists doing bioethics in Western societies have for some years now placed great emphasis on the principle of respect for persons and its derived obligations, both in theoretical analyses and when doing applied ethics in clinical and research contexts. Moral philosophers continue to disagree over the exact scope and meaning of autonomy and over the exact normative weight which should attach to it *vis-à-vis* other principles and obligations such as beneficence and justice. But despite a variety of nuances, the enterprise of applied ethics in Western societies assumes the centrality of autonomy. Those who do applied ethics continue to appeal to respect for autonomy as one of the decisive moral parameters to be considered in identifying and resolving ethical dilemmas.

The principle of respect for persons and the moral obligations associated with it are also very much in evidence in the various codes of ethics produced by national and international health-related agencies and associations since World War II. The major international codes include the Nuremberg Code (1946); the World Health Organization's Definition of Health (1946); the Declaration of Helsinki (1964, revised 1975); the Declaration of Tokyo (on torture, detention, and imprisonment, 1975); and the World Health Organization's Proposed International Guidelines for Biomedical Research involving Human Subjects.

More recently, 26 delegates from ten countries attended the Fourth Bioethics Summit Conference in 1987 in Ottawa and produced a series of proposals entitled, "Towards an International Ethic for Research with Human Beings," which gives central place to respect for persons. A number of medical disciplines also have produced, or are in the process of formulating, international codes of ethics for their members. These codes and guidelines uniformly uphold a strong principle of autonomy.

There are many who take exception to the strong focus in these international codes and guidelines on individual autonomy. Objectors tend to claim that autonomy (often equated with self-determination or individualism) is more or less exclusively a Western notion and preoccupation, one which assumes and promotes an isolation of the individual form his or her social context by focusing on the idea of a self-interested, rational agent existing in competition with others in a manner more or less free of all traces of social and cultural determination. The basic claim is that the Western concept of person implicit in the exaltation of autonomy is both foreign to and destructive of the cultures of many non-Western societies, and should not be included in codes of ethics for other than Western societies. Some critics go further, concluding that the whole enterprise of producing codes of ethics for multi-cultural professions, disciplines, and associations is misguided. It is better, they argue, to allow each society to formulate its own code or set of guidelines that respects and does not threaten its own moral, social, cultural, and economic context and traditions.

This is the basic issue that will be examined in this paper. A number of ideas will be proposed and defended:

1   International codes of ethics and the Western systems of bioethics from which they largely derive can be justified and useful in non-Western societies, but only in so far as they challenge the moral status quo, especially regarding the more repressive and harmful aspects of national, local, or regional cultures, institutions, and moral priorities. If they are to play this role they cannot jettison or reduce the focus on respect for persons and autonomy.

2   However, the meaning and scope of respect for autonomy (as understood in this paper) has nothing in common with the caricature of autonomy that is presented by many of its critics and some of its defenders. No *ideal* of personal autonomy is promoted in this paper or should be in codes of ethics. People should make decisions and choices in accordance with their own values and priorities, and may even decide not to make autonomous decisions. In other words, the form of autonomy that needs to be respected is certainly not the extreme individualism which posits a person isolated from and in opposition to family, neighbors, society, culture, and so forth.

3   When this kind of extremism is avoided, the focus on autonomy in international health and research codes of ethics, as derived from Western systems of bioethics, need not be viewed as essentially foreign, destructive, or insensitive to the aspirations of non-Western cultures. There are indications that in many of these societies respect for autonomy may be a victim of economic and political circumstances, rather than standing in fundamental opposition to the traditions and aspirations of those cultures.

4   Input into the formulation and application of international codes of ethics should include representatives of all the societies and cultures to which that code is directed. At the same time, code-writing committees and organizations should be aware of the dangers and limits of ethical consensus-seeking.

5   It may not be feasible for every society to implement morally desirable policies immediately or at the same pace. There may well be a variety of fundamental institutional and cultural circumstances from which an immoral practice stems. Clearly, these must be confronted and overcome in the interests of substantial moral progress. Indeed, the major problem with health and research codes of ethics and other ethical policies designed to apply internationally may be not their focus on autonomy, but their lack of attention to basic concerns of social justice.

6   Lastly, those international associations and agencies which formulate codes of ethics and moral policies intended to apply in both developed and less developed societies incur an obligation to assist less developed member countries with the infrastructures needed to enable ethical action in health care and research matters. It would be inconsistent and hypocritical to act otherwise. Among the types of assistance required will typically be the training of ethicists and the establishment of ethics committees.

1   Codes of Ethics: Mirrors of Positive Morality or Challenges to Reform?

The emphasis on codes of ethics in this paper should be explained at the outset. They are, of course, a legitimate object of ethical inquiry for many reasons. In this paper they are of interest only in so far as their international versions are a vehicle for the export of a certain aspect of Western ethics or bioethics to non-Western and less developed societies. Those societies are not, of course, their only targets: they are also directed to Western and developed nations. And there are many other vehicles for the export of Western bioethics, for example books, ethics journals, international conferences, and the growing number of health professionals, philosophers, and theologians in many societies who have studied bioethics in the West.

More than any of those other channels, international codes of ethics are readily accessible, distilled and summary statements intended to apply as moral guides in many cultures. That makes them a convenient, but not sufficient, reference point in an inquiry looking at the transportability of moral concepts and moral obligations between cultures. Therefore the inquiry which follows will sometimes go beyond codes of ethics alone and consider the Western system of ethics from which they spring.

A first task must be that of clarifying the primary function this paper envisages for international codes of ethics. Judgments about the appropriateness of a code's contents and focus, in particular concerning the respect for autonomy, depend at least in part on the end these codes are meant to achieve. One disturbing view about professional codes of ethics is that no one should expect them to do more than mirror the positive morality and primary interests of the members of the profession or group which produces them. Caplan, for example, has written:

> I find it surprising that anyone would expect a professional code to serve any goals other than those that are in the self-interest of the professionals who constructed it ... The real value of a code for moral and ethical

discussion lies in its revealing to the outsider where the group stands, what its intentions are, and what objectives it serves. Thus codes are documents worthy of study and critique not because they provide nuanced moral distinctions or standards for behavioral evaluation but because they make the self-interest of professional groups explicit.[1]

Veatch has expressed a similar, though perhaps less cynical view:

> Modern codes can reasonably be expected to reflect the basic ethical views of the organizations that endorsed them. In fact it might be argued that documents that are the product of practitioners rather than theoreticians reflect even more accurately the ethical stance of the group than do more systematic efforts at developing theories of medical ethics.[2]

There is little doubt that many professional codes do little more than reflect the positive morality and value priorities of the professionals involved, though this is not to say that that is all they should do. But if that is to be the goal of international codes of ethics, then our primary question need only be whether such codes involving a major emphasis on autonomy do in fact accurately reflect the present moral principles and priorities of the cultures involved. Obviously, they do not. There is, however, another and nobler goal for these codes, one which justifies calling them codes of "ethics" rather than mere codifying summaries of current standards of practice and primary professional objectives. This second option looks to them as aspiring to universal normative validity, as being valid moral injunctions to reform and improve conduct, customs, laws, and institutions which fall below the articulated general standards.[3] Codes having this goal fall within the tradition of ancient codes of medical ethics inspired by exemplars of practice such as Hippocrates, Percival, Maimonides, and many others, although those earlier models put their emphasis on the principles of beneficence and physician virtue, paying little or no attention to patient autonomy.[4]

Modern examples of international codes in the research and health arenas are, of course, the Nuremberg Code of 1946, and the Declaration of Helsinki of 1964. Neither was by any stretch of the imagination a mere reflection of the moral status quo of those times. On the contrary, both were explicitly formulated in order to correct prevailing abuses by investigators, physicians, governments, and research institutions; both focus especially on the need to obtain voluntary and informed consent from subjects; and both are replete with unqualified uses of the words "should" and "must." They were, and were meant to be, applied universally, and provided no exceptions for particular cultures or societies. A more recent example of a code of ethics claiming general validity in the international context is that of the International Epidemiological Association (IEA), which is in the process of drafting and debating a code of ethics for all its members and member associations around the world. The major portion of that draft code is devoted to moral injunctions about autonomy, informed consent, truth-telling, privacy, and confidentiality.[5] Another recent step toward formulating a new international code of ethics for human research was taken at the Fourth Bioethics Summit Conference held in 1987 in Ottawa.[6] The recommendations which emerged from that conference are by no means mere reflections of existing practice and conventional morality. Rather, they urge those of all societies and cultures to improve their protection of research subjects and face up to new threats to respect for persons.

These international codes of ethics make the claim that there are certain moral principles and obligations which have universal normative validity and which must be respected in all societies no matter what the cultural peculiarities of a given society; that one of these fundamental principles is respect for persons; that in the light of this principle and the obligations it engenders, some current practices are objectively wrong; and that these wrongs can and should be changed.

Given these general claims implicit in the genuinely normative international codes of ethics, the question their framers and defenders must answer is simply this: Granting the fundamental importance in the West of the principle of respect for persons, can the principle of autonomy be promoted in non-Western and less developed societies via codes of ethics (and by other means) without doing serious violence to those cultures? Our answer will be a conditional yes, the conditions being that respect for autonomy be understood and defined in a particular way and that the codes be formulated in cooperative dialogue with people from the member cultures, and adapted and applied with great sensitivity to those cultures.

2 The Meaning and Scope of "Respect for Autonomy"

If codes of ethics are to confront immoral conduct and urge improvement, then they cannot neglect or reduce the emphasis on respect for persons and autonomy. A primary function codes of ethics have set for themselves is that of affirming the right of the individual patient and research subject to be protected from unjustified and harmful incursions by the state, the medical and research establishments, or other institutions. And the most compelling and even indispensable moral basis for such a right is that of the principle requiring respect for personal autonomy.

However, autonomy in this context cannot mean that form of extreme individualism with which autonomy has been equated by some of its defenders and critics alike. If such an equation were accurate, then respect for autonomy would in fact be completely foreign to the cultures of most non-Western and less developed societies, given the importance they assign to family and community. For some time now commentators from many disciplines and perspectives have been critical of the individualism which they see as underlying and fueling Western interpretations of freedom, liberty, autonomy, and rights. Western biomedicine, like other areas of Western thought, has been held by many to be incapable of integration into other societies, in part because it assumes that the individual is prior to, distinct from, and even in conflict with society. Dumont, for example, claimed that this is particularly the case in North America, where society is based more on atomism than holism, fostering relationships more contractual than organic. This, in turn, is said to promote moral codes of rights rather than duties.[7]

Although in many traditions and societies persons are not defined separately from their context, but to varying degrees are defined in socially relative ways, persons in the European, Protestant tradition tend to be seen in essential isolation from social position, role, and nurturing context. Geertz writes that the Western concept of self is identified with the conscious self, the seat of control, not with the physical body.[8] Similarly, for Gordon the ideal modern self "is as free of traces of social and cultural determination as possible. It strives to be its own author, consciously choosing its path, able to disengage itself and step back and judge rationally what it will be, where it will go. Self control by the modern identity is potentially unlimited."[9] Foucault made a similar claim in noting how the self has been objectified, made out to be autonomous, self-determining, not determined even by its own values, traditions, or relations with others.[10] And there is the stark description of the Western concept of person proposed by Kirmayer:

> A rational agent which occupies a space within the body, which itself dwells within the social world. The self has goals which are distinct from, and in many cases in conflict with, the goals of those who occupy the social world outside. The value of the person lies in his strength of will which is defined always in opposition to the other – whether that other be society, nature or the body itself. The person is identical with that rational agency that establishes its unique worth by promoting its own goals over those of others. The potential divisiveness of this individualism and rational self-interest is held in check by appeals to moral obligation.[11]

These depictions of essential agents or persons as conceived in the West, which may reveal attitudes which are still current in practice if not in theory, are telling and important. But it would be wrong to conclude that they capture the essence of what respect for autonomy is all about.

In fact, no serious philosopher or theologian writing in bioethics today advocates such a deformed notion of autonomy. Beauchamp and Childress, for example, write:

> Moral principles are not disembodied rules, cut off from their cultural setting. To interpret autonomy in morality as entailing the reign of subjective principles involves an inherent misunderstanding of both moral belief and ethical theory. This conception wrongly portrays moral principles as formulated by atomized "moral" agents disengaged from a cultural setting ... By its nature morality is not individual-centered ... Virtuous conduct, role responsibilities, acceptable forms of loving, charitable behaviour, respect for persons, and many other moral views are individually assumed, but usually appropriated from established cultural arrangements.[12]

The characteristics of isolation, separation, and contractualism inherent in extreme individualism have been vigorously repudiated by contemporary bioethicists. Callahan, for instance, has written the following:

> This understanding of autonomy is hazardous to moral relationships and moral community. It buys our freedom to be ourselves, and to be free of undue influence by others, at too high a price. It establishes contractual relationships as the principal and highest form of relationships. It elevates isolation and separation as the necessary starting points of human commitments. It presumes that the moral life can be made a wholly voluntary matter ... thus attempting to deny the validity of many uninvited moral obligations that ordinary life with other people usually casts before us.[13]

Just as the individual should not be portrayed as isolated from community, so autonomy should not be understood in isolation from other values and goals. As has been noted, the importance of autonomy lies not in its achievement but in "the uses to which it is put and the moral ends it is fashioned to serve."[14] Whereas respect for autonomy is essential as a protection against paternalism, that achievement alone does not settle all questions about "the relation of autonomy to our duty to others to organize a community in a moral way."[15]

In international codes of ethics, as in bioethics generally, the "principle of respect for autonomy" should be distinguished from what some refer to as the "principle of autonomy." It is in part because the two are so often equated that respect for autonomy seems to some so foreign and threatening when applied to non-Western societies. Whereas the expression "principle of autonomy" can be thought to imply an ideal of autonomy, as if one "ought" to be and act autonomously, "respect for autonomy" implies no such thing. Respect for personal autonomy means just that – an obligation to value the autonomous choices and actions of

others, those made by people who are competent, informed, and acting voluntarily. An autonomous decision has been well defined by Beauchamp and McCullough as one which "derives from the person's own values and beliefs, is based on adequate information and understanding, and is not determined by internal or external constraints that compel the decision."
16

But respect for autonomy does not oblige one to act autonomously, most particularly not in the sense associated with individualism. Nor does it oblige one to make or induce others to act autonomously. One obviously cannot be forced to act autonomously. One may in fact choose not to decide or act autonomously. What this means and how it can be defended in some cultural contexts will be explored below.

To "respect" autonomy involves more than just having a certain attitude. It also means acting. The first sort of act it obliges is a negative one, that of refraining from controlling, coercing, or interfering with the autonomous acts and choices of other persons. But to value or respect personal autonomy entails some positive duties as well. For example, one could hardly value another's personal autonomy without at the same time fostering autonomous decision-making and attempting to make it possible by, for example, disclosing needed information. It does not mean leaving persons in "splendid isolation," simply free from constraints, but calls for efforts to provide or restore opportunity for personal choice. Implicit in this principle is the injunction to facilitate autonomy. This will involve both removing obstacles to it, and creating the conditions in which the autonomy, liberty, and freedom of choice of other persons can be expressed, to the extent of those other persons' capacity and desire to do so.

As already claimed above, respect for personal autonomy is by no means the whole of moral obligation, and international codes of ethics should reflect that fact. First of all, respect for autonomy, which is the basis for the right to self-determination, deals only with that one element (self-determination) of what it means to be a person and to respect persons. This underlines the need to consider respect for personal autonomy as only one of the obligations to be derived from the "umbrella" principle of respect for persons. Respecting autonomy in this sense means valuing and accommodating the reality that persons are embodied within and nurtured by particular histories, places, communities, shared expectations, and manners of coping and surviving – all ingredients of what is called culture.

Secondly, besides respect for autonomy, the other obligations arising from the principle of respect for persons within bioethics are those of protecting nonautonomous persons and those with diminished autonomy, seeking informed consent, and ensuring privacy and confidentiality. All of these should be underlined in international codes of ethics.

Thirdly, in addition to the principle of respect for persons, there are two other fundamental principles of bioethics which give rise to additional moral obligations, specifically the principles of beneficence and justice. Each of these three basic principles is best viewed, not as lexically ordered and binding in that order at all times, but as requiring trade-offs. For example, in some circumstances and situations when they compete, respect for persons in some form could be overridden by the obligation to do good and avoid harm (the principle of beneficence). We need not and cannot consider here the criteria and procedures according to which one principle or another could be overridden in defence of a competing one, but others have proposed and discussed some of these.[17]

3 Respect for Autonomy in Non-Western and Less Developed Societies

Understood and applied in the manner described above, the importance ascribed to respect for autonomy in Western systems of bioethics and reflected in international health and research codes of ethics need not be viewed as foreign to, destructive of, or insensitive to the cultures of non-Western and less developed societies.

It is arguable that versions of the principle of respect for persons already serve as "indigenous" normative principles (along with others) for distinguishing between right and wrong in many non-Western societies. It may well be the case that where these principles, and the rights and obligations to which they give rise, are invisible or submerged, that is not due to essential differences between peoples, or to the fact that people care about radically different things, or to the fact that people in different societies would be incapable of coming to ethical agreement about them on the basis of knowing the relevant facts and reasoning together.[18] It may be doubtful whether the degree of full rationality and shared understanding required in order to achieve ethical agreement between societies is possible, but within certain limits and under certain conditions there may be more agreement than disagreement between peoples on certain fundamental matters.

The underlying reasons why some societies appear to assign less value than others to respect for life, persons, or autonomy may have more to do with the various and different circumstances in which people live, or once lived, such as centuries of coping with hostile natural environments, the threat of neighboring groups, or the ever-present danger of starvation. Circumstances such as the struggle for economic or community survival may account for many attitudes and practices which appear to be objectively wrong in the light of detached ethical analysis, in that the rights and welfare of some individuals may be seriously violated. But the Inuit who abandoned their elderly members to die, the many societies which provide more food and care for their boys than their girls, and those cultures in which important decisions are made by families not individuals, are not necessarily less respectful of life, persons, and autonomy than others. Should certain circumstances of severe threat and hardship, and the attitudes they foster, be mitigated, those peoples may well be quite prepared to change their practices.

In some societies, on the other hand, respect for persons and autonomy may be very important, but may also be overlooked by observers in pursuit of conventional or superficial cultural analyses. It may well be there, but one must know what to look for, and how to find it. As I will suggest below, one such society may be that of Japan.

In support of these possibilities, I will explore, albeit necessarily briefly, a number of pieces of evidence. They are admittedly only loosely related, but they do arguably converge to make plausible the belief that respect for persons and autonomy is not as foreign an idea in many non-Western or underdeveloped societies as some have claimed.

The "Echo Factor" in Cross-cultural Bioethical Agreement   .

One should begin by acknowledging the need for caution in any search for cross-cultural similarities and agreement in bioethics. Given the diffusion of Western biomedicine around the world over many years, it is hardly surprising that Western ethics which went along with it has made some inroads. It has been noted, for example, that in India the ethical codes of Western physicians and of a variety of indigenous medical personnel, including Ayurvedic and Unani practitioners, are almost identical, having obviously been modeled on the British code.[19] Yet it would be hasty to conclude that this constitutes a significant contribution to India and Indian patients, because the British code which was exported was more a code of "colonial etiquette" than of ethics: strong on professional rights and beneficence, weak on patient rights and autonomy. However, the relevant point here is that unless one is aware of the Western antecedents and sources of those Indian codes, one might be inclined to conclude, on the basis of a comparison of the codes alone, that there is a striking cross-cultural similarity in medical ethics between the indigenous and Western codes.

The same danger and need for caution apply to the more recent phenomenon of multinational survey reports on the state of bioethics.[20] There may be a tendency to characterize some bioethical stances and concerns in other societies as being more indigenous than is justified in view of the major inroads made in recent years by North American bioethics, and the fact that many of the "national" reporters are graduates of American bioethics programs. Most appear to be ethicists or physicians not also trained in anthropology or related skills. It is not clear to what extent the observations of these reporters are accurate and comprehensive descriptions of both official and unofficial, articulate and inarticulate moralities of those societies, as opposed to being echoes or reflections of the ethical priorities learned in and imported from North America.

One cannot avoid a degree of skepticism on reading that many countries with very different cultures, traditions, institutions, and needs can come to more or less the same position on some highly contentious ethical issues, ranging from the use of the new reproductive technologies to euthanasia. Consider, for example, this observation by a Spanish ethicist in a recent multinational report on bioethics: "Looking back over all that has happened in the last ten years, it is surprising how closely bioethics in Spain has followed in the footsteps of North America and Central Europe."[21] Indeed, it is so surprising that one is entitled to wonder about the accuracy of the observations and the depth of the roots of bioethics in some of those societies.

One of the dangerous tendencies resulting from bioethics having itself become an international professional enterprise, with a common language and preoccupation, may well be that specific variations based upon different cultural, institutional, political, and belief factors are increasingly ignored. A "one size fits all" approach would be tragic: inauthentic, impoverishing, and a form of bioethical imperialism.

Respect for Autonomy: a Victim of Circumstances?

Having identified a danger, I will now flip the coin and defend the position that respect for persons and autonomy may be indigenous to many non-Western and developing societies, suggesting that when those principles and the conduct they impose are invisible or muted, this is more likely to be due to circumstances such as threats to survival than to people being indifferent or uncaring about individual lives.

Some examples and explanations are in order. A 1986 study of 228 villages in Bangladesh uncovered significantly higher mortality rates for females than for males.[22] Males were provided with better nutrition and health care, resource allocations which the authors attributed to economic and cultural factors. This differential is first evident from the time when breastfeeding is no longer adequate to meet the nutritional needs of a child, at which point parents have to make a decision about allocating scarce and costly supplementary food. Why do they favour male children from this point on? Apparently only men are involved in agricultural production, and women make only a limited direct economic contribution to the household. The productive labor of sons, from adolescence onward, is fundamental to the household economy. Sons therefore represent one of the few forms of economic security against the ever-present risk of the death or incapacitation of the head of the household.

Clearly this practice raises serious ethical questions from the perspective of Western bioethics, specifically in view of the lack of protection afforded to the vulnerable and nonautonomous girls and the unfair distribution of resources. But there is no evidence to suggest that these Bangladesh villagers do not respect the persons and lives of their daughters to the fullest extent possible within their economic context as presently defined, or that they make these choices with anything but regret, or that were their economic circumstances otherwise than they are they would not choose to feed and care for their sons and daughters equally.

A second example is the practice of female circumcision in a number of African countries. This may take the form of clitoridectomy, which involves slitting the hood of the clitoris, or the more drastic procedure of infibulation, in which the clitoris is completely excised and the sides of the vulva are stitched together. Clitoridectomies are usually done at the time girls begin menstruating, about age 12 years. Infibulations are performed on younger girls, from age three to about six or seven. Female circumcision is a traditional means of limiting a woman's ability to enjoy sex, guarding virginity, and discouraging sexual intercourse outside marriage. It is a practice which is still common in more than 20 African countries, among them, for example, Sudan, Somalia, Nigeria, and Kenya. The practice has been outlawed in Kenya since 1982, but such laws have had little effect on such a long-established custom. For over ten years now various groups, often with the support of the UN, have campaigned to end the practice, but change has been slow. These practices are followed by Christians, Muslims, and animists alike. There remains enormous pressure on young girls to be circumcised if they wish to fit into the community and be well respected.

Especially outside urban centres, circumcision is still widely performed by local women, often midwives, using a knife or homemade razor blade and of course without anesthesia or hygienic conditions. Accordingly the health and even the lives of the girls involved are at great risk. Hemorrage, septicemia, and retention of urine, as well as severe shock, occur.

There is increasing demand to have the procedure performed by medical or paramedical personnel in hospitals. That would reduce the health hazards, though not the social pressure to maintain the practice or the violation of the autonomy and bodily integrity of the young girls involved. Given this involvement of medical personnel, despite their education about the continuing health hazards, and the enforced nature of the operation, it is of interest that a 1986 survey of male medical students and female nursing students in Somalia reported that 51 percent of nursing students and 21 percent of medical students saw positive aspects in the practice.[23] The nursing students in Somalia are replacing the unlicensed midwives in rural areas in the performance of these circumcisions. Though 81 percent of the male medical students found the practice to be injurious, 38 percent favored continuing it and 29 percent said they would want their own daughters to be circumcised.

In view of the serious health risks involved and the enforced nature of the procedure, it is clearly objectively wrong by the criteria of Western bioethics. But reprehensible as the practice is, in view of the cultural and economic circumstances of these societies it does not necessarily establish that respect for persons and personal autonomy are principles completely foreign to the parents and other leaders involved. It has been well documented that women in Sudan and other African societies derive their economic security and social status largely from their roles as wives and mothers, and that therefore female virginity at the time of marriage is so important that even a rumor casting doubt on a girl's morality can bar her from marriage and seriously harm her family's honor.[24]

It is at least plausible that should the economic and social circumstances in which those women live be otherwise than they are, should they be gradually changed, the practice of female circumcision would correspondingly and happily be rejected by the Sudanese and other African societies. If that observation is correct, it follows that short-range approaches to this problem, whether by means of prohibitions in codes of ethics, or other attacks focused exclusively on the practice, will not be very effective.[25] The only effective policy in the long run would appear to be one which works towards expanding the status and economic security of women beyond that provided by their role as wives and mothers alone, and thereby removing the circumstance which supports the practice.[26]

Finding Autonomy within Conformity

Are conformity to tradition and subjection to authority sometimes compatible with autonomy? Yes, if one important condition is met: namely, that one autonomously chooses to surrender what could be called "first order" decisions to that authority, tradition, or institution. First order decisions are those concerning whether a practice or form of conduct is right or wrong. One is exercising "second order" autonomy in the selection of another person, authority, tradition, or religious institution, which one allows to make those "first order" decisions. Persons who make that choice, who voluntarily become subservient, for example, to a particular doctor or a particular religion or any other form of heteronomy, give over some or all first order autonomy, but not second order autonomy. As such they are owed respect for their second order autonomy or choices. Thus the principle of respect for autonomy is not incompatible with every form of heteronomy.[27]

If that analysis is applied to the cases discussed in the previous section, can we conclude that the young girls in Bangladesh who are provided with less food and health care than boys, and the young African girls who undergo circumcision, are exercising second order autonomy? Certainly not. Not even when stretched to the limit could the concept of autonomy accommodate those examples. The key condition for second order autonomy, namely that of an "autonomous" choice to let others decide the rightness and wrongness of conduct, cannot be met in those cases. The girls in both situations are too young to understand, and the social pressures brought to bear even on the older African girls make their "decisions" to undergo circumcision at best doubtfully voluntary.

But there are other situations in Western and non-Western societies, developed and less developed societies, in which that analysis may be appropriate and helpful. Consider, for example, the experience of those in Indonesia involved with family planning programs, a major government and health clinic priority. Established programs were apparently technically excellent, but only moderately successful. The rate of acceptance for family planning remained low. It finally became clear that the programs were based on the erroneous assumption that it was the woman herself who made the relevant decisions. As a result, all the education and propaganda efforts were directed exclusively at the wives. In fact, their views on that subject and others were the least important in the family. The major decisions are made by the husband, and on matters such as children and grandchildren the views of the grandparents also are crucially important.[28]

Obviously, it is difficult to characterize the conduct of these Indonesian wives, who accepted or rejected family planning at the behest of their husbands or parents, as the exercise of first order autonomy. But their readiness to allow other family members, as well as the prevailing cultural values and social organization, to determine for them right and wrong conduct in this matter may not be significantly different from the attitude of those born into a particular religion who allow their religious leaders and doctrines to determine right and wrong for them. If the latter case can be described as the exercise of second order autonomy (though not everyone will necessarily agree that it can) then it is difficult to see why the former should not as well.

There is another non-Western society in which the first order/second order autonomy analysis may be still more appropriate, namely that of

Japan. It has long been the standard view that the Japanese have no clear sense of self or interest in individuality, and that they want only to conform, to melt into the larger society, to achieve harmony at all costs, and that they make all important decisions consensually. Respect for personal autonomy is therefore widely assumed to be at odds with Japanese attitudes and culture. One expression of that view is the following: "The Japanese 'person' . . . is a finely honed social being who is trained from birth onwards in conformity, dependency and the suppression of individuality for the sake of group harmony."[29] While that may be an accurate analysis as far as it goes, it does not go far enough. There is much more to be said, another side of the coin. Smith, another ethnographer of Japan, insists:

> It seems to me that the Japanese possess a very clear sense of self, although it differs from our own, and that they regularly behave as though persons are indeed individuals. Western observers are often blinded by our inability to perceive the locus of the self in Japan, and by our unwillingness to accept the low priority given its expression . . . Within the confines of Japanese society, there are indeed some spheres of activity of which the common view is that there is diversity aplenty. The difficulty is that the differences which are pointed out in support of this contention are often so minute that they are scarcely discernible to the eye of the foreigner.[30]

One of the keys to the place and scope of self and autonomy in Japan is the much more muted sense of opposition between the self and others in a society in which autonomous acts are less prized than is social connectedness. Plath has noted that "the American archetype seems more attuned to cultivating a self that knows it is unique in the cosmos, the Japanese archetype to a self that can feel human in the company of others."[31] To a large extent individuals find self-realization by coming to terms with the demands of society, by disciplining themselves to conform to public roles and expectations. There is a strong imperative in Japan to seek the fusion or reintegration of the self with the objective world in which that self lives.[32]

But at the same time, having accomplished that fusion, that mature, not submissive accommodation to society, there is ample, though subtle, evidence to the trained and sensitive eye that the cultivation of one's individual nature, talents, and skills is both expected and encouraged. Smith, quoting Reischauer, writes: "To an extent not even remotely approached in the United States, most Japanese have their own personal literary, artistic or performing skill [which] is not only a means of emotional self-expression, but a treasured element of self-identity."[33] Smith finds further evidence of the fact that the Japanese realize they have an autonomous existence in the recurring themes of popular literature and drama.

Novels, plays, and films make heroes and heroines out of those with strong wills who struggle and often fail to resolve the conflicts that arise in trying to come to terms with the demands of society.[34]

The Japanese may be generally loath to express contentious personal opinions in public; but they have them, they do express them, and on many matters of public interest the public appears to be very well informed. A contemporary medical issue which has made all that quite evident is the ongoing public debate in Japan on brain death and organ transplantation. The debate is lively, opposing views are strongly stated, it is carried on not just in professional journals but in the public media, and it is fully accepted that policy on this issue cannot be changed until there is a public, not just a professional, consensus.[35] This is hardly the stuff of a society composed of passive, self-effacing individuals.

What can we conclude regarding the presence or absence of respect for autonomy in Japan? That it exists and is indigenous is undeniable, though the forms it assumes and the evidence supporting its existence are far more subtle than in Western societies. Is it on balance closer to "first order" or "second order" autonomy, assuming that that distinction is appropriate and helpful in this instance? Given the prominence of consensus and conformity in Japan, one may be inclined to conclude that people there generally tend to yield decisions about the rightness and wrongness of conduct to their traditions and other authorities, and therefore manifest respect only for a second order autonomy. But that degree of consensus and conformity may be expected, indeed inevitable, in a society as culturally and racially homogeneous as Japan. It would be surprising were it otherwise. Must we classify the exercise of autonomy in all homogeneous societies as necessarily of the second-order variety? As well, while consensus and conformity do exist, they are more in the nature of goals toward which the Japanese continually strive than static and fixed realities. In the process of seeking that consensus on moral issues in health care as in other areas, the Japanese arguably manifest healthy individualities and lively autonomies of the first order variety.

Autonomous Health Behavior before the Arrival of Western Medicine

Many commentators have compellingly demonstrated how Western medicine, in contributing to the displacement of indigenous cultures, has jeopardized if not destroyed the potential those societies had to deal with sickness, pain, and vulnerability in personal and autonomous ways. The subject is too enormous and complex to do it any justice here; but for the purposes of this paper the single point to be noted is the extent to which personal autonomy and responsibility in health matters were already present and thriving before the arrival of Western civilization and Western medicine. Far from being a Western import, versions of autonomous health behavior, strongly supported by the cultural context, were indigenous and healthy, more put at risk than enhanced by the advent of Western medicine. What Illich calls "medical civilization" largely displaced both existing interpretations of illness, pain, and death and individual responsibility for coping with them, substituting a new dependence on corporate, institutionalized medicine:

> Modern cosmopolitan medical civilization denies the need for man's acceptance of pain, sickness and death. Medical civilization is planned and organized to kill pain, to eliminate sickness, and to struggle against death. These are new goals, and goals which have never before been guidelines for social life. From being essential experiences with which each of us has to come to terms, pain, sickness and death are transformed by medical civilization into accidents for which people must seek medical treatment. The goals of medical civilization are thus antithetical to every one of the cultures with which it is confronted when it is dumped, as part and parcel of industrial progress, on the so-called under-developed countries.[36]

Illich then notes the effect this development has had on personal responsibility and autonomy:

> As the medical institution assumes the management of suffering, my responsibility for my and your suffering declines. Culturally regulated, autonomous health behaviour is restricted, crippled and paralysed by the expansion of corporate medical care. The effectiveness of persons and of primary groups in self-care is overwhelmed by the competing industrial production of a substitute value.[37]

Two conclusions may be in order. The first is that respect for autonomy in many less developed societies should not be viewed as a destructive import from the West. In the health context the real intrusion and destruction more plausibly resulted from the inability of Western medicine to value, protect, and accommodate the already existing autonomous health behavior and its cultural framework. It is at least arguable that that was not at all due to an over-emphasis on autonomy and individuality in Western biomedicine and medical ethics in those earlier times, but quite the opposite. Beneficence and paternalism were the reigning models in medical practice and medical ethics, in both domestic and exported versions.

This leads to the second conclusion. If autonomous health behavior is (or was) already a reality in less developed societies, then surely it could be respectful of, rather than destructive of, those cultures to place a strong emphasis on respect for autonomy in international codes of ethics and by other means. But, of course, this must be done in the sense we have been advocating, namely one which accommodates interdependence, responsibility, and community. By doing so, Western medicine would be carrying along with it a partial antidote for one of its regrettable by-products, the dependency it creates.

There are a number of important additional criteria which must be met in formulating and applying these international codes of ethics, all of which relate directly or indirectly to establishing the meaning, scope, and context of respect for persons and autonomy in these codes. I will briefly outline some of those proposed criteria in the following sections.

4 Multi-cultural Input in the Formulation and Application of International Codes of Ethics

There is always the real danger that the dominant cultural and national element in a code-writing committee will (often unconsciously) impose its own culturally conditioned values, principles, and priorities as the predominant normative standards. It is no secret that the dominant cultural and national orientation of such committees in the past, whether of health agencies or health profsesions, has been Western. There are at least three reasons why representatives from all the societies and professions to which a code is directed should contribute to it:

1 to correctly identify the abuses and dangers to be addressed;
2 to ensure that the code in question reflects awareness of and sensitivity to different moral and cultural perceptions, as well as cross-cultural commonalities;
3 to strive together to make the code not just a reflection of the moral status quo in any society, but a challenge to all the member societies to improve conduct toward patients and research subjects.

5 The Dangers and Limitations of Seeking Moral Consensus

Given the many different cultures, traditions, economies, political systems, and institutions of the member countries to which international codes of ethics are directed, it is necessary to seek moral consensus for the reasons indicated above. But the dangers and limitations of its pursuit must be acknowledged. Too little consensus can mean that a code of ethics will be treated as irrelevant or intrusive by some member societies; but too much consensus can mean too little ethics. Ethical reasoning and the establishment of the best ethical norms should not in the final analysis be determined by counting heads but by finding the best reasons.

There is danger whichever way one turns in such exercises. To undervalue consensus risks cultural insensitivity and irrelevance. To overvalue it risks a code of ethics which will be culturally non-offensive but heavy on generalities and support for the moral status quo. This is by no means a new dilemma. In large, pluralistic, and secular states the achievement of clear public consensus on contentious moral issues has become increasingly elusive and unlikely, and perhaps the most that can be hoped for is an agreement to negotiate peacefully.[38] That observation may be equally (or more) applicable to efforts to produce international codes of ethics, given the many societies and cultures involved.

The experience of some national bioethics committees and commissions may be both instructive and somewhat depressing when we consider the various sieves through which ethical viewpoints are squeezed on the way to becoming policy.

Since the mid-1970s the committee (or commission) mode has emerged as an extremely important method for both ethical analysis and public policy making in the bioethics field. In many cases the committees are officially appointed by governments to help resolve controversial or technically complex issues in a more academic mode than the rough and tumble of day to day politics allows. Officially appointed committees in turn receive testimony from other committees representing various interest groups, as well as from technical experts and laypeople. The committees then typically seek to reach ethical judgments that are both rationally defensible and politically acceptable to large segments of a given society. In other words, publicly appointed committees frequently seek the middle ground on an issue.[39]

In a democratic, liberal, and pluralist society, such goals and methods may well be the best we can do. That may be so as well for committees mandated to write international codes of ethics. But the trouble with aiming at "middle grounds" is that one is inevitably thereby re-enforcing the moral status quo:[40] and, as already suggested, that is not an attractive goal for codes of ethics. If they are to serve the more noble purpose of repudiating conduct which is wrong, challenging conventional value assumptions and demanding improvement, then those who formulate the codes must insulate themselves as much as possible from political and interest group considerations.

6 Taking the Indirect Route: Forsaking Short-range Approaches

It will not be possible for every society to abandon unethical health care or research practices at the same pace, given the variety of economic, social, and other circumstances which in many cases gave rise to that conduct. This reality underlines the obvious insufficiency of codes of ethics alone when it comes to changing practices. As already suggested earlier in this paper, in many cases it does little or no good to prohibit and campaign against a particular form of conduct while leaving untouched the more fundamental motivating circumstances.

One example considered above was that of female circumcision in Africa, a practice closely linked to the status and economic security of women in that part of the world. Clearly it is the latter circumstances which must be modified first. That is of course a long-range, sensitive, and complex undertaking, involving education and time. Codes of ethics can play a part by directly or indirectly identifying the conduct in question, but that is the first and easiest step.

On the other hand, there are some health problems and diseases against which concerted international efforts can make important progress without necessarily solving or modifying more fundamental circumstances. An example is the eradication of smallpox.

7 The Missing Ingredient in Codes of Ethics: Social Justice

A major defect in most health and research codes of ethics, both national and international, is not that they give too much attention to respect for autonomy, but rather that they give too little to social justice issues. The focus in these codes is usually the narrow one of the doctor and patient or researcher and subject; in some cases it is widened to include the hospital or research institution. The issues tend to be limited to those of autonomy, beneficence, confidentiality, informed consent, and risk/benefit factors. If justice concerns are included, the focus is narrow and little or no attention is directed to distributive justice or social justice issues. More attention in codes and other health policies to issues such as a right of access to adequate health care is badly needed. Another concern should be the obligation of more affluent member countries and professions to distribute research attention and funding for the diseases of concern to developing countries. In 1974, for example, the US spent $400 million on cancer research, but only $25 million on research on tropical diseases.

It is particularly appropriate for epidemiologists to expand their horizons beyond micro-ethical issues to include these macro-ethical concerns. It is, after all, one of the professional mandates of epidemiologists to uncover factors which influence health-related states or events in order to enhance the health of populations and individuals. That "population-based" aspect of epidemiology (as distinct from clinical epidemiology) surely provides an ample justification and duty to attend to economic, environmental, institutional, structural, and political influences when it comes to designing international health care and research codes of ethics for epidemiologists. Serious inequities with severe health-related effects, including famine, poverty, disease, and death, are built into the social and political fabric of many countries.[41]

8 Providing the Infrastructures for Doing Ethics

International codes of ethics are necessarily couched in general terms. They provide for the most part only ethical conclusions, principles, or injunctions, not the careful and difficult ethical reasoning and multidisciplinary collaboration which will be required in applying those principles to specific ethical dilemmas in a variety of circumstances. In other words, the codes at least implicitly require by their very nature and promulgation that ethicists be available to apply them and to train others to do so.

There is then an obligation upon those who formulate these codes to help those countries who do not have the needed expertise to acquire it. In some cases that will involve the provision of opportunities to train ethicists academically and clinically. In other cases it will involve as well assisting less developed societies to establish clinical ethics and research ethics committees. It serves no useful purpose whatsoever to insist upon the evaluation of research protocols everywhere, when some countries have neither the personnel nor the funding to establish such committees.

Notes

1 A. L. Caplan, "Cracking Codes," *Hastings Center Report*, (Aug. 1978), 18. Caplan suggests the following excerpt from the Code of Ethics of the American Chiropractic Association as a good example of self-interest in professional codes: "A wealthy chiropractor should not give advice gratuitously to the affluent. In so doing, he injures his professional brethren. The office of a chiropractor can never be supported as a beneficent one. Hence, it is defrauding the common fund when fees are dispensed with which might rightfully be claimed."

2   R. Veatch, "Codes of Medical Ethics: Ethical Analysis," in W. Reich and L. Walters, eds, *Encyclopedia of Bioethics*, vol. 7, Free Press, New York, 1988.

3   See B. Freedman, "Health Professions, Codes and the Right to Refuse to Treat HIV-Infectious Patients," *Hastings Center Report* (April/May 1988), 20.

4   On the lack of attention to patient autonomy in earlier codes, see e.g. T. L. Beauchamp and L. B. McCullough, *Medical Ethics: The Moral Responsibility of Physicians*, Prentice-Hall, Englewood Cliffs, NJ, 1984. See also R. M. Veatch, *A Theory of Medical Ethics*, Basic Books, New York, 1981.

5   This draft code of the IEA was not yet published when this paper was written, but was made available to and discussed with me by Dr John Last, MD, responsible for the draft and consultations on it.

6   A summary of the discussion and the recommendations of that conference are available in Medical Research Council of Canada, *Towards an International Ethic for Research with Human Beings*, Ottawa, 1988.

7   L. Dumont, *Homo Hierarchicus*, Paladin, London, 1970. See also D. R. Gordon, "Tenacious Assumptions in Western Medicine," in M. Lock and D. R. Gordon, eds, *Biomedicine Examined*, Kluwer, 1988.

8   C. Geertz, "On the Nature of Anthropological Understanding," in *Annual Editions in Anthropology*, Duskin, Guilford, Conn., 1977.

9   Gordon, "Tenacious Assumptions in Western Medicine."

10 M. Foucault, *The Order of Things: The Archeology of the Human Sciences*, Vintage, New York, 1973.

11 L. J. Kirmayer, "Mind and Body as Metaphor: Hidden Values in Biomedicine," in M. Lock and D. R. Gordon, eds, *Biomedicine Examined*, Kluwer, 1988. Renee Fox recently made the following observation about bioethics:

> The weight that bioethics has placed on individualism has relegated more socially-oriented values and ethical questions to a secondary status. The concept and the language of "rights" prevails over those of "responsibility," "obligation" and "duty" in bioethical discourse. The skein of relationships of which the individual is a part, the socio-moral importance of the interdependence of persons, and of reciprocity, solidarity and community between them, have been overshadowed by the insistence on the autonomy of self as the highest moral good. Social and cultural factors have been primarily seen as external constraints that limit individuals. They are rarely viewed as forces that exist "inside", as well as outside individuals, shaping their personhood and enriching their humanity. (R. C. Fox, "The Evolution of American Bioethics," in G. Weisz, ed, *Social Science Perspectives on Medical Ethics*, Kluwer, Dordrecht, 1990, 207)

12 T. L. Beauchamp and J. F. Childress, *Principles of Biomedical Ethics*, 2nd edn, Oxford University Press, Oxford, 1983, 65.

13 D. Callahan, "Autonomy: A Moral Good, Not a Moral Obsession," *Hastings Center Report* (Oct. 1984), 41.

14 Ibid., 42.

15 R. M. Veatch, "Autonomy's Temporary Triumph," *Hastings Center Report* (Oct. 1984), 39.

16 Beauchamp and McCullough, *Medical Ethics*, 44. It should, however, be noted that this definition is quite compatible with making choices for oneself in

keeping with one's own values, which take into account as much as possible the needs and desires of others, of the community at large, as long as doing so reflects internalized values.

17 See for example J. F. Childress, "The Place of Autonomy in Bioethics," *Hastings Center Report* (Jan./Feb. 1990), 12.

18 This line of reasoning, though not applied specifically to autonomy, was suggested by James Rachels in "Can Ethics Provide Answers?", *Hastings Center Report* (June 1980), 32.

19 P. Kunstadter, "Medical Ethics in Cross-Cultural and Multi-Cultural Perspective," (1980) *Social Science and Medicine*, 14B (1980), 289.

20 Some examples of these multinational surveys and analyses are: "Biomedical Ethics: A Multinational View," *Hastings Center Report*, Special Supplement (June 1987); "International Perspectives on Biomedical Ethics," *Hastings Center Report*, Special Supplement (Aug. 1988); "Biomedical Ethics Around the World," *Hastings Center Report* (Dec. 1984), 14; R. M. Veatch, "Medical Ethics in the Soviet Union," *Hastings Center Report* (March/April 1989), 11; H. T. Engelhardt, "Bioethics in the People's Republic of China," *Hastings Center Report* (April 1980), 7.

21 D. Gracia, "Spain: From the Decree to the Proposal," *Hastings Center Report* (June 1987), 29.

22 M. A. Koenig and S. D'Souza, "Sex Differences in Childhood Morality in Rural Bangladesh," *Social Science and Medicine* 22 (1986), 15–22. This example and the next one (female circumcision in Africa), though not some of the conclusions I have drawn, were suggested by Richard W. Lieban in "Medical Anthropology and the Comparative Study of Medical Ethics," in Weisz, ed, *Social Science Perspectives on Medical Ethics*, 221–39.

23 P. G. Gallo, "Views of Future Health Workers in Somalia on Female Circumcision," *Medical Anthropology Quarterly* 17 (1986), 71–3.

24 On the other hand it could perhaps be claimed that there are important differences between these two examples, making the case of female circumcision in Africa a serious devaluation of the girls and violation of the principle of respect for persons because of the nature of the belief system explaining it. In the Bangladesh example there is arguably a factual basis for the better treatment according to boys: for example boys, on average, may be able to do more physical work than girls. But in the case of female circumcision in Africa the basis for the practice is somewhat different. The way non-virgins are treated may be a social reality based upon a cluster of beliefs and attitudes without a grounding in anything as factual or plausible as exists in the Bangladesh example.

25 On the other hand, such denunciations may have some effect. They can force people to try to explain and defend what is indefensible. That very effort and its failure may contribute to a gradual change in attitudes.

26 E. Gruenbaum, "The Movement against Clitoridectomy and Infibulation in Sudan: Public Health Policy and the Women's Movement," *Medical Anthropology Newsletter*, 13 (1982), 4.

414 Edward W. Keyserlingk

27   See for example Childress, "The Place of Autonomy in Bioethics," 13.
28   G. M. Foster and B. G. Anderson, *Medical Anthropology*, Wiley, New York, 1978.
29   M. Lock and C. Honde, "Reaching Consensus about Death: Heart Transplants and Cultural Identity in Japan," in Weisz, ed., *Social Science Perspectives on Medical Ethics*, 99. See also M. Lock, *East Asian Medicine in Urban Japan: Varieties of Medical Experience*, University of California Press, Berkeley, 1980.
30   R. J. Smith, *Japanese Society, Tradition, Self and the Social Order* (Lewis Henry Morgan Lecture Series), Cambridge University Press, Cambridge, 1983, 89, 93.
31   D. W. Plath, *Long Engagements: Maturity in Modern Japan*, Stanford University Press, Stanford, 1980, 218.
32   T. S. Lebra, *Japanese Patterns of Behaviour*, University Press of Hawaii, Honolulu, 1976.
33   Smith, *Japanese Society*, 103.
34   Ibid., 98.
35   Lock and Honde, "Reaching Consensus about Death."
36   I. Illich, *Medical Nemesis, The Expropriation of Health*, McClelland & Stewart, London, 1975, 90.
37   Ibid., 91–2.
38   H. T. Engelhardt, "Bioethics in Pluralist Societies," *Perspectives in Biology and Medicine*, 26 (1982) 64–77; "Allocating Scarce Medical Resources and the Availability of Organ Transplantation," *New England Journal of Medicine* (Special Report), 311 (1984), 66–71.
39   L. Walters, "Ethics and New Reproductive Technologies: An International Review of Committee Statements," *Hastings Center Report*, (Special Supplement) (June 1987), 4.
40   R. Neville made the following comment about the report on research with human subjects produced by the (US) National Commission for the Protection of Human Subjects:

> The present report presents a general consensus about the moral conflicts involved in doing research on people institutionalized as mentally infirm – a consensus that is adequate for recommending sane, cautious policies with a broad base of support. The Commission has done what it was asked to do. Although I believe that it is a proper way of establishing national policy, we must recognize the degree to which this form of deliberation and policy making exerts a conservative force in choosing among a variety of ethical options. Precisely when the underlying value assumptions of our society cry out for reconsideration, social institutions such as the Commission reinforce those assumptions, by rationalizing, coordinating, and making them practically applicable. (R. Neville, "On the National Commission: A Puritan Critique of Consensus Ethics," *Hastings Center Report* 10 (1979), 22)

41   There remains of course the ever-present danger of forcing non-medical concerns into the medical model by assuming that epidemiologists have the training and mandate to attack all problems in the economic, political, and other arenas of life. See e.g. L. E. Goodman and M. J. Goodman, "Prevention, How Misuse of a Concept Undercuts its Worth," *Hastings Center Report*

16 (1986), 26–38. But that danger can surely be mitigated if epidemiologists, and other health professionals, work closely at the "macro" level with those of many other disciplines – anthropologists, economists, political scientists, ethicists, etc.

22
The Functions and Limitations of Professional Codes of Ethics

Dale Beyerstein

Granting that professional codes of ethics are of little use in resolving moral dilemmas, Beyerstein argues that cynicism about the usefulness of such codes is unjustified because they serve other important functions. Cynicism about the possibility of resolving moral dilemmas simply because they cannot be resolved by recourse to codes of ethics is similarly unwarranted. Moral dilemmas can often be resolved by recourse to moral theory. Beyerstein lists four important functions served by a code of ethics and argues that three of them can be fulfilled only if the code represents the consensus of the profession. Any code capable of securing such a consensus is likely to consist of rules for judging obvious cases and general statements that everyone could interpret in a way they find acceptable. It is this generality that makes codes useless for solving moral dilemmas.

Moral dilemmas arise when we must choose ebtween incompatible actions each of which promotes a good we think ought not to be sacrificed. Beyerstein identifies two possibilities for resolving such dilemmas: finding additional morally relevant facts about the situation, or refining our moral theories to yield a clear priority between the contested goods. A professional code of ethics, he suggests, is of no help in either of these tasks. Consequently, being a moral professional involves more than simply following one's professional code; it also involves paying attention to a wider moral theory in reasoning about difficult cases.

This essay, with its emphasis on the regulative functions of professional codes that reflect our judgments about settled, non-controversial cases, provides a useful counterbalance to the essays by Winkler (chapter 19) and Hoffmaster (chapter 20), which focus on deliberation in difficult, problematic cases. Also it is useful to compare Beyerstein's views on the potential power of codes of ethics to solve moral dilemmas with Keyserlingk's views on this subject (chapter 21).

A related version of this paper by J. Paredes, D. Beyerstein, B. Ledwidge, and C. Kogan was presented to the Canadian Psychiatric Association Annual Meeting in 1986, and published in the *Canadian Journal of Psychiatry*, vol. 35, Oct. 1990. I would like to thank Jaime Paredes for comments on this version, as well as Don Brown for useful discussions on this topic. I have also benefited from his "On Professing to be a Profession," *Dialogue* 25/4 (Winter 1986), pp. 753–6, which was a response to D. MacNive, P. MacEwen and C. Paiva, "A Code of Ethics for Canadian Philosophers: A Working Paper," *Dialogue*, 25/1 (Spring 1986), pp. 179–89.

[Note: Although Beyerstein's discussion of codes of ethics has relevance to professional ethics generally, we believe it is most usefully considered in the context of biomedical ethics. Because discussion of codes of ethics has been prominent in the medical field, considering Beyerstein's paper in relation to the others in this section provides a fuller picture of the concerns that have animated that field.]

Many people become cynical about codes of ethics because they suspect that such codes are of no help in resolving moral dilemmas. In fact, some cynics take delight in pointing out holes in their own professional codes that are large enough to drive a truck through, thus making them next to worthless for providing moral guidance. Other cynics speculate on the reason for this: that codes of ethics exist primarily to make professionals *look* moral, not to promote morality in the profession – in other words, to allow professionals to protect themselves, either individually or collectively. It is not my purpose here to either affirm or deny this claim. As far as I can see, it is perfectly possible for professions to design codes of ethics for this purpose; just as it is possible for individual professionals to use the codes of their professions for this purpose. But it is equally possible for whole professions and individuals to use codes for other, more respectable ends; and it is these ends which I wish to explore here.

The point of this paper, then, is not to examine how codes of ethics are *in fact* used, but rather to say a few things about how they *might* be used. My hope is that this will shed some light on the question whether there is any point in a profession's having a code of ethics, and in a professional's ever bothering to consult one. The argument of this paper is twofold: the first point is that the intuition behind the cynicism I have alluded to is perfectly correct – that is, codes of ethics cannot resolve moral dilemmas. The second is that it does not matter very much that codes cannot fulfill this function. Codes of ethics have other purposes than to resolve moral dilemmas; and we have other (and better) means besides codes of ethics to resolve moral dilemmas. Resolving moral dilemmas requires the application of a moral theory which is more general than the moral theory which informs the code of ethics of a particular profession. So the cynicism implied in the above criticism of codes of ethics is misplaced: we simply should not expect the code of ethics to resolve moral dilemmas.

A second sort of cynicism I wish to address holds that moral dilemmas are irresolvable. The usual argument for this view rests upon the correct observation that codes of ethics do not resolve moral dilemmas, but leaps from this premise to the unwarranted conclusion that moral dilemmas are not capable of rational resolution. The reason that this inference is unwarranted is that it ignores the fact that moral theory can be invoked in those cases where codes provide no guidance. Fortunately, it is not my job here to actually resolve any moral dilemmas. My aim is much less ambitious: to simply direct you to the right place, and let you take it from there. I shall begin by distinguishing professional codes from moral theories.

The *Oxford English Dictionary* defines "code" in the sense we are interested in as "a systematic collection or digest of the laws of a country, or of those relating to a particular subject." Two points in this definition are important for our present purposes. First is the emphasis on "systematic": a good code of ethics will present its injunctions in a systematic manner. However, note the second point: the connection with the laws of a country. The laws of the land merely assert what is to be done, or, more usually, what must *not* be done. They do not explain why this is so, or provide the reasons behind these pronouncements. Thus, if the legal system is systematic, a mere inspection of the code is not sufficient to reveal this. It is only by examining the code in the light of legal and moral theory that we can judge the code to be adequate or inadequate.

A code of ethics is essentially a societal code "writ small" – that is, one that governs the conduct of a subset of the population who engage in a particular set of tasks that are not commonly engaged in by the wider public. Since only a small number of people are doing these things, and usually only those people doing them have the knowledge to tell whether they are done well or badly, it would be too cumbersome and without point to have these rules listed in the whole society's code. Instead they can be listed in a code made available to the profession itself and to those who deal directly with these professionals. But the main point of a code is that it is a statement of the rules which govern, or which ought to govern, a profession.

Such a statement of rules will necessarily be incomplete. The point of listing a set of rules is so that people can follow them; and if the list is so long that we cannot find the rules when we want to refer to them, then the list is of no use to us. This is not to say that the rules of the system are or must be incomplete; my point is that the statement of them must be incomplete if the list is to be of any use. For example, the law setting the speed limit at 50 kph on city streets is clear and unambiguous: driving at 51 kph counts as a violation. But if a man is pulled over by a policeman and explains that he was speeding in order to get his wife to the hospital before she delivers the baby, this constitutes an exception to the law, but not one that is recognized in the law itself as an exception. The reason for this is threefold. First, the number of exceptions is so large that the statute could not be learned by the public if all the known exceptions were listed. Secondly, the traffic police officer still would have to use his or her judgment to determine whether this case constituted the type of situation the exception was framed to capture. Third, it is arguable that it would be impossible to state in advance all possible types of situations where an exception ought to be made. So, the procedure we follow is to rely on the individual judgment of the police officer involved at the time. In probably 99.9 percent of cases no exceptions apply, and in only about 0.1 percent of cases is an individual judgment called for. Similarly, the professionals' code of ethics will work very well for the bulk of cases, and it would be foolish to attempt to write into the code provisions for moral dilemmas which will be encountered very rarely, and which require a great deal of moral deliberation to resolve.

A moral theory, on the other hand, is not itself a set of principles, but is an attempt to explain why we place the weight we do on the principles we use to guide our lives; to explain why we rank them in the order we do; and provide reasons for preferring one principle over another when they conflict. Those of us who act in the world, as professionals do, are primarily interested in this function of a moral theory, as a method for providing justifications for what we think we ought to do. In moral dilemmas where two morally good actions are mutually exclusive, a moral theory resolves the dilemma by explaining why one action has a higher value than the other. How does it do this? Actions are done for a purpose, an end, and so what we need when we resolve a conflict between actions is a theory of value: what kinds of things are valuable? Actions? Subjective states such as pleasures, contemplations, intentions, hopes . . . ? How is it that we come to have duties? Is it when the opportunity to do some sort of good presents itself to us, or only when we put ourselves under an obligation, as when we make a promise? Do the duties that we contract when we take on a client give our clients special claims on us, even when they are suffering less, or are generally less morally worthy, than a non-client? Who counts from the moral point of view anyway? Who has interests that we must take into account when we decide what to do? Do fetuses, gerbils, trees, or the environment as a whole have interests? If so, how can we weigh them against our own? These are the kinds of questions that we need to answer in order to solve difficult moral dilemmas. Fortunately we need not answer them now in order for me to make the central point of this paper: that, given the functions that we expect a code of ethics to serve, we find that it will in most cases be helpless in answering these kinds of questions; and therefore helpless in resolving moral dilemmas. To show this I need to outline the functions of a code of ethics.

A professional code serves four functions: (1) it gives guidance to the individual professional; (2) its principles are statements of the agreed-upon standards of ethical practice, and thus provide guidance for ethics committees struck to rule on professional misconduct of members; (3) it is a public pronouncement of the ethical principles agreed upon by the majority of the profession and thus serves to inform clients about what they have a right to expect from their professionals; and (4) it informs other professionals with whom the professional must work about the kind of cooperation they have a right to expect from the professional; and the limits to the cooperation that a professional ought to give. All four of these functions always involve a consensus of the profession. Their point is to announce the moral principles that the profession has already agreed to endorse. Now, this agreement must have been arrived at either by imposition by a group of people whose authority is unquestioned, or by some sort of democratic decision-making process. In the former case, there is little to recommend that decision. Part of what makes someone a professional is that she is thought to have the capacity for independent judgment; therefore it is contrary to the professional *ethos* for her to do something simply because she is told to. This point holds even when the person doing the ordering is another member of the same profession.[1] Therefore, this leaves the second option, that the provision of the code will have been arrived at by the usual methods of democratically arriving at a consensus: negotiation and bargaining. And we know what is the usual result of this process; agreement about that which is obvious, and prevarication over that which is difficult or contentious.

This necessity for compromise severely weakens the first function of a code, to give guidance to individual professionals. While the provisions of the code may be adequate to handle the clear and obvious moral problems that arise, we shall see in a moment, when we examine the nature of moral dilemmas, why the methods of compromise and Trasle-066 are unable to produce a code that is adequate to the task of resolving moral dilemmas.

Now let us turn to the second function of the code we have specified: to state the standards of ethical practice that are invoked by an ethics committee to judge a professional's conduct. These standards must be promulgated in advance, just as a law must, if someone is to be accused of violating it. We consider it unjust to charge a citizen with violating a law that was promulgated after the alleged offense was committed; and it would be similarly unjust for a professional society's disciplinary body to discipline a member for something that is not clearly forbidden by the society's code of ethics in advance of the action which is the subject of the investigation. If a professional stands in front of an ethics committee charged with misconduct, then that person is accused of behavior or judgment which falls very much below the standards of his or her colleagues. Therefore, there must exist an agreed-upon standard which this person has failed to meet.

The third function of the code, that is, its providing a public pronouncement of the ethical principles of the profession, again requires the consensus of the majority of the profession. As already mentioned, this pronouncement serves to inform clients about what they have a right to expect from the professionals with whom they deal; and therefore such a pronouncement would be hypocritical if it were *not* agreed upon by the vast majority. It is for this reason that many provisions in a code tend to be general statements that everyone could interpret in a way he or she finds acceptable. But this generality is precisely what makes these statements useless as a guide to solving a moral dilemma.

The fourth function of a code is to inform other professionals with whom the professional must work about the kind of cooperation they have a right to expect from the professional; and the limits of the cooperation a professional ought to give. Often, in such a case, the individual is pressured by these other professionals to do something he or she morally cannot do; and the code serves to buttress the professional's resolve to resist this pressure, and to provide an authority for the professional's arguments against the other professionals: "I cannot do what you request because our code forbids it." It also indicates to the others that there is no point in simply asking some other member of the profession to do this job, since the other members are bound by the same code. But, again, if the code is to serve this purpose, it must express the resolve of the majority of the profession. If it did not, it would be disingenuous for a professional to state that provision of the code as evidence that this is the case.

Dilemmas sometimes arise in these cases where one professional, who has one set of duties, asks for cooperation from a second professional who has a different, conflicting set of duties. In this sort of case, there will be a conflict between the two professionals' codes of ethics. An example of this sort of conflict between codes would be that of a psychiatrist who is approached by his client's lawyer asking that the client be kept in hospital two weeks longer, although she was ready for discharge, so that the lawyer could have the trial deferred and would therefore have time to prepare her case for court.

In this sort of case, each professional has a code of ethics which enjoins him or her to promote certain ends. So, here, we have a conflict between codes, as well as a conflict about which end – an honest diagnosis or a fair trial – is most important from the moral point of view. It is understandable in these cases that each professional, given his or her training, and the values that led that person into the profession, will come to value things differently. And it is perfectly natural that, having once decided that one of these is the most important, she will struggle to bring it about. But it will not do to say about this sort of case that one professional ought to follow his code and the other professional hers, and both simply ought to try to bring about what their respective codes enjoin. In the sort of dilemma we are considering, both professionals have as their ultimate responsibility to look after the client's over-all interests, and in so far as both professionals are trying to achieve this end, they cannot be indifferent to what ultimately happens. Thus, both professionals must re-examine their codes, and look for guidance from moral theory to determine what ought to happen in this particular case, and which code has to be revised in order to be consistent with that result.

To summarize, then, it appears that three of the four functions of a code of ethics necessarily involve a consensus already having been established among the members of the profession. But with respect to the first function of a moral code, to provide guidance in ethical deliberation, an appeal to what the majority would do cannot, by itself, serve as a moral reason for acting. The reason for this can be seen if we examine briefly the nature of moral deliberation. Moral deliberation necessarily involves the moral agent confronting the situation facing him or her, asking the question, "What ought I to do?" This question is not equivalent to the question, "What is the consensus of my colleagues about what to do?" The question "What ought I to do?" remains to be asked even after finding out what others recommend. That is not, of course, to say that seeking the advice of your colleagues is worthless. Your colleagues' advice may be exactly right. My point is that what *makes* it right has nothing to do with the numbers of people who take it to be so. Therefore, the fact that your professional colleagues have agreed to put a rule in your code does not *make* this the right action.

Moral dilemmas arise when we are faced with incompatible actions, one of which promotes one end, or one person's end, and the other of which promotes some other end, or some other person's end. Thus, we are faced with a trade-off: at most, we can satisfy one of these ends. But this conflict between ends is not all there is to a moral dilemma. This much is common to almost all moral deliberations. The second feature of a dilemma is that we see both ends as ones that we must promote: we recognize a moral loss if we fail to promote either one of these ends, even if the reason we do not promote it is the impossibility of promoting both ends together. In most moral deliberations we encounter, we see the gain from promoting one end as so obviously greater than that to be achieved by any alternative that the sacrifice of the other end is obviously worth it. But in a moral dilemma, we do not see which end to promote: all alternatives seem all to involve ends which we ought not to sacrifice.

Now, it is at this point that I shall actually say something controversial. Up until now, I take it that my remarks about moral theories and moral codes have been merely descriptive, and would be accepted by philosophers no matter which of the available alternative moral theories they might defend.

It seems to me that there are two approaches to the study of moral dilemmas that we might take. One approach focuses on what it is really like to be in a moral dilemma – on the psychological and phenomenological attributes of the situation: the *angst* we experience while we are deliberating about what to do, and the regret and sense of loss we experience after the decision has been made. This is the approach we find in European philosophy and among those who have been influenced by this tradition, as well as in the continent's literature. The other approach focuses on the method of deliberation itself. According to this tradition, if it really were the case that we had no reason to prefer one option in a moral dilemma to the other, then there is no role for reason to play. It would not matter which option we chose, since *ex hypothesi* there is nothing to be gained by the choice. So we really have no deliberation problem, even if we do have a human problem – which the novelist is much better equipped to deal with than the philosopher.

My position is the second one, though I cannot justify it in this paper. All I have space for here is to point out a consequence of this position. It is only when we think that there really is a reason to prefer one course of action over another, but that we just do not yet know what it is, that we have a problem. All we can do is either try to find empirical facts of the situation which we have not yet seen which might make a morally relevant difference, or refine our theories so that this difference will be apparent. Paying attention to our code is of no use in either of these two endeavors.

If I am right, we see something as a moral dilemma, rather than as a usual garden-variety moral problem that we handle every day, precisely because we have not gathered the facts, or have not done enough moral theorizing. Here we have in a nutshell the reason why codes cannot help us resolve moral dilemmas. The articulation of a code always occurs after the real moral deliberation has taken place; after we have put enough thought into a few of our dilemmas to resolve them, so that they are now just moral problems. But in a profession which is advancing, there will be new situations which arise, of sufficient complexity to tax the individual's moral sense, and which have not yet been subjected to the moral deliberation of the entire profession. These will be the moral dilemmas.

I think I have now established the point that we should not look to codes of ethics for the resolution of moral dilemmas. But, given our comparison between codes of ethics and society's laws, this should come as no surprise. Being a moral person in society as a whole involves much more than simply obeying society's laws: it involves paying attention to moral theory. Similarly, being a moral professional who is capable of resolving the moral dilemmas that arise in one's professional life from time to time involves much more than acting in accordance with a profession's code of ethics. It involves, in addition, reasoning about what one is doing by paying attention to a wider moral theory. That was the 'pessimistic' part of this paper. But every paper ought to end on an optimistic note. I actually have two.

First, as I have already mentioned, a code of ethics should serve three other functions, and nothing I have said entails that it cannot perform these tasks adequately. But, more importantly, when we find that our professional codes are inadequate to resolve moral dilemmas, we should remember that we have recourse to moral theory. The reason that some people despair about the prospect of resolving ethical dilemmas with moral theories is that they focus only on the most difficult moral dilemmas that have not been resolved and therefore conclude that moral theory is incapable of resolving moral dilemmas. Such a view is short-sighted. We should remember that professionals make hundreds of moral judgments every day with confidence, without any reason at all to think that these judgments are difficult or controversial. These moral judgments are not moral dilemmas precisely because our commonsense moral theories are adequate to cope with them; we know exactly how to handle the trade-offs between good and bad that arise with them. In these cases, it does not matter whether professional codes of ethics pronounce on what to do when they arise; for the answer is so obvious. On the other hand, genuine moral dilemmas arise infrequently, but these are the ones we remember – for good reason, of course, becuase these are the ones that do require the bulk of our attention. The optimistic though undefended conclusion is that moral theory will help us resolve these difficult cases as well.

NOTES

1   If this is a necessary condition for a vocation counting as a profession, then it would seem to rule out certain vocations – nursing and the military, to name two – as professions. In both these vocations, practitioners take direction, and even orders, from superiors. However, this is the point of the qualification "simply": nurses have come to realize the problem with professionals simply following orders, and have in their codes addressed this issue. The general consensus among nurses is that a nurse ought not to follow an order that violates her professional responsibilities. This does not mean, though, that a nurse must stop to question every order given: it is perfectly consistent with the notion of professional responsibility to follow orders during an emergency, on the general principle(s) that the person giving them is *likely* to know what is best; and/or that when a task requires the cooperation of several people, things will get ruined if one person 'breaks rank' or wastes precious time questioning. So my point is not that it is *always* inconsistent to follow an order. What *is* inconsistent with professionalism is to agree in advance to

follow orders from a superior, no matter what the circumstances. Soldiers come dangerously close to agreeing to this; and for this reason I take the term 'professional soldier' to function like 'professional athlete', the point of the honorific being to distinguish careerists from amateurs.

Index of Proper Names